THE
CONFESSION OF FAITH

of
The Presbyterian Church
in the United States

Together with

THE LARGER CATECHISM
and
THE SHORTER CATECHISM

Declared by the General Assembly at
Augusta, Georgia, December 1861

With amendments that were enacted by the
General Assemblies of 1886, 1939, 1942,
1944, 1959, and 1963

PRINTED FOR THE GENERAL ASSEMBLY
OF THE PRESBYTERIAN CHURCH IN THE UNITED STATES

Atlanta

Revised edition with amendments
Twenty-first printing 1978

International Standard Book Number: 0-8042-3936-3
© Stated Clerk of the General Assembly
of the Presbyterian Church in the United
States 1965
Printed in the United States of America

JOHN KNOX PRESS

Contents

THE ORIGIN AND FORMATION
OF
THE WESTMINSTER
CONFESSION OF FAITH

THE ORIGIN AND FORMATION
OF
THE WESTMINSTER CONFESSION
OF FAITH

✠

As early as 1540, two great types of the reform of religion in northern Europe had made themselves manifest. Luther had molded the one type. Calvin had molded, or begun the molding of, the other. Luther was for retaining of mediaeval doctrine, government, worship, many things—whatever seemed to him desirable and not forbidden in the Word of God. Calvin was for bringing the Church into conformity with the pattern shown in the Word. He would have the Church hold the faith taught in the Word, govern itself according to the principles taught in the Word, and conduct its exercises of worship according to maxims derivable from the Word. He believed in the sufficiency of the Scriptures as a rule of faith and practice, and would have had the Church conform in all respects to Scripture teaching. Lutheranism was the great type of moderate reform in northern Europe. Calvinism was the great type of thoroughgoing reform. Owing to the peculiar genius of the German people and to peculiar favoring providences, Lutheranism prevailed widely throughout north Germany and Scandinavia, but not a few in these regions craved a more thoroughgoing reform. Owing to the peculiar genius of the French, the Dutch, and south Germans, and to favoring providences, Calvinism prevailed in France, in the Netherlands, and in certain south German States and cities; amongst these peoples, however, there were some who had a greater love for features of the mediaeval Church and would have retained them. There were, thus, on the Continent two great types of reform movement, the one dominant in the one quarter, and the other dominant in other quarters. At the same time, in the sphere within which moderate reform pre-

7

vailed there was more or less demand for thoroughgoing reform; and in the sphere within which thoroughgoing reform prevailed there was more or less desire for merely moderate reform.

In England, also, two types of reform were clearly manifest from the early days of Queen Elizabeth, the one a moderate, the other a type tending to thoroughgoing reform, each type indigenous, but each type strengthened by influences from beyond the Channel. The development of these two types of ecclesiastical reform in England was mightily influenced by the action of the crown, the one type being swerved by attraction, the other stimulated by opposition. In no other country did the throne influence the character of reform so greatly. This was owing to the fact, amongst other forces, that the head of the English State had been made the head of the English Church. Henry VIII had, for personal and, in the main, base reasons, revolted from the papal rule; and had secured at the hands of Parliament in 1534 the "Act of Supremacy," which ordered that the king "shall be taken, accepted, and reputed the only Supreme Head in earth of the Church of England . . . and shall have and enjoy annexed and united to the imperial Crown of this realm as well the title and style thereof, as all honours . . . jurisdictions, privileges, authorities, immunities, profits, and commodities, to the said dignity . . . belonging and appertaining: And that our said Sovereign Lord . . . shall have full power and authority from time to time to visit, repress, redress, reform . . . and amend all such errors, heresies, abuses, offences, contempts, and enormities, whatsoever they be, which by any manner spiritual authority or jurisdiction ought or may lawfully be reformed . . ." While Henry vacillated somewhat in his attitude toward the reform movement, owing to political exigencies, and unwittingly furthered Protestantism at times, as in authorizing the publication of the Scriptures in the vernacular, he remained, at heart, a Romanist, in revolt against papal rule, and was hostile to any representative of reform of either type who was bold enough steadily to maintain his convictions. During the reign of his son, Edward, moderate reform was favored. During the reign of Mary, who succeeded Edward, every type of reform was bitterly and relentlessly persecuted. No less than two hundred and eighty persons were burned at the stake, and many hundreds of persons were driven into exile. By the ruthlessness of her opposition Mary did much, however, to fertilize and stimulate the Protestant cause. She was succeeded, in 1558, by her half-sister, Elizabeth. This last representative of the House of Tudor, though at heart holding a religion not very different from the Anglo-Catholicism of her father, so far as she had any religion, was forced by circumstances to favor Protestantism. Naturally, she favored moderate reform and fought thoroughgoing reform. This and her lust for power led her to resist constitutional changes that were proposed in the Church, just where she pleased. An aristocratic hierarchy, though with noble exceptions, naturally also sided with her in repressing both the civil and the religious liberties of the people. With Elizabeth the Tudor dynasty because extinct. The Stuart dynasty succeeded to the throne in the person of James, VI of Scotland, I of England. Brought up under Presbyterian tutelage, but with the blood of tricksters in his veins, he knew and approved the better, but followed the worse way. The party of moderate reform was regarded by him as more in harmony with civil monarchy. Moreover, that party pleased him by approving his fatal *theory of the divine right of kings,* and by endless and unseemly flatteries. His son Charles, who followed him to the throne, swung back toward Roman Catholicism—to Anglo-Catholicism. During these two Stuart reigns the party of moderate reform, enjoying the favor of the court, and tending toward Anglo-Catholicism, united with the court in a bitter effort at repression of the party of thoroughgoing reform. This persecution, together with the spread of Arminianism among the moderate reformers, stimulated into large vigor of life the party tending to thoroughgoing reform.

The party tending to thoroughgoing reform in England in the age of Bloody Mary finds its rootlets in Ridley, Hooper, Latimer, and others, and in part of the work of Cranmer. It finds rootlets reaching further back—to Tyndale, who, prior to his death in 1536, had spread widely his translation of the New Testament in Scotland as well as in England. Some of its rootlets reach even further back—to the followers of Wycliffe and to Wycliffe himself. But while thoroughgoing reform was thus indigenous to England, it received a mighty impulse from the Continent, and particularly from Geneva. Many of those driven

from England by the Marian persecutions found a congenial
exile at Geneva, and became apt and honest pupils of the great
Calvin. At the beginning of Elizabeth's reign they returned thoroughly imbued with those views of Scripture truth which he
taught with a clarity and force elsewhere unparalleled. The Cal-
vinistic theology became the theology of the great men of the
Anglican Church during the first forty years of Elizabeth's reign.
The most of these great men would willingly have tolerated a
more thoroughgoing reform of the government and worship of
the Church. Some of them positively and openly favored further
reform in these departments. But Elizabeth stood in the way.
In 1563 the formularies of the Anglican Church were completed,
containing Protestant doctrines along with a mediaeval hierarchy
and a partially mediaeval cultus. In the following year the queen
began the attempt to enforce a rigid uniformity—an attempt
resulting in the expulsion from the Established Church of many
of the godliest ministers of all England. Further trouble arose
over the private meetings for worship in London at which
Knox's Book of Common Order was used instead of the Liturgy,
and over the more public meetings known as prophesyings—
gatherings of ministers and pious laymen for the study and
exposition of the Scriptures—very important meetings, as proven
in their use in Zurich, Geneva, and Scotland. Elizabeth commanded their suppression. Before Elizabeth had been on the
throne a score of years a considerable number of advocates of
thoroughgoing reform, "who had been led on to substantially
Presbyterian opinions, but discouraged by friends abroad and
debarred by the authorities at home from overtly seceding from
the national church, began to hold secretly private meetings for
mutual conference and prayer, and possibly also for the exercise
of discipline over those who voluntarily joined their associations
and submitted to their guidance. It is even said that a presbytery
was formed at Wandsworth in Surrey, wherein eleven lay-elders
were associated with the lecturer of that congregation and certain
leading Puritan clergymen. But if this was really a formal presbytery, it is probable that it was what was then called the lesser
presbytery or session, not the greater presbytery or *classis* to
which the name is now usually restricted. It is more certain that
when Cartwright, the redoubted leader of this school of Puritans,

was arrested in 1585 and his study searched, a copy was found of a Directory for church-government, which made provision for synods, provincial and national, as well as for presbyteries, greater and lesser. This, according to some authorities, had been subscribed by about five hundred Puritans of this school, and, for some years . . . had, to a certain extent, been carried out, and a church within the church virtually formed."[1] These and all other expressions of thoroughgoing reform Elizabeth did her utmost to stamp out, using the despotic Courts of Star Chamber and High Commission without regard to the feelings and convictions of many of the most patriotic, learned, and Christian of her subjects, but with disastrous failure as the result. Her tyrannical measures called out and developed love for the more biblical form of religion which she persecuted. They multiplied the advocates of thoroughgoing reform, or Puritans, as they came early to be called in England.

It has been said that the chief thing for which the Puritans all along contended was the "principle that the church has no right to burden the consciences of her members in matters of faith and worship with aught that is contrary to or *beside* (*i.e.,* in addition to) the express or implicit teaching of the Word of God," that they would restrict the authority of the church within narrower limits than their opponents; that they did not at first perceive the full import of the principle for which they contended; that they were reluctant to extend it rigidly to the constitution and government of the church as well as to her articles of faith and forms of worship; but that, as the contest proceeded, they could not fail to be led on more and more distinctly to assert it with a fuller consciousness of its far-reaching consequences, and a more earnest longing to bring back the church in constitution and government as well as in faith and worship, to what they believed to be "the pattern showed in the mount."[2] The demand for a further reformation of religion had grown great in England as early as the death of Elizabeth and the succession of James Stuart of Scotland to the English throne. It had been augmented just at the close of the sixteenth century

---

[1]Mitchell, *The Westminster Assembly*, pp. 51 and 52.
[2]Mitchell, *The Westminster Assembly*, p. 61.

by the introduction of Arminianism into England. The demand was fanned into a flame by the arbitrary and retroactive measures of James I, of Charles I, and especially by the measures of Charles and his ministers, Laud and Wentworth.

In 1603, James I, son of Mary Stuart, acceded to the English throne. He was learned but wanting in common sense. A tyrant in politics, a bigot in religion, he thought that he had been commissioned of God to re-establish the Davidic Theocracy in England. He attempted the exercise of absolute authority in his kingdom, dispensing largely with the use of Parliaments. Civil rights were trampled under his feet, religious grievances were multiplied. All this had been presaged in his treatment of the Puritan Millenary petitioners—by his haughty, arrogant, and brutal treatment of their representatives, voiced in his maxims set forth at the Hampton Court Conference: "No bishop, no king"; "A Scottish Presbytery agreeth as well with the monarchy as God with the devil. Now Jack and Tom and Will and Dick shall meet and at their pleasure censure me and my council . . . let that alone"; "I will have one doctrine, one discipline, one religion in substance and ceremony." In order to win a Spanish, or French, princess for wife to his son Charles, he flattered Rome and outraged national sentiment. He ordered the publication of the *Book of Sports,* enjoining games and other festivities after services on the Lord's Day. By such means he arrayed against himself the landed gentry, the merchants, the professional men, and some of the nobility—the classes which stood for Parliamentary government and amongst whom the Puritan movement had its strength. They were indignant at his degradation of the morals of the people, his support of profligates at Court, his development of the Church worship in a Romeward direction.

Charles I inherited the absolutist views of his father in intensified form. He was heir also to the unrest, dissatisfaction, and abhorrence of Stuart arbitrariness which James' measures had created. The conflict went on. Other provocations were given the lovers of liberty and truth. Charles claimed and exercised the authority to levy and collect taxes—an authority which belonged to the Parliament as the representative of the people. He aspired to rule as did Louis XIV of France. The Huguenots of France and the Lutherans of Denmark were going down before Roman Catholics; and King Charles was showing favor to Romanists, had a Romanist wife, and might give them a Roman Catholic king in the next generation. The king and Archbishop Laud were pressing for uniformity of increasing rigidity. A stress was laid on the divine right of Episcopacy which unchurched all non-Episcopal churches. The communion table was turned into an altar. A doctrine of the real presence, hard for the people to distinguish from the Romish, was advocated. Some of the bishops commended the invocations of the saints. Arminius and Arminians at that time favored the pretensions of the king over against the Parliament, and were beginning the revision of the ceremonial in a Romeward direction. They were becoming numerous and prominent, "so that Bishop Morely being asked what the Arminians hold, replied with truth as well as wit, 'They hold the best bishoprics and deaneries in England.'"

The agents of Charles for carrying out his policies in Church and State, William Laud and Wentworth, were men of his spirit, narrow zealots. In enforcing uniformity to his mediaevalized ritual, Laud used the scourge, the pillory, the prison, the cropping of ears, the slitting of noses, and other such gentle persuasives.

The liberties, civil and religious, of England were at stake. A war in behalf of these liberties was at hand. The war in behalf of a more biblical form of religion began in Scotland. The Reformation in essentially the Genevan form had been established in the northern kingdom between 1560 and 1590. The struggle against popery over, a struggle against prelacy, lasting a hundred years, ensued. Against determined opposition, James and his government had succeeded in the re-establishment of Episcopacy in 1610. About the middle of his reign, Charles and Archbishop Laud attempted to conform the Scottish Church to the Anglican model. They proceeded about the business as if the Scots were mere wooden men. In 1636, on the authority of the king alone, a body of canons for the government and discipline of the Scottish Church was issued. The next year, in the same autocratic way, a new liturgy was assigned to the Scots. It was the old English Prayer Book revised in a way thought to savor of Romanism. Popular resentment flamed. The National Covenant (1638) was brought forth and enthusiastically signed, for the defense of the Reformed religion and resistance to innovations. The new regulations were declared abolished. Episcopacy was swept away, and the nation resorted to arms to maintain their liberties.

To get the sinews of war with which to subjugate the Scots, Charles summoned the English Parliament, without which he had ruled for eleven years. Parliament at once set itself to avenge grievances. Charles dissolved it. Almost immediately he was forced to call another. It was in sympathy with the Scots. It had a large leverage over Charles in the fact that by a treaty into which the king had entered, the Scottish army was to be paid before it was disbanded. Parliament knew the value of this lever. It began the rectification of abuses, impeached, and committed to the Tower, Wentworth (Strafford) and Laud, passed a bill to prevent its own dissolution or prorogation except by its own free consent (May, 1641), put religion to the front, passed an ordinance against Laud's ceremonies and the Sunday sports, expelled the bishops from the House of Lords (January, 1642), decreed the hierachy out of existence (November, 1642), the bill to take effect November 5, 1643, enacted the Grand Remonstrance, a restatement of all past grievances against the king, followed by a demand for cabinet ministers, and for the references of Church matters to an Assembly of Divines to be nominated by Parliament.

Charles flung his standards to the breeze. The House of Commons accepted the gage of battle. The war began.

June 12, 1643, the Parliament passed an act entitled "An Ordinance of the Lords and Commons in Parliament for the calling of an Assembly of learned and godly divines and others, to be consulted with by the Parliament, for the settlement of the Government and Liturgy of the Church of England, and for the indicating and clearing of the doctrine of the said Church from false aspersions and interpretations." The persons who were to constitute this Assembly were named in the ordinance. They embraced the finest representatives, with two or three possible exceptions, of the Church of the age. Subsequently about twenty-one ministers were added to make up for the absence of others. The original list contained one hundred and fifty-one names—the names of ten lords, twenty commoners, and one hundred and twenty-one divines—and included, in fair proportions, Moderate Episcopalians, Presbyterians, Independents, and Erastians.

In the original ordinance four bishops were named. Of the other Episcopalians called, five afterwards became bishops. But the Episcopalians mostly refused to attend, partly because the Assembly was not a regular convocation called by the king, and partly because he had expressly condemned the Solemn League and Covenant which, after the Assembly was a few weeks old, became a force determining the character of the work of the Assembly.

The Presbyterians formed the great majority of the Assembly and gained in numbers and influence as time passed. Of these there were two parties—one party holding to a *jure humano* theory of Presbyterianism, the other holding to the *jure divino* theory, *i.e.,* that government by Presbytery is "expressly instituted or commanded" in the New Testament as the proper polity of the Church. This latter party was powerfully re-enforced by the Scottish commissioners to the Assembly who became debating, though not voting, members, after the adoption of the Solemn League and Covenant. The party won an essential triumph for the *jure divino* theory, a strong majority of all the Presbyterians coming to believe that the Lord Jesus is the sole King and Head of the Church, and has appointed a spiritual government in the hands of chosen representatives.

There were only five prominent Independents in the Assembly. They maintained that a local church should not be subject to the jurisdiction of presbyteries and synods, and that such a church has a right to ordain its own ministers.

The Erastians maintained the ecclesiastical supremacy of the civil government in all matters of discipline, and made the Church a department of the State—on the ground that clergymen are merely teachers, and that power of rule in the Church belongs to the civil magistrate. They were willing to concede a *jure humano Presbyterianism,* denied a *jure divino* form of Church government of any kind, and claimed for the State the right to give to the Church any form of government it might please to grant. These constituted a small party, but exercised vast influence because their views harmonized with those of Parliament.

It is to be remembered in this connection that the Long Parliament had the opportunity to select a body for the work of creed construction, fitter therefor than could have been found in any other age in England down to this day, perhaps. Puritanism had been doing its work of making great men in England for a century. It had been aided in that work by all the mental and moral stimulus coming of geographical discovery, of the Great Reformation, of progress along every line of civilization, of advance in national well-being and prestige. The middle of the seventeenth century was, from a moral and spiritual point of view, the greatest age in the history of England to the present. Under the providence of God, the Long Parliament had the noblest age of England to choose the Assembly from; and it chose well as has appeared.

The Westminster Assembly was set to work, at first, on a revision of the Thirty-Nine Articles; but, on October 12, 1643, shortly after the signing of the Solemn League and Covenant, wherein, in order to secure Scottish aid against the king, Parliament had agreed to make the religions of England, Scotland, and Ireland as nearly uniform as possible and to reform religion "according to the Word of God, and the example of the best Reformed churches," Parliament directed the Assembly to "consider among themselves of such a discipline and government as may be most agreeable to God's holy word." Thereupon the Assembly entered at once upon the work of preparing a Directory of Government, Worship and Discipline. Delayed by much controversy with the Independent and Erastian members, they did not complete this portion of their work till near the end of 1644. Then they began work upon the Catechisms and Confession of Faith simultaneously. After progress with both, the Assembly resolved to finish the Confession of Faith first and then construct the Catechisms upon its model. December 3, 1646, they, in a body, presented the finished Confession to Parliament. Parliament recommitted the work that Scripture passages might be attached to every part of it. April 29, 1647, they reported it finished with full Scripture proofs of each separate proposition attached thereto.

The Shorter Catechism was completed and reported to Parliament, November 5, 1647, and the Larger Catechism, April 14, 1648. March 22, 1648, the two Houses held a conference to compare their opinion about the Confession of Faith. Rushworth stated the result as follows: "The Commons this day, at a conference, presented the Lords with a Confession of Faith passed by them, with some alterations (especially concerning questions of discipline), viz.: That they do agree with their Lordships, and so with the Assembly, in the doctrinal part, and desire the same may be made public, that this kingdom and all the Reformed churches of Christendom, may see the Parliament of England differ not in doctrine."

It is plain from the preceding statements that the Westminster Standards were, in form, the standards of the Long Parliament. The Westminster Assembly was appointed by that Parliament. It was supported by that Parliament. Its acts were given validity, so far as political England was concerned, by enactment of that Parliament. The Westminster Assembly was a body called to advise that great Parliament as to the Biblical faith, polity, and worship. It is just as true, however, that the Parliament had taken care to constitute the Assembly of a body of men of uncommon abilities, learning, and godliness; just as true that it framed rules in accord with which the Assembly should do its work. These regulations indicated serious business for the Assembly, and the utmost freedom of discussion. They provided, amongst other things, "that every member, at his first entrance into the Assembly, shall make serious and solemn protestation not to maintain anything but what he believes to be the truth in sincerity, when discovered unto him"; "that what any man undertakes to prove as necessary, he shall make good out of the Scriptures." The rules of procedure were read at the beginning of each week or month. So also was the following vow, framed in accord with one of the regulations: "I do seriously promise and vow in the presence of Almighty God, that in this Assembly, whereof I am a member, I will maintain nothing in the point of doctrine but what I believe to be most agreeable to the Word of God, nor in point of discipline, but what may make most for God's glory and the peace and good will of His Church." The Assembly not only enjoyed, it was encouraged to, the fullest freedom of debate, and to an endeavor to set forth the Bible faith, polity, and worship.

The Assembly had a wide acquaintance with creeds, Greek, Latin, Continental Reformed; but naturally, in accord with the Anglo-Saxon genius, it carried on the line of development begun on English soil in the Thirty-Nine Articles, continued by the framers of the Lambeth Articles (1595), continued further by Archbishop Usher, in the Irish Articles (1615), who was one of the greatest doctrinal Puritans of the time. While the creed of the Westminster Assembly shows striking likeness to the Irish Articles—probably intending thus to make clear its essential agreement with the doctrines of the English and Irish Reformation, it is far abler, fuller, and superior to any of its predecessors, and gives proof that the Assembly was steadily dominated by its aim to state nothing therein which is not expressly taught in the Word of God, or derivable therefrom by good and necessary inference. Working thus it produced not only the most logical and most complete, but the most Biblical and the noblest creed ever yet produced in Christendom.

As soon as completed the Confession of Faith was brought to Scotland, and most favorably received. It was adopted by the Scottish General Assembly, August 27, 1647. The Scottish Parliament endorsed this action, February 7, 1690. In 1729, the old Synod of Philadelphia—the first Presbyterian Synod in North America—in its famous "Adopting Act" adopted the Confession of Faith and Larger and Shorter Catechisms "as the Confession of our Faith."

Although the Westminster Assembly excluded from their Confession everything they regarded as savoring of Erastianism, yet their views as to church establishments led them to concede power to the civil magistrates concerning religious things, which the fathers of American Presbyterianism would not concede. Hence in the "Adopting Act," just referred to, the Synod declared that it did not receive the clauses relating to this subject (some clauses in the twentieth and twenty-third chapters of the Confession) "in any such sense as to suppose the civil magistrate hath a controlling power over Synods with respect to their exercise of ministerial authority; or power to persecute any for their religion; or, in any sense contrary to the Protestant succession to the throne of Great Britain." And, when the Synod was revising and amending its standards in 1787, preparatory to the organization of the General Assembly of the Presbyterian Church, U. S. A., "it took into consideration the last paragraph of the twentieth chapter of the Westminster Confession of Faith; the third paragraph of the twenty-third chapter, and the first paragraph of the thirty-first chapter; and, having made some alterations, agreed that the said paragraphs as now altered be printed for consideration." Thus altered and amended, the Confession and the Catechisms were adopted as the doctrinal part of the Constitution of the Presbyterian Church in the United States of America, and so remained till 1861, and, indeed, until 1903, when other changes were made.

On the organization of the Presbyterian Church in the United States in 1861, it adopted the Standards of the Presbyterian Church in the United States of America from which its constituents had withdrawn. The only amendment in the Confession since 1861, by this Church, has been in striking out the clause in Chapter XXIV, Section 4, making it unlawful to marry a deceased wife's sister.

SPECIAL NOTE.—This historical sketch was ordered by the General Assembly of 1906, and it has appeared in editions of *The Confession of Faith* subsequent to that date. Chapter numbers, paragraphs, and amendment actions referred to in this sketch have not been revised to accord with changes made in the present edition.

THE
CONFESSION OF FAITH

With amendments that were enacted by the the General Assemblies of 1886, 1939, 1942, 1944, 1959, and 1963, and with Revised Proof Texts adopted by the General Assembly of 1910.

Contents

THE CONFESSION OF FAITH

✠

CHAPTER I

Of the Holy Scripture

1. Although the light of nature, and the works of creation and providence, do so far manifest the goodness, wisdom, and power of God, as to leave men inexcusable;[1] yet are they not sufficient to give that knowledge of God, and of his will, which is necessary unto salvation;[2] therefore it pleased the Lord, at sundry times, and in divers manners, to reveal himself, and to declare that his will unto his church;[3] and afterwards for the better pre-

GENERAL NOTE: At several points the Confession of Faith is more specific in its statements than the Scriptures. These statements are inferences drawn from the Scriptures or from statements based on the Scriptures, or from the experience and observation of the Church. In such cases no texts are cited, but reference is made to this General Note.

1. Rom. 1:19, 20. Because that which may be known of God is manifest in them; for God hath shewed *it* unto them. For the invisible things of him from the creation of the world are clearly seen, being understood by the things that are made, *even* his eternal power and Godhead; so that they are without excuse.
Rom. 2:14, 15. For when the Gentiles, which have not the law, do by nature the things contained in the law, these, having not the law, are a law unto themselves: which shew the work of the law written in their hearts, their conscience also bearing witness, and *their* thoughts the mean while accusing or else excusing one another.
Rom. 1:32. Who knowing the judgment of God, that they which commit such things are worthy of death, not only do the same, but have pleasure in them that do them.

2. I Cor. 1:21. For after that in the wisdom of God the world by wisdom knew not God, it pleased God by the foolishness of preaching to save them that believe.
I Cor. 2:13, 14. Which things also we speak, not in the words which man's wisdom teacheth, but which the Holy Ghost teacheth; comparing spiritual things with spiritual. But the natural man receiveth not the things of the Spirit of God: for they are foolishness unto him: neither can he know *them,* because they are spiritually discerned.
I Cor. 2:9-12; Acts 4:12; Rom. 10:13, 14.

3. Heb. 1:1, 2. God, who at sundry times and in divers manners spake in time past unto the fathers by the prophets, hath in these last days spoken unto us by *his* Son.
Gal. 1:11, 12. But I certify you, brethren, that the gospel which was preached of me is not after man. For I neither received it of man, neither was I taught *it,* but by the revelation of Jesus Christ.
Deut. 4:12-14.

serving and propagating of the truth, and for the more sure establishment and comfort of the church against the corruption of the flesh, and the malice of Satan and of the world, to commit the same wholly unto writing;[4] which maketh the Holy Scripture to be most necessary;[5] those former ways of God's revealing his will unto his people being now ceased.[6]

2. Under the name of Holy Scripture, or the word of God written, are now contained all the books of the Old and New Testaments, which are these:

Of the Old Testament

Genesis	II Chronicles	Daniel
Exodus	Ezra	Hosea
Leviticus	Nehemiah	Joel
Numbers	Esther	Amos
Deuteronomy	Job	Obadiah
Joshua	Psalms	Jonah
Judges	Proverbs	Micah
Ruth	Ecclesiastes	Nahum
I Samuel	The Song of Songs	Habakkuk
II Samuel	Isaiah	Zephaniah
I Kings	Jeremiah	Haggai
II Kings	Lamentations	Zechariah
I Chronicles	Ezekiel	Malachi

---

4. Luke 24:27. And beginning at Moses and all the prophets, he expounded unto them in all the scriptures the things concerning himself.

II Tim. 3:16. All scripture *is* given by inspiration of God, and *is* profitable for doctrine, for reproof, for correction, for instruction in righteousness.

Rom. 15:4. For whatsoever things were written aforetime were written for our learning, that we through patience and comfort of the scriptures might have hope.

II Peter 3:15, 16. And account *that* the longsuffering of our Lord *is* salvation; even as our beloved brother Paul also according to the wisdom given unto him hath written unto you; as also in all *his* epistles, speaking in them of these things; in which are some things hard to be understood, which they that are unlearned and unstable wrest, as *they do* also the other scriptures, unto their own destruction.

5. Luke 16:29-31. Abraham saith unto him, They have Moses and the prophets; let them hear them. And he said, Nay, father Abraham: but if one went unto them from the dead, they will repent. And he said unto him, If they hear not Moses and the prophets, neither will they be persuaded, though one rose from the dead.

Heb. 2:1-3; II Tim. 3:15, 16; II Peter 1:10.

6. See General Note, p. 25.

Of the New Testament

Matthew	Ephesians	Hebrews
Mark	Philippians	James
Luke	Colossians	I Peter
John	I Thessalonians	II Peter
Acts of the Apostles	II Thessalonians	I John
Romans	I Timothy	II John
I Corinthians	II Timothy	III John
II Corinthians	Titus	Jude
Galatians	Philemon	Revelation

All which are given by inspiration of God, to be the rule of faith and life.

3. The books commonly called Apocrypha, not being of divine inspiration, are no part of the canon of the Scripture; and therefore are of no authority in the Church of God, nor to be any otherwise approved, or made use of, than other human writings.[7]

4. The authority of the Holy Scripture, for which it ought to be believed and obeyed, dependeth not upon the testimony of any man or church, but wholly upon God (who is truth itself), the author thereof; and therefore it is to be received, because it is the word of God.[8]

5. We may be moved and induced by the testimony of the church to an high and reverent esteem for the Holy Scripture; and the heavenliness of the matter, the efficacy of the doctrine, the majesty of the style, the consent of all the parts, the scope of the whole (which is to give all glory to God), the full discovery it makes of the only way of man's salvation, the many other incomparable excellencies, and the entire perfection thereof, are arguments whereby it doth abundantly evidence itself to be the

---

7. The Canon of Scripture is not established by explicit passages, but by the testimony of Jesus and His Apostles; of ancient manuscripts and versions; of ancient Christian writers and church councils, and by the internal evidence exhibited in the separate books.

8. I Thess. 2:13. For this cause also thank we God without ceasing, because, when ye received the word of God which ye heard of us, ye received it not as the word of men, but as it is in truth, the word of God, which effectually worketh also in you that believe.

II Tim. 3:16. All scripture is given by inspiration of God, and is profitable for doctrine, for reproof, for correction, for instruction in righteousness.

II Peter 1:21; Gal. 1:11, 12.

word of God; yet, notwithstanding, our full persuasion and assurance of the infallible truth and divine authority thereof, is from the inward work of the Holy Spirit, bearing witness by and with the word in our hearts.[9]

6. The whole counsel of God, concerning all things necessary for his own glory, man's salvation, faith, and life, is either expressly set down in Scripture, or by good and necessary consequence may be deduced from Scripture:[10] unto which nothing at any time is to be added, whether by new revelations of the Spirit, or traditions of men.[11] Nevertheless we acknowledge the inward illumination of the Spirit of God to be necessary for the saving understanding of such things as are revealed in the word;[12] and that there are some circumstances concerning the worship of God, and government of the church, common to human actions and societies, which are to be ordered by the light of nature and Christian prudence, according to the general rules of the word, which are always to be observed.[13]

---

9. I Cor. 2:10, 11. But God hath revealed *them* unto us by his Spirit; for the Spirit searcheth all things, yea, the deep things of God. For what man knoweth the things of a man, save the spirit of man which is in him? even so the things of God knoweth no man, but the Spirit of God.
John 16:13, 14. Howbeit when he, the Spirit of truth, is come, he will guide you into all truth: for he shall not speak of himself; but whatsoever he shall hear, *that* shall he speak: and he will shew you things to come. He shall glorify me: for he shall receive of mine, and shall shew *it* unto you.
I Cor. 2:6-9.

10. Mark 7:5-7. Then the Pharisees and scribes asked him, Why walk not thy disciples according to the tradition of the elders, but eat bread with unwashen hands? He answered and said unto them, Well hath Esaias prophesied of you hypocrites, as it is written, This people honoureth me with *their* lips, but their heart is far from me. Howbeit in vain do they worship me, teaching *for* doctrines the commandments of men.

11. This statement is an inference from the sufficiency of the Scriptures.

12. John 6:45. It is written in the prophets, And they shall be all taught of God. Every man therefore that hath heard, and hath learned of the Father, cometh unto me.
I Cor. 2:9, 10, 12. But as it is written, Eye hath not seen, nor ear heard, neither have entered into the heart of man, the things which God hath prepared for them that love him. But God hath revealed *them* unto us by his Spirit: for the Spirit searcheth all things, yea, the deep things of God. . . . Now we have received, not the spirit of the world, but the spirit which is of God; that we might know the things that are freely given to us of God.

13. I Cor. 14:26, 40. How is it then, brethren? when ye come together, every one of you hath a psalm, hath a doctrine, hath a tongue, hath a

7. All things in Scripture are not alike plain in themselves, nor alike clear unto all;[14] yet those things which are necessary to be known, believed, and observed, for salvation, are so clearly propounded and opened in some place of Scripture or other, that not only the learned, but the unlearned, in a due use of the ordinary means, may attain unto a sufficient understanding of them.[15]

8. The Old Testament in Hebrew (which was the native language of the people of God of old), and the New Testament in Greek (which at the time of the writing of it was most generally known to the nations), being immediately inspired by God,[16] and by his singular care and providence kept pure in all ages, are therefore authentical; so as in all controversies of religion the church is finally to appeal unto them.[17] But because these original tongues are not known to all the people of God who have right unto, and interest in, the Scriptures, and are commanded, in the fear of God, to read and search them,[18] therefore they are

---

revelation, hath an interpretation. Let all things be done unto edifying. . . . Let all things be done decently and in order.

I Cor. 11:13, 14. Judge in yourselves: is it comely that a woman pray unto God uncovered? Doth not even nature itself teach you, that, if a man have long hair, it is a shame unto him?

14. II Peter 3:16. As also in all *his* epistles, speaking in them of these things; in which are some things hard to be understood, which they that are unlearned and unstable wrest, as *they do* also the other scriptures, unto their own destruction.

John 16:17. Then said *some* of his disciples among themselves, What is this that he saith unto us, A little while, and ye shall not see me: and again, a little while, and ye shall see me: and, Because I go to the Father?

John 6:60. Many therefore of his disciples, when they had heard *this*, said, This is an hard saying; who can hear it?

15. Ps. 119:105, 130. Thy word *is* a lamp unto my feet, and a light unto my path. . . . The entrance of thy words giveth light; it giveth understanding unto the simple.

Acts 17:11, 12. These were more noble than those in Thessalonica, in that they received the word with all readiness of mind, and searched the scriptures daily, whether those things were so. Therefore many of them believed; also of honourable women which were Greeks, and of men, not a few.

16. See Note under Section 3, figure 7 above.

17. Isaiah 8:20. To the law and to the testimony: if they speak not according to this word, *it is* because *there is* no light in them.

Acts 15:14-18.

18. John 5:39. Search the scriptures; for in them ye think ye have eternal life: and they are they which testify of me.

II Tim. 3:14, 15; II Peter 1:19.

to be translated into the language of every people unto which they come, that the word of God dwelling plentifully in all, they may worship him in an acceptable manner, and, through patience and comfort of the Scriptures, may have hope.[19]

9. The infallible rule of interpretation of Scripture, is the Scripture itself; and therefore, when there is a question about the true and full sense of any scripture (which is not manifold, but one), it may be searched and known by other places that speak more clearly.[20]

10. The Supreme Judge, by which all controversies of religion are to be determined, and all decrees of councils, opinions of

---

19. I Cor. 14:6, 9, 11, 12, 24, 27, 28. Now, brethren, if I come unto you speaking with tongues, what shall I profit you, except I shall speak to you either by revelation, or by knowledge, or by prophesying, or by doctrine? . . . So likewise ye, except ye utter by the tongue words easy to be understood, how shall it be known what is spoken? for ye shall speak into the air. . . . Therefore if I know not the meaning of the voice, I shall be unto him that speaketh a barbarian, and he that speaketh *shall be* a barbarian unto me. Even so ye, forasmuch as ye are zealous of spiritual *gifts*, seek that ye may excel to the edifying of the church. . . . But if all prophesy, and there come in one that believeth not, or *one* unlearned, he is convinced of all, he is judged of all. . . . If any man speak in an *unknown* tongue, *let it be* by two, or at the most *by* three, and *that* by course; and let one interpret. But if there be no interpreter, let him keep silence in the church; and let him speak to himself, and to God.
Matt. 28:19, 20. Go ye therefore, and teach all nations, baptizing them in the name of the Father, and of the Son, and of the Holy Ghost: teaching them to observe all things whatsoever I have commanded you: and, lo, I am with you alway, *even* unto the end of the world. Amen.
Col. 3:16. Let the word of Christ dwell in you richly in all wisdom; teaching and admonishing one another in psalms and hymns and spiritual songs, singing with grace in your hearts to the Lord.
Rom. 15:4. For whatsoever things were written aforetime were written for our learning, that we through patience and comfort of the scriptures might have hope.

20. Matt. 4:5-7. Then the devil taketh him up into the holy city, and setteth him on a pinnacle of the temple, and saith unto him, If thou be the Son of God, cast thyself down: for it is written, He shall give his angels charge concerning thee: and in *their* hands they shall bear thee up, lest at any time thou dash thy foot against a stone. Jesus said unto him, It is written again, Thou shalt not tempt the Lord thy God. Matt. 12:1-7. At that time Jesus went on the sabbath day through the corn; and his disciples were an hungred, and began to pluck the ears of corn, and to eat. But when the Pharisees saw *it*, they said unto him, Behold, thy disciples do that which is not lawful to do upon the sabbath day. But he said unto them, Have ye not read what David did, when he was an hungred, and they that were with him; how he

ancient writers, doctrines of men, and private spirits, are to be examined, and in whose sentence we are to rest, can be no other but the Holy Spirit speaking in the Scripture.[21]

CHAPTER II

Of God, and of the Holy Trinity

1. There is but one only living and true God,[1] who is infinite in being and perfection,[2] a most pure spirit,[3] invisible,[4] without

---

entered into the house of God, and did eat the shewbread, which was not lawful for him to eat, neither for them which were with him, but only for the priests? Or have ye not read in the law, how that on the sabbath days the priests in the temple profane the sabbath, and are blameless? But I say unto you, That in this place is *one* greater than the temple. But if ye had known what *this* meaneth, I will have mercy, and not sacrifice, ye would not have condemned the guiltless.

21. Matt. 22:29, 31. Jesus answered and said unto them, Ye do err, not knowing the scriptures, nor the power of God . . . But as touching the resurrection of the dead, have ye not read that which was spoken unto you by God . . . ?
Acts 28:25. And when they agreed not among themselves, they departed, after that Paul had spoken one word, Well spake the Holy Ghost by Esaias the prophet unto our fathers.
Luke 10:26. He said unto him, What is written in the law? how readest thou?

1. Deut. 6:4. Hear, O Israel: The LORD our God *is* one LORD.
I Cor. 8:4, 6. As concerning therefore the eating of those things that are offered in sacrifice unto idols, we know that an idol *is* nothing in the world, and that *there is* none other God but one. . . . But to us *there is but* one God, the Father, of whom *are* all things, and we in him; and one Lord Jesus Christ, by whom *are* all things, and we by him.
I Thess. 1:9. Ye turned to God from idols to serve the living and true God.
Jer. 10:10. But the LORD *is* the true God, he *is* the living God, and an everlasting king.

2. Jer. 23:24. Can any hide himself in secret places that I shall not see him? saith the LORD. Do not I fill heaven and earth? saith the LORD.
Ps. 147:5. Great *is* our Lord, and of great power: his understanding is infinite.
I Kings 8:27. But will God indeed dwell on the earth? behold, the heaven and heaven of heavens cannot contain thee: how much less this house that I have builded?
Ps. 139.

3. John 4:24. God *is* a Spirit: and they that worship him must worship *him* in spirit and in truth.

4. I Tim. 1:17. Now unto the King eternal, immortal, invisible, the only wise God, *be* honour and glory for ever and ever. Amen.

body, parts, or passions,[5] immutable,[6] immense,[7] eternal,[8] incomprehensible,[9] almighty;[10] most wise,[11] most holy,[12] most free,[13] most absolute,[14] working all things according to the counsel of his own immutable and most righteous will,[15] for his own

---

5. Luke 24:39. Behold my hands and my feet, that it is I myself: handle me, and see; for a spirit hath not flesh and bones, as ye see me have.

   Deut. 4:15, 16. Take ye therefore good heed unto yourselves; for ye saw no manner of similitude on the day *that* the LORD spake unto you in Horeb out of the midst of the fire: lest ye corrupt *yourselves*, and make you a graven image, the similitude of any figure, the likeness of male or female.

6. James 1:17. The Father of lights, with whom is no variableness, neither shadow of turning.

   Mal. 3:6. For I *am* the LORD: I change not.

7. I Kings 8:27. But will God indeed dwell on the earth? behold, the heaven and heaven of heavens cannot contain thee; how much less this house that I have builded?

   Jer. 23:23, 24. *Am* I a God at hand, saith the LORD, and not a God afar off? Can any hide himself in secret places that I shall not see him? saith the LORD. Do not I fill heaven and earth? saith the LORD.

8. Ps. 90:2. Before the mountains were brought forth, or ever thou hadst formed the earth and the world, even from everlasting to everlasting, thou *art* God.

   I Tim. 1:17. Now unto the King eternal, immortal, invisible, the only wise God, *be* honour and glory for ever and ever. Amen.

9. Rom. 11:33. O the depth of the riches both of the wisdom and knowledge of God! how unsearchable *are* his judgments, and his ways past finding out!

   Ps. 145:3. His greatness *is* unsearchable.

10. Rev. 4:8. And the four beasts had each of them six wings about *him;* and *they were* full of eyes within: and they rest not day and night, saying, Holy, holy, holy, Lord God Almighty, which was, and is, and is to come.

11. Rom. 16:27. To God only wise, *be* glory through Jesus Christ for ever. Amen.

12. Isa. 6:3. And one cried unto another, and said, Holy, holy, holy, *is* the LORD of hosts: the whole earth *is* full of his glory.

   Rev. 4:8.

13. Ps. 115:3. But our God *is* in the heavens: he hath done whatsoever he hath pleased.

14. Isa. 44:6. Thus saith the LORD the King of Israel, and his redeemer the LORD of hosts; I *am* the first, and I *am* the last; and beside me *there is* no God.

   Acts 17:24, 25.

15. Eph. 1:11. In whom also we have obtained an inheritance, being predestinated according to the purpose of him who worketh all things after the counsel of his own will.

glory;[16] most loving,[17] gracious, merciful, long-suffering, abundant in goodness and truth, forgiving iniquity, transgression, and sin;[18] the rewarder of them that diligently seek him;[19] and withal most just and terrible in his judgments;[20] hating all sin,[21] and who will by no means clear the guilty.[22]

2. God hath all life, glory, goodness, blessedness, in and of himself;[23] and is alone in and unto himself all-sufficient, not

16. Rom. 11:36. For of him, and through him, and to him, *are* all things: to whom *be* glory for ever. Amen.
Rev. 4:11. Thou art worthy, O Lord, to receive glory and honour and power: for thou hast created all things, and for thy pleasure they are and were created.

17. I John 4:8-10. He that loveth not knoweth not God; for God is love. In this was manifested the love of God toward us, because that God sent his only begotten Son into the world, that we might live through him. Herein is love, not that we loved God, but that he loved us, and sent his Son *to be* the propitiation for our sins.

18. Exod. 34:6, 7. And the LORD passed by before him, and proclaimed, The Lord, The LORD God, merciful and gracious, longsuffering, and abundant in goodness and truth, keeping mercy for thousands, forgiving iniquity and transgression and sin, and that will by no means clear *the guilty*.

19. Heb. 11:6. For he that cometh to God must believe that he is, and *that* he is a rewarder of them that diligently seek him.

20. Neh. 9:32, 33. Now therefore, our God, the great, the mighty, and the terrible God, who keepest covenant and mercy, let not all the trouble seem little before thee, that hath come upon us, on our kings, on our princes, and on our priests, and on our prophets, and on our fathers, and on all thy people, since the time of the kings of Assyria unto this day. Howbeit thou *art* just in all that is brought upon us; for thou hast done right, but we have done wickedly.

21. Hab. 1:13. *Thou art* of purer eyes than to behold evil, and canst not look on iniquity: wherefore lookest thou upon them that deal treacherously, *and* holdest thy tongue when the wicked devoureth *the man that is* more righteous than he?
Ps. 5:5, 6.

22. Exod. 34:7. Keeping mercy for thousands, forgiving iniquity and transgression and sin, and that will by no means clear *the guilty*; visiting the iniquity of the fathers upon the children, and upon the children's children, unto the third and to the fourth *generation*.
Nahum 1:2, 3. God *is* jealous, and the LORD revengeth; the LORD revengeth, and *is* furious; the LORD will take vengeance on his adversaries, and he reserveth *wrath* for his enemies. The LORD *is* slow to anger, and great in power, and will not at all acquit *the wicked*.

23. John 5:26. For as the Father hath life in himself; so hath he given to the Son to have life in himself.
Acts 7:2. And he said, Men, brethren, and fathers, hearken; The God of glory appeared unto our father Abraham, when he was in Mesopotamia, before he dwelt in Charran.
Ps. 119:68. Thou *art* good, and doest good; teach me thy statutes.
I Tim. 6:15. Which in his times he shall shew, *who is* the blessed and only Potentate, the King of kings, and Lord of lords.
Rom. 9:5. Who is over all, God blessed for ever. Amen.

standing in need of any creatures which he hath made, nor deriving any glory from them, but only manifesting his own glory in, by, unto, and upon them:[24] he is the alone fountain of all being, of whom, through whom, and to whom, are all things;[25] and hath most sovereign dominion over them, to do by them, for them, or upon them, whatsoever himself pleaseth.[26] In his sight all things are open and manifest;[27] his knowledge is infinite, infallible, and independent upon the creature;[28] so as nothing is to him contingent or uncertain.[29] He is most holy in all his counsels, in all his works, and in all his commands.[30] To him is due from angels and men, and every other creature, whatsoever worship, service, or obedience he is pleased to require of them.[31]

---

24. Acts 17:24, 25. God that made the world and all things therein, seeing that he is Lord of heaven and earth, dwelleth not in temples made with hands; neither is worshipped with men's hands, as though he needed any thing, seeing he giveth to all life, and breath, and all things.

25. Rom. 11:36. For of him, and through him, and to him, are all things: to whom be glory for ever. Amen.
    Isa. 40:12-17.

26. Dan. 4:25. The most High ruleth in the kingdom of men, and giveth it to whomsoever he will.
    Eph. 1:11. In whom also we have obtained an inheritance, being predestinated according to the purpose of him who worketh all things after the counsel of his own will.

27. Heb. 4:13. Neither is there any creature that is not manifest in his sight: but all things are naked and opened unto the eyes of him with whom we have to do.

28. Rom. 11:33, 34. O the depth of the riches both of the wisdom and knowledge of God! how unsearchable are his judgments, and his ways past finding out! For who hath known the mind of the Lord? or who hath been his counsellor?
    Ps. 147:5. Great is our Lord, and of great power: his understanding is infinite.

29. Isa. 46:9-11. Remember the former things of old: for I am God, and there is none else; I am God, and there is none like me, declaring the end from the beginning, and from ancient times the things that are not yet done, saying, My counsel shall stand, and I will do all my pleasure: calling a ravenous bird from the east, the man that executeth my counsel from a far country: yea, I have spoken it, I will also bring it to pass; I have purposed it, I will also do it.
    Acts 15:18; Ezek. 11:5.

30. Ps. 145:17. The Lord is righteous in all his ways, and holy in all his works.
    Rom. 7:12. Wherefore the law is holy, and the commandment holy, and just, and good.

31. Rev. 7:11, 12. And all the angels stood round about the throne, and about the elders and the four beasts, and fell before the throne on their faces, and worshipped God, saying, Amen: Blessing, and glory,

3. In the unity of the Godhead there be three persons of one substance, power, and eternity: God the Father, God the Son, and God the Holy Ghost.[32] The Father is of none, neither begotten nor proceeding; the Son is eternally begotten of the Father;[33] the Holy Ghost eternally proceeding from the Father and the Son.[34]

CHAPTER III

Of God's Eternal Decrees

1. God from all eternity did by the most wise and holy counsel of his own will, freely and unchangeably ordain whatsoever comes to pass;[1] yet so as thereby neither is God the author of

---

and wisdom, and thanksgiving, and honour, and power, and might, *be* unto our God for ever and ever. Amen.
Rev. 5:12-14.

32. Matt. 28:19. Go ye therefore, and teach all nations, baptizing them in the name of the Father, and of the Son, and of the Holy Ghost. II Cor. 13:14. The grace of the Lord Jesus Christ, and the love of God, and the communion of the Holy Ghost, *be* with you all. Amen.
Matt. 3:16, 17. And Jesus, when he was baptized, went up straightway out of the water: and, lo, the heavens were opened unto him, and he saw the Spirit of God descending like a dove, and lighting upon him: and lo a voice from heaven, saying, This is my beloved Son, in whom I am well pleased.

33. John 1:14, 18. And the Word was made flesh, and dwelt among us, (and we beheld his glory, the glory as of the only begotten of the Father,) full of grace and truth. . . . No man hath seen God at any time; the only begotten Son, which is in the bosom of the Father, he hath declared *him*.
John 17:24.

34. Gal. 4:6. And because ye are sons, God hath sent forth the Spirit of his Son into your hearts, crying, Abba, Father.
John 15:26.

1. Eph. 1:11. In whom also we have obtained an inheritance, being predestinated according to the purpose of him who worketh all things after the counsel of his own will.
Acts 4:27, 28. For of a truth against thy holy child Jesus, whom thou hast anointed, both Herod, and Pontius Pilate, with the Gentiles, and the people of Israel, were gathered together, for to do whatsoever thy hand and thy counsel determined before to be done.
Matt. 10:29, 30. Are not two sparrows sold for a farthing? and one of them shall not fall on the ground without your Father. But the very hairs of your head are all numbered.
Eph. 2:10.

sin;[2] nor is violence offered to the will of the creatures, nor is the liberty or contingency of second causes taken away, but rather established.[3]

2. Although God knows whatsoever may or can come to pass, upon all supposed conditions;[4] yet hath he not decreed anything because he foresaw it as future, or as that which would come to pass, upon such conditions.[5]

3. By the decree of God, for the manifestation of his glory,

---

2. James 1:13. Let no man say when he is tempted, I am tempted of God: for God cannot be tempted with evil, neither tempteth he any man.

I John 1:5. This then is the message which we have heard of him, and declare unto you, that God is light, and in him is no darkness at all.

3. Acts 2:23. Him, being delivered by the determinate counsel and fore-knowledge of God, ye have taken, and by wicked hands have crucified and slain.

Matt. 17:12. But I say unto you, That Elias is come already, and they knew him not, but have done unto him whatsoever they listed. Like-wise shall also the Son of man suffer of them.

Acts 4:27, 28. For of a truth against thy holy child Jesus, whom thou hast anointed, both Herod, and Pontius Pilate, with the Gentiles, and the people of Israel, were gathered together, for to do whatsoever thy hand and thy counsel determined before to be done.

John 19:11; Prov. 16:33; Acts 27:23, 24, 34, 44.

4. I Sam. 23:11, 12. Will the men of Keilah deliver me up into his hand? will Saul come down, as thy servant hath heard? O LORD God of Israel, I beseech thee, tell thy servant. And the LORD said, He will come down. Then said David, Will the men of Keilah deliver me and my men into the hand of Saul? And the LORD said, They will deliver *thee* up.

Matt. 11:21, 23. Woe unto thee, Chorazin! woe unto thee, Bethsaida! for if the mighty works, which were done in you, had been done in Tyre and Sidon, they would have repented long ago in sackcloth and ashes. . . . And thou, Capernaum, which art exalted unto heaven, shalt be brought down to hell: for if the mighty works, which have been done in thee, had been done in Sodom, it would have remained until this day.

Ps. 139:1-4.

5. Rom. 9:11, 13, 16, 18. (For *the children* being not yet born, neither having done any good or evil, that the purpose of God according to election might stand, not of works, but of him that calleth.) . . . As it is written, Jacob have I loved, but Esau have I hated. . . . So then *it is* not of him that willeth, nor of him that runneth, but of God that sheweth mercy. . . . Therefore hath he mercy on whom he will *have mercy,* and whom he will he hardeneth.

II Tim. 1:9. Who hath saved us, and called *us* with an holy calling, not according to our works, but according to his own purpose and grace, which was given us in Christ Jesus before the world began.

Eph. 1:4, 5.

some men and angels are predestinated unto everlasting life,[6] and others fore-ordained to everlasting death.[7]

4. These angels and men, thus predestinated and fore-ordained, are particularly and unchangeably designed; and their number is so certain and definite that it cannot be either increased or diminished.[8]

5. Those of mankind that are predestinated unto life, God, before the foundation of the world was laid,[9] according to his eternal and immutable purpose,[10] and the secret counsel and

---

6. I Tim. 5:21. I charge *thee* before God, and the Lord Jesus Christ, and the elect angels.

Acts 13:48. And when the Gentiles heard this, they were glad, and glorified the word of the Lord: and as many as were ordained to eternal life believed.

Rom. 8:29, 30; John 10:27-29.

7. Matt. 25:41. Then shall he say also unto them on the left hand, Depart from me, ye cursed, into everlasting fire, prepared for the devil and his angels.

Rom. 9:22, 23.

Jude 4. For there are certain men crept in unawares, who were before of old ordained to this condemnation, ungodly men, turning the grace of our God into lasciviousness, and denying the only Lord God, and our Lord Jesus Christ.

8. John 10:14-16, 27-29. I am the good shepherd, and know my *sheep*, and am known of mine. As the Father knoweth me, even so know I the Father: and I lay down my life for the sheep. And other sheep I have, which are not of this fold: them also I must bring, and they shall hear my voice; and there shall be one fold, *and* one shepherd. . . .

My sheep hear my voice, and I know them, and they follow me: and I give unto them eternal life; and they shall never perish, neither shall any *man* pluck them out of my hand. My Father, which gave *them* me, is greater than all; and no *man* is able to pluck *them* out of my Father's hand.

John 6:37-39. All that the Father giveth me shall come to me; and him that cometh to me I will in no wise cast out. For I came down from heaven, not to do mine own will, but the will of him that sent me. And this is the Father's will which hath sent me, that of all which he hath given me I should lose nothing, but should raise it up again at the last day.

John 13:18. I speak not of you all: I know whom I have chosen.

Acts 13:48. And when the Gentiles heard this, they were glad, and glorified the word of the Lord: and as many as were ordained to eternal life believed.

II Tim. 2:19. Nevertheless the foundation of God standeth sure, having this seal, The Lord knoweth them that are his.

9. Eph. 1:4. According as he hath chosen us in him before the foundation of the world.

10. Eph. 1:11. In whom also we have obtained an inheritance, being predestinated according to the purpose of him who worketh all things after the counsel of his own will.

good pleasure of his will,[11] hath chosen in Christ,[12] unto everlasting glory,[13] out of his free grace and love alone, without any foresight of faith or good works, or perseverance in either of them, or any other thing in the creature, as conditions, or causes moving him thereunto;[14] and all to the praise of his glorious grace.[15]

6. As God hath appointed the elect unto glory, so hath he, by the eternal and most free purpose of his will, fore-ordained all the means thereunto.[16] Wherefore they who are elected being fallen in Adam are redeemed by Christ,[17] are effectually called

---

11. Eph. 1:9. Having made known unto us the mystery of his will, according to his good pleasure which he hath purposed in himself.

12. II Tim. 1:9. Who hath saved us, and called us with an holy calling, not according to our works, but according to his own purpose and grace, which was given us in Christ Jesus before the world began.

13. Rom. 8:30. Moreover whom he did predestinate, them he also called: and whom he called, them he also justified: and whom he justified, them he also glorified.
I Peter 5:10. But the God of all grace, who hath called us unto his eternal glory by Christ Jesus.

14. II Tim. 1:9. Who hath saved us, and called us with an holy calling, not according to our works, but according to his own purpose and grace, which was given us in Christ Jesus before the world began.
Eph. 1:6. To the praise of the glory of his grace, wherein he hath made us accepted in the beloved.
Eph. 2:8, 9. For by grace are ye saved through faith; and that not of yourselves: it is the gift of God: Not of works, lest any man should boast.

15. Eph. 1:5, 6, 12. Having predestinated us unto the adoption of children by Jesus Christ to himself, according to the good pleasure of his will, to the praise of the glory of his grace, wherein he hath made us accepted in the beloved. . . . That we should be to the praise of his glory, who first trusted in Christ.

16. Eph. 2:10. For we are his workmanship, created in Christ Jesus unto good works, which God hath before ordained that we should walk in them.
II Thess. 2:13. But we are bound to give thanks alway to God for you, brethren beloved of the Lord, because God hath from the beginning chosen you to salvation through sanctification of the Spirit and belief of the truth.
I Peter 1:2. Elect according to the foreknowledge of God the Father, through sanctification of the Spirit, unto obedience and sprinkling of the blood of Jesus Christ: Grace unto you, and peace, be multiplied.
Eph. 1:4.

17. Rom. 5:19. For as by one man's disobedience many were made sinners, so by the obedience of one shall many be made righteous.
I Thess. 5:9, 10. For God hath not appointed us to wrath, but to obtain salvation by our Lord Jesus Christ, who died for us, that, whether we wake or sleep, we should live together with him.
Titus 2:14. Who gave himself for us, that he might redeem us from all

unto faith in Christ by his Spirit working in due season;[18] are justified,[19] adopted,[20] sanctified,[21] and kept by his power through faith unto salvation.[22] Neither are any other redeemed by Christ, effectually called, justified, adopted, sanctified, and saved, but the elect only.[23]

7. The rest of mankind, God was pleased, according to the unsearchable counsel of his own will, whereby he extendeth or withholdeth mercy as he pleaseth, for the glory of his sovereign

---

iniquity, and purify unto himself a peculiar people, zealous of good works.

18. Rom. 9:11. (For *the children* being not yet born, neither having done any good or evil, that the purpose of God according to election might stand, not of works, but of him that calleth.)

   II Thess. 2:13, 14. But we are bound to give thanks alway to God for you, brethren beloved of the Lord, because God hath from the beginning chosen you to salvation through sanctification of the Spirit and belief of the truth: whereunto he called you by our gospel, to the obtaining of the glory of our Lord Jesus Christ.

   I Cor. 1:9. God *is* faithful, by whom ye were called unto the fellowship of his Son Jesus Christ our Lord.

19. Rom. 8:30. Moreover whom he did predestinate, them he also called: and whom he called, them he also justified: and whom he justified, them he also glorified.

20. Eph. 1:5. Having predestinated us unto the adoption of children by Jesus Christ to himself, according to the good pleasure of his will.

21. Eph. 1:4. According as he hath chosen us in him before the foundation of the world, that we should be holy and without blame before him in love.

   I Thess. 4:3. For this is the will of God, *even* your sanctification.

   II Thess. 2:13. God hath from the beginning chosen you to salvation through sanctification of the Spirit and belief of the truth.

22. I Peter 1:5. Who are kept by the power of God through faith unto salvation.

   John 10:28. And I give unto them eternal life; and they shall never perish, neither shall any *man* pluck them out of my hand.

23. John 17:9. I pray for them: I pray not for the world, but for them which thou hast given me; for they are thine.

   John 6:64, 65. But there are some of you that believe not. For Jesus knew from the beginning who they were that believed not, and who should betray him. And he said, Therefore said I unto you, that no man can come unto me, except it were given unto him of my Father.

   John 8:47. He that is of God heareth God's words: ye therefore hear *them* not, because ye are not of God.

   John 10:26. But ye believe not, because ye are not of my sheep, as I said unto you.

   Acts 13:48. And when the Gentiles heard this, they were glad, and glorified the word of the Lord: and as many as were ordained to eternal life believed.

   I John 2:19. They went out from us, but they were not of us; for if they had been of us, they would *no doubt* have continued with us: but *they went out*, that they might be made manifest that they were not all of us.

power over his creatures, to pass by,[24] and to ordain them to dishonour and wrath for their sin,[25] to the praise of his glorious justice.[26]

8. The doctrine of this high mystery of predestination is to be handled with special prudence and care, that men attending the will of God revealed in his word, and yielding obedience thereunto, may, from the certainty of their effectual vocation, be assured of their eternal election. So shall this doctrine afford matter of praise, reverence, and admiration of God; and of humility, diligence, and abundant consolation to all that sincerely obey the gospel.[27]

CHAPTER IV

Of Creation

1. It pleased God the Father, Son, and Holy Ghost, for the manifestation of the glory of his eternal power, wisdom, and goodness, in the beginning, to create or make of nothing the world, and all things therein, whether visible or invisible, in the space of six days, and all very good.[1]

---

24. Matt. 11:25, 26. At that time Jesus answered and said, I thank thee, O Father, Lord of heaven and earth, because thou hast hid these things from the wise and prudent, and hast revealed them unto babes. Even so, Father: for so it seemed good in thy sight.

25. Rom. 2:8, 9. But unto them that are contentious, and do not obey the truth, but obey unrighteousness, indignation and wrath, tribulation and anguish, upon every soul of man that doeth evil, of the Jew first, and also of the Gentile.
II Thess. 2:10-12. And with all deceivableness of unrighteousness in them that perish; because they received not the love of the truth, that they might be saved. And for this cause God shall send them strong delusion, that they should believe a lie: that they all might be damned who believe not the truth, but had pleasure in unrighteousness.
Rom. 9:14-22.

26. Rev. 15:3, 4. And they sing the song of Moses the servant of God, and the song of the Lamb, saying, Great and marvellous are thy works, Lord God Almighty; just and true are thy ways, thou King of saints. Who shall not fear thee, O Lord, and glorify thy name? for thou only art holy: for all nations shall come and worship before thee; for thy judgments are made manifest. (See preceding context.)

27. See General Note, page 25.

1. Gen. 1:1-3. In the beginning God created the heaven and the earth. And the earth was without form, and void; and darkness was upon the

2. After God had made all other creatures, he created man, male and female,[2] with reasonable and immortal souls,[3] endued with knowledge, righteousness, and true holiness after his own image,[4] having the law of God written in their hearts,[5] and

face of the deep. And the Spirit of God moved upon the face of the waters. And God said, Let there be light: and there was light.

Exod. 20:11. For *in* six days the Lord made heaven and earth, the sea, and all that in them *is*.

Jer. 10:12. He hath made the earth by his power, he hath established the world by his wisdom, and hath stretched out the heavens by his discretion.

Col. 1:16. For by him were all things created, that are in heaven, and that are in earth, visible and invisible, whether *they be* thrones, or dominions, or principalities, or powers: all things were created by him, and for him.

John 1:2, 3. The same was in the beginning with God. All things were made by him; and without him was not anything made that was made.

Heb. 1:2. [God] hath in these last days spoken unto us by *his* Son, whom he hath appointed heir of all things, by whom also he made the worlds.

Heb. 11:3. Through faith we understand that the worlds were framed by the word of God, so that things which are seen were not made of things which do appear.

Ps. 104:24. O Lord, how manifold are thy works! in wisdom hast thou made them all: the earth is full of thy riches.

Gen. 1.

2. Gen. 1:27. So God created man in his *own* image, in the image of God created he him; male and female created he them.

3. Ps. 8:5, 6. For thou hast made him a little lower than the angels, and hast crowned him with glory and honour. Thou madest him to have dominion over the works of thy hands; thou hast put all *things* under his feet.

Gen. 2:19, 20. And out of the ground the Lord God formed every beast of the field, and every fowl of the air; and brought *them* unto Adam to see what he would call them: and whatsoever Adam called every living creature, that *was* the name thereof. And Adam gave names to all cattle, and to the fowl of the air, and to every beast of the field; but for Adam there was not found an help meet for him.

Luke 23:43. And Jesus said unto him, Verily I say unto thee, To day shalt thou be with me in paradise.

Matt. 10:28. And fear not them which kill the body, but are not able to kill the soul: but rather fear him which is able to destroy both soul and body in hell.

4. Gen. 1:26. And God said, Let us make man in our image, after our likeness.

Col. 3:10. And have put on the new *man*, which is renewed in knowledge after the image of him that created him.

Eph. 4:24. And that ye put on the new man, which after God is created in righteousness and true holiness.

5. Rom. 2:14, 15. For when the Gentiles, which have not the law, do by

power to fulfill it; and yet under a possibility of transgressing, being left to the liberty of their own will, which was subject unto change.[6] Besides this law written in their hearts, they received a command not to eat of the tree of the knowledge of good and evil;[7] which while they kept they were happy in their communion with God,[8] and had dominion over the creatures.[9]

CHAPTER V

Of Providence

1. God, the great Creator of all things, doth uphold, direct, dispose, and govern all creatures, actions, and things, from the

---

nature the things contained in the law, these, having not the law, are a law unto themselves: which shew the work of the law written in their hearts, their conscience also bearing witness, and *their* thoughts the mean while accusing or else excusing one another.

6. Gen. 2:16, 17. And the LORD God commanded the man, saying, Of every tree of the garden thou mayest freely eat: but of the tree of the knowledge of good and evil, thou shalt not eat of it: for in the day that thou eatest thereof thou shalt surely die.
Gen. 3:6, 17.

7. Gen. 2:16, 17. And the LORD God commanded the man, saying, Of every tree of the garden thou mayest freely eat: but of the tree of the knowledge of good and evil, thou shalt not eat of it: for in the day that thou eatest thereof thou shalt surely die.

8. Gen. 2:17. But of the tree of the knowledge of good and evil, thou shalt not eat of it: for in the day that thou eatest thereof thou shalt surely die.
Gen. 3:8-11, 23. And they heard the voice of the LORD God walking in the garden in the cool of the day: and Adam and his wife hid themselves from the presence of the LORD God amongst the trees of the garden. And the LORD God called unto Adam, and said unto him, Where *art* thou? And he said, I heard thy voice in the garden, and I was afraid, because I *was* naked; and I hid myself. And he said, Who told thee that thou *wast* naked? Hast thou eaten of the tree, whereof I commanded thee that thou shouldest not eat? . . . Therefore the LORD God sent him forth from the garden of Eden, to till the ground from whence he was taken.

9. Gen. 1:28. And have dominion over the fish of the sea, and over the fowl of the air, and over every living thing that moveth upon the earth.
Ps. 8:6-8.

greatest even to the least,[1] by his most wise and holy providence,[2] according to his infallible foreknowledge,[3] and the free and immutable counsel of his own will,[4] to the praise of the glory of his wisdom, power, justice, goodness, and mercy.[5]

2. Although in relation to the foreknowledge and decree of God, the first cause, all things come to pass immutably and infallibly,[6] yet, by the same providence, he ordereth them to fall

---

1. Neh. 9:6. Thou, *even* thou, *art* Lord alone; thou hast made heaven, the heaven of heavens, with all their host, the earth, and all *things* that *are* therein, the seas, and all that *is* *therein*, and thou preservest them all.

Heb. 1:3. Who being the brightness of *his* glory, and the express image of his person, and upholding all things by the word of his power.

Ps. 135:6. Whatsoever the Lord pleased, *that* did he in heaven, and in earth, in the seas, and all deep places.

Matt. 10:29-31. Are not two sparrows sold for a farthing? and one of them shall not fall on the ground without your Father. But the very hairs of your head are all numbered. Fear ye not therefore, ye are of more value than many sparrows.

Acts 17:25, 28; Matt. 6:26, 30; Job, chapters 38-41.

2. Prov. 15:3. The eyes of the Lord *are* in every place, beholding the evil and the good.

II Chron. 16:9. For the eyes of the Lord run to and fro throughout the whole earth, to shew himself strong in the behalf of *them* whose heart *is* perfect toward him.

Ps. 145:17; 104:24.

3. Acts 15:18. Known unto God are all his works from the beginning of the world.

4. Eph. 1:11. Who worketh all things after the counsel of his own will.
Ps. 33:11. The counsel of the Lord standeth for ever, the thoughts of his heart to all generations.

5. Eph. 3:10. To the intent that now unto the principalities and powers in heavenly *places* might be known by the church the manifold wisdom of God.

Rom. 9:17. For the scripture saith unto Pharaoh, Even for this same purpose have I raised thee up, that I might shew my power in thee, and that my name might be declared throughout all the earth.

Ps. 145.

6. Acts 2:23. Him, being delivered by the determinate counsel and foreknowledge of God, ye have taken, and by wicked hands have crucified and slain.

See under figures 3 and 4 above.

out according to the nature of second causes, either necessarily,[7] freely, or contingently.[8]

3. God, in his ordinary providence, maketh use of means,[9] yet is free to work without,[10] above,[11] and against them, at his pleasure.[12]

---

7. Gen. 8:22. While the earth remaineth, seedtime and harvest, and cold and heat, and summer and winter, and day and night shall not cease. Jer. 31:35. Thus saith the LORD, which giveth the sun for a light by day, and the ordinances of the moon and of the stars for a light by night, which divideth the sea when the waves thereof roar; The LORD of hosts is his name.

8. Exod. 21:13. If a man lie not in wait, but God deliver him into his hand; then I will appoint thee a place whither he shall flee.

   Gen. 50:19, 20. And Joseph said unto them, Fear not: for am I in the place of God? But as for you, ye thought evil against me; but God meant it unto good, to bring to pass, as it is this day, to save much people alive.

   I Kings 22:34. And a certain man drew a bow at a venture, and smote the king of Israel between the joints of the harness: wherefore he said unto the driver of his chariot, Turn thine hand, and carry me out of the host; for I am wounded.

   Isa. 10:6, 7. I will send him against an hypocritical nation, and against the people of my wrath will I give him a charge, to take the spoil, and to take the prey, and to tread them down . . . Howbeit he meaneth not so, neither doth his heart think so; but it is in his heart to destroy and cut off nations not a few.

9. Acts 27:24, 31, 44. Saying, Fear not, Paul; thou must be brought before Cæsar: and, lo, God hath given thee all them that sail with thee. . . . Paul said to the centurion and to the soldiers, Except these abide in the ship, ye cannot be saved. . . . And the rest, some on boards, and some on broken pieces of the ship. And so it came to pass, that they escaped all safe to land.

   Isa. 55:10, 11. For as the rain cometh down, and the snow from heaven, and returneth not thither, but watereth the earth, and maketh it bring forth and bud, that it may give seed to the sower, and bread to the eater: so shall my word be that goeth forth out of my mouth: it shall not return unto me void, but it shall accomplish that which I please, and it shall prosper in the thing whereto I sent it.

10. Hos. 1:7. But I will have mercy upon the house of Judah, and will save them by the LORD their God, and will not save them by bow, nor by sword, nor by battle, by horses, nor by horsemen.

11. Rom. 4:19-21. And being not weak in faith, he considered not his own body now dead, when he was about an hundred years old, neither yet the deadness of Sarah's womb: he staggered not at the promise of God through unbelief; but was strong in faith, giving glory to God; and being fully persuaded that, what he had promised, he was able also to perform.

12. II Kings 6:6. And the man of God said, Where fell it? And he shewed him the place. And he cut down a stick, and cast it in thither; and the iron did swim.

   Dan. 3:27. And the princes, governors, and captains, and the king's counsellors, being gathered together, saw these men, upon whose bodies the

4. The almighty power, unsearchable wisdom, and infinite goodness of God, so far manifest themselves in his providence, that it extendeth itself even to the first fall,[13] and all other sins of angels and men,[14] and that not by a bare permission, but such as hath joined with it a most wise and powerful bounding,[15] and otherwise ordering and governing of them, in a manifold dispensation, to his own holy ends;[16] yet so, as the sinfulness thereof proceedeth only from the creature, and not from God; who being most holy and righteous, neither is nor can be the author or approver of sin.[17]

---

fire had no power, nor was an hair of their head singed, neither were their coats changed, nor the smell of fire had passed on them.

13. This statement is sustained by the doctrines of God's decrees and providence. See citations under Chapter III and Chapter V, Sections 1, 2, 3.

14. Rom. 11:32, 33. For God hath concluded them all in unbelief, that he might have mercy upon all. O the depth of the riches both of the wisdom and knowledge of God! how unsearchable *are* his judgments, and his ways past finding out!

II Sam. 24:1. And again the anger of the LORD was kindled against Israel, and he moved David against them to say, Go, number Israel and Judah.

Acts 4:27, 28. For of a truth against thy holy child Jesus, whom thou hast anointed, both Herod, and Pontius Pilate, with the Gentiles, and the people of Israel, were gathered together, for to do whatsoever thy hand and thy counsel determined before to be done.

See citations under Chapter III and Chapter V, Sections 1, 2, 3.

15. II Kings 19:28. Because thy rage against me and thy tumult is come up into mine ears, therefore I will put my hook in thy nose, and my bridle in thy lips, and I will turn thee back by the way by which thou camest.

Isa. 10:5-7, 12, 15. O Assyrian, the rod of mine anger, and the staff in their hand is mine indignation. I will send him against an hypocritical nation, and against the people of my wrath will I give him a charge, to take the spoil, and to take the prey, and to tread them down like the mire of the streets. Howbeit he meaneth not so, neither doth his heart think so; but *it is* in his heart to destroy and cut off nations not a few. . . . Wherefore it shall come to pass, *that* when the Lord hath performed his whole work upon mount Zion and on Jerusalem, I will punish the fruit of the stout heart of the king of Assyria, and the glory of his high looks. . . . Shall the ax boast itself against him that heweth therewith? *or* shall the saw magnify itself against him that shaketh it? as if the rod should shake *itself* against them that lift it up, *or* as if the staff should lift up *itself, as if it were* no wood.

16. Gen. 50:20. But as for you, ye thought evil against me; *but* God meant it unto good, to bring to pass, as *it is* this day, to save much people alive.

See under figure 15 above.

17. I John 2:16. For all that *is* in the world, the lust of the flesh, and the lust of the eyes, and the pride of life, is not of the Father, but is of the world.

5. The most wise, righteous, and gracious God, doth often-times leave for a season his own children to manifold temptations and the corruption of their own hearts, to chastise them for their former sins, or to discover unto them the hidden strength of corruption and deceitfulness of their hearts, that they be humbled;[18] and to raise them to a more close and constant dependence for their support upon himself, and to make them more watchful against all future occasions of sin, and for sundry other just and holy ends.[19]

6. As for those wicked and ungodly men whom God, as a righteous judge, for former sins, doth blind and harden;[20] from them he not only withholdeth his grace, whereby they might

---

Ps. 50:21. These *things* hast thou done, and I kept silence; thou thoughtest that I was altogether *such an one* as thyself: *but* I will reprove thee, and set *them* in order before thine eyes.

James 1:13, 14. Let no man say when he is tempted, I am tempted of God: for God cannot be tempted with evil, neither tempteth he any man: but every man is tempted, when he is drawn away of his own lust, and enticed.

18. Deut. 8:2. And thou shalt remember all the way which the Lord thy God led thee these forty years in the wilderness, to humble thee, *and* to prove thee, to know what *was* in thine heart, whether thou wouldest keep his commandments, or no.

II Chron. 32:25, 26, 31. But Hezekiah rendered not again according to the benefit *done* unto him; for his heart was lifted up: therefore there was wrath upon him, and upon Judah and Jerusalem. Notwithstanding Hezekiah humbled himself for the pride of his heart, *both* he and the inhabitants of Jerusalem, so that the wrath of the Lord came not upon them in the days of Hezekiah. . . . Howbeit in *the business of* the ambassadors of the princes of Babylon, who sent unto him to enquire of the wonder that was *done* in the land, God left him, to try him, that he might know all *that was* in his heart.

19. II Cor. 12:7-9. And lest I should be exalted above measure through the abundance of the revelations, there was given to me a thorn in the flesh, the messenger of Satan to buffet me, lest I should be exalted above measure. For this thing I besought the Lord thrice, that it might depart from me. And he said unto me, My grace is sufficient for thee: for my strength is made perfect in weakness. Most gladly therefore will I rather glory in my infirmities, that the power of Christ may rest upon me.

Ps. 73; Ps. 77:1-12; Mark 14:66-72; John 21:15-17.

20. Rom. 1:24, 26, 28. Wherefore God also gave them up to uncleanness through the lusts of their own hearts, to dishonour their own bodies between themselves . . . For this cause God gave them up unto vile affections: for even their women did change the natural use into that which is against nature . . . And even as they did not like to retain God in *their* knowledge, God gave them over to a reprobate mind.

Rom. 11:7, 8. What then? Israel hath not obtained that which he seeketh for; but the election hath obtained it, and the rest were blinded

have been enlightened in their understandings, and wrought upon in their hearts;[21] but sometimes also withdraweth the gifts which they had;[22] and exposeth them to such objects as their corruption makes occasion of sin;[23] and withal, giveth them over to their own lusts, the temptations of the world, and the power of Satan;[24] whereby it cometh to pass that they harden themselves, even under those means which God useth for the softening of others.[25]

7. As the providence of God doth, in general, reach to all

(according as it is written, God hath given them the spirit of slumber, eyes that they should not see, and ears that they should not hear;) unto this day.

II Thess. 2:11, 12. And for this cause God shall send them strong delusion, that they should believe a lie: that they all might be damned who believed not the truth, but had pleasure in unrighteousness.

21. Deut. 29:4. Yet the LORD hath not given you an heart to perceive, and eyes to see, and ears to hear, unto this day.

Mark 4:11, 12. And he said unto them, Unto you it is given to know the mystery of the kingdom of God: but unto them that are without, all *these* things are done in parables: that seeing they may see, and not perceive; and hearing they may hear, and not understand; lest at any time they should be converted, and *their* sins should be forgiven them.

22. Matt. 13:12. But whosoever hath not, from him shall be taken away even that he hath.

Matt. 25:29.

23. II Kings 8:12, 13. And Hazael said, Why weepeth my lord? And he answered, Because I know the evil that thou wilt do unto the children of Israel: their strongholds wilt thou set on fire, and their young men wilt thou slay with the sword, and wilt dash their children, and rip up their women with child. And Hazael said, But what, *is* thy servant a dog, that he should do this great thing? And Elisha answered, The LORD hath shewed me that thou *shalt be* king over Syria.

24. Ps. 81:11, 12. But my people would not hearken to my voice; and Israel would none of me. So I gave them up unto their own hearts' lust: *and* they walked in their own counsels.

II Thess. 2:10-12. And with all deceivableness of unrighteousness in them that perish; because they received not the love of the truth, that they might be saved. And for this cause God shall send them strong delusion, that they should believe a lie: that they all might be damned who believed not the truth, but had pleasure in unrighteousness.

25. Exod. 8:15, 32. But when Pharaoh saw that there was respite, he hardened his heart, and hearkened not unto them; as the LORD had said. . . . And Pharaoh hardened his heart at this time also, neither would he let the people go.

II Cor. 2:15, 16. For we are unto God a sweet savour of Christ, in them that are saved, and in them that perish: to the one *we are* the savour of death unto death; and to the other the savour of life unto life. Isa. 8:14; Exod. 7:3; I Peter 2:7, 8; Isa. 6:9, 10; Acts 28:26, 27.

creatures; so, after a most special manner, it taketh care of his church, and disposeth all things to the good thereof.[26]

CHAPTER VI

Of the Fall of Man, of Sin, and of the Punishment Thereof

1. Our first parents, being seduced by the subtilty and temptation of Satan, sinned in eating the forbidden fruit.[1] This their sin God was pleased, according to his wise and holy counsel, to permit, having purposed to order it to his own glory.[2]

2. By this sin they fell from their original righteousness and communion with God,[3] and so became dead in sin,[4] and wholly defiled in all the faculties and parts of soul and body.[5]

---

26. Amos 9:8, 9. Behold the eyes of the Lord GOD are upon the sinful kingdom, and I will destroy it from off the face of the earth; saving that I will not utterly destroy the house of Jacob, saith the LORD. For, lo, I will command, and I will sift the house of Israel among all nations, like as corn is sifted in a sieve, yet shall not the least grain fall upon the earth.
Rom. 8:28. And we know that all things work together for good to them that love God, to them who are the called according to his purpose.
Eph. 1:22. And hath put all things under his feet, and gave him to be the head over all things to the church.
1. Gen. 3:13. And the woman said, The serpent beguiled me, and I did eat.
II Cor. 11:3. But I fear, lest by any means, as the serpent beguiled Eve through his subtilty, so your minds should be corrupted from the simplicity that is in Christ.
Gen. 3:1-14.
2. Rom. 5:19-21. For as by one man's disobedience many were made sinners, so by the obedience of one shall many be made righteous. Moreover the law entered, that the offence might abound. But where sin abounded, grace did much more abound: that as sin hath reigned unto death, even so might grace reign through righteousness unto eternal life by Jesus Christ our Lord.
3. Gen. 3:7, 8. And the eyes of them both were opened, and they knew that they were naked; and they sewed fig leaves together, and made themselves aprons. And they heard the voice of the LORD God walking in the garden in the cool of the day: and Adam and his wife hid themselves from the presence of the LORD God amongst the trees of the garden.
Gen. 2:17. But of the tree of the knowledge of good and evil, thou shalt not eat of it: for in the day that thou eatest thereof thou shalt surely die.
4. Rom. 5:12. Wherefore, as by one man sin entered into the world, and

3. They being the root of all mankind, the guilt of this sin was imputed,[6] and the same death in sin and corrupted nature conveyed to all their posterity, descending from them by ordinary generation.[7]

4. From this original corruption, whereby we are utterly indisposed, disabled, and made opposite to all good, and wholly inclined to all evil,[8] do proceed all actual transgressions.[9]

5. This corruption of nature, during this life, doth remain in those that are regenerated:[10] and although it be through

---

death by sin; and so death passed upon all men, for that all have sinned.
Eph. 2:3. Among whom also we all had our conversation in times past in the lusts of our flesh, fulfilling the desires of the flesh and of the mind; and were by nature the children of wrath, even as others.

5. Gen. 6:5. And GOD saw that the wickedness of man *was* great in the earth, and *that* every imagination of the thoughts of his heart *was* only evil continually.
Jer. 17:9. The heart *is* deceitful above all *things*, and desperately wicked: who can know it?
Rom. 3:10-19; Rom. 8:6-8; Ps. 58:1-5.

6. Acts 17:26. And hath made of one blood all nations of men for to dwell on all the face of the earth, and hath determined the times before appointed, and the bounds of their habitation.
Compare Gen. 2:16, 17, with Rom. 5:12, 15-19; I Cor. 15:21, 22, 45, 49.

7. Ps. 51:5. Behold, I was shapen in iniquity; and in sin did my mother conceive me.
Gen. 5:3. And Adam lived an hundred and thirty years, and begat *a son* in his own likeness, after his image; and called his name Seth.
John 3:6. That which is born of the flesh is flesh; and that which is born of the Spirit is spirit.
Rom. 3:10-18.

8. Rom. 5:6. For when we were yet without strength, in due time Christ died for the ungodly.
Rom. 8:7. Because the carnal mind *is* enmity against God: for it is not subject to the law of God, neither indeed can be.
John 3:6; Rom. 7:18.
Gen. 8:21. And the Lord said . . . The imagination of man's heart *is* evil from his youth.
Rom. 8:7. Because the carnal mind *is* enmity against God: for it is not there is none that understandeth, there is none that seeketh after God. They are all gone out of the way, they are together become unprofitable; there is none that doeth good, no, not one.

9. James 1:14, 15. But every man is tempted, when he is drawn away of his own lust, and enticed. Then when lust hath conceived, it bringeth forth sin: and sin, when it is finished, bringeth forth death.
Matt. 15:19. For out of the heart proceed evil thoughts, murders, adulteries, fornications, thefts, false witness, blasphemies.

10. Rom. 7:14, 17, 18, 23. For we know that the law is spiritual: but I am carnal, sold under sin. . . . Now then it is no more I that do it, but sin that dwelleth in me. For I know that in me (that is, in my flesh,) dwelleth no good thing: for to will is present with me; but *how* to perform that which is good I find not. . . . But I see another law in my

Christ pardoned and mortified, yet both itself, and all the motions thereof, are truly and properly sin.[11]

6. Every sin, both original and actual, being a transgression
of the righteous law of God, and contrary thereunto, doth, in its
own nature, bring guilt upon the sinner,[12] whereby he is bound
over to the wrath of God,[13] and curse of the law,[14] and so made
subject to death,[15] with all miseries spiritual, temporal, and
eternal.[16]

---

members, warring against the law of my mind, and bringing me into
captivity to the law of sin which is in my members.
James 3:2. For in many things we offend all.
I John 1:8, 10. If we say that we have no sin, we deceive ourselves, and
the truth is not in us. . . . If we say that we have not sinned, we make
him a liar, and his word is not in us.
Prov. 20:9. Who can say, I have made my heart clean, I am pure from
my sin?

11. Rom. 7:5, 7, 8, 25. For when we were in the flesh, the motions of
sins, which were by the law, did work in our members to bring forth
fruit unto death. . . . What shall we say then? Is the law sin? God
forbid. Nay, I had not known sin, but by the law: for I had not
known lust, except the law had said, Thou shalt not covet. But sin,
taking occasion by the commandment, wrought in me all manner of
concupiscence. For without the law sin was dead. . . . So then with the
mind I myself serve the law of God; but with the flesh the law of sin.

12. Rom. 3:19. Now we know that what things soever the law saith, it
saith to them who are under the law: that every mouth may be stopped,
and all the world may become guilty before God.
Rom. 2:15. Which shew the work of the law written in their hearts,
their conscience also bearing witness, and their thoughts the mean
while accusing or else excusing one another.
I John 3:4. Whosoever committeth sin transgresseth also the law: for
sin is the transgression of the law.

13. Eph. 2:3. Among whom also we all had our conversation in times past
in the lusts of our flesh, fulfilling the desires of the flesh and of the
mind; and were by nature the children of wrath, even as others.
Rom. 5:12.

14. Gal. 3:10. For as many as are of the works of the law are under the
curse: for it is written, Cursed is every one that continueth not in all
things which are written in the book of the law to do them.

15. Rom. 6:23. For the wages of sin is death.
Gen. 2:17.

16. Eph. 4:18. Having the understanding darkened, being alienated from
the life of God through the ignorance that is in them, because of the
blindness of their heart.
Matt. 25:41. Then shall he say also unto them on the left hand, Depart
from me, ye cursed, into everlasting fire, prepared for the devil and
his angels.
II Thess. 1:9. Who shall be punished with everlasting destruction from
the presence of the Lord, and from the glory of his power.
Rom. 1:21-28; Lev. 26:14 ff.; Deut. 28:15 ff.

CHAPTER VII

Of God's Covenant with Man

1. The distance between God and the creature is so great, that although reasonable creatures do owe obedience unto him as their Creator, yet they could never have any fruition of him, as their blessedness and reward, but by some voluntary condescension on God's part, which he hath been pleased to express by way of covenant.[1]

2. The first covenant made with man was a covenant of works,[2] wherein life was promised to Adam, and in him to his posterity, upon condition of perfect and personal obedience.[3]

3. Man, by his fall, having made himself incapable of life by that covenant, the Lord was pleased to make a second, commonly called the covenant of grace:[4] wherein he freely offered unto sinners life and salvation by Jesus Christ, requiring of them

---

1. See General Note, page 25.

2. Gen. 2:16, 17. And the LORD God commanded the man, saying, Of every tree of the garden thou mayest freely eat: but of the tree of the knowlege of good and evil, thou shalt not eat of it: for in the day that thou eatest thereof thou shalt surely die.

   Gal. 3:10. For as many as are of the works of the law are under the curse: for it is written, Cursed *is* every one that continueth not in all things which are written in the book of the law to do them.

   Hosea 6:7. But they like Adam have transgressed the covenant: there have they dealt treacherously against me. (A.S.V.)

   Rom. 5:12, 19; I Cor. 15:22, 47.

3. Compare Gen. 2:16, 17, with Rom. 5:12-14; Rom. 10:5; Luke 10:25-28; and with the covenants made with Noah and Abraham.

4. Matt. 26:28. For this is my blood of the new testament, which is shed for many for the remission of sins.

   Gal. 3:21. For if there had been a law given which could have given life, verily righteousness should have been by the law.

   Rom. 8:3. For what the law could not do, in that it was weak through the flesh, God sending his own Son in the likeness of sinful flesh, and for sin, condemned sin in the flesh.

   Isa. 42:6. I the LORD have called thee in righteousness, and will hold thine hand, and will keep thee, and give thee for a covenant of the people, for a light of the Gentiles.

   Gen. 3:15. And I will put enmity between thee and the woman, and between thy seed and her seed; it shall bruise thy head, and thou shalt bruise his heel.

   Heb. 10:5-10.

faith in him, that they may be saved,[5] and promising to give unto all those that are ordained unto life, his Holy Spirit, to make them willing and able to believe.[6]

4. This covenant of grace is frequently set forth in the Scripture by the name of a testament, in reference to the death of Jesus Christ, the testator, and to the everlasting inheritance, with all things belonging to it, therein bequeathed.

5. This covenant was differently administered in the time of the law, and in the time of the gospel:[7] under the law it was administered by promises, prophecies, sacrifices, circumcision, the paschal lamb, and other types and ordinances delivered to the people of the Jews, all fore-signifying Christ to come,[8] which

---

5. John 3:16. For God so loved the world, that he gave his only begotten Son, that whosoever believeth in him should not perish, but have everlasting life.

Acts 16:30, 31. And brought them out, and said, Sirs, what must I do to be saved? And they said, Believe on the Lord Jesus Christ, and thou shalt be saved, and thy house.

6. John 3:5-8. Jesus answered, Verily, verily, I say unto thee, Except a man be born of water and *of* the Spirit, he cannot enter into the kingdom of God. That which is born of the flesh is flesh; and that which is born of the Spirit is spirit. Marvel not that I said unto thee, Ye must be born again. The wind bloweth where it listeth, and thou hearest the sound thereof, but canst not tell whence it cometh, and whither it goeth: so is every one that is born of the Spirit.

John 6:37, 44. All that the Father giveth me shall come to me; and him that cometh to me I will in no wise cast out. . . . No man can come to me, except the Father which hath sent me draw him: and I will raise him up at the last day.

Ezek. 36:26, 27. A new heart also will I give you, and a new spirit will I put within you: and I will take away the stony heart out of your flesh, and I will give you an heart of flesh. And I will put my Spirit within you, and cause you to walk in my statutes, and ye shall keep my judgments, and do *them*.

7. Heb. 1:1, 2. God, who at sundry times and in divers manners spake in time past unto the fathers by the prophets, hath in these last days spoken unto us by *his* Son, whom he hath appointed heir of all things, by whom also he made the worlds.

II Cor. 3:6-9. Who also hath made us able ministers of the new testament; not of the letter, but of the spirit: for the letter killeth, but the spirit giveth life. But if the ministration of death, written *and* engraven in stones, was glorious, so that the children of Israel could not stedfastly behold the face of Moses for the glory of his countenance; which *glory* was to be done away: how shall not the ministration of the spirit be rather glorious? For if the ministration of condemnation *be* glory, much more doth the ministration of righteousness exceed in glory.

8. Rom. 4:11. And he received the sign of circumcision, a seal of the righteousness of the faith which *he had yet* being uncircumcised: that he might be the father of all them that believe, though they be not

were for that time sufficient and efficacious, through the operation of the Spirit, to instruct and build up the elect in faith in the promised Messiah,[9] by whom they had full remission of sins, and eternal salvation; and is called the Old Testament.[10]

6. Under the gospel, when Christ the substance was exhibited, the ordinances in which this covenant is dispensed, are the preaching of the word, and the administration of the sacraments of baptism and the Lord's supper;[11] which, though fewer in number, and administered with more simplicity and less outward glory, yet in them it is held forth in more fullness, evidence, and spiritual efficacy,[12] to all nations, both Jews and Gentiles;[13]

---

circumcised; that righteousness might be imputed unto them also. Heb., chapters 8, 9, 10.

9. Heb. 11:13. These all died in faith, not having received the promises, but having seen them afar off, and were persuaded of *them*, and embraced *them*, and confessed that they were strangers and pilgrims on the earth.

John 8:56. Your father Abraham rejoiced to see my day: and he saw *it*, and was glad.

Gal. 3:6-8. Even as Abraham believed God, and it was accounted to him for righteousness. Know ye therefore that they which are of faith, the same are the children of Abraham. And the scripture, foreseeing that God would justify the heathen through faith, preached before the gospel unto Abraham, *saying*, In thee shall all nations be blessed.

10. Acts 15:11. But we believe that through the grace of the Lord Jesus Christ we shall be saved, even as they.

Rom. 3:30. Seeing *it is* one God, which shall justify the circumcision by faith, and uncircumcision through faith.

Gal. 3:8, 9, 14.

11. Matt. 28:19, 20. Go ye therefore, and teach all nations, baptizing them in the name of the Father, and of the Son, and of the Holy Ghost: teaching them to observe all things whatsoever I have commanded you: and, lo, I am with you alway, *even* unto the end of the world. Amen.

I Cor. 11:23-25. For I have received of the Lord that which also I delivered unto you, That the Lord Jesus the *same* night in which he was betrayed took bread: and when he had given thanks, he brake *it*, and said, Take, eat: this is my body, which is broken for you: this do in remembrance of me. After the same manner also *he took* the cup, when he had supped, saying, This cup is the new testament in my blood: this do ye, as oft as ye drink *it*, in remembrance of me.

12. Heb. 8:6-13; II Cor. 3:9-11.

13. Eph. 2:15-19. Having abolished in his flesh the enmity, *even* the law of commandments *contained* in ordinances; for to make in himself of twain one new man, *so* making peace; and that he might reconcile both unto God in one body by the cross, having slain the enmity thereby: and came and preached peace to you which were afar off, and to them that were nigh. For through him we both have access by one Spirit unto the Father. Now therefore ye are no more strangers and

and is called the New Testament. There are not, therefore, two covenants of grace differing in substance, but one and the same under various dispensations.[14]

CHAPTER VIII

Of Christ the Mediator

1. It pleased God, in his eternal purpose, to choose and ordain the Lord Jesus, his only begotten Son, to be the mediator between God and man,[1] the prophet,[2] priest,[3] and king;[4] the head and

------

    foreigners, but fellow-citizens with the saints, and of the household of God.

    See under figure 11 above.

14. Gal. 3:17, 29. And this I say, *that* the covenant, that was confirmed before of God in Christ, the law, which was four hundred and thirty years after, cannot disannul, that it should make the promise of none effect. . . . And if ye *be* Christ's, then are ye Abraham's seed, and heirs according to the promise.

    See context and citations under figure 10 above.

1. Isa. 42:1. Behold my servant, whom I uphold; mine elect, *in whom* my soul delighteth; I have put my spirit upon him: he shall bring forth judgment to the Gentiles.

    I Peter 1:19, 20. But with the precious blood of Christ, as of a lamb without blemish and without spot: who verily was foreordained before the foundation of the world, but was manifest in these last times for you.

    I Tim. 2:5. For *there is* one God, and one mediator between God and men, the man Christ Jesus.

    John 3:16.

2. Acts 3:22. For Moses truly said unto the fathers, A prophet shall the Lord your God raise up unto you of your brethren, like unto me; him shall ye hear in all things whatsoever he shall say unto you.

    Deut. 18:15.

3. Heb. 5:5, 6. So also Christ glorified not himself to be made an high priest; but he that said unto him, Thou art my Son, to day have I begotten thee. As he saith also in another *place,* Thou *art* a priest for ever after the order of Melchisedec.

4. Ps. 2:6. Yet have I set my king upon my holy hill of Zion.

    Luke 1:33. And he shall reign over the house of Jacob for ever; and of his kingdom there shall be no end.

    Isa. 9:6, 7. For unto us a child is born, unto us a son is given: and the government shall be upon his shoulder: and his name shall be called Wonderful, Counsellor, The mighty God, The everlasting Father, The Prince of Peace. Of the increase of *his* government and peace *there shall be* no end, upon the throne of David, and upon his kingdom, to order it, and to establish it with judgment and with justice from henceforth even for ever. The zeal of the Lord of hosts will perform this.

saviour of his church,[5] the heir of all things,[6] and judge of the world;[7] unto whom he did, from all eternity, give a people to be his seed,[8] and to be by him in time redeemed, called, justified, sanctified, and glorified.[9]

2. The Son of God, the second person in the Trinity, being very and eternal God, of one substance, and equal with the Father, did, when the fullness of time was come, take upon him man's nature,[10] with all the essential properties and common

---

5. Eph. 5:23. For the husband is the head of the wife, even as Christ is the head of the church: and he is the saviour of the body.

6. Heb. 1:2. [God] hath in these last days spoken unto us by *his* Son, whom he hath appointed heir of all things.

7. Acts 17:31. Because he hath appointed a day, in the which he will judge the world in righteousness by *that* man whom he hath ordained; *whereof* he hath given assurance unto all *men*, in that he hath raised him from the dead.

II Cor. 5:10. For we must all appear before the judgment seat of Christ; that every one may receive the things *done* in *his* body, according to that he hath done, whether *it be* good or bad.

8. John 17:6. I have manifested thy name unto the men which thou gavest me out of the world: thine they were, and thou gavest them me; and they have kept thy word.

Eph. 1:4. According as he hath chosen us in him before the foundation of the world, that we should be holy and without blame before him in love.

John 6:37, 39. All that the Father giveth me shall come to me; and him that cometh to me I will in no wise cast out. . . . And this is the Father's will which hath sent me, that of all which he hath given me I should lose nothing, but should raise it up again at the last day.

Isa. 53:10. Yet it pleased the LORD to bruise him; he hath put *him* to grief: when thou shalt make his soul an offering for sin, he shall see *his* seed, he shall prolong *his* days, and the pleasure of the LORD shall prosper in his hand.

9. I Tim. 2:5, 6. For *there is* one God, and one mediator between God and men, the man Christ Jesus; who gave himself a ransom for all, to be testified in due time.

Mark 10:45. For even the Son of man came not to be ministered unto, but to minister, and to give his life a ransom for many.

I Cor. 1:30. But of him are ye in Christ Jesus, who of God is made unto us wisdom, and righteousness, and sanctification, and redemption.

Rom. 8:30. Moreover whom he did predestinate, them he also called: and whom he called, them he also justified: and whom he justified, them he also glorified.

10. John 1:1, 14. In the beginning was the Word, and the Word was with God, and the Word was God. . . . And the Word was made flesh and dwelt among us, (and we beheld his glory, the glory as of the only be-gotten of the Father,) full of grace and truth.

I John 5:20. And we know that the Son of God is come, and hath given

infirmities thereof; yet without sin:[11] being conceived by the power of the Holy Ghost, in the womb of the Virgin Mary, of her substance.[12] So that two whole, perfect, and distinct natures, the Godhead and the manhood, were inseparably joined together in one person, without conversion, composition, or confusion.[13] Which person is very God and very man, yet one Christ, the only mediator between God and man.[14]

3. The Lord Jesus in his human nature thus united to the divine, was sanctified and anointed with the Holy Spirit above measure;[15] having in him all the treasures of wisdom and knowl-

---

us an understanding, that we may know him that is true, and we are in him that is true, *even* in his Son Jesus Christ. This is the true God, and eternal life.

Phil. 2:6. Who, being in the form of God, thought it not robbery to be equal with God.

Gal. 4:4. But when the fulness of the time was come, God sent forth his Son, made of a woman, made under the law.

Heb. 2:14. Forasmuch then as the children are partakers of flesh and blood, he also himself likewise took part of the same; that through death he might destroy him that had the power of death, that is, the devil.

11. Heb. 2:17. Wherefore in all things it behooved him to be made like unto *his* brethren, that he might be a merciful and faithful high priest in things *pertaining* to God, to make reconciliation for the sins of the people.

Heb. 4:15. For we have not an high priest which cannot be touched with the feeling of our infirmities; but was in all points tempted like as *we are, yet* without sin.

12. Luke 1:27, 31, 35. To a virgin espoused to a man whose name was Joseph, of the house of David; and the virgin's name *was* Mary. . . . And, behold, thou shalt conceive in thy womb, and bring forth a son, and shalt call his name JESUS. . . . And the angel answered and said unto her, The Holy Ghost shall come upon thee, and the power of the Highest shall overshadow thee: therefore also that holy thing which shall be born of thee shall be called the Son of God.

Gal. 4:4. See under figure 10 above.

13. Col. 2:9. For in him dwelleth all the fulness of the Godhead bodily.

Rom. 9:5. Whose *are* the fathers, and of whom as concerning the flesh Christ *came*, who is over all, God blessed for ever. Amen.

See under figure 12 above.

14. Rom. 1:3, 4. Concerning his Son Jesus Christ our Lord, which was made of the seed of David according to the flesh; and declared *to be* the Son of God with power, according to the spirit of holiness, by the resurrection from the dead.

I Tim. 2:5. For *there is* one God, and one mediator between God and men, the man Christ Jesus.

15. Luke 4:18, 19, 21. The Spirit of the Lord *is* upon me, because he hath anointed me to preach the gospel to the poor; he hath sent me to heal the brokenhearted, to preach deliverance to the captives, and re-

edge,[16] in whom it pleased the Father that all fullness should dwell:[17] to the end that being holy, harmless, undefiled, and full of grace and truth, he might be thoroughly furnished to execute the office of a mediator and surety.[18] Which office he took not unto himself, but was thereunto called by his Father;[19] who put all power and judgment into his hand, and gave him commandment to execute the same.[20]

4. This office the Lord Jesus did most willingly undertake,[21] which, that he might discharge, he was made under the law,[22] and did perfectly fulfill it;[23] endured most grievous torments

---

covering of sight to the blind, to set at liberty them that are bruised, to preach the acceptable year of the Lord. . . . And he began to say unto them, This day is this scripture fulfilled in your ears.

Acts 10:38. How God anointed Jesus of Nazareth with the Holy Ghost and with power: who went about doing good, and healing all that were oppressed of the devil; for God was with him.

16. Col. 2:3. In whom are hid all the treasures of wisdom and knowledge.

17. Col. 1:19. For it pleased *the Father* that in him should all fulness dwell.

18. Heb. 7:26. For such an high priest became us, *who is* holy, harmless, undefiled, separate from sinners, and made higher than the heavens.

John 1:14. And the Word was made flesh, and dwelt among us, (and we beheld his glory, the glory as of the only begotten of the Father,) full of grace and truth.

Luke 4:18-21.

19. Heb. 5:4, 5. And no man taketh this honour unto himself, but he that is called of God, as *was* Aaron. So also Christ glorified not himself to be made an high priest; but he that said unto him, Thou art my Son, to day have I begotten thee.

20. John 5:22, 27. For the Father judgeth no man, but hath committed all judgment unto the Son . . . and hath given him authority to execute judgment also, because he is the Son of man.

Matt. 28:18. And Jesus came and spake unto them, saying, All power is given unto me in heaven and in earth.

21. Ps. 40:7, 8. Then said I, Lo, I come: in the volume of the book *it is* written of me, I delight to do thy will, O my God: yea, thy law *is* within my heart.

Phil. 2:5-8. Let this mind be in you, which was also in Christ Jesus: who, being in the form of God, thought it not robbery to be equal with God: but made himself of no reputation, and took upon him the form of a servant, and was made in the likeness of men: and being found in fashion as a man, he humbled himself, and became obedient unto death, even the death of the cross.

22. Gal. 4:4. But when the fulness of the time was come, God sent forth his Son, made of a woman, made under the law.

23. Matt. 3:15. Thus it becometh us to fulfil all righteousness.

John 17:4. I have glorified thee on the earth: I have finished the work which thou gavest me to do.

immediately in his soul,[24] and most painful sufferings in his body;[25] was crucified and died;[26] was buried, and remained under the power of death, yet saw no corruption.[27] On the third day he arose from the dead,[28] with the same body in which he suffered;[29] with which also he ascended into heaven, and there sitteth at the right hand of his Father,[30] making intercession;[31]

---

24. Matt. 26:37, 38. And he took with him Peter and the two sons of Zebedee, and began to be sorrowful and very heavy. Then saith he unto them, My soul is exceeding sorrowful, even unto death.

Luke 22:44. And being in an agony he prayed more earnestly: and his sweat was as it were great drops of blood falling down to the ground.

Matt. 27:46. And about the ninth hour Jesus cried with a loud voice, saying, Eli, Eli, lama sabachthani? that is to say, My God, my God, why hast thou forsaken me?

25. Matt., chapters 26 and 27.

26. Phil. 2:8. He humbled himself, and became obedient unto death, even the death of the cross.

27. Acts 2:24, 27. Whom God hath raised up, having loosed the pains of death: because it was not possible that he should be holden of it. . . . Because thou wilt not leave my soul in hell, neither wilt thou suffer thine Holy One to see corruption.

Acts 13:37. But he, whom God raised again, saw no corruption.

28. I Cor. 15:4. That he was buried, and that he rose again the third day according to the scriptures.

29. John 20:25, 27. But he said unto them, Except I shall see in his hands the print of the nails, and put my finger into the print of the nails, and thrust my hand into his side, I will not believe. . . . Then saith he to Thomas, Reach hither thy finger, and behold my hands; and reach hither thy hand, and thrust it into my side: and be not faithless, but believing.

30. Luke 24:50, 51. And he led them out as far as to Bethany, and he lifted up his hands, and blessed them. And it came to pass, while he blessed them, he was parted from them, and carried up into heaven.

Acts 1:9. And when he had spoken these things, while they beheld, he was taken up; and a cloud received him out of their sight.

Acts 2:33-36. Therefore being by the right hand of God exalted, and having received of the Father the promise of the Holy Ghost, he hath shed forth this, which we now see and hear. For David is not ascended into the heavens: but he saith himself, The Lord said unto my Lord, Sit thou on my right hand, until I make thy foes thy footstool. Therefore let all the house of Israel know assuredly, that God hath made that same Jesus, whom ye have crucified, both Lord and Christ.

31. Rom. 8:34. Who is even at the right hand of God, who also maketh intercession for us.

Heb. 7:25. Wherefore he is able also to save them to the uttermost that come unto God by him, seeing he ever liveth to make intercession for them.

and shall return to judge men and angels, at the end of the world.[32]

5. The Lord Jesus, by his perfect obedience and sacrifice of himself, which he through the eternal Spirit once offered up unto God, hath fully satisfied the justice of his Father;[33] and purchased not only reconciliation, but an everlasting inheritance in the kingdom of heaven, for all those whom the Father hath given unto him.[34]

---

32. Acts 10:42. And he commanded us to preach unto the people, and to testify that it is he which was ordained of God *to be* the Judge of quick and dead.

Matt. 13:40-42. As therefore the tares are gathered and burned in the fire; so shall it be in the end of this world. The Son of man shall send forth his angels, and they shall gather out of his kingdom all things that offend, and them which do iniquity; and shall cast them into a furnace of fire: there shall be wailing and gnashing of teeth.

Matt. 16:27. For the Son of man shall come in the glory of his Father with his angels; and then he shall reward every man according to his works.

Matt. 25:31-33. When the Son of man shall come in his glory, and all the holy angels with him, then shall he sit upon the throne of his glory: and before him shall be gathered all nations: and he shall separate them one from another, as a shepherd divideth *his* sheep from the goats: and he shall set the sheep on his right hand, but the goats on the left.

II Tim. 4:1. I charge *thee* therefore before God, and the Lord Jesus Christ, who shall judge the quick and the dead at his appearing and his kingdom.

33. Rom. 5:19. For as by one man's disobedience many were made sinners, so by the obedience of one shall many be made righteous.

Heb. 9:14. How much more shall the blood of Christ, who through the eternal Spirit offered himself without spot to God, purge your conscience from dead works to serve the living God?

Rom. 3:25, 26. Whom God hath set forth *to be* a propitiation through faith in his blood, to declare his righteousness for the remission of sins that are past, through the forbearance of God; to declare, *I say*, at this time his righteousness: that he might be just, and the justifier of him which believeth in Jesus.

Heb. 10:14. For by one offering he hath perfected for ever them that are sanctified.

Eph. 5:2.

34. Eph. 1:11, 14. In whom also we have obtained an inheritance, being predestinated according to the purpose of him who worketh all things after the counsel of his own will . . . which is the earnest of our inheritance until the redemption of the purchased possession, unto the praise of his glory.

John 17:2. As thou hast given him power over all flesh, that he should give eternal life to as many as thou hast given him.

6. Although the work of redemption was not actually wrought by Christ till after his incarnation, yet the virtue, efficacy, and benefits thereof were communicated unto the elect, in all ages successively from the beginning of the world, in and by those promises, types, and sacrifices wherein he was revealed, and signified to be the seed of the woman, which should bruise the serpent's head, and the lamb slain from the beginning of the world, being yesterday and today the same and for ever.[35]

7. Christ, in the work of mediation, acteth according to both natures; by each nature doing that which is proper to itself;[36] yet by reason of the unity of the person, that which is proper to one nature is sometimes, in Scripture, attributed to the person denominated by the other nature.[37]

8. To all those for whom Christ hath purchased redemption, he doth certainly and effectually apply and communicate the

---

Rom. 5:10, 11. For if, when we were enemies, we were reconciled to God by the death of his Son, much more, being reconciled, we shall be saved by his life. And not only *so*, but we also joy in God through our Lord Jesus Christ, by whom we have now received the atonement.
Heb. 9:12, 15.

35. Gen. 3:15. And I will put enmity between thee and the woman, and between thy seed and her seed; it shall bruise thy head, and thou shalt bruise his heel.

Rev. 13:8. And all that dwell upon the earth shall worship him, whose names are not written in the book of life of the Lamb slain from the foundation of the world.

Heb. 13:8. Jesus Christ the same yesterday, and to day, and for ever. See citations under Chapter VII, Section 5, figures 9 and 10.

36. I Peter 3:18. For Christ also hath once suffered for sins, the just for the unjust, that he might bring us to God, being put to death in the flesh, but quickened by the Spirit.

Heb. 9:14. How much more shall the blood of Christ, who through the eternal Spirit offered himself without spot to God, purge your conscience from dead works to serve the living God?

John 10:17, 18. Therefore doth my Father love me, because I lay down my life, that I might take it again. No man taketh it from me, but I lay it down of myself. I have power to lay it down, and I have power to take it again. This commandment have I received of my Father.

37. Acts 20:28. Feed the church of God, which he hath purchased with his own blood.

John 3:13. And no man hath ascended up to heaven, but he that came down from heaven, *even* the Son of man which is in heaven.

I John 3:16. Hereby perceive we the love *of God*, because he laid down his life for us.

same;[38] making intercession for them,[39] and revealing unto them, in and by the word, the mysteries of salvation;[40] effectually persuading them by his Spirit to believe and obey; and governing their hearts by his word and Spirit;[41] overcoming all their enemies by his almighty power and wisdom, in such manner and ways as are most consonant to his wonderful and unsearchable dispensation.[42]

CHAPTER IX

Of the Holy Spirit

1. The Holy Spirit, the third person in the Trinity, proceeding from the Father and the Son, of the same substance and equal in power and glory, is, together with the Father and the Son, to be believed in, loved, obeyed, and worshipped throughout all ages.

---

38. John 6:37, 39. All that the Father giveth me shall come to me; and him that cometh to me I will in no wise cast out. . . . And this is the Father's will which hath sent me, that of all which he hath given me I should lose nothing, but should raise it up again at the last day. John 10:16. And other sheep I have, which are not of this fold: them also I must bring, and they shall hear my voice.
39. I John 2:1. If any man sin, we have an advocate with the Father, Jesus Christ the righteous.
    Rom. 8:34. It is Christ that died, yea rather, that is risen again, who is even at the right hand of God, who also maketh intercession for us.
40. John 15:15. For all things that I have heard of my Father I have made known unto you.
    John 17:6. I have manifested thy name unto the men which thou gavest me out of the world: thine they were, and thou gavest them me; and they have kept thy word.
    Gal. 1:11, 12; Eph. 1:7-9.
41. Rom. 8:9, 14. But ye are not in the flesh, but in the Spirit, if so be that the Spirit of God dwell in you. Now if any man have not the Spirit of Christ, he is none of his. . . . For as many as are led by the Spirit of God, they are the sons of God.
    Titus 3:4, 5. But after that the kindness and love of God our Saviour toward man appeared, not by works of righteousness which we have done, but according to his mercy he saved us, by the washing of regeneration, and renewing of the Holy Ghost.
    Rom. 15:18, 19; John 17:17.
42. Ps. 110:1. The Lord said unto my Lord, Sit thou at my right hand, until I make thine enemies thy footstool.
    I Cor. 15:25, 26. For he must reign, till he hath put all enemies under his feet. The last enemy that shall be destroyed is death.
    Mal. 4:2, 3; Col. 2:15.

Paragraph I
    II Cor. 13:14. The grace of the Lord Jesus Christ, and the love of

2. He is the Lord and Giver of life, everywhere present, and is the source of all good thoughts, pure desires, and holy counsels in men. By him the prophets were moved to speak the word of God, and all the writers of the Holy Scriptures inspired to record infallibly the mind and will of God. The dispensation of the gospel is especially committed to him. He prepares the way for it, accompanies it with his persuasive power, and urges its message upon the reason and conscience of men, so that they who reject its merciful offer are not only without excuse, but are also guilty of resisting the Holy Spirit.

God, and the communion of the Holy Ghost, *be* with you all. Amen. John 15:26. But when the Comforter is come, whom I will send unto you from the Father, *even* the Spirit of truth, which proceedeth from the Father, he shall testify of me.

Matt. 28:19; Matt. 3:16, 17; Luke 1:35.

Eph. 4:30. And grieve not the holy Spirit of God, whereby ye are sealed unto the day of redemption.

Heb. 10:29. Of how much sorer punishment, suppose ye, shall he be thought worthy, who hath trodden under foot the Son of God, and hath counted the blood of the covenant, wherewith he was sanctified, an unholy thing, and hath done despite unto the Spirit of grace? I Cor. 10:10, 11; Rev. 22:17.

Eph. 2:18-20, 22. For through him we both have access by one Spirit unto the Father. . . . and are built upon the foundation of the apostles and prophets, Jesus Christ himself being the chief corner *stone* . . . in whom ye also are builded together for an habitation of God through the Spirit.

John 14:26. But the Comforter, *which is* the Holy Ghost, whom the Father will send in my name, he shall teach you all things, and bring all things to your remembrance, whatsoever I have said unto you. John 16:7; Gal. 4:6.

Acts 5:3, 4. But Peter said, Ananias, why hath Satan filled thine heart to lie to the Holy Ghost . . . why hast thou conceived this thing in thine heart? thou hast not lied unto men, but unto God.

Acts 16:6, 7. Now when they . . . were forbidden of the Holy Ghost to preach the word in Asia, after they were come to Mysia, they assayed to go into Bithynia: but the Spirit suffered them not.

Mark 3:29. But he that shall blaspheme against the Holy Ghost hath never forgiveness, but is in danger of eternal damnation.

Rom. 8:26, 27; I John 2:20-27.

Paragraph 2

Eph. 4:30. And grieve not the holy Spirit of God, whereby ye are sealed unto the day of redemption.

Eph. 5:9. For the fruit of the Spirit *is* in all goodness and righteousness and truth.

Gen. 1:2. And the earth was without form, and void; and darkness *was* upon the face of the deep. And the Spirit of God moved upon the face of the waters.

3. The Holy Spirit, whom the Father is ever willing to give to all who ask him, is the only efficient agent in the application of redemption. He regenerates men by his grace, convicts them of sin, moves them to repentance, and persuades and enables them to embrace Jesus Christ by faith. He unites all believers to Christ, dwells in them as their Comforter and Sanctifier, gives to them the spirit of Adoption and Prayer, and performs all those gracious offices by which they are sanctified and sealed unto the day of redemption.

John 3:5. Jesus answered . . . Except a man be born of water and *of* the Spirit, he cannot enter into the kingdom of God.

Acts 2:1-21.

Gal. 5:22-25. But the fruit of the Spirit is love, joy, peace, longsuffering, gentleness, goodness, faith, meekness, temperance: against such there is no law. And they that are Christ's have crucified the flesh with the affections and lusts. If we live in the Spirit, let us also walk in the Spirit.

John 16:8-11. And when he is come, he will reprove the world of sin, and of righteousness, and of judgment: of sin, because they believe not on me; of righteousness, because I go to my Father, and ye see me no more; of judgment, because the prince of this world is judged.

II Peter 1:21. For the prophecy came not in old time by the will of man: but holy men of God spake *as they were* moved by the Holy Ghost.

II Tim. 3:16. All scripture *is* given by inspiration of God, and *is* profitable for doctrine, for reproof, for correction, for instruction in righteousness.

I Cor. 2:10. But God hath revealed *them* unto us by his Spirit: for the Spirit searcheth all things, yea, the deep things of God.

I Peter 1:11.

John 16:13-15. Howbeit when he, the Spirit of truth, is come, he will guide you into all truth: for he shall not speak of himself; but whatsoever he shall hear, *that* shall he speak: and he will shew you things to come. He shall glorify me: for he shall receive of mine, and shall shew *it* unto you. All things that the Father hath are mine: therefore said I, that he shall take of mine, and shall shew *it* unto you.

Acts 7:51.

I Thess. 5:19. Quench not the Spirit.

Eph. 4:30.

Ps. 104:30. Thou sendest forth thy spirit, they are created: and thou renewest the face of the earth.

Paragraph 3

John 3:1-8.

Acts 2:38. Then Peter said unto them, Repent, and be baptized every one of you in the name of Jesus Christ for the remission of sins, and ye shall receive the gift of the Holy Ghost.

Luke 11:13. If ye then, being evil, know how to give good gifts unto

4. By the indwelling of the Holy Spirit all believers being vitally united to Christ, who is the Head, are thus united one to another in the church, which is his body. He calls and anoints ministers for their holy office, qualifies all other officers in the

---

your children: how much more shall *your* heavenly Father give the Holy Spirit to them that ask him?

I Cor. 12:3. Wherefore I give you to understand, that no man speaking by the Spirit of God calleth Jesus accursed: and *that* no man can say that Jesus is the Lord, but by the Holy Ghost.

John 7:37-39.

John 16:13. Howbeit when he, the Spirit of truth, is come, he will guide you into all truth: for he shall not speak of himself; but whatsoever he shall hear, *that* shall he speak: and he will shew you things to come.

John 16:7-11.

Rev. 22:17. And the Spirit and the bride say, Come. And let him that heareth say, Come. And let him that is athirst come. And whosoever will, let him take the water of life freely.

Titus 3:5-7. Not by works of righteousness which we have done, but according to his mercy he saved us, by the washing of regeneration, and renewing of the Holy Ghost; which he shed on us abundantly through Jesus Christ our Saviour; that being justified by his grace, we should be made heirs according to the hope of eternal life.

II Thess. 2:13. But we are bound to give thanks alway to God for you, brethren beloved of the Lord, because God hath from the beginning chosen you to salvation through sanctification of the Spirit and belief of the truth.

Gal. 4:6. And because ye are sons, God hath sent forth the Spirit of his Son into your hearts, crying, Abba, Father.

I John 4:2. Hereby know ye the Spirit of God: Every spirit that confesseth that Jesus Christ is come in the flesh is of God.

Rom. 8:14, 17, 26, 27. For as many as are led by the Spirit of God, they are the sons of God. . . . and if children, then heirs; heirs of God, and joint-heirs with Christ; if so be that we suffer with *him*, that we may be also glorified together. . . . Likewise the Spirit also helpeth our infirmities: for we know not what we should pray for as we ought: but the Spirit itself maketh intercession for us with groanings which cannot be uttered. And he that searcheth the hearts knoweth what *is* the mind of the Spirit, because he maketh intercession for the saints according to *the will of* God.

Eph. 4:30. And grieve not the holy Spirit of God, whereby ye are sealed unto the day of redemption.

I Cor. 2:13, 14. Which things also we speak, not in the words which man's wisdom teacheth, but which the Holy Ghost teacheth; comparing spiritual things with spiritual. But the natural man receiveth not the things of the Spirit of God: for they are foolishness unto him: neither can he know *them,* because they are spiritually discerned.

Paragraph 4

Eph. 2:14-18. For he is our peace, who hath made both one, and hath broken down the middle wall of partition *between us;* having abolished in his flesh the enmity, *even* the law of commandments *contained* in ordinances; for to make in himself of twain one new man, *so* mak-

church for their special work, and imparts various gifts and graces to its members. He gives efficacy to the word and to the ordinances of the gospel. By him the church will be preserved, increased, purified, and at last made perfectly holy in the presence of God.

CHAPTER X

Of the Gospel

1. God in infinite and perfect love, having provided in the covenant of grace, through the mediation and sacrifice of the Lord Jesus Christ, a way of life and salvation, sufficient for and adapted to the whole lost race of man, doth freely offer this salvation to all men in the gospel.

---

ing peace; and that he might reconcile both unto God in one body by the cross, having slain the enmity thereby: and came and preached peace to you which were afar off, and to them that were nigh. For through him we both have access by one Spirit unto the Father.
Eph. 4:1-6.
Eph. 5:18. And be not drunk with wine, wherein is excess; but be filled with the Spirit.
Acts 2:4. And they were all filled with the Holy Ghost, and began to speak with other tongues, as the Spirit gave them utterance.
Acts 13:2. As they ministered to the Lord, and fasted, the Holy Ghost said, Separate me Barnabas and Saul for the work whereunto I have called them.
I Cor. 12.
II Peter 1:19-21. We have also a more sure word of prophecy; whereunto ye do well that ye take heed, as unto a light that shineth in a dark place, until the day dawn, and the day star arise in your hearts: knowing this first, that no prophecy of the scripture is of any private interpretation. For the prophecy came not in old time by the will of man: but holy men of God spake *as they were* moved by the Holy Ghost.
I Thess. 1:5, 6. For our gospel came not unto you in word only, but also in power, and in the Holy Ghost, and in much assurance; as ye know what manner of men we were among you for your sake. And ye became followers of us, and of the Lord, having received the word in much affliction, with joy of the Holy Ghost.
John 20:22, 23. And when he had said this, he breathed on *them*, and saith unto them, Receive ye the Holy Ghost: whose soever sins ye remit, they are remitted unto them; *and* whose soever *sins* ye retain, they are retained.
Matt. 28:19, 20. Go ye therefore, and teach all nations, baptizing them in the name of the Father, and of the Son, and of the Holy Ghost: teaching them to observe all things whatsoever I have commanded you: and, lo, I am with you alway, *even* unto the end of the world. Amen.
Paragraph 1
Rev. 22:17. And the Spirit and the bride say, Come. And let him that heareth say, Come. And let him that is athirst come. And whosoever will, let him take the water of life freely.

2. In the gospel God declares his love for the world and his desire that all men should be saved; reveals fully and clearly the only way of salvation; promises eternal life to all who truly repent and believe in Christ; invites and commands all to embrace the offered mercy; and by his Spirit accompanying the word pleads with men to accept his gracious invitation.

John 3:16. For God so loved the world, that he gave his only begotten Son, that whosoever believeth in him should not perish, but have everlasting life.

I John 2:1, 2. My little children, these things I write unto you, that ye sin not. And if any man sin, we have an advocate with the Father, Jesus Christ the righteous: and he is the propitiation for our sins: and not for our's only, but also for *the sins of* the whole world.

Acts 2:38, 39. Then Peter said unto them, Repent, and be baptized every one of you in the name of Jesus Christ for the remission of sins, and ye shall receive the gift of the Holy Ghost. For the promise is unto you, and to your children, and to all that are afar off, *even* as many as the Lord our God shall call.

Matt. 11:28-30. Come unto me, all *ye* that labour and are heavy laden, and I will give you rest. Take my yoke upon you, and learn of me; for I am meek and lowly in heart: and ye shall find rest unto your souls. For my yoke *is* easy, and my burden is light.

II Cor. 5:14-19.

Titus 2:11. For the grace of God that bringeth salvation hath appeared to all men.

Heb. 2:9. But we see Jesus, who was made a little lower than the angels for the suffering of death, crowned with glory and honour; that he by the grace of God should taste death for every man.

Luke 24:46, 47. And said unto them, Thus it is written, and thus it behoved Christ to suffer, and to rise from the dead the third day: and that repentance and remission of sins should be preached in his name among all nations, beginning at Jerusalem.

Paragraph 2

Matt. 28:19, 20. Go ye therefore, and teach all nations, baptizing them in the name of the Father, and of the Son, and of the Holy Ghost: teaching them to observe all things whatsoever I have commanded you: and, lo, I am with you alway, *even* unto the end of the world. Amen.

Acts 4:12. Neither is there salvation in any other: for there is none other name under heaven given among men, whereby we must be saved.

John 6:37-40. All that the Father giveth me shall come to me; and him that cometh to me I will in no wise cast out. For I came down from heaven, not to do mine own will, but the will of him that sent me. And this is the Father's will which hath sent me, that of all which he hath given me I should lose nothing, but should raise it up again at the last day. And this is the will of him that sent me, that every one which seeth the Son, and believeth on him, may have everlasting life: and I will raise him up at the last day.

John 17:3. And this is life eternal, that they might know thee the only true God, and Jesus Christ, whom thou hast sent.

Acts 16:31. And they said, Believe on the Lord Jesus Christ, and thou shalt be saved, and thy house.

Acts 2:38. Then Peter said unto them, Repent, and be baptized every

3. It is the duty and privilege of everyone who hears the gospel immediately to accept its merciful provisions; and they who continue in impenitence and unbelief incur aggravated guilt and perish by their own fault.

---

one of you in the name of Jesus Christ for the remission of sins, and ye shall receive the gift of the Holy Ghost.

Gal. 2:16-20.

Rom. 1:16, 17. For I am not ashamed of the gospel of Christ: for it is the power of God unto salvation to every one that believeth; to the Jew first, and also to the Greek. For therein is the righteousness of God revealed from faith to faith: as it is written, The just shall live by faith.

Rom. 4:5. But to him that worketh not, but believeth on him that justifieth the ungodly, his faith is counted for righteousness.

Acts 13:38, 39, 48. Be it known unto you . . . that through this man is preached unto you the forgiveness of sins: and by him all that believe are justified from all things, from which ye could not be justified by the law of Moses. . . . And when the Gentiles heard this, they were glad, and glorified the word of the Lord: and as many as were ordained to eternal life believed.

II Peter 3:9. The Lord is not slack concerning his promise, as some men count slackness; but is longsuffering to us-ward, not willing that any should perish, but that all should come to repentance.

Matt. 11:28-30. Come unto me, all ye that labour and are heavy laden, and I will give you rest. Take my yoke upon you, and learn of me; for I am meek and lowly in heart: and ye shall find rest unto your souls. For my yoke is easy, and my burden is light.

Mark 1:14, 15. Now after that John was put in prison, Jesus came into Galilee, preaching the gospel of the kingdom of God, and saying, The time is fulfilled, and the kingdom of God is at hand: repent ye, and believe the gospel.

Acts 17:30. And the times of this ignorance God winked at; but now commandeth all men every where to repent.

Rev. 22:17. And the Spirit and the bride say, Come. And let him that heareth say, Come. And let him that is athirst come. And whosoever will, let him take the water of life freely.

Ezek. 33:11. Say unto them, As I live, saith the Lord God, I have no pleasure in the death of the wicked; but that the wicked turn from his way and live: turn ye, turn ye from your evil ways; for why will ye die, O house of Israel?

Isa. 1:18.

Luke 13:34.

Paragraph 3

Heb. 2:3. How shall we escape, if we neglect so great salvation; which at the first began to be spoken by the Lord, and was confirmed unto us by them that heard him . . . ?

Heb. 12:25. See that ye refuse not him that speaketh. For if they escaped not who refused him that spake on earth, much more shall not we escape, if we turn away from him that speaketh from heaven.

Acts 13:46. Then Paul and Barnabas waxed bold, and said, It was necessary that the word of God should first have been spoken to you: but seeing ye put it from you, and judge yourselves unworthy of everlasting life, lo, we turn to the Gentiles.

Matt. 10:32, 33. Whosoever therefore shall confess me before men, him will I confess also before my Father which is in heaven. But whosoever

4. Since there is no other way of salvation than that revealed in the gospel, and since in the divinely established and ordinary method of grace faith cometh by hearing the word of God, Christ hath commissioned his church to go into all the world and to make disciples of all nations. All believers are, therefore, under obligation to sustain the ordinances of the Christian religion where they are already established, and to contribute by their prayers, gifts, and personal efforts to the extension of the kingdom of Christ throughout the whole earth.

---

shall deny me before men, him will I also deny before my Father which is in heaven.

Luke 12:47, 48. And that servant, which knew his lord's will, and prepared not *himself,* neither did according to his will, shall be beaten with many *stripes.* But he that knew not, and did commit things worthy of stripes, shall be beaten with few *stripes.* For unto whomsoever much is given, of him shall be much required: and to whom men have committed much, of him they will ask the more.

Heb. 10:29. Of how much sorer punishment, suppose ye, shall he be thought worthy, who hath trodden under foot the Son of God, and hath counted the blood of the covenant, wherewith he was sanctified, an unholy thing, and hath done despite unto the Spirit of grace?

Paragraph 4

Acts 4:12. Neither is there salvation in any other: for there is none other name under heaven given among men, whereby we must be saved.

Matt. 28:19, 20. Go ye therefore, and teach all nations, baptizing them in the name of the Father, and of the Son, and of the Holy Ghost: teaching them to observe all things whatsoever I have commanded you: and, lo, I am with you alway, *even* unto the end of the world. Amen.

Acts 1:8. But ye shall receive power, after that the Holy Ghost is come upon you: and ye shall be witnesses unto me both in Jerusalem, and in all Judæa, and in Samaria, and unto the uttermost part of the earth.

Rom. 10:13-15. For whosoever shall call upon the name of the Lord shall be saved. How then shall they call on him in whom they have not believed? and how shall they believe in him of whom they have not heard? and how shall they hear without a preacher? and how shall they preach, except they be sent? as it is written, How beautiful are the feet of them that preach the gospel of peace, and bring glad tidings of good things!

Heb. 10:19-25. Having therefore, brethren, boldness to enter into the holiest by the blood of Jesus, by a new and living way, which he hath consecrated for us, through the veil, that is to say, his flesh; and *having* an high priest over the house of God; let us draw near with a true heart in full assurance of faith, having our hearts sprinkled from an evil conscience, and our bodies washed with pure water. Let us hold fast the profession of *our* faith without wavering; (for he *is* faithful that promised;) and let us consider one another to provoke unto love and to good works: not forsaking the assembling of ourselves together, as the manner of some *is;* but exhorting *one another:* and so much the more, as ye see the day approaching.

Gal. 3:28. There is neither Jew nor Greek, there is neither bond nor

CHAPTER XI

Of Free Will

1. God hath endued the will of man with that natural liberty, that it is neither forced, nor by any absolute necessity of nature determined to good or evil.[1]

2. Man, in his state of innocency, had freedom and power to will and to do that which is good and well-pleasing to God;[2] but yet mutably, so that he might fall from it.[3]

---

free, there is neither male nor female: for ye are all one in Christ Jesus.
I Cor. 16:1, 2. Now concerning the collection for the saints, as I have given order to the churches of Galatia, even so do ye. Upon the first *day* of the week let every one of you lay by him in store, as *God* hath prospered him, that there be no gatherings when I come.
Matt. 9:36-38. But when he saw the multitudes, he was moved with compassion on them, because they fainted, and were scattered abroad, as sheep having no shepherd. Then saith he unto his disciples, The harvest truly *is* plenteous, but the labourers *are* few; pray ye therefore the Lord of the harvest, that he will send forth labourers into his harvest.
Acts 13:2-4. As they ministered to the Lord, and fasted, the Holy Ghost said, Separate me Barnabas and Saul for the work whereunto I have called them. And when they had fasted and prayed, and laid *their* hands on them, they sent *them* away. So they, being sent forth by the Holy Ghost, departed unto Seleucia; and from thence they sailed to Cyprus.
Col. 3:16. Let the word of Christ dwell in you richly in all wisdom; teaching and admonishing one another in psalms and hymns and spiritual songs, singing with grace in your hearts to the Lord.
Rev. 22:17. And the Spirit and the bride say, Come. And let him that heareth say, Come. And let him that is athirst come. And whosoever will, let him take the water of life freely.
Col. 1:28, 29. Whom we preach, warning every man, and teaching every man in all wisdom; that we may present every man perfect in Christ Jesus: whereunto I also labour, striving according to his working, which worketh in me mightily.

1. Deut. 30:19. I call heaven and earth to record this day against you, *that* I have set before you life and death, blessing and cursing: therefore choose life, that both thou and thy seed may live.
   John 7:17. If any man will do his will, he shall know of the doctrine, whether it be of God, or *whether* I speak of myself.
   Rev. 22:17. And the Spirit and the bride say, Come. And let him that heareth say, Come. And let him that is athirst come. And whosoever will, let him take the water of life freely.
   James 1:14. But every man is tempted, when he is drawn away of his own lust, and enticed.
   John 5:40. And ye will not come to me, that ye might have life.

2. Gen. 1:26. And God said, Let us make man in our image, after our likeness. See under figure 1 above.

3. Gen. 2:16, 17. And the Lord God commanded the man, saying, Of every tree of the garden thou mayest freely eat: but of the tree of the knowledge of good and evil, thou shalt not eat of it: for in the day that thou eatest thereof thou shalt surely die.

3. Man, by his fall into a state of sin, hath wholly lost all ability of will to any spiritual good accompanying salvation;[4] so as a natural man, being altogether averse from that good,[5] and dead in sin,[6] is not able, by his own strength, to convert himself, or to prepare himself thereunto.[7]

4. When God converteth a sinner and translateth him into the state of grace, he freeth him from his natural bondage under sin, and, by his grace alone, enableth him freely to will and to do that which is spiritually good;[8] yet so as that, by reason of

---

Gen. 3:6. And when the woman saw that the tree *was* good for food, and that it *was* pleasant to the eyes, and a tree to be desired to make *one* wise, she took of the fruit thereof, and did eat, and gave also unto her husband with her; and he did eat.

4. Rom. 5:6. For when we were yet without strength, in due time Christ died for the ungodly.
Rom. 8:7. Because the carnal mind *is* enmity against God: for it is not subject to the law of God, neither indeed can be.
John 15:5. For without me ye can do nothing.

5. Rom. 3:10, 12. As it is written, There is none righteous, no, not one . . . They are all gone out of the way, they are together become unprofitable; there is none that doeth good, no, not one.
Rom. 8:7. Because the carnal mind *is* enmity against God: for it is not subject to the law of God, neither indeed can be.

6. Eph. 2:1, 5. And you *hath he quickened*, who were dead in trespasses and sins . . . hath quickened us together with Christ, (by grace ye are saved).
Col. 2:13. And you, being dead in your sins and the uncircumcision of your flesh, hath he quickened together with him, having forgiven you all trespasses.

7. John 6:44, 65. No man can come to me, except the Father which hath sent me draw him . . . And he said, Therefore said I unto you, that no man can come unto me, except it were given unto him of my Father.
I Cor. 2:14. But the natural man receiveth not the things of the Spirit of God: for they are foolishness unto him: neither can he know *them*, because they are spiritually discerned.
Rom. 8:8. So then they that are in the flesh cannot please God.
Eph. 2:2-5.
Titus 3:3-5. But after that the kindness and love of God our Saviour toward man appeared, not by works of righteousness which we have done, but according to his mercy he saved us, by the washing of regeneration, and renewing of the Holy Ghost.

8. Col. 1:13. Who hath delivered us from the power of darkness, and hath translated *us* into the kingdom of his dear Son.
John 8:34, 36. Jesus answered them, Verily, verily, I say unto you, Whosoever committeth sin is the servant of sin. . . . If the Son therefore shall make you free, ye shall be free indeed.
Phil. 2:13. For it is God which worketh in you both to will and to do of *his* good pleasure.
Rom. 6:18, 22. Being then made free from sin, ye became the servants of righteousness. . . . But now being made free from sin, and become servants to God, ye have your fruit unto holiness, and the end everlasting life.

his remaining corruption, he doth not perfectly, nor only, will that which is good, but doth also will that which is evil.[9]

5. The will of man is made perfectly and immutably free to good alone, in the state of glory[10] only.[11]

CHAPTER XII

Of Effectual Calling

1. All those whom God hath predestinated unto life, and those only, he is pleased, in his appointed and accepted time, effectually to call, by his word and Spirit, out of that state of sin and death in which they are by nature, to grace and salvation by Jesus Christ:[1] enlightening their minds, spiritually and sav-

---

9. Gal. 5:17. For the flesh lusteth against the Spirit, and the Spirit against the flesh: and these are contrary the one to the other: so that ye cannot do the things that ye would.
Rom. 7:15. For that which I do I allow not: for what I would, that do I not; but what I hate, that do I. See context.

10. I John 3:2. Beloved, now are we the sons of God, and it doth not yet appear what we shall be: but we know that, when he shall appear, we shall be like him; for we shall see him as he is.
Rev. 22:3, 4. And his servants shall serve him: and they shall see his face; and his name *shall be* in their foreheads.

11. II Chron. 6:36. If they sin against thee, (for *there is* no man which sinneth not).
I John 1:8-10. If we say that we have no sin, we deceive ourselves, and the truth is not in us. If we confess our sins, he is faithful and just to forgive us *our* sins, and to cleanse us from all unrighteousness. If we say that we have not sinned, we make him a liar, and his word is not in us.
I John 2:1-6. My little children, these things write I unto you, that ye sin not. And if any man sin, we have an advocate with the Father, Jesus Christ the righteous: and he is the propitiation for our sins: and not for ours only, but also for *the sins of* the whole world. And hereby we do know that we know him, if we keep his commandments. He that saith, I know him, and keepeth not his commandments, is a liar, and the truth is not in him. But whoso keepeth his word, in him verily is the love of God perfected: hereby know we that we are in him. He that saith he abideth in him ought himself also so to walk, even as he walked.
Ps. 17:15. As for me, I will behold thy face in righteousness: I shall be satisfied, when I awake, with thy likeness.

1. Rom. 11:7. What then? Israel hath not obtained that which he seeketh for; but the election hath obtained it, and the rest were blinded.
Rom. 8:30. Moreover whom he did predestinate, them he also called: and whom he called, them he also justified.
II Thess. 2:13, 14. God hath from the beginning chosen you to salvation through sanctification of the Spirit and belief of the truth: whereunto he called you by our gospel, to the obtaining of the glory of our Lord Jesus Christ.

ingly, to understand the things of God,[2] taking away their heart
of stone, and giving unto them an heart of flesh;[3] renewing
their wills, and by his almighty power determining them to that
which is good;[4] and effectually drawing them to Jesus Christ;[5]
yet so as they come most freely, being made willing by his grace.[6]

2. This effectual call is of God's free and special grace alone,
not from anything at all foreseen in man,[7] who is altogether
passive therein, until, being quickened and renewed by the Holy

---

Rom. 8:2. For the law of the Spirit of life in Christ Jesus hath made me
free from the law of sin and death.

II Tim. 1:9, 10. Who hath saved us, and called *us* with an holy calling,
not according to our works, but according to his own purpose and grace,
which was given us in Christ Jesus before the world began, but is now
made manifest by the appearing of our Saviour Jesus Christ, who hath
abolished death, and hath brought life and immortality to light
through the gospel.

2. Acts 26:18. To open their eyes, *and* to turn *them* from darkness to
light, and *from* the power of Satan unto God, that they may receive forgiveness of sins, and inheritance among them which are sanctified by
faith that is in me.

I Cor. 2:10, 12. But God hath revealed *them* unto us by his Spirit: for the
Spirit searcheth all things, yea, the deep things of God. . . . Now we have
received, not the spirit of the world, but the spirit which is of God; that
we might know the things that are freely given to us of God.

3. Ezek. 36:26. A new heart also will I give you, and a new spirit will I put
within you: and I will take away the stony heart out of your flesh, and I
will give you an heart of flesh.

4. Ezek. 11:19. And I will give them one heart, and I will put a new spirit
within you.

Ezek. 36:27. And I will put my spirit within you, and cause you to walk
in my statutes, and ye shall keep my judgments, and do *them*.

Phil. 2:13. For it is God which worketh in you both to will and to do of
his good pleasure.

Phil. 4:13. I can do all things through Christ which strengtheneth me.

Deut. 30:6. And the LORD thy God will circumcise thine heart, and the
heart of thy seed, to love the LORD thy God with all thine heart, and
with all thy soul, that thou mayest live.

5. John 6:44, 45. No man can come to me, except the Father which hath
sent me draw him . . . Every man therefore that hath heard, and hath
learned of the Father, cometh unto me.

6. John 6:37. All that the Father giveth me shall come to me; and him that
cometh to me I will in no wise cast out.

See under figure 5 above.

7. II Tim. 1:9. Who hath saved us, and called *us* with an holy calling, not
according to our works, but according to his own purpose and grace,
which was given us in Christ Jesus before the world began.

Titus 3:4, 5. But after that the kindness and love of God our Saviour toward man appeared, not by works of righteousness which we have done,
but according to his mercy he saved us, by the washing of regeneration,
and renewing of the Holy Ghost.

Rom. 9:11. For *the children* being not yet born, neither having done

Spirit,[8] he is thereby enabled to answer this call, and to embrace the grace offered and conveyed in it.[9]

3. Elect infants, dying in infancy, are regenerated and saved by Christ through the Spirit, who worketh when, and where, and how he pleaseth. So also are all other elect persons who are incapable of being outwardly called by the ministry of the word.[10]

4. Others, not elected, although they may be called by the ministry of the word, and may have some common operations of the Spirit, yet they never truly come to Christ, and therefore cannot be saved:[11] much less can men, not professing the Chris-

---

any good or evil, that the purpose of God according to election might stand, not of works, but of him that calleth.
Eph. 2:4, 5, 8, 9.

8. I Cor. 2:14. But the natural man receiveth not the things of the Spirit of God: for they are foolishness unto him: neither can he know *them*, because they are spiritually discerned.
Rom. 8:7. Because the carnal mind *is* enmity against God: for it is not subject to the law of God, neither indeed can be.
Eph. 2:5. Even when we were dead in sins, hath quickened us together with Christ, (by grace ye are saved).

9. John 6:37. All that the Father giveth me shall come to me; and him that cometh to me I will in no wise cast out.
Ezek. 36:27. And I will put my spirit within you, and cause you to walk in my statutes, and ye shall keep my judgments, and do *them*.
John 5:25. Verily, verily, I say unto you, The hour is coming, and now is, when the dead shall hear the voice of the Son of God: and they that hear shall live.

10. Acts 4:12. Neither is there salvation in any other: for there is none other name under heaven given among men, whereby we must be saved.
John 3:8. The wind bloweth where it listeth, and thou hearest the sound thereof, but canst not tell whence it cometh, and whither it goeth: so is every one that is born of the Spirit.

11. Matt. 22:14. For many are called, but few *are* chosen.
Matt. 13:20, 21. But he that receiveth the seed into stony places, the same is he that heareth the word, and anon with joy receiveth it; yet hath he not root in himself, but dureth for a while: for when tribulation or persecution ariseth because of the word, by and by he is offended.
John 6:64-66. But there are some of you that believe not. For Jesus knew from the beginning who they were that believed not, and who should betray him. And he said, Therefore said I unto you, that no man can come unto me, except it were given unto him of my Father. From that *time* many of his disciples went back, and walked no more with him.
John 8:24. I said therefore unto you, that ye shall die in your sins: for if ye believe not that I am *he*, ye shall die in your sins.
I John 2:19. They went out from us, but they were not of us; for if they had been of us, they would *no doubt* have continued with us: but *they went out*, that they might be made manifest that they were not all of us.
Heb. 6:4-6.

tian religion, be saved in any other way whatsoever,[12] be they never so diligent to frame their lives according to the light of nature, and the law of that religion they do profess; and to assert and maintain that they may is without warrant of the word of God.[13]

CHAPTER XIII

Of Justification

1. Those whom God effectually calleth, he also freely justifieth:[14] not by infusing righteousness into them, but by pardoning their sins, and by accounting and accepting their persons as righteous; not for anything wrought in them, or done by them, but for Christ's sake alone; not by imputing faith itself, the act of believing, or any other evangelical obedience to them, as their righteousness; but by imputing the obedience and satisfaction of Christ unto them,[15] they receiving and resting on him

---

12. Acts 4:12. Neither is there salvation in any other: for there is none other name under heaven given among men, whereby we must be saved.

John 14:6. Jesus saith unto him, I am the way, the truth, and the life: no man cometh unto the Father, but by me.

John 17:3. And this is life eternal, that they might know thee the only true God, and Jesus Christ, whom thou hast sent.

13. II John 9-11. Whosoever trangresseth, and abideth not in the doctrine of Christ, hath not God. He that abideth in the doctrine of Christ, he hath both the Father and the Son. If there come any unto you, and bring not this doctrine, receive him not into *your* house, neither bid him God speed: for he that biddeth him God speed is partaker of his evil deeds.

Gal. 1:8. But though we, or an angel from heaven, preach any other gospel unto you than that which we have preached unto you, let him be accursed.

14. Rom. 8:30. Whom he called, them he also justified.

Rom. 3:24. Being justified freely by his grace through the redemption that is in Christ Jesus.

15. Rom. 4:5-8. But to him that worketh not, but believeth on him that justifieth the ungodly, his faith is counted for righteousness. Even as David also describeth the blessedness of the man, unto whom God imputeth righteousness without works, *saying*, Blessed *are* they whose iniquities are forgiven, and whose sins are covered. Blessed *is* the man to whom the Lord will not impute sin.

II Cor. 5:19, 21. To wit, that God was in Christ, reconciling the world unto himself, not imputing their trespasses unto them; and hath committed unto us the word of reconciliation. . . . For he hath made him *to be* sin for us, who knew no sin; that we might be made the righteousness of God in him.

and his righteousness by faith; which faith they have not of them-selves, it is the gift of God.[16]

2. Faith, thus receiving and resting on Christ and his righteous-ness, is the alone instrument of justification;[17] yet is it not alone in the person justified, but is ever accompanied with all other saving graces, and is no dead faith, but worketh by love.[18]

3. Christ, by his obedience and death, did fully discharge the debt of all those that are thus justified, and did make a proper, real, and full satisfaction to his Father's justice in their behalf.[19]

Titus 3:5, 7. Not by works of righteousness which we have done, but ac-cording to his mercy he saved us, by the washing of regeneration, and re-newing of the Holy Ghost . . . that being justified by his grace, we should be made heirs according to the hope of eternal life.

Eph. 1:7. In whom we have redemption through his blood, the forgive-ness of sins, according to the riches of his grace.

Jer. 23:6; Rom. 3:22, 24, 25, 27, 28; I Cor. 1:30, 31; Rom. 5:17-19.

16. Phil. 3:9. And be found in him, not having mine own righteousness, which is of the law, but that which is through the faith of Christ, the righteous-ness which is of God by faith.

Eph. 2:8. For by grace are ye saved through faith; and that not of your-selves: *it is* the gift of God.

Acts 13:38, 39.

17. John 1:12. But as many as received him, to them gave he power to be-come the sons of God, *even* to them that believe on his name.

Rom. 3:28. Therefore we conclude that a man is justified by faith with-out the deeds of the law.

Rom. 5:1. Therefore being justified by faith, we have peace with God through our Lord Jesus Christ.

18. James 2:17, 22, 26. Even so faith, if it hath not works, is dead, being alone. . . . Seest thou how faith wrought with his works, and by works was faith made perfect . . . For as the body without the spirit is dead, so faith with-out works is dead also.

Gal. 5:6. For in Jesus Christ neither circumcision availeth any thing, nor uncircumcision; but faith which worketh by love.

19. Rom. 5:8-10, 19. But God commendeth his love toward us, in that, while we were yet sinners, Christ died for us. Much more then, being now jus-tified by his blood, we shall be saved from wrath through him. For if, when we were enemies, we were reconciled to God by the death of his Son, much more, being reconciled, we shall be saved by his life. . . . For as by one man's disobedience many were made sinners, so by the obedience of one shall many be made righteous.

I Cor. 15:3. For I delivered unto you first of all that which I also received, how that Christ died for our sins according to the scriptures.

II Cor. 5:21. For he hath made him *to be* sin for us, who knew no sin; that we might be made the righteousness of God in him.

I Peter 2:24. Who his own self bare our sins in his own body on the tree.

I Peter 3:18. For Christ also hath once suffered for sins, the just for the unjust, that he might bring us to God, being put to death in the flesh, but quickened by the Spirit.

Heb. 10:10, 14. By the which will we are sanctified through the offering

Yet inasmuch as he was given by the Father for them,[20] and his obedience and satisfaction accepted in their stead,[21] and both freely, not for anything in them, their justification is only of free grace;[22] that both the exact justice and rich grace of God might be glorified in the justification of sinners.[23]

4. God did, from all eternity, decree to justify all the elect;[24] and Christ did, in the fullness of time, die for their sins and rise again for their justification:[25] nevertheless they are not justified until the Holy Spirit doth, in due time, actually apply Christ unto them.[26]

---

of the body of Jesus Christ once *for all*. . . . For by one offering he hath perfected for ever them that are sanctified.
Isa. 53.

20. Rom. 8:32. He that spared not his own Son, but delivered him up for us all, how shall he not with him also freely give us all things?
John 3:16. For God so loved the world, that he gave his only begotten Son, that whosoever believeth in him should not perish, but have everlasting life.

21. II Cor. 5:21. For he hath made him *to be* sin for us, who knew no sin; that we might be made the righteousness of God in him.
Isa. 53:6. All we like sheep have gone astray; we have turned every one to his own way; and the Lord hath laid on him the iniquity of us all.

22. Rom. 3:24. Being justified freely by his grace through the redemption that is in Christ Jesus.
Rom. 6:23. For the wages of sin *is* death; but the gift of God *is* eternal life through Jesus Christ our Lord.
Eph. 1:7. In whom we have redemption through his blood, the forgiveness of sins, according to the riches of his grace.
Eph. 2:6-9.

23. Rom. 3:26. To declare, *I say*, at this time his righteousness: that he might be just, and the justifier of him which believeth in Jesus.
Eph. 2:7. That in the ages to come he might shew the exceeding riches of his grace in *his* kindness toward us through Christ Jesus.

24. I Peter 1:2, 19, 20. Elect according to the foreknowledge of God the Father, through sanctification of the Spirit, unto obedience and sprinkling of the blood of Jesus Christ . . . but with the precious blood of Christ, as of a lamb without blemish and without spot: who verily was foreordained before the foundation of the world, but was manifest in these last times for you.
Rom. 8:30.

25. Gal. 4:4. But when the fulness of the time was come, God sent forth his Son, made of a woman, made under the law.
I Tim. 2:6. Who gave himself a ransom for all, to be testified in due time.
Rom. 4:25. Who was delivered for our offences, and was raised again for our justification.

26. John 3:5, 18, 36. Jesus answered, Verily, verily, I say unto thee, Except a man be born of water and *of* the Spirit, he cannot enter into the kingdom of God. . . . He that believeth on him is not condemned: but he that believeth not is condemned already, because he hath not believed in the name of the only begotten Son of God. . . . He that believeth on the Son

5. God doth continue to forgive the sins of those that are justified;[27] and although they can never fall from the state of justification,[28] yet they may by their sins fall under God's fatherly displeasure, and not have the light of his countenance restored
unto them, until they humble themselves, confess their sins, beg
pardon, and renew their faith and repentance.[29]

6. The justification of believers under the Old Testament was,
in all these respects, one and the same with the justification of
believers under the New Testament.[30]

CHAPTER XIV

Of Adoption

1. All those that are justified, God vouchsafeth, in and for his
only Son Jesus Christ, to make partakers of the grace of adop-

hath everlasting life: and he that believeth not the Son shall not see
life; but the wrath of God abideth on him.
Gal. 2:16. Knowing that a man is not justified by the works of the law,
but by the faith of Jesus Christ, even we have believed in Jesus Christ,
that we might be justified by the faith of Christ, and not by the works of
the law: for by the works of the law shall no flesh be justified.
Titus 3:4-7.

27. Matt. 6:12. And forgive us our debts, as we forgive our debtors.
I John 1:9. If we confess our sins, he is faithful and just to forgive us *our*
sins, and to cleanse us from all unrighteousness.
I John 2:1. If any man sin, we have an advocate with the Father, Jesus
Christ the righteous.

28. Luke 22:32. But I have prayed for thee, that thy faith fail not: and when
thou art converted, strengthen thy brethren.
John 10:28. And I give unto them eternal life; and they shall never perish, neither shall any *man* plunk them out of my hand.
Heb. 10:14. For by one offering he hath perfected for ever them that are
sanctified.
Phil. 1:6. Being confident of this very thing, that he which hath begun a
good work in you will perform *it* until the day of Jesus Christ.
I John 2:19. They went out from us, but they were not of us; for if they
had been of us, they would *no doubt* have continued with us: but *they
went out,* that they might be made manifest that they were not all of us.

29. Ps. 89:31-33. If they break my statutes, and keep not my commandments; then will I visit their transgression with the rod, and their iniquity
with stripes. Nevertheless my lovingkindness will I not utterly take from
him, nor suffer my faithfulness to fail.
Ps. 32:5. I acknowledged my sin unto thee, and mine iniquity have I
not hid. I said, I will confess my transgressions unto the Lord; and thou
forgavest the iniquity of my sin.
Matt. 26:75. And Peter remembered the word of Jesus . . . And he went
out, and wept bitterly.
Ps. 51:7-12; I Cor. 11:30, 32.

30. Heb. 11:13. These all died in faith, not having received the promises, but
having seen them afar off, and were persuaded of *them,* and embraced

tion:[1] by which they are taken into the number, and enjoy the liberties and privileges of the children of God;[2] have his name put upon them;[3] receive the Spirit of adoption;[4] have access to the throne of grace with boldness;[5] are enabled to cry, Abba, Father;[6] are pitied,[7] protected,[8] provided for,[9] and chastened by

---

them, and confessed that they were strangers and pilgrims on the earth. John 8:56. Your father Abraham rejoiced to see my day: and he saw it, and was glad.

Gal. 3:6-8. Even as Abraham believed God, and it was accounted to him for righteousness. Know ye therefore that they which are of faith, the same are the children of Abraham. And the scripture, foreseeing that God would justify the heathen through faith, preached before the gospel unto Abraham, saying, In thee shall all nations be blessed.

Acts 15:11. But we believe that through the grace of the Lord Jesus Christ we shall be saved, even as they.

Rom. 3:30. Seeing it is one God, which shall justify the circumcision by faith, and uncircumcision through faith.

Gal. 3:8, 9, 14.

1. Eph. 1:5. Having predestinated us unto the adoption of children by Jesus Christ to himself, according to the good pleasure of his will.
Gal. 4:4, 5. God sent forth his Son, made of a woman, made under the law, to redeem them that were under the law, that we might receive the adoption of sons.

2. John 1:12. But as many as received him, to them gave he power to become the sons of God, even to them that believe on his name.
Rom. 8:17. And if children, then heirs; heirs of God, and joint-heirs with Christ.

3. Rev. 3:12. Him that overcometh will I make a pillar in the temple of my God, and he shall go no more out: and I will write upon him the name of my God, and the name of the city of my God, which is new Jerusalem, which cometh down out of heaven from my God: and I will write upon him my new name.

4. Rom. 8:15. For ye have not received the spirit of bondage again to fear; but ye have received the Spirit of adoption, whereby we cry, Abba, Father.

5. Eph. 3:12. In whom we have boldness and access with confidence by the faith of him.
Heb. 4:16. Let us therefore come boldly unto the throne of grace, that we may obtain mercy, and find grace to help in time of need.
Rom. 5:2.

6. Gal. 4:6. And because ye are sons, God hath sent forth the Spirit of his Son into your hearts, crying, Abba, Father.

7. Ps. 103:13. Like as a father pitieth his children, so the LORD pitieth them that fear him.

8. Prov. 14:26. In the fear of the LORD is strong confidence: and his children shall have a place of refuge.
Ps. 27:1-3. The LORD is my light and my salvation; whom shall I fear? the LORD is the strength of my life; of whom shall I be afraid? When the wicked, even mine enemies and my foes, came upon me to eat up my flesh, they stumbled and fell. Though an host should encamp against me, my heart shall not fear: though war should rise against me, in this will I be confident.

9. Matt. 6, 30, 32. Wherefore, if God so clothe the grass of the field,

him as by a father;[10] yet never cast off,[11] but sealed to the day of redemption,[12] and inherit the promises,[13] as heirs of everlasting salvation.[14]

CHAPTER XV

Of Sanctification

1. They who are effectually called and regenerated, having a new heart and a new spirit created in them, are further sanctified, really and personally, through the virtue of Christ's death and resurrection, by his word and Spirit dwelling in them;[1] the dominion of the whole body of sin is destroyed,[2] and the several

---

which to day is, and to morrow is cast into the oven, *shall he* not much more *clothe* you, O ye of little faith? . . . for your heavenly Father knoweth that ye have need of all these things.

I Peter 5:7. Casting all your care upon him; for he careth for you.

10. Heb. 12:6. For whom the Lord loveth he chasteneth, and scourgeth every son whom he receiveth.

11. Lam. 3:31. For the LORD will not cast off for ever.

Heb. 13:5. *Let your* conversation *be* without covetousness; *and be* content with such things as ye have: for he hath said, I will never leave thee, nor forsake thee.

12. Eph. 4:30. Whereby ye are sealed unto the day of redemption.

13. Heb. 6:12. That ye be not slothful, but followers of them who through faith and patience inherit the promises.

14. I Peter 1:4. To an inheritance incorruptible, and undefiled, and that fadeth not away, reserved in heaven for you.

Heb. 1:14. Are they not all ministering spirits, sent forth to minister for them who shall be heirs of salvation?

1. Acts 20:32. And now, brethren, I commend you to God, and to the word of his grace, which is able to build you up, and to give you an inheritance among all them which are sanctified.

Rom. 6:5, 6. For if we have been planted together in the likeness of his death, we shall be also *in the likeness* of *his* resurrection: knowing this, that our old man is crucified with *him*, that the body of sin might be destroyed, that henceforth we should not serve sin.

John 17:17. Sanctify them through thy truth: thy word is truth.

Eph. 5:26. That he might sanctify and cleanse it with the washing of water by the word.

II Thess. 2:13. But we are bound to give thanks alway to God for you, brethren beloved of the Lord, because God hath from the beginning chosen you to salvation through sanctification of the Spirit and belief of the truth.

2. Rom. 6:6, 14. Knowing this, that our old man is crucified with *him*, that the body of sin might be destroyed, that henceforth we should not serve sin. . . . For sin shall not have dominion over you: for ye are not under the law, but under grace.

lusts thereof are more and more weakened and mortified,[3] and they more and more quickened and strengthened, in all saving graces,[4] to the practice of true holiness, without which no man shall see the Lord.[5]

2. This sanctification is throughout in the whole man,[6] yet imperfect in this life: there abideth still some remnants of corruption in every part, whence ariseth a continual and irreconcilable war, the flesh lusting against the Spirit, and the Spirit against the flesh.[7]

3. In which war, although the remaining corruption for a time may much prevail,[8] yet, through the continual supply of strength from the sanctifying Spirit of Christ, the regenerate part doth

---

3. Rom. 8:13. For if ye live after the flesh, ye shall die: but if ye through the Spirit do mortify the deeds of the body, ye shall live.

Gal. 5:24. And they that are Christ's have crucified the flesh with the affections and lusts.

Col. 3:5. Mortify therefore your members which are upon the earth; fornication, uncleanness, inordinate affection, evil concupiscence, and covetousness, which is idolatry.

4. Col. 1:11. Strengthened with all might, according to his glorious power, unto all patience and longsuffering with joyfulness.

II Peter 3:13, 14. Nevertheless we, according to his promise, look for new heavens and a new earth, wherein dwelleth righteousness. Wherefore, beloved, seeing that ye look for such things, be diligent that ye may be found of him in peace, without spot, and blameless.

Eph. 3:16-19.

5. II Cor. 7:1. Having therefore these promises, dearly beloved, let us cleanse ourselves from all filthiness of the flesh and spirit, perfecting holiness in the fear of God.

Heb. 12:14. Follow peace with all *men,* and holiness, without which no man shall see the Lord.

6. I Thess. 5:23. And the very God of peace sanctify you wholly; and I *pray God* your whole spirit and soul and body be preserved blameless unto the coming of our Lord Jesus Christ.

7. I John 1:10. If we say that we have not sinned, we make him a liar, and his word is not in us.

Phil. 3:12. Not as though I had already attained, either were already perfect: but I follow after, if that I may apprehend that for which also I am apprehended of Christ Jesus.

Gal. 5:17. For the flesh lusteth against the Spirit, and the Spirit against the flesh: and these are contrary the one to the other: so that ye cannot do the things that ye would.

Rom. 7:18, 23.

8. Rom. 7:23. But I see another law in my members, warring against the law of my mind, and bringing me into captivity to the law of sin which is in my members.

overcome:[9] and so the saints grow in grace,[10] perfecting holiness
in the fear of God.[11]

CHAPTER XVI

Of Saving Faith

1. The grace of faith, whereby the elect are enabled to believe
to the saving of their souls, is the work of the Spirit of Christ in
their hearts;[1] and is ordinarily wrought by the ministry of the
word:[2] by which also, and by the administration of the sacraments, and prayer, it is increased and strengthened.[3]

2. By this faith, a Christian believeth to be true whatsoever is
revealed in the word, for the authority of God himself speaking
therein;[4] and acteth differently, upon that which each particular

---

9. Rom. 6:14. For sin shall not have dominion over you: for ye are not
under the law, but under grace.
I John 5:4. For whatsoever is born of God overcometh the world: and
this is the victory that overcometh the world, *even* our faith.
Eph. 4:16. From whom the whole body fitly joined together and compacted by that which every joint supplieth, according to the effectual
working in the measure of every part, maketh increase of the body
unto the edifying of itself in love.

10. II Peter 3:18. But grow in grace, and *in* the knowledge of our Lord and
Saviour Jesus Christ.
II Cor. 3:18. But we all, with open face beholding as in a glass the
glory of the Lord, are changed into the same image from glory to glory,
even as by the Spirit of the Lord.

11. II Cor. 7:1. Having therefore these promises, dearly beloved, let us
cleanse ourselves from all filthiness of the flesh and spirit, perfecting
holiness in the fear of God.

1. I Cor. 12:3. No man can say that Jesus is the Lord, but by the Holy
Ghost.
Eph. 2:8. For by grace are ye saved through faith; and that not of your-
selves: *it is* the gift of God.
Heb. 12:2.

2. Rom. 10:14, 17. How shall they believe in him of whom they have not
heard? and how shall they hear without a preacher? . . . So then faith
cometh by hearing, and hearing by the word of God.

3. I Peter 2:2. As newborn babes, desire the sincere milk of the word,
that ye may grow thereby.
Acts 20:32. And now, brethren, I commend you to God, and to the
word of his grace, which is able to build you up, and to give you an inheritance among all them which are sanctified.
Matt. 28:19; I Cor. 11:23-29; II Cor. 12:8-10.

4. I Thess. 2:13. For this cause also thank we God without ceasing, be-

passage thereof containeth; yielding obedience to the commands, trembling at the threatenings, and embracing the promises of God for this life, and that which is to come. But the principal acts of saving faith are, accepting, receiving, and resting upon Christ alone for justification, sanctification, and eternal life, by virtue of the covenant of grace.

3. This faith is different in degrees, weak or strong;[5] may be often and many ways assailed and weakened, but gets the victory;[6] growing up in many to the attainment of a full assurance through Christ,[7] who is both the author and finisher of our faith.[8]

---

cause, when ye received the word of God which ye heard of us, ye received *it* not *as* the word of men, but as it is in truth, the word of God, which effectually worketh also in you that believe.

I John 5:10. He that believeth on the Son of God hath the witness in himself: he that believeth not God hath made him a liar; because he believeth not the record that God gave of his Son.

Acts 24:14. Believing all things which are written in the law and in the prophets.

5. Matt. 6:30. *Shall he* not much more *clothe* you, O ye of little faith?

Matt. 8:10. When Jesus heard *it,* he marvelled, and said to them that followed, Verily I say unto you, I have not found so great faith, no, not in Israel.

Rom. 4:19, 20. And being not weak in faith, he comsidered not his own body now dead, when he was about an hundred years old, neither yet the deadness of Sarah's womb: he staggered not at the promise of God through unbelief; but was strong in faith, giving glory to God.

6. Luke 22:31, 32. And the Lord said, Simon, Simon, behold, Satan hath desired *to have* you, that he may sift *you* as wheat: but I have prayed for thee, that thy faith fail not: and when thou art converted, strengthen thy brethren.

I Cor. 10:13. There hath no temptation taken you but such as is common to man: but God *is* faithful, who will not suffer you to be tempted above that ye are able; but will with the temptation also make a way to escape, that ye may be able to bear *it.*

7. Heb. 6:11, 12. And we desire that every one of you do shew the same diligence to the full assurance of hope unto the end: that ye be not slothful, but followers of them who through faith and patience inherit the promises.

Heb. 10:22. Let us draw near with a true heart in full assurance of faith, having our hearts sprinkled from an evil conscience, and our bodies washed with pure water.

II Tim. 1:12. For I know whom I have believed, and am persuaded that he is able to keep that which I have committed unto him against that day.

8. Heb. 12:2. Looking unto Jesus the author and finisher of *our* faith.

CHAPTER XVII

Of Repentance unto Life

1. Repentance unto life is an evangelical grace,[1] the doctrine whereof is to be preached by every minister of the gospel, as well as that of faith in Christ.[2]

2. By it a sinner, out of the sight and sense, not only of the danger, but also of the filthiness and odiousness of his sins, as contrary to the holy nature and righteous law of God, and upon the apprehension of his mercy in Christ to such as are penitent, so grieves for, and hates his sins, as to turn from them all unto God,[3] purposing and endeavoring to walk with him in all the ways of his commandments.[4]

---

1. Acts 11:18. When they heard these things, they held their peace, and glorified God, saying, Then hath God also to the Gentiles granted repentance unto life.

2. Luke 24:47. And that repentance and remission of sins should be preached in his name among all nations, beginning at Jerusalem.
   Mark 1:15. And saying, The time is fulfilled, and the kingdom of God is at hand: repent ye, and believe the gospel.
   Acts 20:21. Testifying both to the Jews, and also to the Greeks, repentance toward God, and faith toward our Lord Jesus Christ.

3. Ezek. 18:30, 31. Repent, and turn *yourselves* from all your transgressions; so iniquity shall not be your ruin. Cast away from you all your transgressions, whereby ye have transgressed; and make you a new heart and a new spirit: for why will ye die, O house of Israel?
   Ezek. 36:31. Then shall ye remember your own evil ways, and your doings that *were* not good, and shall loathe yourselves in your own sight for your iniquities and for your abominations.
   Ps. 51:4. Against thee, thee only, have I sinned, and done *this* evil in thy sight: that thou mightest be justified when thou speakest, *and* be clear when thou judgest.
   Jer. 31:18, 19. I have surely heard Ephraim bemoaning himself *thus;* Thou hast chastised me, and I was chastised, as a bullock unaccustomed *to the yoke:* turn thou me, and I shall be turned; for thou *art* the Lord my God. Surely after that I was turned, I repented; and after that I was instructed, I smote upon *my* thigh: I was ashamed, yea, even confounded, because I did bear the reproach of my youth.
   II Cor. 7:11. For behold this selfsame thing, that ye sorrowed after a godly sort, what carefulness it wrought in you, yea, *what* clearing of yourselves, yea, *what* indignation, yea, *what* fear, yea, *what* vehement desire, yea, *what* zeal, yea, *what* revenge! In all *things* ye have approved yourselves to be clear in this matter.

4. Ps. 119:59, 106. I thought on my ways, and turned my feet unto thy testimonies. . . . I have sworn, and I will perform *it,* that I will keep thy righteous judgments.
   John 14:23. Jesus answered and said unto him, If a man love me, he will keep my words.

3. Although repentance be not to be rested in as any satisfaction for sin, or any cause of the pardon thereof,[5] which is the act of God's free grace in Christ;[6] yet is it of such necessity to all sinners, that none may expect pardon without it.[7]

4. As there is no sin so small but it deserves damnation;[8] so there is no sin so great that it can bring damnation upon those who truly repent.[9]

5. Men ought not to content themselves with a general repentance, but it is every man's duty to endeavor to repent of his particular sins, particularly.[10]

6. As every man is bound to make private confession of his

---

5. Titus 3:5. Not by works of righteousness which we have done, but according to his mercy he saved us, by the washing of regeneration, and renewing of the Holy Ghost.

Acts 5:31. Him hath God exalted with his right hand *to be* a Prince and a Saviour, for to give repentance to Israel, and forgiveness of sins.

6. Rom. 3:24. Being justified freely by his grace through the redemption that is in Christ Jesus.

Eph. 1:7. In whom we have redemption through his blood, the forgiveness of sins, according to the riches of his grace.

7. Luke 13:3. I tell you, Nay: but, except ye repent, ye shall all likewise perish.

Acts 17:30.

8. Rom. 6:23. For the wages of sin *is* death.

Matt. 12:36. But I say unto you, That every idle word that men shall speak, they shall give account thereof in the day of judgment.

James 2:10. For whosoever shall keep the whole law, and yet offend in one *point,* he is guilty of all.

9. Isa. 55:7. Let the wicked forsake his way, and the unrighteous man his thoughts: and let him return unto the Lord, and he will have mercy upon him; and to our God, for he will abundantly pardon.

Rom. 8:1. *There is* therefore now no condemnation to them which are in Christ Jesus.

Isa. 1:18. Come now, and let us reason together, saith the Lord: though your sins be as scarlet, they shall be as white as snow; though they be red like crimson, they shall be as wool.

10. Ps. 19:13. Keep back thy servant also from presumptuous *sins;* let them not have dominion over me: then shall I be upright, and I shall be innocent from the great transgression.

Luke 19:8. And Zacchæus stood, and said unto the Lord; Behold, Lord, the half of my goods I give to the poor; and if I have taken any thing from any man by false accusation, I restore *him* fourfold.

I Tim. 1:13, 15. Who was before a blasphemer, and a persecutor, and injurious: but I obtained mercy, because I did *it* ignorantly in unbelief. . . . This *is* a faithful saying, and worthy of all acceptation, that Christ Jesus came into the world to save sinners; of whom I am chief. Dan. 9; Neh. 9.

sins to God, praying for the pardon thereof,[11] upon which, and
the forsaking of them, he shall find mercy:[12] so he that scandal-
izeth his brother, or the church of Christ, ought to be willing,
by a private or public confession and sorrow for his sin, to declare his repentance to those that are offended;[13] who are thereupon to be reconciled to him, and in love to receive him.[14]

CHAPTER XVIII

Of Good Works

1. Good works are only such as God hath commanded in his
holy word,[1] and not such as, without the warrant thereof, are

---

11. Ps. 32:5, 6. I acknowledged my sin unto thee, and mine iniquity have
I not hid. I said, I will confess my transgressions unto the LORD; and
thou forgavest the iniquity of my sin. For this shall every one that is
godly pray unto thee in a time when thou mayest be found: surely in
the floods of great waters they shall not come nigh unto him.
Ps. 51:4, 5, 7, 9, 14.

12. Prov. 28:13. He that covereth his sins shall not prosper: but whoso
confesseth and forsaketh *them* shall have mercy.
I John 1:9. If we confess our sins, he is faithful and just to forgive us
our sins.

13. James 5:16. Confess *your* faults one to another, and pray one for
another, that ye may be healed. The effectual fervent prayer of a
righteous man availeth much.
Luke 17:3, 4. Take heed to yourselves: If thy brother trespass against
thee, rebuke him; and if he repent, forgive him. And if he trespass
against thee seven times in a day, and seven times in a day turn again
to thee, saying, I repent; thou shalt forgive him.
Josh. 7:19. And Joshua said unto Achan, My son, give, I pray thee,
glory to the LORD God of Israel, and make confession unto him; and
tell me now what thou hast done; hide *it* not from me.
Ps. 51.

14. II Cor. 2:7, 8. So that contrariwise ye *ought* rather to forgive *him,*
and comfort *him,* lest perhaps such a one should be swallowed up with
overmuch sorrow. Wherefore I beseech you that ye would confirm
your love toward him.
Gal. 6:1, 2. Brethren, if a man be overtaken in a fault, ye which are
spiritual, restore such an one in the spirit of meekness; considering
thyself, lest thou also be tempted. Bear ye one another's burdens,
and so fulfil the law of Christ.

1. Deut. 12:32. What thing soever I command you, observe to do it: thou
shalt not add thereto, nor diminish from it.
Ps. 119:9. Wherewithal shall a young man cleanse his way? by taking
heed *thereto* according to thy word.
Matt. 28:20. Teaching them to observe all things whatsoever I have
commanded you.
Luke 10:25, 26. And, behold, a certain lawyer stood up, and tempted

devised by men out of blind zeal, or upon any pretense of good intention.[2]

2. These good works, done in obedience to God's commandments, are the fruits and evidences of a true and lively faith:[3] and by them believers manifest their thankfulness,[4] strengthen their assurance,[5] edify their brethren,[6] adorn the profession of the gospel,[7] stop the mouths of the adversaries,[8] and glorify God,[9]

---

him, saying, Master, what shall I do to inherit eternal life? He said unto him, What is written in the law? how readest thou?

II Peter 1:19. We have also a more sure word of prophecy; whereunto ye do well that ye take heed, as unto a light that shineth in a dark place, until the day dawn, and the day star arise in your hearts.

2. Matt. 15:9. But in vain they do worship me, teaching *for* doctrines the commandments of men.

Isa. 29:13. Wherefore the Lord said, Forasmuch as this people draw near *me* with their mouth, and with their lips do honour me, but have removed their heart far from me, and their fear toward me is taught by the precepts of men.

John 16:2. They shall put you out of the synagogues: yea, the time cometh, that whosoever killeth you will think that he doeth God service.

I Sam. 15:22, 23.

Col. 2:20-23.

3. James 2:18, 22. Yea, a man may say, Thou hast faith, and I have works: shew me thy faith without thy works, and I will shew thee my faith by my works. . . . Seest thou how faith wrought with his works, and by works was faith made perfect?

4. Ps. 116:12, 13. What shall I render unto the LORD *for* all his benefits toward me? I will take the cup of salvation, and call upon the name of the LORD.

Col. 3:17. And whatsoever ye do in word or deed, *do* all in the name of the Lord Jesus, giving thanks to God and the Father by him.

I Chron. 29:6-9.

5. I John 2:3, 5. And hereby we do know that we know him, if we keep his commandments. . . . But whoso keepeth his word, in him verily is the love of God perfected: hereby know we that we are in him.

II Peter 1:5-10.

6. II Cor. 9:2. For I know the forwardness of your mind, for which I boast of you to them of Macedonia, that Achaia was ready a year ago; and your zeal hath provoked very many.

Matt. 5:16. Let your light so shine before men, that they may see your good works, and glorify your Father which is in heaven.

7. Titus 2:5. *To be* discreet, chaste, keepers at home, good, obedient to their own husbands, that the word of God be not blasphemed.

I Tim. 6:1. Let as many servants as are under the yoke count their own masters worthy of all honour, that the name of God and *his* doctrine be not blasphemed.

Titus 2:9-12.

8. I Peter 2:15. For so is the will of God, that with well doing ye may put to silence the ignorance of foolish men.

9. I Peter 2:12. Having your conversation honest among the Gentiles: that,

whose workmanship they are, created in Christ Jesus thereunto,[10] that, having their fruit unto holiness, they may have the end, eternal life.[11]

3. Their ability to do good works is not at all of themselves, but wholly from the Spirit of Christ.[12] And that they may be enabled thereunto, besides the graces they have already received, there is required an actual influence of the same Holy Spirit to work in them to will and to do of his good pleasure;[13] yet are they not hereupon to grow negligent, as if they were not bound to perform any duty unless upon a special motion of the Spirit; but they ought to be diligent in stirring up the grace of God that is in them.[14]

4. They, who in their obedience, attain to the greatest height which is possible in this life, are so far from being able to super-

---

whereas they speak against you as evil doers, they may by *your* good works, which they shall behold, glorify God in the day of visitation.

Phil. 1:11. Being filled with the fruits of righteousness, which are by Jesus Christ, unto the glory and praise of God.

John 15:8. Herein is my Father glorified, that ye bear much fruit.

10. Eph. 2:10. For we are his workmanship, created in Christ Jesus unto good works, which God hath before ordained that we should walk in them.

11. Rom. 6:22. But now being made free from sin, and become servants to God, ye have your fruit unto holiness, and the end everlasting life.

12. John 15:5, 6. I am the vine, ye *are* the branches: He that abideth in me, and I in him, the same bringeth forth much fruit: for without me ye can do nothing. If a man abide not in me, he is cast forth as a branch, and is withered; and men gather them, and cast *them* into the fire. Ezek. 36:26, 27.

13. Phil. 2:13. For it is God which worketh in you both to will and to do of *his* good pleasure.

Phil. 4:13. I can do all things through Christ which strengtheneth me.

II Cor. 3:5. Not that we are sufficient of ourselves to think any thing as of ourselves; but our sufficiency *is* of God.

14. Phil. 2:12. Wherefore, my beloved, as ye have always obeyed, not as in my presence only, but now much more in my absence, work out your own salvation with fear and trembling.

Heb. 6:11, 12. And we desire that every one of you do shew the same diligence to the full assurance of hope unto the end: that ye be not slothful, but followers of them who **through faith** and patience inherit the promises.

Isa. 64:7. And *there is* none that calleth upon thy name, that stirreth up himself to take hold of thee: for thou hast hid thy face from us, and hast consumed us, because of our iniquities.

II Peter 1:3, 5, 10, 11; II Tim. 1:6; Jude 20, 21.

erogate and to do more than God requires, that they fall short of much which in duty they are bound to do.[15]

5. We cannot, by our best works, merit pardon of sin, or eternal life, at the hand of God, because of the great disproportion that is between them and the glory to come, and the infinite distance that is between us and God, whom by them we can neither profit, nor satisfy for the debt of our former sins;[16] but when we have done all we can, we have done but our duty, and are unprofitable servants:[17] and because, as they are good, they proceed from his Spirit;[18] and as they are wrought by us, they are defiled and mixed with so much weakness and imperfection that they cannot endure the severity of God's judgment.[19]

6. Yet notwithstanding, the persons of believers being accepted through Christ, their good works also are accepted in him,[20] not

---

15. Luke 17:10. So likewise ye, when ye shall have done all those things which are commanded you, say, We are unprofitable servants: we have done that which was our duty to do.
Gal. 5:17. For the flesh lusteth against the Spirit, and the Spirit against the flesh: and these are contrary the one to the other: so that ye cannot do the things that ye would.

16. Rom. 3:20. Therefore by the deeds of the law there shall no flesh be justified in his sight: for by the law *is* the knowledge of sin.
Rom. 4:2, 4, 6. For if Abraham were justified by works, he hath *whereof* to glory; but not before God. . . . Now to him that worketh is the reward not reckoned of grace, but of debt. . . . Even as David also describeth the blessedness of the man, unto whom God imputeth righteousness without works.
Eph. 2:8, 9. For by grace are ye saved through faith; and that not of yourselves: *it is* the gift of God: not of works, lest any man should boast.
Titus 3:5-7; Rom. 8:18.

17. See citations under 15 above.

18. Gal. 5:22, 23. But the fruit of the Spirit is love, joy, peace, longsuffering, gentleness, goodness, faith, meekness, temperance.

19. Isa. 64:6. But we are all as an unclean *thing,* and all our righteousnesses *are* as filthy rags; and we all do fade as a leaf; and our iniquities, like the wind, have taken us away.
Ps. 143:2. And enter not into judgment with thy servant: for in thy sight shall no man living be justified.
Ps. 130:3. If thou, Lord, shouldest mark iniquities, O Lord, who shall stand?
Gal. 5:17; Rom. 7:15, 18.

20. Eph. 1:6. To the praise of the glory of his grace, wherein he hath made us accepted in the beloved.
I Peter 2:5. Ye also, as lively stones, are built up a spiritual house, an holy priesthood, to offer up spiritual sacrifices, acceptable to God by Jesus Christ.
Gen. 4:4. And Abel, he also brought of the firstlings of his flock and of

as though they were in this life wholly unblamable and unreprovable in God's sight;[21] but that he, looking upon them in his Son, is pleased to accept and reward that which is sincere, although accompanied with many weaknesses and imperfections.[22]

7. Works done by unregenerate men, although for the matter of them they may be things which God commands, and of good use both to themselves and others;[23] yet because they proceed not from a heart purified by faith;[24] nor are done in a right manner, according to the word;[25] nor to a right end, the glory of God;[26] they are therefore sinful, and cannot please God, or

---

the fat thereof. And the LORD had respect unto Abel and to his offering. Heb. 11:4.

21. I Cor. 4:3, 4. But with me it is a very small thing that I should be judged of you, or of man's judgment: yea, I judge not mine own self. For I know nothing by myself; yet am I not hereby justified: but he that judgeth me is the Lord.
Ps. 143:2. And enter not into judgment with thy servant: for in thy sight shall no man living be justified.

22. II Cor. 8:12. For if there be first a willing mind, *it is* accepted according to that a man hath, *and* not according to that he hath not.
Heb. 6:10. For God *is* not unrighteous to forget your work and labour of love, which ye have shewed toward his name, in that ye have ministered to the saints, and do minister.

23. II Kings 10:30, 31. And the LORD said unto Jehu, Because thou hast done well in executing *that which is* right in mine eyes, *and* hast done unto the house of Ahab according to all that *was* in mine heart, thy children of the fourth *generation* shall sit on the throne of Israel. But Jehu took no heed to walk in the law of the LORD God of Israel with all his heart: for he departed not from the sins of Jeroboam, which made Israel to sin.
Phil. 1:15, 16, 18. Some indeed preach Christ even of envy and strife; and some also of good will: the one preach Christ of contention, not sincerely, supposing to add affliction to my bonds . . . What then? notwithstanding, every way, whether in pretence or in truth, Christ is preached; and I therein do rejoice.

24. Heb. 11:4, 6. By faith Abel offered unto God a more excellent sacrifice than Cain, by which he obtained witness that he was righteous, God testifying of his gifts: and by it he being dead yet speaketh. . . . But without faith *it is* impossible to please *him*: for he that cometh to God must believe that he is, and *that* he is a rewarder of them that diligently seek him.
Gen. 4:3-5.

25. I Cor. 13:3. And though I bestow all my goods to feed *the poor,* and though I give my body to be burned, and have not charity, it profiteth me nothing.
Isa. 1:12. When ye come to appear before me, who hath required this at your hand, to tread my courts?

26. Matt. 6:2, 5, 16. Therefore when thou doest *thine* alms, do not sound a trumpet before thee, as the hypocrites do in the synagogues and in the streets, that they may have glory of men. Verily I say unto you,

make a man meet to receive grace from God.[27] And yet their neglect of them is more sinful, and displeasing unto God.[28]

CHAPTER XIX

Of the Perseverance of the Saints

1. They whom God hath accepted in his Beloved, effectually called and sanctified by his Spirit, can neither totally nor finally fall away from the state of grace: but shall certainly persevere therein to the end, and be eternally saved.[1]

They have their reward. . . . And when thou prayest, thou shalt not be as the hypocrites *are*: for they love to pray standing in the synagogues and in the corners of the streets, that they may be seen of men. Verily I say unto you, They have their reward. . . . Moreover, when ye fast, be not as the hypocrites, of a sad countenance: for they disfigure their faces, that they may appear unto men to fast. Verily I say unto you, They have their reward.
Rom. 14:23. For whatsoever *is* not of faith is sin.

27. Titus 1:15. Unto them that are defiled and unbelieving *is* nothing pure; but even their mind and conscience is defiled.
Prov. 15:8. The sacrifice of the wicked *is* an abomination to the LORD: but the prayer of the upright *is* his delight.
Prov. 28:9. He that turneth away his ear from hearing the law, even his prayer *shall be* abomination.

28. Matt. 25:24-28. Then he which had received the one talent came and said, Lord, I knew thee that thou art an hard man, reaping where thou hast not sown, and gathering where thou hast not strawed: and I was afraid, and went and hid thy talent in the earth: lo, *there* thou hast *that is* thine. His lord answered and said unto him, *Thou* wicked and slothful servant, thou knewest that I reap where I sowed not, and gather where I have not strawed: Thou oughtest therefore to have put my money to the exchangers, and *then* at my coming I should have received mine own with usury. Take therefore the talent from him, and give *it* unto him which hath ten talents.
Matt. 25:41-45. Then shall he say also unto them on the left hand, Depart from me, ye cursed, into everlasting fire, prepared for the devil and his angels: for I was an hungred, and ye gave me no meat: I was thirsty, and ye gave me no drink: I was a stranger, and ye took me not in: naked, and ye clothed me not: sick, and in prison, and ye visited me not. . . . Then shall he answer them, saying, Verily I say unto you, Inasmuch as ye did *it* not to one of the least of these, ye did *it* not to me.
Matt. 23:23. Woe unto you, scribes and Pharisees, hypocrites! for ye pay tithe of mint and anise and cummin, and have omitted the weightier *matters* of the law, judgment, mercy, and faith: these ought ye to have done, and not to leave the other undone.

1. Phil 1:6. Being confident of this very thing, that he which hath begun a good work in you will perform *it* until the day of Jesus Christ.
John 10:28, 29. And I give unto them eternal life; and they shall never perish, neither shall any *man* pluck them out of my hand. My Father, which gave *them* me, is greater than all; and no *man* is able to pluck *them* out of my Father's hand.
Jer. 32:40. And I will make an everlasting covenant with them, that I

2. This perseverance of the saints depends, not upon their own free-will, but upon the immutability of the decree of election, flowing from the free and unchangeable love of God the Father;[2] upon the efficacy of the merit and intercession of Jesus Christ;[3] the abiding of the Spirit and of the seed of God within them;[4] and the nature of the covenant of grace;[5] from all which ariseth also the certainty and infallibility thereof.[6]

---

will not turn away from them, to do them good; but I will put my fear in their hearts, that they shall not depart from me.
I John 3:9; I Peter 1:5, 9.

2. II Tim. 2:19. Nevertheless the foundation of God standeth sure, having this seal, The Lord knoweth them that are his.
Jer. 31:3. The LORD hath appeared of old unto me, *saying,* Yea, I have loved thee with an everlasting love: therefore with lovingkindness have I drawn thee.
Eph. 1:4, 5. He hath chosen us in him before the foundation of the world, that we should be holy and without blame before him in love: having predestinated us unto the adoption of children by Jesus Christ to himself, according to the good pleasure of his will.
John 13:1. Now before the feast of the passover, when Jesus knew that his hour was come that he should depart out of this world unto the Father, having loved his own which were in the world, he loved them unto the end.
Rom. 8:35-39.

3. Heb. 10:10, 14. By the which will we are sanctified through the offering of the body of Jesus Christ once *for all.* . . . For by one offering he hath perfected for ever them that are sanctified.
John 17:11, 24. And now I am no more in the world, but these are in the world, and I come to thee. Holy Father, keep through thine own name those whom thou hast given me, that they may be one, as we are. . . . Father, I will that they also, whom thou hast given me, be with me where I am; that they may behold my glory, which thou hast given me: for thou lovedst me before the foundation of the world.
Heb. 7:25. Wherefore he is able also to save them to the uttermost that come unto God by him, seeing he ever liveth to make intercession for them.
Heb. 9:12-15; Rom. 8:32-39; Luke 22:32.

4. John 14:16, 17. And I will pray the Father, and he shall give you another Comforter, that he may abide with you for ever; *even* the Spirit of truth; whom the world cannot receive, because it seeth him not, neither knoweth him: but ye know him; for he dwelleth with you, and shall be in you.
I John 2:27. But the anointing which ye have received of him abideth in you, and ye need not that any man teach you: but as the same anointing teacheth you of all things, and is truth, and is no lie, and even as it hath taught you, ye shall abide in him.
I John 3:9. Whosoever is born of God doth not commit sin; for his seed remaineth in him: and he cannot sin, because he is born of God.

5. Jer. 32:40. And I will make an everlasting covenant with them, that I will not turn away from them, to do them good; but I will put my fear in their hearts, that they shall not depart from me.
Heb. 8:10-12.

6. II Thess. 3:3. But the Lord is faithful, who shall stablish you, and keep *you* from evil.

3. Nevertheless they may, through the temptations of Satan and of the world, the prevalency of corruption remaining in them, and the neglect of the means of their preservation, fall into grievous sins; and for a time continue therein:[7] whereby they incur God's displeasure,[8] and grieve his Holy Spirit;[9] come to be deprived of some measure of their graces and comforts;[10] have their hearts hardened,[11] and their consciences wounded;[12] hurt and

---

I John 2:19. They went out from us, but they were not of us; for if they had been of us, they would *no doubt* have continued with us: but *they went out,* that they might be made manifest that they were not all of us.

John 10:28. They shall never perish.

I Thess. 5:23, 24; Heb. 6:17-20.

7. Matt. 26:70, 72, 74. But he denied before *them* all, saying, I know not what thou sayest. . . . And again he denied with an oath, I do not know the man. . . . Then began he to curse and to swear, *saying,* I know not the man.

II Sam. 12:9, 13. Wherefore hast thou despised the commandment of the Lord, to do evil in his sight? thou hast killed Uriah the Hittite with the sword, and hast taken his wife *to be* thy wife, and hast slain him with the sword of the children of Ammon. . . . And David said unto Nathan, I have sinned against the Lord. And Nathan said unto David, The Lord also hath put away thy sin; thou shalt not die.

8. Isa. 64:7, 9. For thou hast hid thy face from us, and hast consumed us, because of our iniquities. . . . Be not wroth very sore, O Lord, neither remember iniquity for ever: behold, see, we beseech thee, we *are* all thy people.

II Sam. 11:27. And when the mourning was past, David sent and fetched her to his house, and she became his wife, and bare him a son. But the thing that David had done displeased the Lord.

9. Eph. 4:30. And grieve not the Holy Spirit of God, whereby ye are sealed unto the day of redemption.

10. Ps. 51:8, 10, 12. Make me to hear joy and gladness; *that* the bones *which* thou hast broken may rejoice. . . . Create in me a clean heart, O God; and renew a right spirit within me. . . . Restore unto me the joy of thy salvation; and uphold me *with thy* free spirit.

Rev. 2:4. Nevertheless I have *somewhat* against thee, because thou hast left thy first love.

11. Mark 6:52. For they considered not *the miracle* of the loaves: for their heart was hardened.

Ps. 95:8. Harden not your heart, as in the provocation, *and* as *in* the day of temptation in the wilderness.

12. Ps. 32:3, 4. When I kept silence, my bones waxed old through my roaring all the day long. For day and night thy hand was heavy upon me: my moisture is turned into the drought of summer.

Ps. 51:8. Make me to hear joy and gladness; *that* the bones *which* thou hast broken may rejoice.

scandalize others,[13] and bring temporal judgments upon themselves.[14]

CHAPTER XX

Of the Assurance of Grace and Salvation

1. Although hypocrites, and other unregenerate men, may vainly deceive themselves with false hopes and carnal presumptions: of being in the favor of God and estate of salvation;[1] which hope of theirs shall perish:[2] yet such as truly believe in the Lord Jesus, and love him in sincerity, endeavoring to walk in all good conscience before him, may in this life be certainly assured that they are in a state of grace,[3] and may rejoice in the hope of the glory of God: which hope shall never make them ashamed.[4]

---

13. II Sam. 12:14. Howbeit, because by this deed thou hast given great occasion to the enemies of the LORD to blaspheme, the child also *that is* born unto thee shall surely die.
Ezek. 16:54. That thou mayest bear thine own shame, and mayest be confounded in all that thou hast done, in that thou art a comfort unto them.

14. II Sam. 12:10. Now therefore the sword shall never depart from thine house; because thou hast despised me, and hast taken the wife of Uriah the Hittite to be thy wife.
Ps. 89:31, 32. If they break my statutes, and keep not my commandments; then will I visit their transgression with the rod, and their iniquity with stripes.
I Cor. 11:32. But when we are judged, we are chastened of the Lord, that we should not be condemned with the world.

1. Deut. 29:19. I shall have peace, though I walk in the imagination of mine heart, to add drunkenness to thirst.
John 8:41. Ye do the deeds of your father. Then said they to him, We be not born of fornication; we have one Father, *even* God.

2. Matt. 7:22, 23. Many will say to me in that day, Lord, Lord, have we not prophesied in thy name? and in thy name have cast out devils? and in thy name done many wonderful works? And then will I profess unto them, I never knew you: depart from me, ye that work iniquity.

3. II Tim. 1:12. I know whom I have believed, and am persuaded that he is able to keep that which I have committed unto him against that day.
I John 2:3. And hereby we do know that we know him, if we keep his commandments.
I John 5:13. These things have I written unto you that believe on the name of the Son of God; that ye may know that ye have eternal life, and that ye may believe on the name of the Son of God.
I John 3:14, 18, 19, 21, 24.

4. Rom. 5:2, 5. By whom also we have access by faith into this grace wherein we stand, and rejoice in hope of the glory of God. . . . and hope

2. This certainty is not a bare conjectural and probable persuasion, grounded upon a fallible hope; but an infallible assurance of faith,[5] founded upon the divine truth of the promises of salvation,[6] the inward evidence of those graces unto which these promises are made,[7] the testimony of the Spirit of adoption witnessing with our spirits that we are the children of God;[8] which Spirit is the earnest of our inheritance, whereby we are sealed to the day of redemption.[9]

3. This infallible assurance doth not so belong to the essence of faith but that a true believer may wait long and conflict with many difficulties before he be partaker of it:[10] yet, being enabled

---

maketh not ashamed; because the love of God is shed abroad in our hearts by the Holy Ghost which is given unto us.
See citations under 3 above.

5. Heb. 6:11, 12. And we desire that every one of you do shew the same diligence to the full assurance of hope unto the end: that ye be not slothful, but followers of them who through faith and patience inherit the promises.
See citations under 3 and 4 above.

6. Heb. 6:17, 18. Wherein God, willing more abundantly to shew unto the heirs of promise the immutability of his counsel, confirmed it by an oath: that by two immutable things, in which it was impossible for God to lie, we might have a strong consolation, who have fled for refuge to lay hold upon the hope set before us.
II Peter 1:4, 5. Whereby are given unto us exceeding great and precious promises: that by these ye might be partakers of the divine nature, having escaped the corruption that is in the world through lust. And beside this, giving all diligence, add to your faith virtue; and to virtue knowledge.

7. II Peter 1:10, 11. Wherefore the rather, brethren, give diligence to make your calling and election sure: for if ye do these things, ye shall never fall: for so an entrance shall be ministered unto you abundantly into the everlasting kingdom of our Lord and Saviour Jesus Christ.
I John 3:14. We know that we have passed from death unto life, because we love the brethren.

8. Rom. 8:15, 16. For ye have not received the spirit of bondage again to fear; but ye have received the Spirit of adoption, whereby we cry, Abba, Father. The Spirit itself beareth witness with our spirit, that we are the children of God.

9. Eph. 1:13, 14. In whom ye also trusted, after that ye heard the word of truth, the gospel of your salvation: in whom also after that ye believed, ye were sealed with that Holy Spirit of promise, which is the earnest of our inheritance until the redemption of the purchased possession, unto the praise of his glory.
II Cor. 1:21, 22. Now he which stablisheth us with you in Christ, and hath anointed us, is God; who hath also sealed us, and given the earnest of the Spirit in our hearts.

10. Isa. 50:10. Who is among you that feareth the LORD, that obeyeth the voice of his servant, that walketh in darkness, and hath no light? let him trust in the name of the LORD, and stay upon his God.

by the Spirit to know the things which are freely given him of God, he may, without extraordinary revelation, in the right use of ordinary means, attain thereunto.[11] And therefore it is the duty of everyone to give all diligence to make his calling and election sure; that thereby his heart may be enlarged in peace and joy in the Holy Ghost, in love and thankfulness to God, and in strength and cheerfulness in the duties of obedience, the proper fruits of this assurance: so far is it from inclining men to looseness.[12]

4. True believers may have the assurance of their salvation divers ways shaken, diminished, and intermitted; as, by negligence in preserving of it; by falling into some special sin, which woundeth the conscience, and grieveth the Spirit; by some sudden or vehement temptation; by God's withdrawing the light of his countenance, and suffering even such as fear him to walk in darkness and to have no light:[13] yet are they never utterly destitute of that seed of God, and life of faith, that love of Christ

---

I John 5:13. These things have I written unto you that believe on the name of the Son of God; that ye may know that ye have eternal life, and that ye may believe on the name of the Son of God.
Ps. 73; 77; 88.

11. I Cor. 2:12. Now we have received, not the spirit of the world, but the spirit which is of God: that we might know the things that are freely given to us of God.
I John 4:13. Hereby know we that we dwell in him, and he in us, because he hath given us of his Spirit.
Ps. 77:10-20; Ps. 73.
See citations under Section 2 above.

12. II Peter 1:10. Wherefore the rather, brethren, give diligence to make your calling and election sure: for if ye do these things, ye shall never fall.
Rom. 6:1, 2. What shall we say then? Shall we continue in sin, that grace may abound? God forbid. How shall we, that are dead to sin, live any longer therein?
Titus 2:11, 12, 14. For the grace of God that bringeth salvation hath appeared to all men, teaching us that, denying ungodliness and wordly lusts, we should live soberly, righteously, and godly, in this present world . . . who gave himself for us, that he might redeem us from all iniquity, and purify unto himself a peculiar people, zealous of good works.

13. Ps. 51:8, 12, 14. Make me to hear joy and gladness; *that* the bones *which* thou hast broken may rejoice. . . . Restore unto me the joy of thy salvation; and uphold me *with thy* free spirit. . . . Deliver me from bloodguiltiness, O God, thou God of my salvation: *and* my tongue shall sing aloud of thy righteousness.
Eph. 4:30. And grieve not the Holy Spirit of God, whereby ye are sealed unto the day of redemption.
Ps. 77:1-10; Matt. 26:69-72; Ps. 31:22; Ps. 88; Isa. 50:10.

and the brethren, that sincerity of heart and conscience of duty, out of which, by the operation of the Spirit, this assurance may in due time be revived,[14] and by the which, in the meantime, they are supported from utter despair.[15]

CHAPTER XXI

Of the Law of God

1. God gave to Adam a law, as a covenant of works, by which he bound him and all his posterity to personal, entire, exact, and perpetual obedience; promised life upon the fulfilling, and threatened death upon the breach of it; and endued him with power and ability to keep it.

2. This law, after his fall, continued to be a perfect rule of righteousness; and, as such, was delivered by God upon mount Sinai in ten commandments, and written in two tables;[1] the first

-----

14. I John 3:9. Whosoever is born of God doth not commit sin; for his seed remaineth in him: and he cannot sin, because he is born of God.
Luke 22:32. But I have prayed for thee, that thy faith fail not.
Ps. 73:15. If I say, I will speak thus; behold, I should offend *against* the generation of thy children.
Ps. 51:8, 12. Make me to hear joy and gladness; *that* the bones *which* thou hast broken may rejoice. . . . Restore unto me the joy of thy salvation; and uphold me *with thy* free spirit.
Isa. 50:10.

15. Micah 7:7-9. Therefore I will look unto the LORD; I will wait for the God of my salvation: my God will hear me. Rejoice not against me, O mine enemy: when I fall, I shall arise; when I sit in darkness, the LORD *shall be* a light unto me. I will bear the indignation of the LORD, because I have sinned against him, until he plead my cause, and execute judgment for me: he will bring me forth to the light, *and* I shall behold his righteousness.

1. Gal. 3:12. And the law is not of faith: but, The man that doeth them shall live in them.
Hos. 6:7. But they like Adam have transgressed the covenant: there have they dealt treacherously against me. (A.S.V.)
Gen. 2:16, 17. And the LORD God commanded the man, saying, Of every tree of the garden thou mayest freely eat: but of the tree of the knowledge of good and evil, thou shalt not eat of it: for in the day that thou eatest thereof thou shalt surely die.
Compare Rom. 5:12-14; I Cor. 15:22; Luke 10:25-28, and the covenants made with Noah and Abraham.
Gen. 1:26. And God said, Let us make man in our image, after our likeness.
Deut. 30:19. I call heaven and earth to record this day against you, *that* I have set before you life and death, blessing and cursing: therefore choose life, that both thou and thy seed may live.
John 7:17. If any man will do his will, he shall know of the doctrine, whether it be of God, or *whether* I speak of myself.

four commandments containing our duty toward God, and the other six our duty to man.[2]

3. Besides this law, commonly called moral, God was pleased to give to the people of Israel, as a church under age, ceremonial laws, containing several typical ordinances, partly of worship, prefiguring Christ, his graces, actions, sufferings, and benefits;[3] and partly holding forth divers instructions of moral duties.[4] All which ceremonial laws are now abrogated under the New Testament.[5]

Rev. 22:17. And the Spirit and the bride say, Come. And let him that heareth say, Come. And let him that is athirst come. And whosoever will, let him take the water of life freely.

James 1:14. But every man is tempted, when he is drawn away of his own lust, and enticed.

James 1:25. But whoso looketh into the perfect law of liberty, and continueth *therein*, he being not a forgetful hearer, but a doer of the work, this man shall be blessed in his deed.

James 2:8, 10. If ye fulfil the royal law according to the scripture, Thou shalt love thy neighbour as thyself, ye do well. . . . For whosoever shall keep the whole law, and yet offend in one *point*, he is guilty of all.

Rom. 3:19. Now we know that what things soever the law saith, it saith to them who are under the law.

Deut. 5:32. Ye shall observe to do therefore as the LORD your God hath commanded you: ye shall not turn aside to the right hand or to the left.

Deut. 10:4. And he wrote on the tables, according to the first writing, the ten commandments, which the LORD spake unto you in the mount out of the midst of the fire in the day of the assembly: and the LORD gave them unto me.

Exod. 34:1; Rom. 13:8, 9.

2. Matt. 22:37-40. Jesus said unto him, Thou shalt love the Lord thy God with all thy heart, and with all thy soul, and with all thy mind. This is the first and great commandment. And the second *is* like unto it, Thou shalt love thy neighbour as thyself. On these two commandments hang all the law and the prophets.

Exod. 20:3-18.

3. Heb. 10:1. For the law having a shadow of good things to come, *and* not the very image of the things, can never with those sacrifices which they offered year by year continually make the comers thereunto perfect.

Gal. 4:1-3. Now I say, *That* the heir, as long as he is a child, differeth nothing from a servant, though he be lord of all; but is under tutors and governors until the time appointed of the father. Even so we, when we were children, were in bondage under the elements of the world.

Col. 2:17. Which are a shadow of things to come; but the body *is* of Christ.

Heb. 9.

4. See Lev. 5:1-6; 6:1-7, and similar passages.

5. Mark 7:18, 19. Perceive ye not, that whatsoever from without goeth into the man, *it* cannot defile him; because it goeth not into his heart,

4. To them also, as a body politic, he gave sundry judicial laws, which expired together with the state of that people, not obliging any other, now, further than the general equity thereof may require.[6]

5. The moral law doth forever bind all, as well justified persons as others, to the obedience thereof; and that not only in regard of the matter contained in it, but also in respect of the authority of God the Creator who gave it.[7] Neither doth Christ in the gospel any way dissolve, but much strengthen, this obligation.[8]

---

but into his belly, and goeth out into the draught? *This he said*, making all meats clean. (A.S.V.)

Gal. 2:4. And that because of false brethren unawares brought in, who came in privily to spy out our liberty which we have in Christ Jesus, that they might bring us into bondage.

Col. 2:17. Which are a shadow of things to come; but the body *is* of Christ.

Eph. 2:15, 16. Having abolished in his flesh the enmity, *even* the law of commandments *contained* in ordinances; for to make in himself of twain one new man, *so* making peace; and that he might reconcile both unto God in one body by the cross, having slain the enmity thereby.

6. Matt. 5:38, 39. Ye have heard that it hath been said, An eye for an eye, and a tooth for a tooth: but I say unto you, That ye resist not evil.

I Cor. 9:8-10. Say I these things as a man? or saith not the law the same also? For it is written in the law of Moses, Thou shalt not muzzle the mouth of the ox that treadeth out the corn. Doth God take care for oxen? or saith he *it* altogether for our sakes? For our sakes, no doubt, *this* is written: that he that plougheth should plough in hope; and that he that thresheth in hope should be partaker of his hope.

Exod., chapters 21 and 22.

7. Rom. 13:8, 9. Owe no man any thing, but to love one another: for he that loveth another hath fulfilled the law. For this, Thou shalt not commit adultery, Thou shalt not kill, Thou shalt not steal, Thou shalt not bear false witness, Thou shalt not covet; and if *there be* any other commandment, it is briefly comprehended in this saying, namely, Thou shalt love thy neighbour as thyself.

I John 2:3, 4, 7. And hereby we do know that we know him, if we keep his commandments. He that saith, I know him, and keepeth not his commandments, is a liar, and the truth is not in him. . . . Brethren, I write no new commandment unto you, but an old commandment which ye had from the beginning.

Rom. 3:31. Do we then make void the law through faith? God forbid: yea, we establish the law.

Rom. 6:15. What then? shall we sin, because we are not under the law, but under grace? God forbid.

See citations under Section 2 above.

8. Matt. 5:18, 19. For verily I say unto you, Till heaven and earth pass, one jot or one tittle shall in no wise pass from the law, till all be fulfilled. Whosoever therefore shall break one of these least commandments, and shall teach men so, he shall be called the least in the kingdom of

6. Although true believers be not under the law as a covenant of works, to be thereby justified or condemned;[9] yet is it of great use to them, as well as to others; in that, as a rule of life, informing them of the will of God and their duty, it directs and binds them to walk accordingly;[10] discovering also the sinful pollutions of their nature, hearts, and lives;[11] so as, examining themselves thereby, they may come to further conviction of, humiliation for, and hatred against sin;[12] together with a clearer sight of the need they have of Christ, and the perfection of his obedience.[13] It is likewise of use to the regenerate, to restrain their corruptions, in that it forbids sin,[14] and the threatenings of it serve to show what even their sins deserve, and what afflictions in this life they may expect for them, although freed from the

---

heaven: but whosoever shall do and teach *them,* the same shall be called great in the kingdom of heaven.
James 2:8; Rom. 3:31.

9. Rom. 6:14. For sin shall not have dominion over you: for ye are not under the law, but under grace.
Rom. 8:1. *There is* therefore now no condemnation to them which are in Christ Jesus.
Gal. 4:4, 5; Acts 13:39.

10. Rom. 7:12. Wherefore the law *is* holy, and the commandment holy, and just, and good.
Ps. 119:5. O that my ways were directed to keep thy statutes!
I Cor. 7:19. Circumcision is nothing, and uncircumcision is nothing, but the keeping of the commandments of God.
Gal. 5:14, 18, 23.

11. Rom. 7:7. What shall we say then? *Is* the law sin? God forbid. Nay, I had not known sin, but by the law: for I had not known lust, except the law had said, Thou shalt not covet.
Rom. 3:20. For by the law *is* the knowledge of sin.

12. Rom. 7:9, 14, 24. For I was alive without the law once: but when the commandment came, sin revived, and I died. . . . For we know that the law is spiritual: but I am carnal, sold under sin. . . . O wretched man that I am! who shall deliver me from the body of this death?

13. Gal. 3:24. Wherefore the law was our schoolmaster *to bring us* unto Christ, that we might be justified by faith.
Rom. 8:3, 4. For what the law could not do, in that it was weak through the flesh, God sending his own Son in the likeness of sinful flesh, and for sin, condemned sin in the flesh: that the righteousness of the law might be fulfilled in us who walk not after the flesh, but after the Spirit.
Rom. 7:24, 25.

14. James 2:11. For he that said, Do not commit adultery, said also, Do not kill. Now if thou commit no adultery, yet if thou kill, thou art become a transgressor of the law.
Ps. 119:128. Therefore I esteem all *thy* precepts *concerning* all *things* to be right; *and* I hate every false way.

curse thereof threatened in the law.[15] The promises of it, in like manner, show them God's approbation of obedience, and what blessings they may expect upon the performance thereof;[16] although not as due to them by the law as a covenant of works: so as a man's doing good, and refraining from evil, because the law encourageth to the one, and deterreth from the other, is no evidence of his being under the law, and not under grace.[17]

7. Neither are the forementioned uses of the law contrary to the grace of the gospel, but do sweetly comply with it:[18] the Spirit of Christ subduing and enabling the will of man to do that freely and cheerfully, which the will of God, revealed in the law, requireth to be done.[19]

CHAPTER XXII

Of Christian Liberty, and Liberty of Conscience

1. The liberty which Christ hath purchased for believers under the gospel consists in their freedom from the guilt of sin,

---

15. Ezra 9:13, 14. And after all that is come upon us for our evil deeds, and for our great trespass, seeing that thou our God hast punished us less than our iniquities *deserve,* and hast given us *such* deliverance as this; should we again break thy commandments, and join in affinity with the people of these abominations? wouldest not thou be angry with us till thou hadst consumed *us,* so that *there should be* no remnant nor escaping?
    Ps. 89:30-34.

16. Ps. 37:11. But the meek shall inherit the earth; and shall delight themselves in the abundance of peace.
    Ps. 19:11. Moreover by them is thy servant warned: *and* in keeping of them *there is* great reward.
    Lev. 26:3-13; Eph. 6:2; Matt. 5:5.

17. Rom. 6:12, 14. Let not sin therefore reign in your mortal body, that ye should obey it in the lusts thereof. . . . For sin shall not have dominion over you: for ye are not under the law, but under grace.
    Heb. 12:28, 29. Wherefore we receiving a kingdom which cannot be moved, let us have grace whereby we may serve God acceptably with reverence and godly fear: For our God *is* a consuming fire.
    I Peter 3:8-12; Ps. 34:12-16.

18. See citations under Section 6, above.

19. See citations under Chapter X, Section 1.
    Gal. 3:13. Christ hath redeemed us from the curse of the law, being made a curse for us: for it is written, Cursed *is* every one that hangeth on a tree.

the condemning wrath of God, the curse of the moral law;[1] and in their being delivered from this present evil world, bondage to Satan, and dominion of sin,[2] from the evil of afflictions, the sting of death, the victory of the grave, and everlasting damnation;[3] as also in their free access to God,[4] and their yielding obedience unto him, not out of slavish fear, but a childlike love, and a willing mind.[5] All which were common also to believers under the law;[6] but under the New Testament, the liberty of Christians is further enlarged in their freedom from the yoke of the ceremonial law, to which the Jewish church was subjected;[7]

---

1. Titus 2:14. Who gave himself for us, that he might redeem us from all iniquity, and purify unto himself a peculiar people, zealous of good works.
   I Thess. 1:10. And to wait for his Son from heaven, whom he raised from the dead, *even* Jesus, which delivered us from the wrath to come.
2. Gal. 1:4. Who gave himself for our sins, that he might deliver us from this present evil world, according to the will of God and our Father.
   Acts 26:18. To open their eyes, *and* to turn *them* from darkness to light, and *from* the power of Satan unto God, that they may receive forgiveness of sins, and inheritance among them which are sanctified by faith that is in me.
   Col. 1:13. Who hath delivered us from the power of darkness, and hath translated *us* into the kingdom of his dear Son.
   Rom. 6:14. For sin shall not have dominion over you: for ye are not under the law, but under grace.
3. Ps. 119:71. *It is* good for me that I have been afflicted; that I might learn thy statutes.
   I Cor. 15:56, 57. The sting of death *is* sin; and the strength of sin *is* the law. But thanks *be* to God, which giveth us the victory through our Lord Jesus Christ.
   Rom. 8:1.
4. Rom. 5:2. By whom also we have access by faith into this grace wherein we stand.
5. Rom. 8:14, 15. For as many as are led by the Spirit of God, they are the sons of God. For ye have not received the spirit of bondage again to fear; but ye have received the Spirit of adoption, whereby we cry, Abba, Father.
   Eph. 2:18. For through him we both have access by one Spirit unto the Father.
   Gal. 4:6. And because ye are sons, God hath sent forth the Spirit of his Son into your hearts, crying, Abba, Father.
   Heb. 10:19. Having therefore, brethren, boldness to enter into the holiest by the blood of Jesus.
   I John 4:18.
6. Gal. 3:9, 14. So then they which be of faith are blessed with the faithful Abraham. . . . that the blessing of Abraham might come on the Gentiles through Jesus Christ; that we might receive the promise of the Spirit through faith.
   See citations under Chapter VIII, Section 6.
7. Gal. 5:1. Stand fast therefore in the liberty wherewith Christ hath made us free, and be not entangled again with the yoke of bondage.

and in greater boldness of access to the throne of grace,[8] and in fuller communications of the free Spirit of God, than believers under the law did ordinarily partake of.[9]

2. God alone is Lord of the conscience, and hath left it free from the doctrines and commandments of men which are in anything contrary to his word, or beside it in matters of faith or worship.[10] So that to believe such doctrines, or to obey such commandments out of conscience, is to betray true liberty of conscience;[11] and the requiring an implicit faith, and an absolute and blind obedience, is to destroy liberty of conscience, and reason also.[12]

Acts 15:10. Now therefore why tempt ye God, to put a yoke upon the neck of the disciples, which neither our fathers nor we were able to bear?
Gal. 4:1-3, 6.

8. Heb. 4:14, 16. Seeing then that we have a great high priest, that is passed into the heavens, Jesus the Son of God, let us hold fast *our* profession. . . . Let us therefore come boldly unto the throne of grace, that we may obtain mercy, and find grace to help in time of need.
Heb. 10:19, 20. Having therefore, brethren, boldness to enter into the holiest by the blood of Jesus, by a new and living way, which he hath consecrated for us, through the veil, that is to say, his flesh.

9. John 7:38, 39. He that believeth on me, as the scripture hath said, out of his belly shall flow rivers of living water. (But this spake he of the Spirit, which they that believe on him should receive: for the Holy Ghost was not yet *given*; because that Jesus was not yet glorified.)
II Cor. 3:13, 17, 18.

10. Rom. 14:4. Who art thou that judgeth another man's servant? to his own master he standeth or falleth. Yea, he shall be holden up: for God is able to make him stand.
Acts 4:19. But Peter and John answered and said unto them, Whether it be right in the sight of God to hearken unto you more than unto God, judge ye.
Acts 5:29. Then Peter and the *other* apostles answered and said, We ought to obey God rather than men.
I Cor. 7:23; Matt. 23:8-10; II Cor. 1:24; Matt. 15:9.

11. Gal. 2:3, 4. But neither Titus, who was with me, being a Greek, was compelled to be circumcised: and that because of false brethren unawares brought in, who came in privily to spy out our liberty which we have in Christ Jesus, that they might bring us into bondage.
Col. 2:20, 22, 23. Wherefore if ye be dead with Christ from the rudiments of the world, why, as though living in the world, are ye subject to ordinances . . . which all are to perish with the using; after the commandments and doctrines of men? Which things have indeed a shew of wisdom in will worship, and humility, and neglecting of the body; not in any honour to the satisfying of the flesh.
Gal. 5:1.

12 Hosea 5:11. Ephraim *is* oppressed *and* broken in judgment, because he willingly walked after the commandment.
Rev. 13:12, 16, 17.

3. They who, upon pretense of Christian liberty, do practice any sin, or cherish any lust, do thereby destroy the end of Christian liberty; which is, that, being delivered out of the hands of our enemies, we might serve the Lord without fear, in holiness and righteousness before him, all the days of our life.[13]

4. And because the powers which God hath ordained, and the liberty which Christ hath purchased, are not intended by God to destroy, but mutually to uphold and preserve one another; they who, upon pretense of Christian liberty, shall oppose any lawful power, or the lawful exercise of it, whether it be civil or ecclesiastical, resist the ordinance of God.[14] And for their publishing of such opinions, or maintaining of such practices, as are contrary to the light of nature, or to the known principles of Christianity, whether concerning faith, worship, or conversation; or to the power of godliness; or such erroneous opinions or practices as, either in their own nature, or in the manner of publishing or maintaining them, are destructive to the external peace and order which Christ hath established in the church: they may lawfully be called to account, and proceeded against by the censures of the church.[15]

---

13. Gal. 5:13. For, brethren, ye have been called unto liberty; only *use* not liberty for an occasion to the flesh, but by love serve one another.
   I Peter 2:16. As free, and not using *your* liberty for a cloke of maliciousness, but as the servants of God.
   Luke 1:74, 75. That he would grant unto us, that we being delivered out of the hand of our enemies might serve him without fear, in holiness and righteousness before him, all the days of our life.
   II Peter 2:19; John 8:34.

14. I Peter 2:13, 14, 16. Submit yourselves to every ordinance of man for the Lord's sake: whether it be to the king, as supreme; or unto governors, as unto them that are sent by him for the punishment of evildoers, and for the praises of them that do well. . . . As free, and not using *your* liberty for a cloke of maliciousness, but as the servants of God.
   Heb. 13:17. Obey them that have the rule over you, and submit yourselves: for they watch for your souls, as they that must give account, that they may do it with joy, and not with grief: for that *is* unprofitable for you.
   Rom. 13:1-8.

15. I Cor. 5:1, 5, 11, 13. It is reported commonly *that there is* fornication among you, and such fornication as is not so much as named among the Gentiles, that one should have his father's wife. . . . to deliver such an one unto Satan for the destruction of the flesh, .that the spirit may be saved in the day of the Lord Jesus. . . . But now I have written unto you not to keep company, if any man that is called a brother be a fornicator, or covetous, or an idolater, or a railer, or a drunkard, or an extortioner; with such an one no not to eat. . . . But them that are without God

CHAPTER XXIII

Of Religious Worship
and the Sabbath Day

1. The light of nature showeth that there is a God, who hath lordship and sovereignty over all; is good, and doeth good unto all; and is therefore to be feared, loved, praised, called upon, trusted in, and served with all the heart, and with all the soul, and with all the might.[1] But the acceptable way of worshipping the true God is instituted by himself, and so limited by his own revealed will, that he may not be worshipped according to the imaginations and devices of men, or the suggestions of Satan, under any visible representation or any other way not prescribed in the Holy Scripture.[2]

---

judgeth. Therefore put away from among yourselves that wicked person. Titus 1:13. This witness is true. Wherefore rebuke them sharply, that they may be sound in the faith.

Matt. 18:17, 18. And if he shall neglect to hear them, tell *it* unto the church: but if he neglect to hear the church, let him be unto thee as a heathen man and a publican. Verily I say unto you, Whatsoever ye shall bind on earth shall be bound in heaven: and whatsoever ye shall loose on earth shall be loosed in heaven.

II Thess. 3:14. And if any man obey not our word by this epistle, note that man, and have no company with him, that he may be ashamed.

Titus 3:10. A man that is an heretic after the first and second admonition reject.

1. Rom. 1:19, 20. Because that which may be known of God is manifest in them; for God hath shewed *it* unto them. For the invisible things of him from the creation of the world are clearly seen, being understood by the things that are made, *even* his eternal power and Godhead; so that they are without excuse.

Jer. 10:7. Who would not fear thee, O King of nations? for to thee doth it appertain: forasmuch as among all the wise *men* of the nations, and in all their kingdoms, *there is* none like unto thee.

Ps. 19:1-6. The heavens declare the glory of God; and the firmament sheweth his handywork. Day unto day uttereth speech, and night unto night sheweth knowledge. *There is* no speech nor language, *where* their voice is not heard. Their line is gone out through all the earth, and their words to the end of the world. In them hath he set a tabernacle for the sun, which *is* as a bridegroom coming out of his chamber, *and* rejoiceth as a strong man to run a race. His going forth *is* from the end of the heaven, and his circuit unto the ends of it: and there is nothing hid from the heat thereof.

2. Deut. 12:32. What thing soever I command you, observe to do it: thou shalt not add thereto, nor diminish from it.

Matt. 15:9. But in vain they do worship me, teaching *for* doctrines the commandments of men.

2. Religious worship is to be given to God, the Father, Son, and Holy Ghost; and to him alone:[3] not to angels, saints, or any other creature:[4] and since the fall, not without a Mediator; nor in the mediation of any other but of Christ alone.[5]

3. Prayer with thanksgiving, being one special part of religious worship,[6] is by God required of all men;[7] and that it may be accepted, it is to be made in the name of the Son,[8] by the help

---

Matt. 4:9, 10. And saith unto him, All these things will I give thee, if thou wilt fall down and worship me. Then saith Jesus unto him, Get thee hence, Satan: for it is written, Thou shalt worship the Lord thy God, and him only shalt thou serve.

Acts 17:24, 25. God that made the world and all things therein, seeing that he is Lord of heaven and earth, dwelleth not in temples made with hands; neither is worshipped with men's hands, as though he needed any thing, seeing he giveth to all life, and breath, and all things.

Exod. 20:4-6; Deut. 4:15-20; Col. 2:20-23.

3. John 5:23. That all *men* should honour the Son, even as they honour the Father. He that honoureth not the Son honoureth not the Father which hath sent him.

II Cor. 13:14. The grace of the Lord Jesus Christ, and the love of God, and the communion of the Holy Ghost, *be* with you all. Amen.

Matt. 4:10. Then said Jesus unto him, Get thee hence, Satan: for it is written, Thou shalt worship the Lord thy God, and him only shalt thou serve.

Rev. 5:11-13.

4. Col. 2:18. Let no man beguile you of your reward in a voluntary humility and worshipping of angels.

Rev. 19:10. And I fell at his feet to worship him. And he said unto me, See *thou do it* not: I am thy fellowservant, and of thy brethren that have the testimony of Jesus: worship God.

Rom. 1:25. Who changed the truth of God into a lie, and worshipped and served the creature more than the Creator, who is blessed for ever. Amen.

5. John 14:6. Jesus saith unto him, I am the way, the truth, and the life: no man cometh unto the Father, but by me.

I Tim. 2:5. For *there is* one God, and one mediator between God and men, the man Christ Jesus.

Eph. 2:18. For through him we both have access by one Spirit unto the Father.

6. Phil. 4:6. Be careful for nothing; but in every thing by prayer and supplication with thanksgiving let your requests be made known unto God.

7. Luke 18:1. And he spake a parable unto them *to this end,* that men ought always to pray, and not to faint.

I Tim. 2:8. I will therefore that men pray every where, lifting up holy hands, without wrath and doubting.

8. John 14:13, 14. And whatsoever ye shall ask in my name, that will I do, that the Father may be glorified in the Son. If ye shall ask any thing in my name, I will do *it.*

of his Spirit,[9] according to his will,[10] with understanding, reverence, humility, fervency, faith, love, and perseverance;[11] and, if vocal, in a known tongue.[12]

4. Prayer is to be made for things lawful,[13] and for all sorts of men living, or that shall live hereafter;[14] but not for the dead.[15]

5. The reading of the Scriptures with godly fear;[17] the sound

---

9. Rom. 8:26. Likewise the Spirit also helpeth our infirmities: for we know not what we should pray for as we ought: but the Spirit itself maketh intercession for us with groanings which cannot be uttered.

10. I John 5:14. And this is the confidence that we have in him, that, if we ask any thing according to his will, he heareth us.

11. Ps. 47:7. For God is the King of all the earth: sing ye praises with understanding.
    Heb. 12:28. Let us have grace, whereby we may serve God acceptably with reverence and godly fear.
    Gen. 18:27. I have taken upon me to speak unto the Lord, which am but dust and ashes.
    James 5:16. The effectual fervent prayer of a righteous man availeth much.
    Eph. 6:18. Praying always with all prayer and supplication in the Spirit, and watching thereunto with all perseverance and supplication for all saints.
    James 1:6, 7; Mark 11:24; Matt. 6:12, 14, 15; Col. 4:2.

12. I Cor. 14:14. For if I pray in an *unknown* tongue, my spirit prayeth, but my understanding is unfruitful.

13. I John 5:14. And this is the confidence that we have in him, that, if we ask any thing according to his will, he heareth us.

14. I Tim. 2:1, 2. I exhort therefore, that, first of all, supplications, prayers, intercessions, *and* giving of thanks, be made for all men; for kings, and *for* all that are in authority; that we may lead a quiet and peaceable life in all godliness and honesty.
    John 17:20. Neither pray I for these alone, but for them also which shall believe on me through their word.
    II Sam. 7:29. Therefore now let it please thee to bless the house of thy servant, that it may continue for ever before thee: for thou, O Lord God, hast spoken *it:* and with thy blessing let the house of thy servant be blessed for ever.

15. This statement is based on the absence of any command to pray for the dead, and of any example in the Scripture of such prayer.
    I John 5:14.

16. Original note 16 removed by amendment enacted by the General Assembly in 1939.

17. Acts 15:21. For Moses of old time hath in every city them that preach him, being read in the synagogues every sabbath day.
    Acts 17:11. These were more noble than those in Thessalonica, in that they received the word with all readiness of mind, and searched the scriptures daily, whether those things were so.
    Rev. 1:3. Blessed *is* he that readeth, and they that hear the words of this prophecy, and keep those things which are written therein: for the time *is* at hand.

preaching,[18] and conscionable hearing of the word, in obedience unto God with understanding, faith, and reverence;[19] singing of psalms with grace in the heart;[20] as, also, the due administration and worthy receiving of the sacraments instituted by Christ; are all parts of the ordinary religious worship of God:[21] besides religious oaths,[22] and vows,[23] solemn fastings,[24] and thanksgivings upon special occasion;[25] which are, in their several times and seasons, to be used in an holy and religious manner.[26]

---

18. II Tim. 4:2. Preach the word; be instant in season, out of season; reprove, rebuke, exhort with all longsuffering and doctrine.

19. James 1:22. But be ye doers of the word, and not hearers only, deceiving your own selves.
Acts 10:33. Immediately therefore I sent to thee; and thou hast well done that thou art come. Now therefore are we all here present before God, to hear all things that are commanded thee of God.
Heb. 4:2. For unto us was the gospel preached, as well as unto them: but the word preached did not profit them, not being mixed with faith in them that heard it.
Matt. 13:19; Isa. 66:2.

20. Col. 3:16. Let the word of Christ dwell in you richly in all wisdom; teaching and admonishing one another in psalms and hymns and spiritual songs, singing with grace in your hearts to the Lord.
Eph. 5:19; James 5:13.

21. Matt. 28:19. Go ye therefore, and teach all nations, baptizing them in the name of the Father, and of the Son, and of the Holy Ghost.
Acts 2:42. And they continued stedfastly in the apostles' doctrine and fellowship, and in breaking of bread, and in prayers.
I Cor. 11:23-29.

22. Deut. 6:13. Thou shalt fear the LORD thy God, and serve him, and shalt swear by his name.

23. Ps. 116:14. I will pay my vows unto the LORD now in the presence of all his people.
Isa. 19:21. And the LORD shall be known to Egypt, and the Egyptians shall know the LORD in that day, and shall do sacrifice and oblation; yea, they shall vow a vow unto the LORD, and perform it.
Neh. 10:29.

24. Joel 2:12. Therefore also now, saith the LORD, turn ye even to me with all your heart, and with fasting, and with weeping, and with mourning.
Matt. 9:15. Can the children of the bridechamber mourn, as long as the bridegroom is with them? but the days will come, when the bridegroom shall be taken from them, and then shall they fast.
I Cor. 7:5. Defraud ye not one the other, except it be with consent for a time, that ye may give yourselves to fasting and prayer; and come together again, that Satan tempt you not for your incontinency.
Esther 4:16.

25. Ps. 107.

26. John 4:24. God is a Spirit: and they that worship him must worship him in spirit and in truth.
Heb. 10:22. Let us draw near with a true heart in full assurance of

6. Neither prayer, nor any other part of religious worship, is now, under the gospel, either tied unto, or made more acceptable by, any place in which it is performed, or towards which it is directed:[27] but God is to be worshipped everywhere[28] in spirit and in truth;[29] as in private families[30] daily,[31] and in secret each one by himself,[32] so more solemnly in the public assemblies, which are not carelessly or willfully to be neglected or forsaken, when God, by his word or providence, calleth thereunto.[33]

7. As it is of the law of nature that, in general, a due proportion of time be set apart for the worship of God; so, in his word, by a positive, moral, and perpetual commandment, binding all

---

faith, having our hearts sprinkled from an evil conscience, and our bodies washed with pure water.

27. John 4:21. Jesus saith unto her, Woman, believe me, the hour cometh, when ye shall neither in this mountain, nor yet at Jerusalem, worship the Father.

28. Mal. 1:11. From the rising of the sun even unto the going down of the same my name *shall be* great among the Gentiles; and in every place incense *shall be* offered unto my name, and a pure offering: for my name *shall be* great among the heathen, saith the LORD of hosts.
I Tim. 2:8. I will therefore that men pray every where, lifting up holy hands, without wrath and doubting.

29. John 4:23, 24. But the hour cometh, and now is, when the true worshippers shall worship the Father in spirit and in truth: for the Father seeketh such to worship him. God *is* a Spirit: and they that worship him must worship *him* in spirit and in truth.

30. Deut. 6:7. And thou shalt teach them diligently unto thy children, and shalt talk of them when thou sittest in thine house, and when thou walkest by the way, and when thou liest down, and when thou risest up.
Job 1:5. And it was so, when the days of *their* feasting were gone about, that Job sent and sanctified them, and rose up early in the morning, and offered burnt offerings *according* to the number of them all: for Job said, It may be that my sons have sinned, and cursed God in their hearts. Thus did Job continually.
Acts 10:2. A devout *man*, and one that feared God with all his house, which gave much alms to the people, and prayed to God alway.

31. Matt. 6:11. Give us this day our daily bread.

32. Matt. 6:6. But thou, when thou prayest, enter into thy closet, and when thou hast shut thy door, pray to thy Father which is in secret; and thy Father which seeth in secret shall reward thee openly.
Eph. 6:18.

33. Isa. 56:7. Mine house shall be called an house of prayer for all people.
Heb. 10:25. Not forsaking the assembling of ourselves together, as the manner of some *is*; but exhorting *one another*: and so much the more, as ye see the day approaching.
Acts 2:42. And they continued stedfastly in the apostles' doctrine and fellowship, and in breaking of bread, and in prayers.
Luke 4:16; Acts 13:42.

men in all ages, he hath particularly appointed one day in seven for a Sabbath, to be kept holy unto him:[34] which, from the beginning of the world to the resurrection of Christ, was the last day of the week; and, from the resurrection of Christ, was changed into the first day of the week, which in Scripture is called the Lord's day, and is to be continued to the end of the world as the Christian Sabbath.[35]

8. This Sabbath is then kept holy unto the Lord when men, after a due preparing of their hearts, and ordering of their common affairs beforehand, do not only observe an holy rest all the day from their own works, words, and thoughts about their worldly employments and recreations;[36] but also are taken up

34. Exod. 20:8-11. Remember the sabbath day, to keep it holy. Six days shalt thou labour, and do all thy work: but the seventh day *is* the sabbath of the LORD thy God: *in it* thou shalt not do any work, thou, nor thy son, nor thy daughter, thy manservant, nor thy maidservant, nor thy cattle, nor thy stranger that *is* within thy gates: for *in* six days the LORD made heaven and earth, the sea, and all that in them *is*, and rested the seventh day: wherefore the LORD blessed the sabbath day, and hallowed it.
Isa. 56:2, 4, 6. Blessed *is* the man *that* doeth this, and the son of man *that* layeth hold on it; that keepeth the sabbath from polluting it, and keepeth his hand from doing any evil. . . . For thus saith the Lord unto the eunuchs that keep my sabbaths, and choose *the things* that please me, and take hold of my covenant . . . Also the sons of the stranger, that join themselves to the LORD, to serve him, and to love the name of the LORD, to be his servants, every one that keepeth the sabbath from polluting it, and taketh hold of my covenant.

35. I Cor. 16:1, 2. Now concerning the collection for the saints, as I have given order to the churches of Galatia, even so do ye. Upon the first *day* of the week let every one of you lay by him in store, as *God* hath prospered him, that there be no gatherings when I come.
Acts 20:7. And upon the first *day* of the week, when the disciples came together to break bread, Paul preached unto them, ready to depart on the morrow; and continued his speech until midnight.
These texts are cited in connection with the example of the apostles and the early church.

36. Exod. 16:23, 25, 26, 29, 30. And he said unto them, This *is that* which the LORD hath said, To morrow *is* the rest of the holy sabbath unto the LORD: bake *that* which ye will bake to day, and seethe that ye will seethe; and that which remaineth over lay up for you to be kept until the morning. . . . And Moses said, Eat that to day; for to day *is* a sabbath unto the LORD: to day ye shall not find it in the field. Six days ye shall gather it; but on the seventh day, *which is* the sabbath, in it there shall be none. . . . See, for that the LORD hath given you the sabbath, therefore he giveth you on the sixth day the bread of two days; abide ye every man in his place, let no man go out of his place on the seventh day. So the people rested on the seventh day.
Exod. 31:15, 16. Six days may work be done; but in the seventh *is* the sabbath of rest, holy to the LORD: whosoever doeth *any* work in the

the whole time in the public and private exercises of his worship, and in the duties of necessity and mercy.[37]

CHAPTER XXIV

Of Lawful Oaths and Vows

1. A lawful oath is a part of religious worship,[1] wherein upon just occasion, the person swearing solemnly calleth God to witness what he asserteth or promiseth; and to judge him according to the truth or falsehood of what he sweareth.[2]

2. The name of God only is that by which men ought to swear, and therein it is to be used with all holy fear and reverence;[3] therefore to swear vainly or rashly by that glorious and dreadful name, or to swear at all by any other thing, is sinful, and to be abhorred.[4] Yet, as, in matters of weight and moment,

---

sabbath day, he shall surely be put to death. Wherefore the children of Israel shall keep the sabbath, to observe the sabbath throughout their generations, *for* a perpetual covenant.
Isa. 58:13; Neh. 13:15-22; Luke 23:56.

37. Isa. 58:13. If thou turn away thy foot from the sabbath, *from* doing thy pleasure on my holy day; and call the sabbath a delight, the holy of the LORD, honourable; and shalt honour him, not doing thine own ways, nor finding thine own pleasure, nor speaking *thine own* words.
Matt. 12:1-13.

1. Deut. 10:20. Thou shalt fear the LORD thy God; him shalt thou serve, and to him shalt thou cleave, and swear by his name.

2. II Cor. 1:23. Moreover I call God for a record upon my soul, that to spare you I came not as yet unto Corinth.
II Chron. 6:22, 23. If a man sin against his neighbour, and an oath be laid upon him to make him swear, and the oath come before thine altar in this house; then hear thou from heaven, and do, and judge thy servants, by requiting the wicked, by recompensing his way upon his own head; and by justifying the righteous, by giving him according to his righteousness.
Exod. 20:7. Thou shalt not take the name of the LORD thy God in vain; for the LORD will not hold him guiltless that taketh his name in vain.

3. Deut. 6:13. Thou shalt fear the LORD thy God, and serve him, and shalt swear by his name.

4. Jer. 5:7. How shall I pardon thee for this? thy children have forsaken me, and sworn by *them that are* no gods: when I had fed them to the full, they then committed adultery, and assembled themselves by troops in the harlots' houses.
James 5:12. But above all things, my brethren, swear not, neither by heaven, neither by the earth, neither by any other oath: but let your yea be yea; and *your* nay, nay; lest ye fall into condemnation.

an oath is warranted by the word of God, under the New Testament, as well as under the Old, so a lawful oath, being imposed by lawful authority, in such matters ought to be taken.[5]

3. Whosoever taketh an oath ought duly to consider the weightiness of so solemn an act, and therein to avouch nothing but what he is fully persuaded is the truth. Neither may any man bind himself by oath to anything but what is good and just, and what he believeth so to be, and what he is able and resolved to perform. Yet it is a sin to refuse an oath touching anything that is good and just, being imposed by lawful authority.[6]

4. An oath is to be taken in the plain and common sense of the words, without equivocation or mental reservation.[7] It cannot oblige to sin; but in anything not sinful, being taken, it binds to performance, although to a man's own hurt:[8] nor is it to be violated, although made to heretics or infidels.[9]

Matt. 5:37. But let your communication be, Yea, yea; Nay, nay: for whatsoever is more than these cometh of evil.
Exod. 20:7.

5. I Kings 8:31. If any man trespass against his neighbour, and an oath be laid upon him to cause him to swear, and the oath come before thine alter in this house.
Ezra 10:5. Then arose Ezra, and made the chief priests, the Levites, and all Israel, to swear that they should do according to this word. And they sware.
Matt. 26:63, 64. But Jesus held his peace. And the high priest answered and said unto him, I adjure thee by the living God, that thou tell us whether thou be the Christ, the Son of God. Jesus saith unto him, Thou hast said: nevertheless I say unto you, Hereafter shall ye see the Son of man sitting on the right hand of power, and coming in the clouds of heaven.

6. See citations under Section 2, above.

7. Ps. 24:4. He that hath clean hands, and a pure heart; who hath not lifted up his soul unto vanity, nor sworn deceitfully.
Jer. 4:2. And thou shalt swear, The LORD liveth, in truth, in judgment, and in righteousness; and the nations shall bless themselves in him, and in him shall they glory.

8. Ps. 15:4. In whose eyes a vile person is contemned; but he honoureth them that fear the LORD. *He that* sweareth to *his own* hurt, and changeth not.

9. Ezek. 17:16, 18. *As* I live, saith the Lord GOD, surely in the place *where* the king *dwelleth* that made him king, whose oath he despised, and whose covenant he brake, *even* with him in the midst of Babylon he shall die. . . . Seeing he despised the oath by breaking the covenant, when, lo, he had given his hand, and hath done all these *things,* he shall not escape.
Josh. 9:18, 19. And the children of Israel smote them not, because the princes of the congregation had sworn unto them by the LORD God of Israel. And all the congregation murmured against the princes. But

5. A vow is of the like nature with a promissory oath, and ought to be made with the like religious care, and to be performed with the like faithfulness.[10]

6. It is not to be made to any creature, but to God alone:[11] and that it may be accepted, it is to be made voluntarily, out of faith and conscience of duty, in way of thankfulness for mercy received, or for obtaining of what we want; whereby we more strictly bind ourselves to necessary duties, or to other things, so far and so long as they may fitly conduce thereunto.[12]

7. No man may vow to do anything forbidden in the word of God, or what would hinder any duty therein commanded, or which is not in his own power, and for the performance whereof he hath no promise or ability from God.[13] In which respects, monastical vows of perpetual single life, professed poverty, and regular obedience, are so far from being degrees of higher perfection, that they are superstitious and sinful snares, in which no Christian may entangle himself.

---

all the princes said unto all the congregation, We have sworn unto them by the LORD God of Israel: now therefore we may not touch them.
II Sam. 21:1.

10. Ps. 66:13, 14. I will pay thee my vows, which my lips have uttered, and my mouth hath spoken, when I was in trouble.

Ps. 61:8. So will I sing praise unto thy name for ever, that I may daily perform my vows.

Deut. 23:21, 23. When thou shalt vow a vow unto the LORD thy God, thou shalt not slack to pay it: for the LORD thy God will surely require it of thee; and it would be sin in thee. . . . That which is gone out of thy lips thou shalt keep and perform; *even* a freewill offering, according as thou hast vowed unto the LORD thy God, which thou hast promised with thy mouth.

11. Ps. 76:11. Vow, and pay unto the LORD your God: let all that be round about him bring presents unto him that ought to be feared.
Jer. 44:25, 26.

12. Ps. 50:14. Offer unto God thanksgiving; and pay thy vows unto the most High.

Gen. 28:20-22. And Jacob vowed a vow, saying, If God will be with me, and will keep me in this way that I go, and will give me bread to eat, and raiment to put on, so that I come again to my father's house in peace; then shall the LORD be my God: and this stone, which I have set *for* a pillar, shall be God's house: and of all that thou shalt give me I will surely give the tenth unto thee.

Compare with the above I Sam. 1:11; Ps. 132:2-5.

13. Num. 30:5, 8, 12, 13.

CHAPTER XXV

Of the Civil Magistrate

1. God, the Supreme Lord and King of all the world, hath ordained civil magistrates to be under him over the people, for his own glory and the public good; and to this end, hath armed them with the power of the sword, for the defense and encouragement of them that are good, and for the punishment of evildoers.[1]

2. It is lawful for Christians to accept and execute the office of a magistrate, when called thereunto;[2] in the managing whereof, as they ought especially to maintain piety, justice, and peace, according to the wholesome laws of each commonwealth,[3] so, for that end, they may lawfully, now under the New Testament, wage war upon just and necessary occasions.[4]

---

1. Rom. 13:1, 3, 4. Let every soul be subject unto the higher powers. For there is no power but of God: the powers that be are ordained of God. . . . For rulers are not a terror to good works, but to the evil. Wilt thou then not be afraid of the power? do that which is good, and thou shalt have praise of the same: for he is the minister of God to thee for good. But if thou do that which is evil, be afraid; for he beareth not the sword in vain: for he is the minister of God, a revenger to *execute* wrath upon him that doeth evil.

   I Peter 2:13, 14. Submit yourselves to every ordinance of man for the Lord's sake: whether it be to the king, as supreme; or unto governors, as unto them that are sent by him for the punishment of evildoers, and for the praise of them that do well.

2. Prov. 8:15, 16. By me kings reign, and princes decree justice. By me princes rule, and nobles, *even* all the judges of the earth.

   See citations under Section 1, above.

3. Ps. 82:3, 4. Defend the poor and fatherless: do justice to the afflicted and needy. Deliver the poor and needy: rid *them* out of the hand of the wicked.

   I Peter 2:13. Submit yourselves to every ordinance of man for the Lord's sake: whether it be to the king as supreme.

   See citations under Section 1, above.

4. Rom. 13:1-4. Let every soul be subject unto the higher powers. For there is no power but of God: the powers that be are ordained of God. Whosoever therefore resisteth the power, resisteth the ordinance of God: and they that resist shall receive to themselves damnation. For rulers are not a terror to good works, but to the evil. Wilt thou then not be afraid of the power? do that which is good, and thou shalt have praise of the same: for he is the minister of God to thee for good. But if thou do that which is evil, be afraid; for he beareth not the sword in vain: for he is the minister of God, a revenger to *execute* wrath upon him that doeth evil.

   Luke 3:14. And the soldiers likewise demanded of him, saying, And

3. Civil magistrates may not assume to themselves the administration of the word and sacraments; or the power of the keys of the kingdom of heaven; or, in the least, interfere in matters of faith.[5] Yet, as nursing fathers, it is the duty of civil magistrates to protect the church of our common Lord, without giving the preference to any denomination of Christians above the rest, in such a manner that all ecclesiastical persons whatever shall enjoy the full, free, and unquestioned liberty of discharging every part of their sacred functions, without violence or danger. And, as Jesus Christ hath appointed a regular government and discipline in his church, no law of any commonwealth should interfere with, let, or hinder, the due exercise thereof, among the voluntary members of any denomination of Christians, according to their own profession and belief. It is the duty of civil magistrates to protect the person and good name of all their people, in such an effectual manner as that no person be suffered, either upon pretense of religion or infidelity, to offer any indignity, violence, abuse, or injury to any other person whatsoever: and to take order, that all religious and ecclesiastical assemblies be held without molestation or disturbance.[6]

---

what shall we do? And he said unto them, Do violence to no man, neither accuse *any* falsely; and be content with your wages.

Matt. 8:9. For I am a man under authority, having soldiers under me: and I say to this *man*, Go, and he goeth; and to another, Come, and he cometh; and to my servant, Do this, and he doeth *it*.

Acts 10:1, 2. There was a certain man in Cæsarea called Cornelius, a centurion of the band called the Italian *band*, a devout *man*, and one that feared God with all his house, which gave much alms to the people, and prayed to God alway.

5. Matt. 16:19. And I will give unto thee the keys of the kingdom of heaven: and whatsoever thou shalt bind on earth shall be bound in heaven: and whatsoever thou shalt loose on earth shall be loosed in heaven.

I Cor. 4:1. Let a man so account of us, as of the ministers of Christ, and stewards of the mysteries of God.

John 18:36. Jesus answered, My kingdom is not of this world.

Eph. 4:11, 12. And he gave some, apostles; and some, prophets: and some, evangelists; and some, pastors and teachers; for the perfecting of the saints, for the work of the ministry, for the edifying of the body of Christ.

II Chron. 26:18. And they withstood Uzziah the king, and said unto him, *It appertaineth* not unto thee, Uzziah, to burn incense unto the Lord, but to the priests the sons of Aaron, that are consecrated to burn incense: go out of the sanctuary; for thou hast trespassed; neither *shall it be* for thine honour from the Lord God.

6. See General Note, page 25.

4. It is the duty of the people to pray for magistrates,[7] to honor their persons,[8] to pay them tribute and other dues,[9] to obey their lawful commands, and to be subject to their authority, for conscience' sake.[10] Infidelity, or difference in religion, doth not make void the magistrate's just and legal authority, nor free the people from their due obedience to him:[11] from which ecclesiastical persons are not exempted;[12] much less hath the Pope any power or jurisdiction over them in their dominions, or over any of their people; and least of all to deprive them of their dominions or lives, if he shall judge them to be heretics, or upon any other pretense whatsoever.[13]

CHAPTER XXVI

Of Marriage and Divorce

1. Marriage is a union between one man and one woman, designed of God to last so long as they both shall live.[1]

---

7. I Tim. 2:1, 2. I exhort therefore, that, first of all, supplications, prayers, intercessions, *and* giving of thanks, be made for all men; for kings, and *for* all that are in authority; that we may lead a quiet and peaceable life in all godliness and honesty.

8. I Peter 2:17. Fear God. Honour the king.

9. Rom. 13:6, 7. For for this cause pay ye tribute also: for they are God's ministers, attending continually upon this very thing. Render therefore to all their dues: tribute to whom tribute *is due*; custom to whom custom; fear to whom fear; honour to whom honour.

10. Rom. 13:5. Wherefore *ye* must needs be subject, not only for wrath, but for conscience sake.
    Titus 3:1. Put them in mind to be subject to principalities and powers, to obey magistrates, to be ready to every good work.

11. This is an inference from the duties just stated.

12. Rom. 13:1. Let every soul be subject unto the higher powers.
    Acts 25:10, 11. Then said Paul, I stand at Cæsar's judgment seat, where I ought to be judged: to the Jews have I done no wrong, as thou very well knowest. For if I be an offender, or have committed any thing worthy of death, I refuse not to die: but if there be none of these things whereof these accuse me, no man may deliver me unto them. I appeal unto Cæsar.

13. This is an inference from the doctrine of the civil magistrate, and from duties incumbent on believers with respect to him.

1. Gen. 2:23, 24. And Adam said, This *is* now bone of my bones, and flesh of my flesh: she shall be called Woman, because she was taken out of Man. Therefore shall a man leave his father and his mother, and shall cleave unto his wife: and they shall be one flesh.
   I Cor. 7:2, 39. Nevertheless, *to avoid* fornication, let every man have

2. Marriage is designed for the mutual help of husband and wife;[2] for the safeguarding, undergirding, and development of their moral and spiritual character;[3] for the propagation of children and the rearing of them in the discipline and instruction of the Lord.[4]

his own wife, and let every woman have her own husband. . . . The wife is bound by the law as long as her husband liveth; but if her husband be dead, she is at liberty to be married to whom she will; only in the Lord.

Matt. 19:4-6. And he answered and said unto them, Have ye not read, that he which made *them* at the beginning made them male and female, and said, For this cause shall a man leave father and mother, and shall cleave to his wife: and they twain shall be one flesh? Wherefore they are no more twain, but one flesh. What therefore God hath joined together, let not man put asunder.

Eph. 5:28, 31, 33. So ought men to love their wives as their own bodies. He that loveth his wife loveth himself. . . . For this cause shall a man leave his father and mother, and shall be joined unto his wife, and they two shall be one flesh. . . . Nevertheless let every one of you in particular so love his wife even as himself; and the wife *see* that she reverence *her* husband.

I Cor. 13:8, 13; Matt. 5:31, 32; Mark 10:5-9; Rom. 7:2, 3.

2. Gen. 2:18, 24. And the LORD God said, *It is* not good that the man should be alone; I will make him an help meet for him. . . . Therefore shall a man leave his father and his mother, and shall cleave unto his wife: and they shall be one flesh.

3. Gen. 1:27, 28. So God created man in his *own* image, in the image of God created he him; male and female created he them. And God blessed them, and God said unto them, Be fruitful, and multiply, and replenish the earth, and subdue it: and have dominion over the fish of the sea, and over the fowl of the air, and over every living thing that moveth upon the earth.

Eph. 5:22, 23. Wives, submit yourselves unto your own husbands, as unto the Lord. For the husband is the head of the wife, even as Christ is the head of the church: and he is the saviour of the body.

Col. 3:18, 19. Wives, submit yourselves unto your own husbands, as it is fit in the Lord. Husbands, love *your* wives, and be not bitter against them.

Gen. 2:18-25; I Cor. 7:3-5, 9, 36.

4. Gen. 1:27, 28. So God created man in his *own* image, in the image of God created he him; male and female created he them. And God blessed them, and God said unto them, Be fruitful, and multiply, and replenish the earth, and subdue it: and have dominion over the fish of the sea, and over the fowl of the air, and over every living thing that moveth upon the earth.

Gen. 9:1. And God blessed Noah and his sons, and said unto them, Be fruitful, and multiply, and replenish the earth.

Mal. 2:15. And did not he make one? Yet had he the residue of the spirit. And wherefore one? That he might seek a godly seed. Therefore take heed to your spirit, and let none deal treacherously against the wife of his youth.

Matt. 18:5, 6, 10, 14. And whoso shall receive one such little child in my name receiveth me. But whoso shall offend one of these little ones which believe in me, it were better for him that a millstone were

3. All persons who are able with judgment to give their consent may marry,[5] except within the limits of blood relationship forbidden by Scripture,[6] and such marriages are valid before God in the eyes of the church.[7] But no marriage can be fully and securely Christian in spirit or in purpose unless both partners are committed to a common Christian faith and to a deeply shared intention of building a Christian home. Evangelical Christians should seek as partners in marriage only persons who hold in common a sound basis of evangelical faith.[8]

---

hanged about his neck, and *that* he were drowned in the depth of the sea. . . . Take heed that ye despise not one of these little ones; for I say unto you, That in heaven their angels do always behold the face of my Father which is in heaven. . . . Even so it is not the will of your Father which is in heaven, that one of these little ones should perish.
Matt. 19:14. But Jesus said, Suffer little children, and forbid them not, to come unto me: for of such is the kingdom of heaven.
Eph. 6:1-4. Children, obey your parents in the Lord: for this is right. Honour thy father and mother; which is the first commandment with promise; that it may be well with thee, and thou mayest live long on the earth. And, ye fathers, provoke not your children to wrath: but bring them up in the nurture and admonition of the Lord.
Col. 3:20, 21. Children, obey *your* parents in all things: for this is well pleasing unto the Lord. Fathers, provoke not your children *to anger*, lest they be discouraged.
Mark 10:13-16; Luke 18:15-17.

5. Gen. 1:27, 28. So God created man in his *own* image, in the image of God created he him; male and female created he them. And God blessed them, and God said unto them, Be fruitful, and multiply, and replenish the earth, and subdue it: and have dominion over the fish of the sea, and over the fowl of the air, and over every living thing that moveth upon the earth.

6. Mark 6:18. For John had said unto Herod, It is not lawful for thee to have thy brother's wife.
I Cor. 5:1. It is reported commonly *that there is* fornication among you, and such fornication as is not so much as named among the Gentiles, that one should have his father's wife.
Lev. 18:6-18.

7. Mark 1:30. But Simon's wife's mother lay sick of a fever, and anon they tell him of her.
John 2:1, 2. And the third day there was a marriage in Cana of Galilee; and the mother of Jesus was there: and both Jesus was called, and his disciples, to the marriage.
I Tim. 5:14. I will therefore that the younger women marry, bear children, guide the house, give none occasion to the adversary to speak reproachfully.
Heb. 13:4. Marriage *is* honourable in all, and the bed undefiled: but whoremongers and adulterers God will judge.
I Cor. 7:7, 36; I Cor. 9:5; I Tim. 4:3.

8. I Cor. 7, especially v. 39. The wife is bound by the law as long as her husband liveth; but if her husband be dead, she is at liberty to be married to whom she will; only in the Lord.

4. Marriage for the Christian has religious as well as civil significance.[9] The distinctive contribution of the church in performing the marriage ceremony is to affirm the divine institution of marriage;[10] to invoke God's blessing upon those who enter into the marital relationship in accordance with his word;[11] to hear the vows of those who desire to be married; and to assure the married partners of God's grace within their new relationship.[12]

5. It is the divine intention that persons entering the marriage covenant become inseparably united, thus allowing for no dissolution save that caused by the death of either husband or wife.[13] However, the weaknesses of one or both partners may lead

---

II Cor. 6:14, 15. Be ye not unequally yoked together with unbelievers: for what fellowship hath righteousness with unrighteousness? and what communion hath light with darkness? and what concord hath Christ with Belial? or what part hath he that believeth with an infidel?

9. Prov. 18:22. *Whoso* findeth a wife findeth a good *thing,* and obtaineth favour of the Lord.
Matt. 19:6. Wherefore they are no more twain, but one flesh. What therefore God hath joined together, let not man put asunder.
Eph. 5:29, 30, 32. For no man ever yet hated his own flesh; but nourisheth and cherisheth it, even as the Lord the church: for we are members of his body, of his flesh, and of his bones. . . . This is a great mystery: but I speak concerning Christ and the church.
Mark 10:9, 11, 12.

10. Gen. 1:27, 28. So God created man in his *own* image, in the image of God created he him; male and female created he them. And God blessed them, and God said unto them, Be fruitful, and multiply, and replenish the earth, and subdue it: and have dominion over the fish of the sea, and over the fowl of the air, and over every living thing that moveth upon the earth.

11. Mark 10:9. What therefore God hath joined together, let not man put asunder.

12. Eph. 5:22, 23. Wives, submit yourselves unto your own husbands, as unto the Lord. For the husband is the head of the wife, even as Christ is the head of the church: and he is the saviour of the body.

13. Gen. 2:23, 24. And Adam said, This *is* now bone of my bones, and flesh of my flesh: she shall be called Woman, because she was taken out of Man. Therefore shall a man leave his father and his mother, and shall cleave unto his wife: and they shall be one flesh.
Matt. 5:31, 32. It hath been said, Whosoever shall put away his wife, let him give her a writing of divorcement: but I say unto you, That whosoever shall put away his wife, saving for the cause of fornication, causeth her to commit adultery: and whosoever shall marry her that is divorced committeth adultery.
Mark 10:5-9. And Jesus answered and said unto them, For the hardness of your heart he wrote you this precept. But from the beginning of the creation God made them male and female. For this cause shall a man leave his father and mother, and cleave to his wife; and they twain

to gross and persistent denial of the marriage vows so that marriage dies at the heart and the union becomes intolerable; yet only in cases of extreme, unrepented-of, and irremediable unfaithfulness (physical or spiritual) should separation or divorce be considered. Such separation or divorce is accepted as permissible only because of the failure of one or both of the partners, and does not lessen in any way the divine intention for indissoluble union.[14]

6. The remarriage of divorced persons may be sanctioned by the church, in keeping with the redemptive gospel of Christ, when sufficient penitence for sin and failure is evident, and a

---

shall be one flesh: so then they are no more twain, but one flesh. What therefore God hath joined together, let not man put asunder.

Rom. 7:2, 3. For the woman which hath an husband is bound by the law to *her* husband so long as he liveth; but if the husband be dead, she is loosed from the law of *her* husband. So then if, while *her* husband liveth, she be married to another man, she shall be called an adulteress: but if her husband be dead, she is free from that law; so that she is no adulteress, though she be married to another man.

I Cor. 7:2, 10, 11, 39. Nevertheless, *to avoid* fornication, let every man have his own wife, and let every woman have her own husband. . . . And unto the married I command, *yet* not I, but the Lord, Let not the wife depart from *her* husband: but and if she depart, let her remain unmarried, or be reconciled to *her* husband: and let not the husband put away *his* wife. . . . The wife is bound by the law as long as her husband liveth; but if her husband be dead, she is at liberty to be married to whom she will; only in the Lord.

Eph. 5:28, 31, 33. So ought men to love their wives as their own bodies. He that loveth his wife loveth himself. . . . For this cause shall a man leave his father and mother, and shall be joined unto his wife, and they two shall be one flesh. . . . Nevertheless let every one of you in particular so love his wife even as himself; and the wife *see* that she reverence *her* husband.

Matt. 19:4-9; I Cor. 13:4-13.

14. Mark 10:4-9. And they said, Moses suffered to write a bill of divorcement, and to put *her* away. And Jesus answered and said unto them, For the hardness of your heart he wrote you this precept. But from the beginning of the creation God made them male and female. For this cause shall a man leave his father and mother, and cleave to his wife; and they twain shall be one flesh: so than they are no more twain, but one flesh. What therefore God hath joined together, let not man put asunder.

I Cor. 7:12, 13, 15. But to the rest speak I, not the Lord: If any brother hath a wife that believeth not, and she be pleased to dwell with him, let him not put her away. And the woman which hath an husband that believeth not, and if he be pleased to dwell with her, let her not leave him. . . . But if the unbelieving depart, let him depart. A brother or a sister is not under bondage in such *cases*: but God hath called us to peace.

Matt. 19:7-9.

firm purpose of and endeavor after Christian marriage is manifested.[15]

7. Divorced persons should give prayerful thought to discover if God's vocation for them is to remain unmarried, since one failure in this realm raises serious question as to the rightness and wisdom of undertaking another union.[16]

---

15. II Sam. 12:13. And David said unto Nathan, I have sinned against the LORD. And Nathan said unto David, The LORD also hath put away thy sin; thou shalt not die.

Neh. 9:17. And refused to obey, neither were mindful of thy wonders that thou didst among them; but hardened their necks, and in their rebellion appointed a captain to return to their bondage: but thou *art* a God ready to pardon, gracious and merciful, slow to anger, and of great kindness, and forsookest them not.

Ps. 32:5. I acknowledged my sin unto thee, and mine iniquity have I not hid. I said, I will confess my transgressions unto the LORD; and thou forgavest the iniquity of my sin.

Ps. 130:4. But *there is* forgiveness with thee, that thou mayest be feared.

Matt. 12:31a. Wherefore I say unto you, All manner of sin and blasphemy shall be forgiven unto men . . .

Matt. 21:31, 32. Whether of them twain did the will of *his* father? They say unto him, The first. Jesus saith unto them, Verily I say unto you, That the publicans and the harlots go into the kingdom of God before you. For John came unto you in the way of righteousness, and ye believed him not: but the publicans and the harlots believed him: and ye, when ye had seen *it*, repented not afterward, that ye might believe him.

John 8:3, 11. And the scribes and Pharisees brought unto him a woman taken in adultery . . . And Jesus said unto her, Neither do I condemn thee: go, and sin no more.

Rom. 3:23. For all have sinned, and come short of the glory of God.

Gal. 6:1. Brethren, if a man be overtaken in a fault, ye which are spiritual, restore such an one in the spirit of meekness; considering thyself, lest thou also be tempted.

I Tim. 2:4. Who will have all men to be saved, and to come unto the knowledge of the truth.

Heb. 7:25. Wherefore he is able also to save them to the uttermost that come unto God by him, seeing he ever liveth to make intercession for them. ,

I John 1:9. If we confess our sins, he is faithful and just to forgive us *our* sins, and to cleanse us from all unrighteousness.

I John 2:1, 2. My little children, these things write I unto you, that ye sin not. And if any man sin, we have an advocate with the Father, Jesus Christ the righteous: and he is the propitiation for our sins: and not for our's only, but also for *the sins of* the whole world.

Luke 7:36-50; Luke 15:11-32; John 3:16, 17; Rom. 10:9, 10.

16. Matt. 5:31, 32. It hath been said, Whosoever shall put away his wife, let him give her a writing of divorcement: but I say unto you, That whosoever shall put away his wife, saving for the cause of fornication, causeth her to commit adultery: and whosoever shall marry her that is divorced committeth adultery.

I Cor. 7:10, 11, 20, 32-35. And unto the married I command, *yet* not I, but the Lord, Let not the wife depart from *her* husband: but and if she depart, let her remain unmarried, or be reconciled to *her* husband: and

CHAPTER XXVII

Of the Church

1. The catholic or universal church, which is invisible, consists of the whole number of the elect, that have been, are, or shall be gathered into one, under Christ the head thereof; and is the spouse, the body, the fullness of him that filleth all in all.[1]

2. The visible church, which is also catholic or universal under the gospel (not confined to one nation as before under the law), consists of all those throughout the world that profess the true religion,[2] together with their children;[3] and is the kingdom of

---

let not the husband put away *his* wife. . . . Let every man abide in the same calling wherein he was called. . . . But I would have you without carefulness. He that is unmarried careth for the things that belong to the Lord, how he may please the Lord: but he that is married careth for the things that are of the world, how he may please *his* wife. There is difference *also* between a wife and a virgin. The unmarried woman careth for the things of the Lord, that she may be holy both in body and in spirit: but she that is married careth for the things of the world, how she may please *her* husband. And this I speak for your own profit; not that I may cast a snare upon you, but for that which is comely, and that ye may attend upon the Lord without distraction.
Mark 10:11; Luke 16:18.

1. Eph. 1:22, 23. And hath put all *things* under his feet, and gave him *to be* the head over all *things* to the church, which is his body, the fulness of him that filleth all in all.
Col. 1:18. And he is the head of the body, the church.
Eph. 5:23, 27, 32.

2. I Cor. 1:2. Unto the church of God which is at Corinth, to them that are sanctified in Christ Jesus, called *to be* saints, with all that in every place call upon the name of Jesus Christ our Lord, both theirs and ours.
I Cor. 12:12, 13. For as the body is one, and hath many members, and all the members of that one body, being many, are one body: so also *is* Christ. For by one Spirit are we all baptized into one body, whether *we be* Jews or Gentiles, whether *we be* bond or free; and have been all made to drink into one Spirit.
Rom. 15:9-12.

3. Gen. 17:7. And I will establish my covenant between me and thee and thy seed after thee in their generations for an everlasting covenant, to be a God unto thee, and to thy seed after thee.
See context. Compare Gal. 3:7, 9, 14; Rom. 4.
Acts 2:39. For the promise is unto you, and to your children, and to all that are afar off, *even* as many as the Lord our God shall call.
I Cor. 7:14. For the unbelieving husband is sanctified by the wife, and the unbelieving wife is sanctified by the husband: else were your children unclean; but now are they holy.
Mark 10:13-16. And they brought young children to him, that he should touch them: and *his* disciples rebuked those that brought *them.* But when Jesus saw *it,* he was much displeased, and said unto them, Suffer the lit-

the Lord Jesus Christ;[4] the house and family of God,[5] through which men are ordinarily saved and union with which is essential to their best growth and service.[6]

3. Unto this catholic visible church, Christ hath given the ministry, oracles, and ordinances of God, for the gathering and perfecting of the saints, in this life, to the end of the world: and doth by his own presence and Spirit, according to his promise, make them effectual thereunto.[7]

4. This catholic church hath been sometimes more, sometimes less, visible.[8] And particular churches, which are members

---

tle children to come unto me, and forbid them not: for of such is the kingdom of God. Verily I say unto you, Whosoever shall not receive the kingdom of God as a little child, he shall not enter therein. And he took them up in his arms, put *his* hands upon them, and blessed them.

4. Matt. 13:47. Again, the kingdom of heaven is like unto a net, that was cast into the sea, and gathered of every kind.
Col. 1:13. Who hath delivered us from the power of darkness, and hath translated *us* into the kingdom of his dear Son.
Isa. 9:7.

5. Eph. 2:19. Now therefore ye are no more strangers and foreigners, but fellowcitizens with the saints, and of the household of God.

6. Matt. 28:19. Go ye therefore, and teach all nations, baptizing them in the name of the Father, and of the Son, and of the Holy Ghost.
Acts 2:38. Then Peter said unto them, Repent, and be baptized every one of you in the name of Jesus Christ for the remission of sins, and ye shall receive the gift of the Holy Ghost.
I Cor. 12:13. For by one Spirit are we all baptized into one body, whether *we be* Jews or Gentiles, whether *we be* bond or free; and have been all made to drink into one Spirit.
Matt. 26:26-28. And as they were eating, Jesus took bread, and blessed *it*, and brake *it*, and gave *it* to the disciples, and said, Take, eat; this is my body. And he took the cup, and gave thanks, and gave *it* to them, saying, Drink ye all of it; for this is my blood of the new testament, which is shed for many for the remission of sins.

7. Eph. 4:11-13. And he gave some, apostles; and some, prophets; and some, evangelists; and some, pastors and teachers; for the perfecting of the saints, for the work of the ministry, for the edifying of the body of Christ: till we all come in the unity of the faith, and of the knowledge of the Son of God, unto a perfect man, unto the measure of the stature of the fulness of Christ.
Isa. 59:21. As for me, this *is* my covenant with them, saith the LORD; My spirit that *is* upon thee, and my words which I have put in thy mouth, shall not depart out of thy mouth, nor out of the mouth of thy seed, nor out of the mouth of thy seed's seed, saith the LORD, from henceforth and for ever.
Matt. 28:19, 20.

8. Rom. 11:3, 4. Lord, they have killed thy prophets, and digged down thine altars; and I am left alone, and they seek my life. But what saith the answer of God unto him? I have reserved to myself seven thousand men who have not bowed the knee to *the image of* Baal.

thereof, are more or less pure, according as the doctrine of the gospel is taught and embraced, ordinances administered, and public worship performed more or less purely in them.[9]

5. The purest churches under heaven are subject both to mixture and error:[10] and some have so degenerated as to become apparently no churches of Christ.[11] Nevertheless, there shall be always a church on earth, to worship God according to his will.[12]

Acts 9:31. Then had the churches rest throughout all Judæa and Galilee and Samaria, and were edified; and walking in the fear of the Lord, and in the comfort of the Holy Ghost, were multiplied.

9. I Cor. 5:6, 7. Your glorying *is* not good. Know ye not that a little leaven leaveneth the whole lump? Purge out therefore the old leaven, that ye may be a new lump, as ye are unleavened. For even Christ our passover is sacrificed for us.

Rev. 2, 3.

10. Matt. 13:24-30, 47, 48. Another parable put he forth unto them, saying, The kingdom of heaven is likened unto a man which sowed good seed in his field: but while men slept, his enemy came and sowed tares among the wheat, and went his way. But when the blade was sprung up, and brought forth fruit, then appeared the tares also. So the servants of the householder came and said unto him, Sir, didst not thou sow good seed in thy field? from whence then hath it tares? He said unto them, An enemy hath done this. The servants said unto him, Wilt thou then that we go and gather them up? But he said, Nay; lest while ye gather up the tares, ye root up also the wheat with them. Let both grow together until the harvest: and in the time of harvest I will say to the reapers, Gather ye together first the tares, and bind them in bundles to burn them: but gather the wheat into my barn. . . . Again, the kingdom of heaven is like unto a net, that was cast into the sea, and gathered of every kind: which, when it was full, they drew to shore, and sat down, and gathered the good into vessels, but cast the bad away.

11. Rom. 11:18-22. Boast not against the branches. But if thou boast, thou bearest not the root, but the root thee. Thou wilt say then, The branches were broken off, that I might be graffed in. Well; because of unbelief they were broken off, and thou standest by faith. Be not highminded, but fear: for if God spared not the natural branches, *take heed* lest he also spare not thee. Behold therefore the goodness and severity of God: on them which fell, severity; but toward thee, goodness, if thou continue in *his* goodness: otherwise thou also shalt be cut off.

Rev. 18:2. And he cried mightily with a strong voice, saying, Babylon the great is fallen, is fallen, and is become the habitation of devils, and the hold of every foul spirit, and a cage of every unclean and hateful bird.

12. Matt. 16:18. And I say also unto thee, That thou art Peter, and upon this rock I will build my church; and the gates of hell shall not prevail against it.

Ps. 102:28. The children of thy servants shall continue, and their seed shall be established before thee.

Matt. 28:19, 20.

6. The Lord Jesus Christ is the only head of the church,[13] and the claim of any man to be the vicar of Christ and the head of the church, is without warrant in fact or in Scripture, even anti-Christian, a usurpation dishonoring to the Lord Jesus Christ.

CHAPTER XXVIII

Of the Communion of Saints

1. All saints being united to Jesus Christ their head, by his Spirit and by faith, have fellowship with him in his graces, sufferings, death, resurrection, and glory:[1] and, being united to one another in love, they have communion in each other's gifts and graces,[2] and are obliged to the performance of such duties, public

---

13. Col. 1:18. And he is the head of the body, the church: who is the beginning, the firstborn from the dead; that in all *things* he might have the preeminence.

1. I John 1:3. That which we have seen and heard declare we unto you, that ye also may have fellowship with us: and truly our fellowship *is* with the Father, and with his Son Jesus Christ.
Eph. 3:16-19. That he would grant you, according to the riches of his glory, to be strengthened with might by his Spirit in the inner man; that Christ may dwell in your hearts by faith; that ye, being rooted and grounded in love, may be able to comprehend with all saints what *is* the breadth, and length, and depth, and height; and to know the love of Christ, which passeth knowledge, that ye might be filled with all the fulness of God.
John 1:16. And of his fulness have all we received, and grace for grace.
Phil. 3:10. That I may know him, and the power of his resurrection, and the fellowship of his sufferings, being made conformable unto his death.
Rom. 6:5, 6. For if we have been planted together in the likeness of his death, we shall be also *in the likeness* of *his* resurrection: knowing this, that our old man is crucified with *him*, that the body of sin might be destroyed, that henceforth we should not serve sin.
Rom. 8:17. And if children, then heirs; heirs of God, and joint-heirs with Christ; if so be that we suffer with *him*, that we may be also glorified together.

2. Eph. 4:15, 16. But speaking the truth in love, may grow up into him in all things, which is the head, *even* Christ: from whom the whole body fitly joined together and compacted by that which every joint supplieth, according to the effectual working in the measure of every part, maketh increase of the body unto the edifying of itself in love.
I John 1:3, 7. That which we have seen and heard declare we unto you, that ye also may have fellowship with us: and truly our fellowship *is* with the Father, and with his Son Jesus Christ. . . . But if we walk in the light, as he is in the light, we have fellowship one with another, and the blood of Jesus Christ his Son cleanseth us from all sin.

and private, as do conduce to their mutual good, both in the inward and outward man.[3]

2. Saints by their profession are bound to maintain an holy fellowship and communion in the worship of God, and in performing such other spiritual services as tend to their mutual edification;[4] as also in relieving each other in outward things, according to their several abilities and necessities. Which communion, as God offereth opportunity, is to be extended unto all those who, in every place, call upon the name of the Lord Jesus.[5]

3. This communion which the saints have with Christ, doth not make them in any wise partakers of the substance of his Godhead, or to be equal with Christ in any respect: either of which to affirm, is impious and blasphemous.[6] Nor doth their communion one with another as saints, take away or infringe the title or property which each man hath in his goods and possessions.[7]

---

3. I Thess. 5:11, 14. Wherefore comfort yourselves together, and edify one another, even as also ye do. . . . Now we exhort you, brethren, warn them that are unruly, comfort the feebleminded, support the weak, be patient toward all *men*.
Gal. 6:10. As we have therefore opportunity, let us do good unto all *men*, especially unto them who are of the household of faith.
I John 3:16-18.

4. Heb. 10:24, 25. And let us consider one another to provoke unto love and to good works: not forsaking the assembling of ourselves together, as the manner of some *is*; but exhorting *one another*: and so much the more, as ye see the day approaching.
Acts 2:42, 46. And they continued stedfastly in the apostles' doctrine and fellowship, and in breaking of bread, and in prayers. . . . And they, continuing daily with one accord in the temple, and breaking bread from house to house, did eat their meat with gladness and singleness of heart.
I Cor. 11:20.

5. I John 3:17. But whoso hath this world's good, and seeth his brother have need, and shutteth up his bowels *of compassion* from him, how dwelleth the love of God in him?
Acts 11:29, 30. Then the disciples, every man according to his ability, determined to send relief unto the brethren which dwelt in Judæa: which also they did, and sent it to the elders by the hands of Barnabas and Saul.
II Cor., chapters 8 and 9.

6. Col. 1:18. And he is the head of the body, the church: who is the beginning, the firstborn from the dead; that in all *things* he might have the preeminence.
I Cor. 8:6. But to us *there is but* one God, the Father, of whom *are* all things, and we in him; and one Lord Jesus Christ, by whom *are* all things, and we by him.
Ps. 14:7.

7. Acts 5:4. Whiles it remained, was it not thine own? and after it was

CHAPTER XXIX

Of the Sacraments

1. Sacraments are holy signs and seals of the covenant of grace, immediately instituted by God,[1] to represent Christ and his benefits, and to confirm our interest in him:[2] as also to put a visible difference between those that belong unto the church, and the rest of the world;[3] and solemnly to engage them to the service of God in Christ, according to his word.[4]

---

sold, was it not in thine own power? why hast thou conceived this thing in thine heart? thou hast not lied unto men, but unto God.

1. Gen. 17:9-11. And God said unto Abraham, Thou shalt keep my covenant therefore, thou, and thy seed after thee in their generations. This *is* my covenant, which ye shall keep, between me and you and thy seed after thee; Every man child among you shall be circumcised. And ye shall circumcise the flesh of your foreskin; and it shall be a token of the covenant betwixt me and you.
Exod. 13:9, 10. And it shall be for a sign unto thee upon thine hand, and for a memorial between thine eyes, that the LORD's law may be in thy mouth: for with a strong hand hath the Lord brought thee out of Egypt. Thou shalt therefore keep this ordinance in his season from year to year.
Rom. 4:11; Exod. 12:3-20.

2. I Cor. 10:16. The cup of blessing which we bless, is it not the communion of the blood of Christ? The bread which we break, is it not the communion of the body of Christ?
I Cor. 11:25, 26. After the same manner also *he took* the cup, when he had supped, saying, This cup is the new testament in my blood: this do ye, as oft as ye drink *it*, in remembrance of me. For as often as ye eat this bread, and drink this cup, ye do shew the Lord's death till he come.
Gal. 3:27. For as many of you as have been baptized into Christ have put on Christ.

3. Exod. 12:48. And when a stranger shall sojourn with thee and will keep the passover to the LORD, let all his males be circumcised, and then let him come near and keep it; and he shall be as one that is born in the land: for no uncircumcised person shall eat thereof.
Heb. 13:10. We have an altar, whereof they have no right to eat which serve the tabernacle.
I Cor. 11:27-29. Wherefore whosoever shall eat this bread, and drink *this* cup of the Lord, unworthily, shall be guilty of the body and blood of the Lord. But let a man examine himself, and so let him eat of *that* bread, and drink of *that* cup. For he that eateth and drinketh unworthily, eateth and drinketh damnation to himself, not discerning the Lord's body.

4. Rom. 6:3, 4. Know ye not, that so many of us as were baptized into Jesus Christ were baptized into his death? Therefore we are buried with him by baptism into death: that like as Christ was raised up from the dead by the glory of the Father, even so we also should walk in newness of life.

2. There is in every sacrament a spiritual relation, or sacramental union, between the sign and the thing signified; whence it comes to pass that the names and effects of the one are attributed to the other.[5]

3. The grace which is exhibited in or by the sacraments, rightly used, is not conferred by any power in them; neither doth the efficacy of a sacrament depend upon the piety or intention of him that doth administer it, but upon the work of the Spirit,[6] and the word of institution, which contains, together with a precept authorizing the use thereof, a promise of benefit to worthy receivers.[7]

4. There be only two sacraments ordained by Christ our Lord in the gospel, that is to say, baptism and the supper of the Lord:[8]

I Cor. 10:14-16. Wherefore, my dearly beloved, flee from idolatry. I speak as to wise men; judge ye what I say. The cup of blessing which we bless, is it not the communion of the blood of Christ? The bread which we break, is it not the communion of the body of Christ? See context.

5. Gen. 17:10. This *is* my covenant, which ye shall keep, between me and you and thy seed after thee; Every man child among you shall be circumcised.
Matt. 26:27, 28. And he took the cup, and gave thanks, and gave *it* to them, saying, Drink ye all of it; for this is my blood of the new testament, which is shed for many for the remission of sins.
Titus 3:5. Not by works of righteousness which we have done, but according to his mercy he saved us, by the washing of regeneration, and renewing of the Holy Ghost.

6. Rom. 2:28, 29. For he is not a Jew, which is one outwardly; neither *is that* circumcision, which is outward in the flesh: but he *is* a Jew, which is one inwardly; and circumcision *is that* of the heart, in the spirit, *and* not in the letter; whose praise *is* not of men, but of God.
I Cor. 3:7. So then neither is he that planteth any thing, neither he that watereth; but God that giveth the increase.
I Cor. 6:11. And such were some of you: but ye are washed, but ye are sanctified, but ye are justified in the name of the Lord Jesus, and by the Spirit of our God.
John 3:5. Jesus answered, Verily, verily, I say unto thee, Except a man be born of water and *of* the Spirit, he cannot enter into the kingdom of God.
Acts 8:13-23.

7. John 6:63. It is the Spirit that quickeneth; the flesh profiteth nothing: the words that I speak unto you, *they* are spirit, and *they* are life.

8. Matt. 28:19. Go ye therefore, and teach all nations, baptizing them in the name of the Father, and of the Son, and of the Holy Ghost.
I Cor. 11:20, 23. When ye come together therefore into one place, *this* is not to eat the Lord's supper. . . . For I have received of the Lord that which also I delivered unto you, That the Lord Jesus the *same* night in which he was betrayed took bread.

neither of which may be dispensed by any but by a minister of the word, lawfully ordained.[9]

5. The sacraments of the Old Testament, in regard of the spiritual things thereby signified and exhibited, were, for substance, the same with those of the New.[10]

CHAPTER XXX

Of Baptism

1. Baptism is a sacrament of the New Testament, ordained by Jesus Christ,[1] not only for the solemn admission of the party baptized into the visible church,[2] but also to be unto him a sign and seal of the covenant of grace,[3] of his ingrafting into Christ,[4] of regeneration,[5] of remission of sins,[6] and of his giving up unto

---

9. See General Note, page 25.

10. Col. 2:11, 12. In whom also ye are circumcised with the circumcision made without hands, in putting off the body of the sins of the flesh by the circumcision of Christ: buried with him in baptism, wherein also ye are risen with *him* through the faith of the operation of God, who hath raised him from the dead.

I Cor. 5:7, 8. For even Christ our passover is sacrificed for us: therefore let us keep the feast, not with old leaven, neither with the leaven of malice and wickedness; but with the unleavened *bread* of sincerity and truth.

1. Matt. 28:19. Go ye therefore, and teach all nations, baptizing them in the name of the Father, and of the Son, and of the Holy Ghost.

2. Acts 2:41. Then they that gladly received his word were baptized: and the same day there were added *unto* them about three thousand souls.

Acts 10:47. Can any man forbid water, that these should not be baptized, which have received the Holy Ghost as well as we?

3. Rom. 4:11. And he received the sign of circumcision, a seal of the righteousness of the faith which *he had yet* being uncircumcised: that he might be the father of all them that believe, though they be not circumcised; that righteousness might be imputed unto them also. Compare with Gal. 3:29; Col. 2:11, 12.

4. Gal. 3:27. For as many of you as have been baptized into Christ have put on Christ.

Rom. 6:3, 4. Know ye not, that so many of us as were baptized into Jesus Christ were baptized into his death? Therefore we are buried with him by baptism into death: that like as Christ was raised up from the dead by the glory of the Father, even so we also should walk in newness of life.

5. Titus 3:5. He saved us, by the washing of regeneration, and renewing of the Holy Ghost.

6. Acts 2:38. Peter said unto them, Repent, and be baptized every one of you in the name of Jesus Christ for the remission of sins.

Mark 1:4; Acts 22:16.

God, through Jesus Christ, to walk in newness of life:[7] which sacrament is, by Christ's own appointment, to be continued in his church until the end of the world.[8]

2. The outward element to be used in this sacrament is water, wherewith the party is to be baptized in the name of the Father, and of the Son, and of the Holy Ghost,[9] by a minister of the gospel, lawfully called thereunto.[10]

3. Dipping of the person into the water is not necessary; but baptism is rightly administered by pouring or sprinkling water upon the person.[11]

4. Not only those that do actually profess faith in and obedi-

---

7. Rom. 6:3, 4. Know ye not, that so many of us as were baptized into Jesus Christ were baptized into his death? Therefore we are buried with him by baptism into death: that like as Christ was raised up from the dead by the glory of the Father, even so we also should walk in newness of life.

8. Matt. 28:19, 20. Go ye therefore, and teach all nations, baptizing them in the name of the Father, and of the Son, and of the Holy Ghost: teaching them to observe all things whatsoever I have commanded you: and, lo, I am with you alway, *even* unto the end of the world.

9. Acts 10:47. Can any man forbid water, that these should not be baptized, which have received the Holy Ghost . . . ?

   Acts 8:36, 38. And as they went on *their* way, they came unto a certain water: and the eunuch said, See, *here is* water; what doth hinder me to be baptized? . . . And he commanded the chariot to stand still: and they went down both into the water, both Philip and the eunuch; and he baptized him.

   Matt. 28:19. Go ye therefore, and teach all nations, baptizing them in the name of the Father, and of the Son, and of the Holy Ghost.

   Eph. 4:11-13.

10. See General Note, page 25.

11. Mark 7:4. And *when they come* from the market, except they wash [Greek, be baptized], they eat not. And many other things there be, which they have received to hold, *as* the washing [Greek, baptizing] of cups, and pots, brasen vessels, and of tables.

    Acts 1:5. For John truly baptized with water; but ye shall be baptized with the Holy Ghost not many days hence.

    Acts 2:3, 4, 17. And there appeared unto them cloven tongues like as of fire, and it sat upon each of them. And they were all filled with the Holy Ghost, and began to speak with other tongues, as the Spirit gave them utterance. . . . And it shall come to pass in the last days, saith God, I will pour out of my Spirit upon all flesh: and your sons and your daughters shall prophesy, and your young men shall see visions, and your old men shall dream dreams.

    Acts 11:15, 16. And as I began to speak, the Holy Ghost fell on them, as on us at the beginning. Then remembered I the word of the Lord, how that he said, John indeed baptized with water; but ye shall be baptized with the Holy Ghost.

    Heb. 9:10, 19-21.

ence unto Christ,[12] but also the infants of one or both believing
parents are to be baptized.[13]

5. Although it be a great sin to contemn or neglect this ordinance,[14] yet grace and salvation are not so inseparably annexed
unto it as that no person can be regenerated or saved without
it,[15] or that all that are baptized are undoubtedly regenerated.[16]

---

12. See citations under Section 1 above.

13. Gen. 17:7, 9-10. And I will establish my covenant between me and
thee and thy seed after thee in their generations for an everlasting covenant, to be a God unto thee, and to thy seed after thee. . . . And God
said unto Abraham, Thou shalt keep my covenant therefore, thou, and
thy seed after thee in their generations. This *is* my covenant, which ye
shall keep, between me and you and thy seed after thee; Every man child
among you shall be circumcised.
Gal. 3:9, 14. So then they which be of faith are blessed with faithful
Abraham. . . . that the blessing of Abraham might come on the Gentiles through Jesus Christ; that we might receive the promise of the
Spirit through faith.
Rom. 4:11, 12. And he received the sign of circumcision, a seal of the
righteousness of the faith which *he had yet* being uncircumcised: that
he might be the father of all them that believe, though they be not circumcised; that righteousness might be imputed unto them also: and
the father of circumcision to them who are not of the circumcision
only, but who also walk in the steps of that faith of our father Abraham, which *he had* being *yet* uncircumcised.
Acts 2:38, 39. Repent, and be baptized every one of you in the name of
Jesus Christ for the remission of sins, and ye shall receive the gift of
the Holy Ghost. For the promise is unto you, and to your children, and
to all that are afar off, *even* as many as the Lord our God shall call.
Acts 16:14, 15, 33; Col. 2:11, 12; I Cor. 7:14; Mark 10:13-16; Luke
18:15, 16.

14. Luke 7:30. But the Pharisees and lawyers rejected the counsel of God
against themselves, being not baptized of him.
Gen. 17:14. And the uncircumcised man child whose flesh of his foreskin is not circumcised, that soul shall be cut off from his people; he
hath broken my covenant.

15. Rom. 4:11. And he received the sign of circumcision, a seal of the
righteousness of the faith which *he had yet* being uncircumcised: that
he might be the father of all them that believe, though they be not
circumcised; that righteousness might be imputed unto them also.
Luke 23:40-43. But the other answering rebuked him, saying, Dost
not thou fear God, seeing thou art in the same condemnation? And we
indeed justly; for we receive the due reward of our deeds: but this
man hath done nothing amiss. And he said unto Jesus, Lord, remember me when thou comest into thy kingdom. And Jesus said unto him,
Verily I say unto thee, To day shalt thou be with me in paradise.
Acts 10:45-47.

16. Acts 8:13, 23. Then Simon himself believed also: and when he was
baptized, he continued with Philip, and wondered, beholding the miracles and signs which were done. . . . For I perceive that thou art in the
gall of bitterness, and *in* the bond of iniquity.

6. The efficacy of baptism is not tied to that moment of time wherein it is administered;[17] yet, notwithstanding, by the right use of this ordinance the grace promised is not only offered, but really exhibited and conferred by the Holy Ghost, to such (whether of age or infants) as that grace belongeth unto, according to the counsel of God's own will, in his appointed time.[18]

7. The sacrament of baptism is but once to be administered to any person.[19]

CHAPTER XXXI

Of the Lord's Supper

1. Our Lord Jesus, in the night wherein he was betrayed, instituted the sacrament of his body and blood, called the Lord's Supper, to be observed in his church unto the end of the world; for the perpetual remembrance of the sacrifice of himself in his death, the sealing all benefits thereof unto true believers, their spiritual nourishment and growth in him, their further engagement in and to all duties which they owe unto him; and to be a bond and pledge of their communion with him, and with each other, as members of his mystical body.[1]

---

17. John 3:5, 8. Verily, verily, I say unto thee, Except a man be born of water and *of* the Spirit, he cannot enter into the kingdom of God. . . . The wind bloweth where it listeth, and thou hearest the sound thereof, but canst not tell whence it cometh, and whither it goeth: so is every one that is born of the Spirit.
    Rom. 4:11. And he received the sign of circumcision, a seal of the righteousness of the faith which *he had yet* being uncircumcised.
18. Gal. 3:27. For as many of you as have, been baptized into Christ have put on Christ.
    Eph. 1:4, 5. According as he hath chosen us in him before the foundation of the world, that we should be holy and without blame before him in love: having predestinated us unto the adoption of children by Jesus Christ to himself, according to the good pleasure of his will.
    Eph. 5:25, 26. Christ also loved the church, and gave himself for it; that he might sanctify and cleanse it with the washing of water by the word.
    Acts 2:38-41; Acts 16:31, 33.
19. There is no command, and no adequate example for the repetition of baptism.
1. I Cor. 11:23-26. For I have received of the Lord that which also I delivered unto you, That the Lord Jesus the *same* night in which he was betrayed took bread: and when he had given thanks, he brake *it*, and said, Take, eat: this is my body, which is broken for you: this do in

2. In this sacrament Christ is not offered up to his Father, nor any real sacrifice made at all for remission of sins of the quick or dead, but a commemoration of that one offering up of himself, by himself, upon the cross, once for all, and a spiritual oblation of all possible praise unto God for the same; so that the so-called sacrifice of the mass is most contradictory to Christ's one sacrifice, the only propitiation for all the sins of the elect.[2]

3. The Lord Jesus hath, in this ordinance, appointed his ministers to declare his word of institution to the people, to pray, and bless the elements of bread and wine, and thereby to set them apart from a common to an holy use; and to take and break the bread, to take the cup, and (they communicating also themselves) to give both to the communicants.[3]

4. Private masses, or receiving this sacrament by a priest, or

---

remembrance of me. After the same manner also *he took* the cup, when he had supped, saying, This cup is the new testament in my blood: this do ye, as oft as ye drink *it*, in remembrance of me. For as often as ye eat this bread, and drink this cup, ye do shew the Lord's death till he come.

Matt. 26:26, 27; Luke 22:19, 20.

I Cor. 10:16, 17, 21. The cup of blessing which we bless, is it not the communion of the blood of Christ? The bread which we break, is it not the communion of the body of Christ? For we *being* many are one bread, *and* one body: for we are all partakers of that one bread. . . . Ye cannot drink the cup of the Lord, and the cup of devils: ye cannot be partakers of the Lord's table, and of the table of devils.

I Cor. 12:13. For by one Spirit are we all baptized into one body, whether *we be* Jews or Gentiles, whether *we be* bond or free; and have been all made to drink into one Spirit.

2. Heb. 9:22, 25, 26, 28. And almost all things are by the law purged with blood; and without shedding of blood is no remission. . . . nor yet that he should offer himself often, as the high priest entereth into the holy place every year with blood of others; for then must he often have suffered since the foundation of the world: but now once in the end of the world hath he appeared to put away sin by the sacrifice of himself. . . . So Christ was once offered to bear the sins of many; and unto them that look for him shall he appear the second time without sin unto salvation.

Matt. 26:26, 27. And as they were eating, Jesus took bread, and blessed *it*, and brake *it*, and gave *it* to the disciples, and said, Take, eat; this is my body. And he took the cup, and gave thanks, and gave *it* to them, saying, Drink ye all of it.

Luke 22:19, 20. And he took bread, and gave thanks, and brake *it*, and gave unto them, saying, This is my body which is given for you: this do in remembrance of me. Likewise also the cup after supper, saying, This cup *is* the new testament in my blood, which is shed for you.

Heb. 10:11, 12, 14, 18.

3. See citations under Sections 1, 2.

any other, alone; as likewise the denial of the cup to the people; worshipping the elements, the lifting them up, or carrying them about for adoration, and the reserving them for any pretended religious use, are all contrary to the nature of this sacrament, and to the institution of Christ.[4]

5. The outward elements in this sacrament, duly set apart to the uses ordained by Christ, have such relation to him crucified, as that truly, yet sacramentally only, they are sometimes called by the name of the things they represent, to wit, the body and blood of Christ;[5] albeit, in substance and nature, they still remain truly, and only, bread and wine, as they were before.[6]

6. That doctrine which maintains a change of the substance of bread and wine, into the substance of Christ's body and blood (commonly called transubstantiation) by consecration of a priest, or by any other way, is repugnant, not to Scripture alone, but even to common sense and reason; overthroweth the nature of the sacrament; and hath been, and is, the cause of manifold superstitions, yea, of gross idolatries.[7]

7. Worthy receivers, outwardly partaking of the visible elements in this sacrament, do then also inwardly by faith, really and indeed, yet not carnally and corporally, but spiritually, receive and feed upon Christ crucified, and all benefits of his death: the body and blood of Christ being then not corporally or carnally in, with, or under the bread and wine; yet as really, but spiritually, present to the faith of believers in that ordinance, as the elements themselves are to their outward senses.[8]

---

4. Matt. 15:9. But in vain they do worship me, teaching *for* doctrines the commandements of men.
NOTE.—There is not the least appearance of a warrant for any of these things, either in precept or example, in any part of the word of God. See all the places in which the ordinance is mentioned.

5. Matt. 26:26-28. And as they were eating, Jesus took bread, and blessed *it,* and brake *it,* and gave *it* to the disciples, and said, Take, eat; this is my body. And he took the cup, and gave thanks, and gave *it* to them, saying, Drink ye all of it; for this is my blood of the new testament, which is shed for many for the remission of sins.

6. I Cor. 11:26, 27. For as often as ye eat this bread, and drink this cup, ye do shew the Lord's death till he come. Wherefore whosoever shall eat this bread, and drink *this* cup of the Lord, unworthily, shall be guilty of the body and blood of the Lord.

7. These statements are inferences from the doctrine of the sacraments, and do not require specific Scripture proofs.

8. I Cor. 10:16. The cup of blessing which we bless, is it not the com-

8. Although ignorant and wicked men receive the outward elements in this sacrament, yet they receive not the thing signified thereby; but by their unworthy coming thereunto are guilty of the body and blood of the Lord, and bring judgment on themselves.[9]

CHAPTER XXXII

Of Church Censures

1. The Lord Jesus, as king and head of his church, hath therein appointed a government in the hand of church officers, distinct from the civil magistrate.[1]

2. To these officers the keys of the kingdom of heaven are committed, by virtue whereof they have power respectively to retain and remit sins, to shut that kingdom against the impenitent, both by the word and censures; and to open it unto penitent sinners, by the ministry of the gospel, and by absolution from censures, as occasion shall require.[2]

---

munion of the blood of Christ? The bread which we break, is it not the communion of the body of Christ?

John 6:53-58. See Note under Section 6, above.

9. I Cor. 11:27, 29. Wherefore whosoever shall eat this bread, and drink *this* cup of the Lord, unworthily, shall be guilty of the body and blood of the Lord. . . . For he that eateth and drinketh unworthily, eateth and drinketh damnation [judgement] to himself, not discerning the Lord's body.

I Cor. 10:21. Ye cannot drink the cup of the Lord, and the cup of devils: ye cannot be partakers of the Lord's table, and of the table of devils.

I Cor. 5:6, 7, 13; II Thess. 3:6, 14, 15.

1. John 18:36. Jesus answered, My kingdom is not of this world: if my kingdom were of this world, then would my servants fight, that I should not be delivered to the Jews: but now is my kingdom not from hence.

Isa. 9:6, 7. For unto us a child is born, unto us a son is given: and the government shall be upon his shoulder: and his name shall be called Wonderful, Counsellor, The mighty God, The everlasting Father, The Prince of Peace. Of the increase of *his* government and peace *there shall be* no end, upon the throne of David, and upon his kingdom, to order it, and to establish it with judgment and with justice from henceforth even for ever. The zeal of the LORD of hosts will perform this.

I Cor. 12:28. And God hath set some in the church, first apostles, secondarily prophets, thirdly teachers, after that miracles, then gifts of healing, helps, governments, diversities of tongues.

I Tim. 5:17. Let the elders that rule well be counted worthy of double honour, especially they who labour in the word and doctrine.

2. Matt. 16:19. And I will give unto thee the keys of the kingdom of

3. Church censures are necessary for the reclaiming and gaining of offending brethren; for deterring of others from like offenses; for purging out of that leaven which might infect the whole lump; for vindicating the honor of Christ, and the holy profession of the gospel; and for preventing the wrath of God, which might justly fall upon the church, if they should suffer his covenant, and the seals thereof, to be profaned by notorious and obstinate offenders.[3]

4. For the better attaining of these ends, the officers of the church are to proceed by admonition, suspension from the sacrament of the Lord's Supper for a season, and by excommunication from the church, according to the nature of the crime, and demerit of the person.[4]

---

heaven: and whatsoever thou shalt bind on earth shall be bound in heaven: and whatsoever thou shalt loose on earth shall be loosed in heaven.

Matt. 18:17, 18. And if he shall neglect to hear them, tell *it* unto the church: but if he neglect to hear the church, let him be unto thee as an heathen man and a publican. Verily I say unto you, Whatsoever ye shall bind on earth shall be bound in heaven: and whatsoever ye shall loose on earth shall be loosed in heaven.

John 20:21-23. Then said Jesus to them again, Peace *be* unto you: as *my* Father hath sent me, even so send I you. And when he had said this, he breathed on *them*, and saith unto them, Receive ye the Holy Ghost: whose soever sins ye remit, they are remitted unto them; *and* whose soever *sins* ye retain, they are retained.

II Cor. 2:6-8. Sufficient to such a man *is* this punishment, which *was* inflicted of many. So that contrariwise ye *ought* rather to forgive *him*, and comfort *him*, lest perhaps such a one should be swallowed up with overmuch sorrow. Wherefore I beseech you that ye would confirm *your* love toward him.

3. I Tim. 5:20. Them that sin rebuke before all, that others also may fear.

I Tim. 1:20. Of whom is Hymenæus and Alexander; whom I have delivered unto Satan, that they may learn not to blaspheme.

Jude 23. And others save with fear, pulling *them* out of the fire; hating even the garment spotted by the flesh.

I Cor. 5; I Cor. 11:27-34; II Sam. 12:14.

4. I Thess. 5:12. And we beseech you, brethren, to know them which labour among you, and are over you in the Lord, and admonish you.

II Thess. 3:6, 14. Now we command you, brethren, in the name of our Lord Jesus Christ, that ye withdraw yourselves from every brother that walketh disorderly, and not after the tradition which he received of us. . . . And if any man obey not our word by this epistle, note that man, and have no company with him, that he may be ashamed.

I Cor. 5:4, 5, 13. In the name of our Lord Jesus Christ, when ye are gathered together, and my spirit, with the power of our Lord Jesus

CHAPTER XXXIII

Of Synods and Councils

1. For the better government and further edification of the church, there ought to be such assemblies as are commonly called synods or councils: and it belongeth to the overseers and other rulers of the particular churches, by virtue of their office, and the power which Christ hath given them for edification, and not for destruction, to appoint such assemblies; and to convene together in them, as often as they shall judge it expedient for the good of the church.[1]

2. It belongeth to synods and councils, ministerially, to determine controversies of faith, and cases of conscience; to set down rules and directions for the better ordering of the public worship of God, and government of his church; to receive complaints in cases of mal-administration, and authoritatively to determine the same: which decrees and determinations, if consonant to the word of God, are to be received with reverence and submission, not only for their agreement with the word, but also for the power whereby they are made, as being an ordinance of God, appointed thereunto in his word.[2]

3. All synods or councils since the apostles' times, whether general or particular, may err, and many have erred; therefore they are not to be made the rule of faith or practice, but to be used as a help in both.[3]

4. Synods and councils are to handle or conclude nothing but that which is ecclesiastical: and are not to intermeddle with civil

---

Christ, to deliver such an one unto Satan for the destruction of the flesh, that the spirit may be saved in the day of the Lord Jesus. . . . Therefore put away from among yourselves that wicked person.

Matt. 18:17. And if he shall neglect to hear them, tell *it* unto the church: but if he neglect to hear the church, let him be unto thee as an heathen man and a publican.
Titus 3:10.

1. Acts 15.

2. Acts 16:4. And as they went through the cities, they delivered them the decrees for to keep, that were ordained of the apostles and elders which were at Jerusalem.
Acts 15:15, 19, 24, 27-31; Matt. 18:17-20.

3. See General Note, page 25.

affairs which concern the commonwealth unless by way of humble petition in cases extraordinary; or by way of advice for satisfaction of conscience, if they be thereunto required by the civil magistrate.[4]

CHAPTER XXXIV

Of the State of Man after Death, and of the Resurrection of the Dead

1. The bodies of men, after death, return to dust, and see corruption;[1] but their souls (which neither die nor sleep), having an immortal subsistence, immediately return to God who gave them.[2] The souls of the righteous, being then made perfect in holiness, are received into the highest heavens, where they behold the face of God in light and glory, waiting for the full redemption of their bodies;[3] and the souls of the wicked are cast into hell, where they remain in torments and utter darkness,

---

4. Luke 12:13, 14. And one of the company said unto him, Master, speak to my brother, that he divide the inheritance with me. And he said unto him, Man, who made me a judge or a divider over you?

John 18:36. Jesus answered, My kingdom is not of this world: if my kingdom were of this world, then would my servants fight, that I should not be delivered to the Jews: but now is my kingdom not from hence.

Matt. 22:21. They say unto him, Cæsar's. Then saith he unto them, Render therefore unto Cæsar the things which are Cæsar's; and unto God the things that are God's.

1. Gen. 3:19. In the sweat of thy face shalt thou eat bread, till thou return unto the ground; for out of it wast thou taken: for dust thou *art,* and unto dust shalt thou return.

Acts 13:36. For David, after he had served his own generation by the will of God, fell on sleep, and was laid unto his fathers, and saw corruption.

2. Luke 23:43. And Jesus said unto him, Verily I say unto thee, To day shalt thou be with me in paradise.

Phil. 1:23. For I am in a strait betwixt two, having a desire to depart, and to be with Christ; which is far better.

II Cor. 5:6-8. Therefore *we are* always confident, knowing that, whilst we are at home in the body, we are absent from the Lord: (for we walk by faith, not by sight:) we are confident, *I say,* and willing rather to be absent from the body, and to be present with the Lord.

3. Luke 16:23. And in hell he lift up his eyes, being in torments, and seeth Abraham afar off, and Lazarus in his bosom.

Rom. 8:23. And not only *they,* but ourselves also, which have the firstfruits of the Spirit, even we ourselves groan within ourselves, waiting for the adoption, *to wit,* the redemption of our body.

See under figure 2 above.

reserved to the judgment of the great day.[4] Besides these two places for souls separated from their bodies, the Scripture acknowledgeth none.

2. At the last day, such as are found alive shall not die, but be changed:[5] and all the dead shall be raised up with the self-same bodies, and none other, although with different qualities, which shall be united again to their souls for ever.[6]

3. The bodies of the unjust shall, by the power of Christ, be raised to dishonor; the bodies of the just, by his Spirit, unto honor, and be made conformable to his own glorious body.[7]

CHAPTER XXXV

Of the Last Judgment

1. God hath appointed a day, wherein he will judge the world in righteousness by Jesus Christ,[1] to whom all power and judg-

---

4. Luke 16:23, 24. And in hell he lift up his eyes, being in torments, and seeth Abraham afar off, and Lazarus in his bosom. And he cried and said, Father Abraham, have mercy on me, and send Lazarus, that he may dip the tip of his finger in water, and cool my tongue; for I am tormented in this flame.
   II Peter 2:9. The Lord knoweth how to deliver the godly out of temptations, and to reserve the unjust unto the day of judgment to be punished.

5. I Thess. 4:17. Then we which are alive *and* remain shall be caught up together with them in the clouds, to meet the Lord in the air: and so shall we ever be with the Lord.
   I Cor. 15:51, 52. Behold, I shew you a mystery; We shall not all sleep, but we shall all be changed, in a moment, in the twinkling of an eye, at the last trump: for the trumpet shall sound, and the dead shall be raised incorruptible, and we shall be changed.

6. I Cor. 15:42-44. So also *is* the resurrection of the dead. It is sown in corruption; it is raised in incorruption: it is sown in dishonour; it is raised in glory: it is sown in weakness; it is raised in power: it is sown a natural body; it is raised a spiritual body. There is a natural body, and there is a spiritual body.
   See preceding context.

7. Acts 24:15. And have hope toward God, which they themselves also allow, that there shall be a resurrection of the dead, both of the just and unjust.
   John 5:28, 29. Marvel not at this: for the hour is coming, in the which all that are in the graves shall hear his voice, and shall come forth; and they that have done good, unto the resurrection of life; and they that have done evil, unto the resurrection of damnation.
   Phil. 3:21. Who shall change our vile body, that it may be fashioned like unto his glorious body, according to the working whereby he is able even to subdue all things unto himself.

1. Acts 17:31. Because he hath appointed a day, in the which he will

ment is given of the Father.[2] In which day, not only the apostate angels shall be judged; but likewise all persons, that have lived upon earth, shall appear before the tribunal of Christ, to give an account of their thoughts, words, and deeds; and to receive according to what they have done in the body, whether good or evil.[3]

2. The end of God's appointing this day, is for the manifestation of the glory of his mercy in the eternal salvation of the elect;[4] and of his justice in the damnation of the reprobate, who are wicked and disobedient.[5] For then shall the righteous go

judge the world in righteousness by *that* man whom he hath ordained; *whereof* he hath given assurance unto all *men,* in that he hath raised him from the dead.

Matt. 25:31-34.

2. John 5:22, 27. For the Father judgeth no man, but hath committed all judgment unto the Son . . . and hath given him authority to execute judgment also, because he is the Son of man.

3. Jude 6. And the angels which kept not their first estate, but left their own habitation, he hath reserved in everlasting chains under darkness unto the judgment of the great day.

II Peter 2:4. For if God spared not the angels that sinned, but cast *them* down to hell, and delivered *them* into chains of darkness, to be reserved unto judgment.

II Cor. 5:10. For we must all appear before the judgment seat of Christ; that every one may receive the things *done* in *his* body, according to that he hath done, whether *it be* good or bad.

Rom. 2:16. In the day when God shall judge the secrets of men by Jesus Christ according to my gospel.

Rom. 14:10, 12. But why dost thou judge thy brother? or why dost thou set at nought thy brother? for we shall all stand before the judgment seat of Christ. . . . So then every one of us shall give account of himself to God.

Matt. 12:36, 37; I Cor. 3:13-15.

4. Rom. 9:23. And that he might make known the riches of his glory on the vessels of mercy, which he had afore prepared unto glory.

Eph. 2:4-7. But God, who is rich in mercy, for his great love wherewith he loved us, even when we were dead in sins, hath quickened us together with Christ, (by grace ye are saved;) and hath raised *us* up together, and made *us* sit together in heavenly *places* in Christ Jesus: that in the ages to come he might shew the exceeding riches of his grace in *his* kindness toward us through Christ Jesus.

5. Rom. 2:5, 6. But after thy hardness and impenitent heart treasurest up into thyself wrath against the day of wrath and revelation of the righteous judgment of God; who will render to every man according to his deeds.

II Thess. 1:7, 8. The Lord Jesus shall be revealed from heaven with his mighty angels, in flaming fire taking vengeance on them that know not God, and that obey not the gospel of our Lord Jesus Christ.

into everlasting life, and receive that fullness of joy and refreshing which shall come from the presence of the Lord:[6] but the wicked, who know not God, and obey not the gospel of Jesus Christ, shall be cast into eternal torments, and punished with everlasting destruction from the presence of the Lord, and from the glory of his power.[7]

3. As Christ would have us to be certainly persuaded that there shall be a day of judgment, both to deter all men from sin, and for the greater consolation of the godly in their adversity:[8] so will he have that day unknown to men, that they may shake off all carnal security, and be always watchful, because they

---

6. Matt. 25:31-34. When the Son of man shall come in his glory, and all the holy angels with him, then shall he sit upon the throne of his glory: and before him shall be gathered all nations: and he shall separate them one from another, as a shepherd divideth *his* sheep from the goats: and he shall set the sheep on his right hand, but the goats on the left. Then shall the King say unto them on his right hand, Come, ye blessed of my Father, inherit the kingdom prepared for you from the foundation of the world.
II Thess. 1:7. And to you who are troubled rest with us, when the Lord Jesus shall be revealed from heaven with his mighty angels.
Ps. 16:11. Thou wilt shew me the path of life: in thy presence *is* fulness of joy; at thy right hand *there are* pleasures for evermore.

7. Matt. 25:41, 46. Then shall he say also unto them on the left hand, Depart from me, ye cursed, into everlasting fire, prepared for the devil and his angels . . . And these shall go away into everlasting punishment.
II Thess. 1:9. Who shall be punished with everlasting destruction from the presence of the Lord, and from the glory of his power.
Mark 9:47, 48. And if thine eye offend thee, pluck it out: it is better for thee to enter into the kingdom of God with one eye, than having two eyes to be cast into hell fire: where their worm dieth not, and the fire is not quenched.

8. II Cor. 5:11. Knowing therefore the terror of the Lord, we persuade men; but we are made manifest unto God; and I trust also are made manifest in your consciences.
II Thess. 1:5-7. *Which is* a manifest token of the righteous judgment of God, that ye may be counted worthy of the kingdom of God, for which ye also suffer: seeing *it is* a righteous thing with God to recompense tribulation to them that trouble you; and to you who are troubled rest with us, when the Lord Jesus shall be revealed from heaven with his mighty angels.
Luke 21:27, 28. And then shall they see the Son of man coming in a cloud with power and great glory. And when these things begin to come to pass, then look up, and lift up your heads; for your redemption draweth nigh.
II Peter 3:11, 14. *Seeing* then *that* all these things shall be dissolved, what manner *of persons* ought ye to be in *all* holy conversation and godliness . . . Wherefore, beloved, seeing that ye look for such things, be diligent that ye may be found of him in peace, without spot, and blameless.

know not at what hour the Lord will come; and may be ever prepared to say, Come, Lord Jesus, come quickly.[9] Amen.

---

9. Mark 13:35-37. Watch ye therefore: for ye know not when the master of the house cometh, at even, or at midnight, or at the cockcrowing, or in the morning: lest coming suddenly he find you sleeping. And what I say unto you I say unto all, Watch.

Luke 12:35, 36. Let your loins be girded about, and *your* lights burning; and ye yourselves like unto men that wait for their Lord, when he will return from the wedding; that when he cometh and knocketh, they may open unto him immediately.

Rev. 22:20. He which testifieth these things saith, Surely I come quickly. Amen. Even so come, Lord Jesus.
See Matt. 24:36, 42-44.

THE
LARGER CATECHISM

With amendment to Answer of Question 156 enacted by the
General Assembly of 1939 and Scripture Proofs
approved by the General Assembly of 1910.

THE
LARGER CATECHISM

✠

Q. 1. *What is the chief and highest end of man?*

A. Man's chief and highest end is to glorify God,[1] and fully to enjoy him forever.[2]

GENERAL NOTE.—At several points the Larger Catechism is more specific in its statements than in Scriptures. These statements are inferences from the Scriptures, or from statements based on the Scriptures, or from the experience and observation of the Church. In such cases no texts are cited; but reference is made to this general note.

1. Rom. 11:36. For of him, and through him, and to him, *are* all things: to whom *be* glory for ever. Amen.

   I Cor. 10:31. Whether therefore ye eat, or drink, or whatsoever ye do, all to the glory of God.

2. Ps. 73:24-26. Thou shalt guide me with thy counsel, and afterward receive me *to* glory. Whom have I in heaven . but *thee?* and *there is* none upon earth *that* I desire beside thee. My flesh and my heart faileth: *but* God *is* the strength of my heart, and my portion for ever.

   John 17:22, 24. The glory which thou gavest me I have given them . . . Father, I will that they also, whom thou hast given me, be with me where I am; that they may behold my glory, which thou hast given me.

Q. 2. *How doth it appear that there is a God?*

A. The very light of nature in man, and the works of God, declare plainly that there is a God;[1] but his word and Spirit only, do sufficiently and effectually reveal him unto men for their salvation.[2]

1. Rom. 1:19, 20. Because that which may be known of God is manifest in them; for God hath shewed *it* unto them. For the invisible things of him from the creation of the world are clearly seen, being understood by the things that are made, *even* his eternal power and Godhead; so that they are without excuse.

   Ps. 19:1-4.

2. I Cor. 1:21. For after that in the wisdom of God the world by wisdom knew not God, it pleased God by the foolishness of preaching to save them that believe.

   I Cor. 2:9, 10. But as it is written, Eye hath not seen, nor ear heard, neither have entered into the heart of man, the things which God hath prepared for them that love him. But God hath revealed *them* unto us by his Spirit: for the Spirit searcheth all things, yea, the deep things of God.

Q. 3. *What is the word of God?*

A. The holy Scriptures of the Old and New Testaments are the word of God, the only rule of faith and obedience.[1]

1. Gal. 1:8, 9. But though we, or an angel from heaven, preach any other gospel unto you than that which we have preached unto you, let him be accursed. As we said before, so say I now again, If any *man* preach any other gospel unto you than that ye have received, let him be accursed.

   Isa. 8:20. To the law and to the testimony: if they speak not according to this word, *it is* because *there is* no light in them.

   Luke 16:29, 31; II Tim. 3:15-17.

Q. 4. *How doth it appear that the Scriptures are the word of God?*

A. The Scriptures manifest themselves to be the word of God, by their majesty and purity; by the consent of all the parts, and the scope of the whole, which is to give all glory to God; by their light and power to convince and convert sinners, to comfort and build up believers unto salvation.[1] But the Spirit of God, bearing witness by and with the Scriptures in the heart of man, is alone able fully to persuade it that they are the very word of God.[2]

1. See General Note, p. 145.
2. John 16:13, 14. Howbeit when he, the Spirit of truth, is come, he will guide you into all truth: for he shall not speak of himself; but whatsoever he shall hear, *that* shall he speak: and he will shew you things to come. He shall glorify me: for he shall receive of mine, and shall shew *it* unto you.

   I Cor. 2:6-9.

Q. 5. *What do the Scriptures principally teach?*

A. The Scriptures principally teach, what man is to believe concerning God, and what duty God requires of man.[1]

1. See General Note, p. 145.

What Man Ought to Believe Concerning God

Q. 6. *What do the Scriptures make known of God?*

A. The Scriptures make known what God is,[1] the persons in the Godhead,[2] his decrees,[3] and the execution of his decrees.[4]

1. John 4:24. God *is* a Spirit.

   Exod. 34:6, 7. And the LORD passed by before him, and proclaimed, The LORD, The LORD God, merciful and gracious, longsuffering, and abundant in goodness and truth, keeping mercy for thousands, forgiving iniquity and transgression and sin, and that will by no means clear *the guilty;* visiting the iniquity of the fathers upon the children, and upon the children's children, unto the third and to the fourth *generation.*

2. Matt. 28:19. Go ye therefore, and teach all nations, baptizing them in the name of the Father, and of the Son, and of the Holy Ghost.

II Cor. 13:14. The grace of the Lord Jesus Christ, and the love of God, and the communion of the Holy Ghost, *be* with you all. Amen.

3. Eph. 1:11. In whom also we have obtained an inheritance, being predestinated according to the purpose of him who worketh all things after the counsel of his own will.

See the context.

4. Acts 4:27, 28. For of a truth against thy holy child Jesus . . . both Herod, and Pontius Pilate, with the Gentiles, and the people of Israel, were gathered together, for to do whatsoever thy hand and thy counsel determined before to be done.

Isa. 42:9.

Q. 7. *What is God?*

A. God is a Spirit,[1] in and of himself infinite in being,[2] glory, blessedness, and perfection;[3] all-sufficient,[4] eternal,[5] unchangeable,[6] incomprehensible,[7] everywhere present,[8] almighty;[9] know-

1. John 4:24. God *is* a Spirit.

2. I Kings 8:27. But will God indeed dwell on the earth? behold, the heaven and heaven of heavens cannot contain thee; how much less this house that I have builded?

Isa. 40:20.

3. See General Note, p. 145.

4. Acts 17:24, 25. God that made the world and all things therein, seeing that he is Lord of heaven and earth, dwelleth not in temples made with hands; neither is worshipped with men's hands, as though he needed any thing, seeing he giveth to all life, and breath, and all things.

5. Ps. 90:2. Before the mountains were brought forth, or ever thou hadst formed the earth and the world, even from everlasting to everlasting, thou *art* God.

6. Mal. 3:6. For I *am* the LORD, I change not; therefore ye sons of Jacob are not consumed.

James 1:17.

7. Rom. 11:33. O the depth of the riches both of the wisdom and knowledge of God! how unsearchable *are* his judgments, and his ways past finding out!

8. Jer. 23:24. Can any hide himself in secret places that I shall not see him? saith the LORD. Do not I fill heaven and earth? saith the LORD.

Ps. 139.

9. Rev. 4:8. And the four beasts had each of them six wings about *him;* and *they were* full of eyes within: and they rest not day and night, saying, Holy, holy, holy, Lord God Almighty, which was, and is, and is to come.

ing all things,[10] most wise,[11] most holy,[12] most just,[13] most merciful and gracious, long-suffering, and abundant in goodness and truth.[14]

10. Heb. 4:13. Neither is there any creature that is not manifest in his sight: but all things *are* naked and opened unto the eyes of him with whom we have to do.
Ps. 147:5.

11. Rom. 16:27. To God only wise, *be* glory through Jesus Christ for ever. Amen.

12. Isa. 6:3. And one cried unto another, and said, Holy, holy, holy, *is* the LORD of hosts: the whole earth *is* full of his glory.
Rev. 15:4. Who shall not fear thee, O Lord, and glorify thy name? for *thou* only *art* holy.

13. Deut. 32:4. *He is* the Rock, his work *is* perfect: for all his ways *are* judgment: a God of truth and without iniquity, just and right *is* he.

14. Exod. 34:6. And the LORD passed by before him, and proclaimed, The LORD, The LORD God, merciful and gracious, longsuffering, and abundant in goodness and truth.

Q. 8. *Are there more gods than one?*

A. There is but one only, the living and true God.[1]

1. Deut. 6:4. Hear, O Israel: The LORD our God *is* one LORD.
1. Cor. 8:4, 6. *There is* none other God but one. . . . But to us *there is but* one God, the Father, of whom *are* all things.
Jer. 10:10. But the LORD *is* the true God, he *is* the living God, and an everlasting king.

Q. 9. *How many persons are there in the Godhead?*

A. There be three persons in the Godhead: the Father, the Son, and the Holy Ghost; and these three are one true, eternal God, the same in substance, equal in power and glory; although distinguished by their personal properties.[1]

1. Matt. 3:16, 17. And Jesus, when he was baptized, went up straightway out of the water: and, lo, the heavens were opened unto him, and he saw the Spirit of God descending like a dove, and lighting upon him: and lo a voice from heaven, saying, This is my beloved Son, in whom I am well pleased.
Matt. 28:19. Go ye therefore, and teach all nations, baptizing them in the name of the Father, and of the Son, and of the Holy Ghost.
II Cor. 13:14. The grace of the Lord Jesus Christ, and the love of God, and the communion of the Holy Ghost, *be* with you all. Amen.

Q. 10. *What are the personal properties of the three persons in the Godhead?*

A. It is proper to the Father to beget the Son,[1] and to the Son to be begotten of the Father,[2] and to the Holy Ghost to proceed from the Father and the Son, from all eternity.[3]

1. Heb. 1:5. For unto which of the angels said he at any time, Thou art my Son, this day have I begotten thee? And again, I will be to him a Father, and he shall be to me a Son?

2. John 1:14. And the Word was made flesh, and dwelt among us, (and we beheld his glory, the glory as of the only begotten of the Father,) full of grace and truth.

3. Gal. 4:6. And because ye are sons, God hath sent forth the Spirit of his Son into your hearts, crying, Abba, Father.

   John 15:26. But when the Comforter is come, whom I will send unto you from the Father, *even* the Spirit of truth, which proceedeth from the Father, he shall testify of me.

Q. 11. *How doth it appear that the Son and the Holy Ghost are God equal with the Father?*

A. The Scriptures manifest that the Son and the Holy Ghost are God equal with the Father, ascribing unto them such names,[1] attributes,[2] works,[3] and worship,[4] as are proper to God only.

1. Jer. 23:6. And this *is* his name whereby he shall be called, THE LORD OUR RIGHTEOUSNESS.

   I. John 5:20. And we are in him that is true, *even* in his Son Jesus Christ. This is the true God, and eternal life.

   Ps. 45:6. Thy throne, O God, *is* for ever and ever.

   Acts 5:3,4. But Peter said, Ananias, why hath Satan filled thine heart to lie to the Holy Ghost . . . ? . . . thou hast not lied unto men, but unto God.

2. John 1:1. In the beginning was the Word, and the Word was with God, and the Word was God.

   Isa. 9:6. For unto us a child is born, unto us a son is given: and the government shall be upon his shoulder: and his name shall be called Wonderful, Counsellor, The mighty God, The everlasting Father, The Prince of Peace.

   John 2:24, 25. But Jesus did not commit himself unto them, because he knew all *men*, and needed not that any should testify of man: for he knew what was in man.

   I Cor. 2:10, 11. But God hath revealed *them* unto us by his Spirit: for the Spirit searcheth all things, yea, the deep things of God. For what man knoweth the things of a man, save the spirit of man which is in him? Even so the things of God knoweth no man, but the Spirit of God.

   Heb. 9:14. How much more shall the blood of Christ, who through the eternal Spirit offered himself without spot to God, purge your conscience from dead works to serve the living God?

3. Col. 1:16. For by him were all things created, that are in heaven, and that are in earth, visible and invisible, whether *they be* thrones, or dominions, or principalities, or powers: all things were created by him, and for him.

Gen. 1:2. And the earth was without form, and void; and darkness *was* upon the face of the deep. And the Spirit of God moved upon the face of the waters.

Ps. 104:30; John 1:3.

4. Matt. 28:19. Go ye therefore, and teach all nations, baptizing them in the name of the Father, and of the Son, and of the Holy Ghost.

II Cor. 13:14. The grace of the Lord Jesus Christ, and the love of God, and the communion of the Holy Ghost *be* with you all. Amen.

Q. 12. *What are the decrees of God?*

A. God's decrees are the wise, free, and holy acts of the counsel of his will, whereby, from all eternity, he hath, for his own glory, unchangeably foreordained whatsoever comes to pass in time,[1] especially concerning angels and men.

1. Eph. 1:4, 11. According as he hath chosen us in him before the foundation of the world, that we should be holy and without blame before him in love . . . in whom also we have obtained an inheritance, being predestinated according to the purpose of him who worketh all things after the counsel of his own will.

Acts 4:27, 28. For of a truth against thy holy child Jesus, whom thou hast anointed, both Herod, and Pontius Pilate, with the Gentiles, and the people of Israel, were gathered together, for to do whatsoever thy hand and thy counsel determined before to be done.

Ps. 33:11. The counsel of the LORD standeth for ever, the thoughts of his heart to all generations.

Q. 13. *What hath God especially decreed concerning angels and men?*

A. God, by an eternal and immutable decree, out of his mere love, for the praise of his glorious grace, to be manifested in due time, hath elected some angels to glory;[1] and, in Christ, hath chosen some men to eternal life, and the means thereof;[2] and also, according to his sovereign power, and the unsearchable counsel of his own will (whereby he extendeth or withholdeth

1. I Tim. 5:21. I charge *thee* before God, and the Lord Jesus Christ, and the elect angels.

2. Eph. 1:4-6. According as he hath chosen us in him before the foundation of the world, that we should be holy and without blame before him in love: having predestinated us unto the adoption of children by Jesus Christ to himself, according to the good pleasure of his will, to the praise of the glory of his grace, wherein he hath made us accepted in the beloved.

II Thess. 2:13, 14. But we are bound to give thanks alway to God for you, brethren beloved of the Lord, because God hath from the beginning chosen you to salvation through sanctification of the Spirit and belief of the truth: whereunto he called you by our gospel, to the obtaining of the glory of our Lord Jesus Christ.

I Peter 1:2.

favor as he pleaseth) hath passed by, and fore-ordained the rest
to dishonor and wrath, to be for their sin inflicted, to the praise
of the glory of his justice.[3]

3. Rom. 9:17, 18, 21, 22. For the scripture saith unto Pharaoh, Even for
this same purpose have I raised thee up, that I might shew my power
in thee, and that my name might be declared throughout all the earth.
Therefore hath he mercy on whom he will *have mercy*, and whom he
will he hardeneth . . . Hath not the potter power over the clay, of the
same lump to make one vessel unto honour, and another unto dishonour? *What* if God, willing to shew *his* wrath, and to make his
power known, endured with much longsuffering the vessels of wrath
fitted to destruction.

Jude 4. For there are certain men crept in unawares, who were before
of old ordained to this condemnation, ungodly men, turning the grace
of our God into lasciviousness, and denying the only Lord God, and
our Lord Jesus Christ.

Matt. 11:25, 26; II Tim. 2:20.

Q. 14. *How doth God execute his decrees?*

A. God executeth his decrees in the works of creation and
providence, according to his infallible foreknowledge, and the
free and immutable counsel of his own will.[1]

1. Eph. 1:11. In whom also we have obtained an inheritance, being predestinated according to the purpose of him who worketh all things after the counsel of his own will.

I Peter 1:1, 2. Peter, an apostle of Jesus Christ, to the strangers scattered throughout Pontus, Galatia, Cappadocia, Asia, and Bithynia,
elect according to the foreknowledge of God the Father, through sanctification of the Spirit, unto obedience and sprinkling of the blood of
Jesus Christ: Grace unto you, and peace, be multiplied.

Q. 15. *What is the work of creation?*

A. The work of creation is that wherein God did in the beginning, by the word of his power, make of nothing, the world
and all things therein for himself, within the space of six days,
and all very good.[1]

1. Heb. 11:3. Through faith we understand that the worlds were framed
by the word of God, so that things which are seen were not made of
things which do appear.

Rev. 4:11. Thou art worthy, O Lord, to receive glory and honour and
power: for thou hast created all things, and for thy pleasure they are
and were created.

Gen. 1.

Q. 16. *How did God create angels?*

A. God created all the angels, spirits,[1] immortal,[2] holy,[3] excelling in knowledge,[4] mighty in power;[5] to execute his commandments, and to praise his name,[6] yet subject to change.[7]

1. Ps. 104:4. Who maketh his angels spirits; his ministers a flaming fire.
   Col. 1:16. For by him were all things created, that are in heaven, and that are in earth, visible and invisible, whether *they be* thrones, or dominions, or principalities, or powers: all things were created by him, and for him.
2. Luke 20:36. Neither can they die any more: for they are equal unto the angels; and are the children of God, being the children of the resurrection.
3. Gen. 1:31. And God saw every thing that he had made, and, behold, *it was* very good.
4. Matt. 24:36. But of that day and hour knoweth no *man*, no, not the angels of heaven, but my Father only.
5. II Thess. 1:7. And to you who are troubled rest with us, when the Lord Jesus shall be revealed from heaven with his mighty angels.
6. Ps. 103:20, 21. Bless the LORD, ye his angels, that excel in strength, that do his commandments, hearkening unto the voice of his word. Bless ye the LORD, all *ye* his hosts; *ye* ministers of his, that do his pleasure.
7. II Peter 2:4. For if God spared not the angels that sinned, but cast *them* down to hell, and delivered *them* into chains of darkness, to be reserved unto judgment.

Q. 17. *How did God create man?*

A. After God had made all other creatures, he created man, male and female;[1] formed the body of the man of the dust of the ground,[2] and the woman of the rib of the man;[3] endued them with living, reasonable, and immortal souls;[4] made them after his own image,[5] in knowledge,[6] righteousness and holiness,[7] having the law of God written in their hearts,[8] and power to fulfill it, with dominion over the creatures;[9] yet subject to fall.[10]

1. Gen. 1:27. So God created man in his *own* image, in the image of God created he him; male and female created he them.
2. Gen. 2:7. And the LORD God formed man *of* the dust of the ground.
3. Gen. 2:22. And the rib, which the LORD God had taken from man, made he a woman, and brought her unto the man.
4. Gen. 2:7. And the LORD God formed man *of* the dust of the ground, and breathed into his nostrils the breath of life; and man became a living soul.
   Matt. 10:28; Luke 23:43.
5. Gen. 1:27. So God created man in his *own* image, in the image of God created he him.
6. Col. 3:10. And have put on the new *man*, which is renewed in knowledge after the image of him that created him.
   Gen. 2:19, 20.
7. Eph. 4:24. And that ye put on the new man, which after God is created in righteousness and true holiness.

8. Rom. 2:14, 15. For when the Gentiles, which have not the law, do by nature the things contained in the law, these, having not the law, are a law unto themselves: which shew the work of the law written in their hearts, their conscience also bearing witness, and *their* thoughts the mean while accusing or else excusing one another.

9. Gen. 1:28. And God blessed them, and God said unto them, Be fruitful, and multiply, and replenish the earth, and subdue it: and have dominion over the fish of the sea, and over the fowl of the air, and over every living thing that moveth upon the earth.

10. Gen. 2:16, 17. And the LORD God commanded the man, saying, Of every tree of the garden thou mayest freely eat: but of the tree of the knowledge of good and evil, thou shalt not eat of it: for in the day that thou eatest thereof thou shalt surely die.

Gen. 3:6.

Q. 18. *What are God's works of providence?*

A. God's works of providence are his most holy,[1] wise,[2] and powerful preserving,[3] and governing all his creatures;[4] ordering them, and all their actions,[5] to his own glory.[6]

1. Ps. 145:17. The LORD *is* righteous in all his ways, and holy in all his works.

2. Ps. 104:24. O LORD, how manifold are thy works! in wisdom hast thou made them all.

Isa. 28:29. This also cometh forth from the LORD of hosts, *which* is wonderful in counsel, *and* excellent in working.

3. Heb. 1:3. Who being the brightness of *his* glory, and the express image of his person, and upholding all things by the word of his power.

4. Ps. 103:19. The LORD hath prepared his throne in the heavens; and his kingdom ruleth over all.

Job, chapters 38—41.

5. Matt. 10:29, 30. Are not two sparrows sold for a farthing? and one of them shall not fall on the ground without your Father. But the very hairs of your head are all numbered.

Gen. 45:7. And God sent me before you to preserve you a posterity in the earth, and to save your lives by a great deliverance.

Ps. 135:6. Whatsoever the Lord pleased, *that* did he in heaven, and in earth, in the seas, and all deep places.

6. Rom. 11:36. For of him, and through him, and to him, *are* all things: to whom *be* glory for ever. Amen.

Isa. 63:14. So didst thou lead thy people, to make thyself a glorious name.

Q. 19. *What is God's providence toward the angels?*

A. God by his providence permitted some of the angels, willfully and irrecoverably, to fall into sin and damnation,[1] limiting and ordering that, and all their sins, to his own glory;[2] and established the rest in holiness and happiness;[3] employing them all, at his pleasure, in the administrations of his power, mercy, and justice.[4]

1. Jude 6. And the angels which kept not their first estate, but left their own habitation, he hath reserved in everlasting chains under darkness unto the judgment of the great day.
   II Peter 2:4.

2. Job 1:12. And the LORD said unto Satan, Behold, all that he hath *is* in thy power; only upon himself put not forth thine hand.
   Luke 10:17; Matt. 8:31.

3. I Tim. 5:21. I charge *thee* before God, and the Lord Jesus Christ, and the elect angels.
   Mark 8:38; Heb. 12:22.

4. Ps. 104:4. Who maketh his angels spirits; his ministers a flaming fire.
   Heb. 1:14. Are they not all ministering spirits, sent forth to minister for them who shall be heirs of salvation?

Q. 20. *What was the providence of God toward man in the estate in which he was created?*

A. The providence of God toward man in the estate in which he was created was, the placing him in paradise, appointing him to dress it, giving him liberty to eat of the fruit of the earth,[1] putting the creatures under his dominion,[2] ordaining marriage for his help,[3] affording him communion with himself,[4] and instituting the Sabbath;[5] entering into a covenant of life with him, upon condition of personal, perfect, and perpetual obedience,[6] of which the tree of life was a pledge; and forbidding to eat of the tree of the knowledge of good and evil, upon pain of death.[7]

1. Gen. 2:8. And the LORD God planted a garden eastward in Eden; and there he put the man whom he had formed.
   Gen. 2:15, 16. And the LORD God took the man, and put him into the garden of Eden to dress it and to keep it. And the LORD God commanded the man, saying, Of every tree of the garden thou mayest freely eat.

2. Gen. 1:28. And God blessed them, and God said unto them, Be fruitful, and multiply, and replenish the earth, and subdue it: and have dominion over the fish of the sea, and over the fowl of the air, and over every living thing that moveth upon the earth.

3. Gen. 2:18. And the LORD God said, *It is* not good that the man should be alone; I will make him an help meet for him.

4. Gen. 1:27, 28. So God created man in his *own* image, in the image of God created he him; male and female created he them. And God blessed them, and God said unto them, Be fruitful, and multiply, and replenish the earth, and subdue it: and have dominion over the fish of the sea, and over the fowl of the air, and over every living thing that moveth upon the earth.

5. Gen. 2:3. And God blessed the seventh day, and sanctified it: because that in it he had rested from all his work which God created and made.

6. Compare Gen. 2:16, 17, with Rom. 5:12-14; 10:5; Luke 10:25-28, and with the covenants made with Noah and Abraham.

7. Gen. 2:17. But of the tree of the knowledge of good and evil, thou shalt not eat of it: for in the day that thou eatest thereof thou shalt surely die.

Q. 21. *Did man continue in that estate wherein God at first created him?*

A. Our first parents, being left to the freedom of their own will, through the temptation of Satan, transgressed the commandment of God, in eating the forbidden fruit, and thereby fell from the estate of innocency wherein they were created.[1]

1. Gen. 3:6-8, 13. And when the woman saw that the tree *was* good for food, and that it *was* pleasant to the eyes, and a tree to be desired to make *one* wise, she took of the fruit thereof, and did eat, and gave also unto her husband with her; and he did eat . . . and they knew that they *were* naked . . . and Adam and his wife hid themselves from the presence of the Lord God amongst the trees of the garden . . . And the Lord God said unto the woman, What *is* this *that* thou hast done? And the woman said, The serpent beguiled me, and I did eat.
II Cor. 11:3.

Q. 22. *Did all mankind fall in that first transgression?*

A. The covenant being made with Adam, as a public person, not for himself only, but for his posterity, all mankind, descending from him by ordinary generation,[1] sinned in him, and fell with him in that first transgression.[2]

1. Acts 17:26. And hath made of one blood all nations of men.
See under figure 6 above.

2. Gen. 2:17. But of the tree of the knowledge of good and evil, thou shalt not eat of it: for in the day that thou eatest thereof thou shalt surely die. Compare with Rom. 5:12-20, and with I Cor. 15:21, 22.

Q. 23. *Into what estate did the fall bring mankind?*

A. The fall brought mankind into an estate of sin and misery.[1]

1. Rom. 5:12. Wherefore, as by one man sin entered into the world, and death by sin; and so death passed upon all men, for that all have sinned.
Gal. 3:10. For as many as are of the works of the law are under the curse: for it is written, Cursed *is* every one that continueth not in all things which are written in the book of the law to do them.

Q. 24. *What is sin?*

A. Sin is any want of conformity unto, or transgression of, any law of God, given as a rule to the reasonable creature.[1]

1. Rom. 3:23. For all have sinned, and come short of the glory of God.
   I John 3:4. Sin is the transgression of the law.

   James 4:17. Therefore to him that knoweth to do good, and doeth it not,
   to him it is sin.

Q. 25. *Wherein consists the sinfulness of that estate whereinto man fell?*

A. The sinfulness of that estate whereinto man fell, consisteth in the guilt of Adam's first sin,[1] the want of that righteousness wherein he was created, and the corruption of his nature, whereby he is utterly indisposed, disabled, and made opposite unto all that is spiritually good, and wholly inclined to all evil, and that continually;[2] which is commonly called original sin, and from which do proceed all actual transgressions.[3]

1. Rom. 5:12, 19. Wherefore, as by one man sin entered into the world, and death by sin; and so death passed upon all men, for that all have sinned . . . by one man's disobedience many were made sinners.
   I Cor. 15:22.
2. Rom. 5:6. For when we were yet without strength, in due time Christ died for the ungodly.
   Eph. 2:1-3. And you *hath he quickened*, who were dead in trespasses and sins; wherein in time past ye walked according to the course of this world, according to the prince of the power of the air, the spirit that now worketh in the children of disobedience: among whom also we all had our conversation in times past in the lusts of our flesh, fulfilling the desires of the flesh and of the mind; and were by nature the children of wrath, even as others.
   Rom. 8:7, 8. Because the carnal mind *is* enmity against God: for it is not subject to the law of God, neither indeed can be. So then they that are in the flesh cannot please God.
   Gen. 6:5. And God saw that the wickedness of man *was* great in the earth, and *that* every imagination of the thoughts of his heart *was* only evil continually.
   Rom. 3:10-20; Ps. 51:5; 58:3.
3. James 1:14, 15. But every man is tempted, when he is drawn away of his own lust, and enticed. Then when lust hath conceived, it bringeth forth sin: and sin, when it is finished, bringeth forth death.
   Matt. 15:19. For out of the heart proceed evil thoughts, murders, adulteries, fornications, thefts, false witness, blasphemies.

Q. 26. *How is original sin conveyed from our first parents unto their posterity?*

A. Original sin is conveyed from our first parents unto their posterity by natural generation, so as all that proceed from them in that way, are conceived and born in sin.[1]

1. Ps. 51:5. Behold, I was shapen in iniquity; and in sin did my mother conceive me.
   John 3:6. That which is born of the flesh is flesh.

Q. 27. *What misery did the fall bring upon mankind?*

A. The fall brought upon mankind the loss of communion with God,[1] his displeasure and curse; so as we are by nature children of wrath,[2] bondslaves to Satan,[3] and justly liable to all punishments in this world and that which is to come.[4]

1. Gen. 3:8, 24. And they heard the voice of the LORD God walking in the garden in the cool of the day: and Adam and his wife hid themselves from the presence of the LORD God amongst the trees of the garden . . . So he drove out the man; and he placed at the east of the garden of Eden Cherubims, and a flaming sword which turned every way, to keep the way of the tree of life.
2. Eph. 2:2, 3. Wherein in time past ye walked according to the course of this world, according to the prince of the power of the air, the spirit that now worketh in the children of disobedience: among whom also we all had our conversation in times past in the lusts of our flesh, fulfilling the desires of the flesh and of the mind; and were by nature the children of wrath, even as others.
3. II Tim. 2:26. And that they may recover themselves out of the snare of the devil. who are taken captive by him at his will.
   Luke 11:21, 22. When a strong man armed keepeth his palace, his goods are in peace: but when a stronger than he shall come upon him, and overcome him, he taketh from him all his armour wherein he trusted, and divideth his spoils.
   Heb. 2:14. Forasmuch then as the children are partakers of flesh and blood, he also himself likewise took part of the same; that through death he might destroy him that had the power of death, that is, the devil.
4. Rom. 6:23. The wages of sin is death.
   Rom. 5:14.

Q. 28. *What are the punishments of sin in this world?*

A. The punishments of sin in this world, are either inward, as blindness of mind,[1] a reprobate sense,[2] strong delusions,[3] hardness of heart,[4] horror of conscience,[5] and vile affections:[6] or outward, as the curse of God upon the creatures for our sake,[7] and all other evils that befall us in our bodies, names, estates, relations, and employments;[8] together with death itself.[9]

1. Eph. 4:18. Having the understanding darkened, being alienated from the life of God through the ignorance that is in them, because of the blindness of their heart.
2. Rom. 1:28. Even as they did not like to retain God in their knowledge, God gave them over to a reprobate mind, to do those things which are not convenient.
3. II Thess. 2:11. And for this cause God shall send them strong delusion, that they should believe a lie.
4. Rom. 2:5. But after thy hardness and impenitent heart treasurest up unto thyself wrath against the day of wrath and revelation of the righteous judgment of God.

5. Isa. 33:14. The sinners in Zion are afraid; fearfulness hath surprised the hypocrites. Who among us shall dwell with the devouring fire? who among us shall dwell with everlasting burnings?

    Gen. 4:13, 14; Matt. 27:4; Heb. 10:27.

6. Rom. 1:26. For this cause God gave them up unto vile affections.

7. Gen. 3:17. Because thou hast hearkened unto the voice of thy wife, and hast eaten of the tree, of which I commanded thee, saying, Thou shalt not eat of it: cursed *is* the ground for thy sake; in sorrow shalt thou eat *of* it all the days of thy life.

8. Deut. 28:15-68.

9. Rom. 6:21, 23. What fruit had ye then in those things whereof ye are now ashamed? for the end of those things *is* death. . . . the wages of sin *is* death.

Q. 29. *What are the punishments of sin in the world to come?*

A. The punishments of sin in the world to come are, everlasting separation from the comfortable presence of God, and most grievous torments in soul and body, without intermission, in hell-fire forever.[1]

1. II Thess. 1:9. Who shall be punished with everlasting destruction from the presence of the Lord, and from the glory of his power.

    Mark 9:43, 44. To go into hell, into the fire that never shall be quenched: where their worm dieth not, and the fire is not quenched.

    Luke 16:24, 26. Send Lazarus, that he may dip the tip of his finger in water, and cool my tongue; for I am tormented in this flame. . . . between us and you there is a great gulf fixed: so that they which would pass from hence to you cannot; neither can they pass to us, that *would come* from thence.

    Matt. 25:41, 46; Rev. 14:11; John 3:36.

Q. 30. *Doth God leave all mankind to perish in the estate of sin and misery?*

A. God doth not leave all men to perish in the estate of sin and misery, into which they fell by the breach of the first covenant, commonly called the covenant of works;[1] but of his mere love and mercy delivereth his elect out of it, and bringeth them into an estate of salvation by the second covenant, commonly called the covenant of grace.[2]

1. I Thess. 5:9. For God hath not appointed us to wrath, but to obtain salvation by our Lord Jesus Christ.

2. Titus 3:4-7. But after that the kindness and love of God our Saviour toward man appeared, not by works of righteousness which we have done, but according to his mercy he saved us, by the washing of regeneration, and renewing of the Holy Ghost; which he shed on us abundantly through Jesus Christ our Saviour; that being justified by his grace, we should be made heirs according to the hope of eternal life.

Titus 1:2. In hope of eternal life, which God, that cannot lie, promised before the world began.

Gal 3:21; Rom. 3:20-22.

Q. 31. *With whom was the covenant of grace made?*

A. The covenant of grace was made with Christ as the second Adam, and in him with all the elect as his seed.[1]

1. I Cor. 15:22, 45. For as in Adam all die, even so in Christ shall all be made alive. . . . And so it is written, The first man Adam was made a living soul; the last Adam *was made* a quickening spirit.

Eph. 1:4. According as he hath chosen us in him before the foundation of the world, that we should be holy and without blame before him in love.

II Tim. 1:9. Who hath saved us, and called *us* with an holy calling, not according to our works, but according to his own purpose and grace, which was given us in Christ Jesus before the world began.

Isa. 53:10, 11; Heb. 2:10, 11, 14.

Q. 32. *How is the grace of God manifested in the second covenant?*

A. The grace of God is manifested in the second covenant, in that he freely provideth and offereth to sinners a mediator,[1] and life and salvation by him;[2] and requiring faith as the condition to interest them in him,[3] promiseth and giveth his Holy Spirit to all his elect, to work in them that faith, with all other saving graces;[4] and to enable them unto all holy obedience,[5] as the evidence of the truth of their faith[6] and of their thankfulness to God,[7] and as the way which he hath appointed them to salvation.[8]

1. I Tim. 2:5. For *there is* one God, and one mediator between God and men, the man Christ Jesus.
2. I John 5:11, 12. And this is the record, that God hath given to us eternal life and this life is in his Son. He that hath the Son hath life.
3. John 3:16. For God so loved the world, that he gave his only begotten Son, that whosoever believeth in him should not perish, but have everlasting life.

John 1:12. But as many as received him, to them gave he power to become the sons of God, *even* to them that believe on his name.

John 3:36.
4. John 1:12, 13. But as many as received him, to them gave he power to become the sons of God, *even* to them that believe on his name: which were born, not of blood, nor of the will of the flesh, nor of the will of man, but of God.

John 3:5, 6, 8. Jesus answered, Verily, verily, I say unto thee, Except a man be born of water and *of* the Spirit, he cannot enter into the kingdom of God. That which is born of the flesh is flesh; and that which is born of the Spirit is spirit . . . The wind bloweth where it listeth, and thou hearest the sound thereof, but canst not tell whence it cometh, and whither it goeth: so is every one that is born of the Spirit.

Gal. 5:22, 23. But the fruit of the Spirit is love, joy, peace, longsuffering, gentleness, goodness, faith, meekness, temperance: against such there is no law.

5. Ezek. 36:27. And I will put my spirit within you, and cause you to walk in my statutes, and ye shall keep my judgments, and do *them*.

6. James 2:18, 22. Yea, a man may say, Thou hast faith, and I have works: shew me thy faith without thy works, and I will shew thee my faith by my works. . . . Seest thou how faith wrought with his works, and by works was faith made perfect?

7. II Cor. 5:14, 15. For the love of Christ constraineth us; because we thus judge, that if one died for all, then were all dead: and *that* he died for all, that they which live should not henceforth live unto themselves, but unto him which died for them, and rose again.

8. Eph. 2:10. For we are his workmanship, created in Christ Jesus unto good works, which God hath before ordained that we should walk in them.

Titus 2:14; 3:8.

Q. 33. *Was the covenant of grace always administered after one and the same manner?*

A. The covenant of grace was not always administered after the same manner, but the administrations of it under the Old Testament were different from those under the New.[1]

1. II Cor. 3:6. Who also hath made us able ministers of the new testament; not of the letter, but of the spirit.
   Heb. 1:1, 2; 8:7, 8 ff.

Q. 34. *How was the covenant of grace administered under the Old Testament?*

A. The covenant of grace was administered under the Old Testament, by promises,[1] prophecies,[2] sacrifices,[3] circumcision,[4] the passover,[5] and other types and ordinances; which did all fore-signify Christ then to come, and were for that time sufficient to build up the elect in faith in the promised Messiah,[6] by whom they then had full remission of sin and eternal salvation.[7]

1. Rom. 15:8. Now I say that Jesus Christ was a minister of the circumcision for the truth of God, to confirm the promises *made* unto the fathers.
   Acts 3:20.
2. Acts 3:20, 24.
3. Heb. 10:1.
4. Rom. 4:11.
5. I Cor. 5:7; Exod. 12:14, 17, 24.
6. Heb. 11:13. These all died in faith, not having received the promises,

but having seen them afar off, and were persuaded of *them,* and embraced *them,* and confessed that they were strangers and pilgrims on the earth.

7. Gal. 3:7-9. Know ye therefore that they which are of faith, the same are the children of Abraham. And the Scripture, foreseeing that God would justify the heathen through faith, preached before the gospel unto Abraham, *saying,* In thee shall all nations be blessed. So then they which be of faith are blessed with faithful Abraham.

Heb. 11.

Q. 35. *How is the covenant of grace administered under the New Testament?*

A. Under the New Testament, when Christ the substance was exhibited, the same covenant of grace was, and still is to be, administered in the preaching of the word,[1] and the administration of the sacraments of baptism,[2] and the Lord's supper;[3] in which grace and salvation are held forth in more fullness, evidence, and efficacy to all nations.[4]

1. Matt. 28:19, 20. Go ye therefore, and teach all nations . . . teaching them to observe all things whatsoever I have commanded you.

2. Matt. 28:19. Go ye therefore, and teach all nations, baptizing them in the name of the Father, and of the Son, and of the Holy Ghost.

3. I Cor. 11:23-26. For I have received of the Lord that which also I delivered unto you, That the Lord Jesus the *same* night in which he was betrayed took bread: and when he had given thanks, he brake *it,* and said, Take, eat: this is my body, which is broken for you: this do in remembrance of me. After the same manner also *he took* the cup, when he had supped, saying, This cup is the new testament in my blood: this do ye, as oft as ye drink *it,* in remembrance of me. For as often as ye eat this bread, and drink this cup, ye do shew the Lord's death till he come.

4. Heb. 8:6, 7. But now hath he obtained a more excellent ministry, by how much also he is the mediator of a better covenant, which was established upon better promises. For if that first *covenant* had been faultless, then should no place have been sought for the second.

Q. 36. *Who is the Mediator of the covenant of grace?*

A. The only Mediator of the covenant of grace is the Lord Jesus Christ,[1] who being the eternal Son of God, of one substance and equal with the Father, in the fullness of time became man, and so was, and continues to be, God and man, in two entire distinct natures, and one person, forever.[2]

1. I Tim. 2:5. For *there is* one God, and one mediator between God and men, the man Christ Jesus.

2. John 1:1. In the beginning was the Word, and the Word was with God, and the Word was God.

John 10:30. I and *my* Father are one.

Phil. 2:6. Who, being in the form of God, thought it not robbery to be equal with God.

Gal. 4:4. But when the fulness of the time was come, God sent forth his Son, made of a woman.

Col. 2:9. For in him dwelleth all the fulness of the Godhead bodily.

Phil. 2:5-11.

Q. 37. *How did Christ, being the Son of God, become man?*

A. Christ, the Son of God, became man by taking to himself a true body, and a reasonable soul,[1] being conceived by the power of the Holy Ghost, in the womb of the Virgin Mary, of her substance, and born of her,[2] yet without sin.[3]

1. John 1:14. And the Word was made flesh, and dwelt among us.
   Matt. 26:38. My soul is exceeding sorrowful, even unto death.
2. Luke 1:31, 35, 42. And, behold, thou shalt conceive in thy womb, and bring forth a son, and shalt call his name JESUS. . . . The Holy Ghost shall come upon thee, and the power of the Highest shall overshadow thee: therefore also that holy thing which shall be born of thee shall be called the Son of God. . . . Blessed *art* thou among women, and blessed *is* the fruit of thy womb.

   Gal. 4:4. God sent forth his Son, made of a woman.
3. Heb. 4:15. For we have not an high priest which cannot be touched with the feeling of our infirmities; but was in all points tempted like as *we are, yet* without sin.

Q. 38. *Why was it requisite that the Mediator should be God?*

A. It was requisite that the Mediator should be God; that he might sustain and keep the human nature from sinking under the infinite wrath of God, and the power of death; give worth and efficacy to his sufferings, obedience, and intercession; and to satisfy God's justice, procure his favor, purchase a peculiar people, give his Spirit to them, conquer all their enemies, and bring them to everlasting salvation.[1]

1. See General Note, p. 145.

Q. 39. *Why was it requisite that the Mediator should be man?*

A. It was requisite that the Mediator should be man; that he might advance our nature, perform obedience to the law,[1] suffer and make intercession for us in our nature,[2] have a fellow-feeling of our infirmities;[3] that we might receive the adoption of sons,[4] and have comfort and access with boldness unto the throne of grace.[5]

1. Rom. 5:19. By the obedience of one shall many be made righteous.
   Gal. 4:4, 5. But when the fulness of the time was come, God sent forth his Son, made of a woman, made under the law, to redeem them that were under the law, that we might receive the adoption of sons.

2. Heb. 2:14. Forasmuch then as the children are partakers of flesh and blood, he also himself likewise took part of the same; that through death he might destroy him that had the power of death.

Heb. 7:24, 25. But this *man*, because he continueth ever, hath an unchangeable priesthood. Wherefore he is able also to save them to the uttermost that come unto God by him, seeing he ever liveth to make intercession for them.

3. Heb. 4:15. For we have not an high priest which cannot be touched with the feeling of our infirmities; but was in all points tempted like as *we are, yet* without sin.

4. Gal. 4:5. To redeem them that were under the law, that we might receive the adoption of sons.

5. Heb. 4:14-16. Seeing then that we have a great high priest, that is passed into the heavens, Jesus the Son of God, let us hold fast *our* profession. For we have not an high priest which cannot be touched with the feeling of our infirmities; but was in all points tempted like as *we are, yet* without sin. Let us therefore come bodly unto the throne of grace, that we may obtain mercy, and find grace to help in time of need.

Q. 40. *Why was it requisite that the Mediator should be God and man in one person?*

A. It was requisite that the Mediator who was to reconcile God and man, should himself be both God and man, and this in one person; that the proper works of each nature might be accepted of God for us, and relied on by us, as the works of the whole person.[1]

1. See General Note, p. 145.

Q. 41. *Why was our Mediator called Jesus?*

A. Our Mediator was called Jesus, because he saveth his people from their sins.[1]

1. Matt. 1:21. And she shall bring forth a son, and thou shalt call his name JESUS: for he shall save his people from their sins.

Q. 42. *Why was our Mediator called Christ?*

A. Our Mediator was called Christ, because he was anointed with the Holy Ghost above measure;[1] and so set apart, and fully furnished with all authority and ability,[2] to execute the office of prophet,[3] priest,[4] and king of his church, in the estate both of his humiliation and exaltation.[5]

1. John 3:34. God giveth not the Spirit by measure *unto him.*
   Luke 4:18-21.

2. Luke 4:14. And Jesus returned in the power of the Spirit into Galilee: and there went out a fame of him through all the region round about.
   Heb. 9:14. How much more shall the blood of Christ, who through the

eternal Spirit offered himself without spot to God, purge your conscience from dead works to serve the living God?

Matt. 28:18-20. And Jesus came and spake unto them, saying, All power is given unto me in heaven and in earth. Go ye therefore, and teach all nations, baptizing them in the name of the Father, and of the Son, and of the Holy Ghost: teaching them to observe all things whatsoever I have commanded you: and, lo, I am with you alway, *even* unto the end of the world. Amen.

3. Acts 3:22. For Moses truly said unto the fathers, A prophet shall the Lord your God raise up unto you of your brethren, like unto me; him shall ye hear in all things whatsoever he shall say unto you.

Luke 4:18, 21.

4. Heb. 5:5, 6. So also Christ glorified not himself to be made an high priest; but he that said unto him, Thou art my Son, to day have I begotten thee. As he saith also in another *place*, Thou *art* a priest for ever after the order of Melchisedec.

Heb. 4:14, 15.

5. Rev. 19:16. And he hath on *his* vesture and on his thigh a name written, KING OF KINGS, AND LORD OF LORDS.

Isa. 9:6, 7; Ps. 2:6.

Q. 43. *How doth Christ execute the office of a prophet?*

A. Christ executeth the office of a prophet, in his revealing to the church in all ages,[1] by his Spirit and word,[2] in divers ways of administration, the whole will of God, in all things concerning their edification and salvation.[3]

1. John 1:1, 4. In the beginning was the Word, and the Word was with God, and the Word was God. . . . In him was life; and the life was the light of men.

2. II Peter 1:21. For the prophecy came not in old time by the will of man: but holy men of God spake *as they were* moved by the Holy Ghost.

II Cor. 2:9, 10. For to this end also did I write, that I might know the proof of you, whether ye be obedient in all things. To whom ye forgive any thing, I *forgive* also: for if I forgave any thing, to whom I forgave *it*, for your sakes *forgave I it* in the person of Christ.

3. Eph. 4:11-13. And he gave some, apostles; and some, prophets; and some, evangelists; and some, pastors and teachers; for the perfecting of the saints, for the work of the ministry, for the edifying of the body of Christ: till we all come in the unity of the faith, and of the knowledge of the Son of God, unto a perfect man, unto the measure of the stature of the fulness of Christ.

John 20:31.

Q. 44. *How doth Christ execute the office of a priest?*

A. Christ executeth the office of a priest, in his once offering himself a sacrifice without spot to God,[1] to be a reconciliation for the sins of his people;[2] and in making continual intercession for them.[3]

1. Heb. 9:14, 28. How much more shall the blood of Christ, who through

the eternal Spirit offered himself without spot to God, purge your conscience . . . so Christ was once offered to bear the sins of many.

2. Heb. 2:17. That he might be a merciful and faithful high priest in things *pertaining* to God, to make reconciliation for the sins of the people.

3. Heb. 7:25. Wherefore he is able also to save them to the uttermost that come unto God by him, seeing he ever liveth to make intercession for them.

Q. 45. *How doth Christ execute the office of a king?*

A. Christ executeth the office of a king, in calling out of the world a people to himself;[1] and giving them officers,[2] laws,[3] and censures, by which he visibly governs them;[4] in bestowing saving grace upon his elect,[5] rewarding their obedience,[6] and correcting them for their sins,[7] preserving and supporting them under all their temptations and sufferings;[8] restraining and overcoming all their enemies,[9] and powerfully ordering all things for his own glory,[10] and their good;[11] and also in taking vengeance on the rest, who know not God, and obey not the gospel.[12]

1. John 10:16, 27. And other sheep I have, which are not of this fold: them also I must bring, and they shall hear my voice; and there shall be one fold, *and* one shepherd. . . . My sheep hear my voice, and I know them, and they follow me.

   Isa. 55:5. Behold, thou shalt call a nation *that* thou knowest not, and nations *that* knew not thee shall run unto thee because of the LORD thy God, and for the Holy One of Israel; for he hath glorified thee.

2. I Cor. 12:28. And God hath set some in the church, first apostles, secondarily prophets, thirdly teachers, after that miracles, then gifts of healings, helps, governments, diversities of tongues.

   Eph. 4:11, 12.

3. Matt. 28:19, 20. Go ye therefore, and teach all nations, baptizing them in the name of the Father, and of the Son, and of the Holy Ghost: teaching them to observe all things whatsoever I have commanded you: and, lo, I am with you alway, *even* unto the end of the world. Amen.

4. Matt. 18:17, 18. And if he shall neglect to hear them, tell *it* unto the church: but if he neglect to hear the church, let him be unto thee as an heathen man and a publican. Verily I say unto you, Whatsoever ye shall bind on earth shall be bound in heaven: and whatsoever ye shall loose on earth shall be loosed in heaven.

   I Cor. 5:4, 5; I Tim. 5:20; Titus 3:10.

5. Acts 5:31. Him hath God exalted with his right hand *to be* a Prince and a Saviour, for to give repentance to Israel, and forgiveness of sins.

6. Rev. 22:12. And, behold, I come quickly; and my reward *is* with me, to give every man according as his work shall be.

   Matt. 25:34-36; Rom. 2:7.

7. Rev. 3:19. As many as I love, I rebuke and chasten.

   Heb. 12:6, 7.

8. II Cor. 12:9, 10. And he said unto me, My grace is sufficient for thee: for my strength is made perfect in weakness. Most gladly therefore will I

rather glory in my infirmities, that the power of Christ may rest upon me. Therefore I take pleasure in infirmities, in reproaches, in necessities, in persecutions, in distresses for .Christ's sake: for when I am weak, then am I strong.

Rom. 8:35-39.

9. I Cor. 15:25. For he must reign, till he hath put all enemies under his feet.

Acts 12:17. But he, beckoning unto them with the hand to hold their peace, declared unto them how the Lord had brought him out of the prison. And he said, Go shew these things unto James, and to the brethren. And he departed, and went into another place.

Acts 18:9, 10. Then spake the Lord to Paul in the night by a vision, Be not afraid, but speak, and hold not thy peace: for I am with thee, and no man shall set on thee to hurt thee: for I have much people in this city.

10. Rom. 14:11. As I live, saith the Lord, every knee shall bow to me, and every tongue shall confess to God.

Col. 1:18. And he is the head of the body, the church: who is the beginning, the firstborn from the dead; that in all *things* he might have the preeminence.

Matt. 28:19, 20.

11. Rom. 8:28. And we know that all things work together for good to them that love God, to them who are the called according to *his* purpose.

12. II Thess. 1:8. In flaming fire taking vengeance on them that know not God, and that obey not the gospel of our Lord Jesus Christ.

Ps. 2:9. Thou shalt break them with a rod of iron; thou shalt dash them in pieces like a potter's vessel.

Q. 46. *What was the estate of Christ's humiliation?*

A. The estate of Christ's humiliation was that low condition, wherein he, for our sakes, emptying himself of his glory, took upon him the form of a servant, in his conception and birth, life, death, and after his death until his resurrection.[1]

1. Phil. 2:6-8. Who, being in the form of God, thought it not robbery to be equal with God: but made himself of no reputation, and took upon him the form of a servant, and was made in the likeness of men: and being found in fashion as a man, he humbled himself, and became obedient unto death, even the death of the cross.

II Cor. 8:9. For ye know the grace of our Lord Jesus Christ, that, though he was rich, yet for your sakes he became poor, that ye through his poverty might be rich.

Gal. 4:4.

Q. 47. *How did Christ humble himself in his conception and birth?*

A. Christ humbled himself in his conception and birth, in that, being from all eternity the Son of God in the bosom of the Father, he was pleased in the fullness of time to become the Son of man, made of a woman of low estate, and to be born of her, with divers circumstances of more than ordinary abasement.[1]

1. John 1:18. No man hath seen God at any time; the only begotten Son, which is in the bosom of the Father, he hath declared *him*.
See citations under Q. 46 above.

Q. 48. *How did Christ humble himself in his life?*

A. Christ humbled himself in his life, by subjecting himself to the law,[1] which he perfectly fulfilled,[2] and by conflicting with the indignities of the world,[3] temptations of Satan,[4] and infirmities in his flesh; whether common to the nature of man, or particularly accompanying that his low condition.[5]

1. Gal. 4:4. God sent forth his Son, made of a woman, made under the law.
2. Matt. 3:15. And Jesus answering said unto him, Suffer *it to be so* now: for thus it becometh us to fulfil all righteousness. Then he suffered him. John 19:30. When Jesus therefore had received the vinegar, he said, It is finished: and he bowed his head, and gave up the ghost.
Rom. 5:19.
3. Heb. 12:2, 3. Looking unto Jesus the author and finisher of *our* faith; who for the joy that was set before him endured the cross, despising the shame, and is set down at the right hand of the throne of God. For consider him that endured such contradiction of sinners against himself, lest ye be wearied and faint in your minds.
Isa. 53:2, 3; Ps. 22:6.
4. Matt. 4:1. Then was Jesus led up of the Spirit into the wilderness to be tempted of the devil.
See verses 2-12; Luke 4:1-14.
5. Heb. 2:17, 18. Wherefore in all things it behooved him to be made like unto *his* brethren . . . for in that he himself hath suffered being tempted, he is able to succour them that are tempted.
Heb. 4:15; Isa. 52:13, 14.

Q. 49. *How did Christ humble himself in his death?*

A. Christ humbled himself in his death, in that having been betrayed by Judas,[1] forsaken by his disciples,[2] scorned and rejected by the world,[3] condemned by Pilate, and tormented by his persecutors;[4] having also conflicted with the terrors of death and the powers of darkness, felt and borne the weight of God's wrath,[5] he laid down his life an offering for sin,[6] enduring the painful, shameful, and cursed death of the cross.[7]

1. Matt. 27:4. Saying, I have sinned in that I have betrayed the innocent blood. And they said, What *is that* to us? see thou *to that*.
2. Matt. 26:56. Then all the disciples forsook him, and fled.
3. Luke 18:32, 33. For he shall be delivered unto the Gentiles, and shall be mocked, and spitefully entreated, and spitted on: and they shall scourge *him*, and put him to death: and the third day he shall rise again.
Isa. 53:3.

4. Matt. 27:26. And when he had scourged Jesus, he delivered *him* to be crucified.
John 19:34; Luke 22:63, 64.

5. Luke 22:44. And being in an agony he prayed more earnestly: and his sweat was as it were great drops of blood falling down to the ground.
Matt. 27:46. And about the ninth hour Jesus cried with a loud voice . . . Eli, Eli, lama sabachthani? . . . My God, my God, why hast thou forsaken me?
Rom. 8:32.

6. Rom. 4:25. Who was delivered for our offences, and was raised again for our justification.
I Cor. 15:3, 4; Isa. 53:10.

7. Phil. 2:8. And being found in fashion as a man, he humbled himself, and became obedient unto death, even the death of the cross.
Heb. 12:2; Gal. 3:13.

Q. 50. *Wherein consisted Christ's humiliation after his death?*

A. Christ's humiliation after his death consisted in his being buried,[1] and continuing in the state of the dead, and under the power of death till the third day,[2] which hath been otherwise expressed in these words, He descended into hell.

1. I Cor. 15:3, 4. For I delivered unto you first of all that which I also received, how that Christ died for our sins according to the scriptures; and that he was buried, and that he rose again the third day according to the scriptures.

2. Matt. 12:40. For as Jonas was three days and three nights in the whale's belly; so shall the Son of man be three days and three nights in the heart of the earth.
Luke 18:33. And they shall scourge *him*, and put him to death: and the third day he shall rise again.

Q. 51. *What was the estate of Christ's exaltation?*

A. The estate of Christ's exaltation comprehendeth his resurrection,[1] ascension,[2] sitting at the right hand of the Father,[3] and his coming again to judge the world.[4]

1. I Cor. 15:4. And that he rose again the third day according to the scriptures.

2. Luke 24:51. And it came to pass, while he blessed them, he was parted from them, and carried up into heaven.
Acts 1:9-11.

3. Eph. 1:20. And set *him* at his own right hand.

4. Acts 1:11. This same Jesus, which is taken up from you into heaven, shall so come in like manner as ye have seen him go into heaven.
Acts 17:31.

Q. 52. *How was Christ exalted in his resurrection?*

A. Christ was exalted in his resurrection, in that, not having seen corruption in death (of which it was not possible for him to be held),[1] and having the very same body in which he suffered, with the essential properties thereof[2] (but without mortality and other common infirmities belonging to this life), really united to his soul,[3] he rose again from the dead the third day by his own power;[4] whereby he declared himself to be the Son of God,[5] to have satisfied divine justice,[6] to have vanquished death and him that had the power of it,[7] and to be Lord of quick and dead.[8] All which he did as a public person,[9] the head of his church,[10] for their justification,[11] quickening in grace,[12] support against enemies,[13] and to assure them of their resurrection from the dead at the last day.[14]

1. Acts 2:24. Whom God hath raised up, having loosed the pains of death: because it was not possible that he should be holden of it.
   Ps. 16:10. For thou wilt not leave my soul in hell; neither wilt thou suffer thine Holy One to see corruption.
2. Luke 24:39. Behold my hands and my feet, that it is I myself: handle me, and see; for a spirit hath not flesh and bones, as ye see me have.
3. Rev. 1:18. I *am* he that liveth, and was dead; and, behold, I am alive for evermore, Amen; and have the keys of hell and of death.
4. John 10:18. No man taketh it from me, but I lay it down of myself. I have power to lay it down, and I have power to take it again.
5. Rom. 1:4. And declared *to be* the Son of God with power, according to the spirit of holiness, by the resurrection from the dead.
6. Rom. 4:25. Who was delivered for our offences, and was raised again for our justification.
   I Cor. 15:17.
7. Heb. 2:14. That through death he might destroy him that had the power of death, that is, the devil.
   Rev. 1:18.
8. Rom. 14:9. For to this end Christ both died, and rose, and revived, that he might be Lord both of the dead and living.
9. I Cor. 15:21, 22. For since by man *came* death, by man *came* also the resurrection of the dead. For as in Adam all die, even so in Christ shall all be made alive.
10. Eph. 1:22, 23. And gave him *to be* the head over all *things* to the church, which is his body, the fulness of him that filleth all in all.
    Col. 1:18.
11. Rom. 4:25. Who was delivered for our offences, and was raised again for our justification.
12. Eph. 2:5, 6. Even when we were dead in sins, hath quickened us together with Christ . . . and hath raised *us* up together, and made *us* sit together in heavenly *places* in Christ Jesus.
    Col. 2:12.
13. I Cor. 15:25, 26. For he must reign, till he hath put all enemies under his feet. The last enemy *that* shall be destroyed *is* death.
    Acts 12:17; Acts 18:9, 10.
14. I Cor. 15:20. But now is Christ risen from the dead, *and* become the first-fruits of them that slept.
    I Thess. 4:13-18.

Q. 53. *How was Christ exalted in his ascension?*

A. Christ was exalted in his ascension, in that having, after his resurrection, often appeared unto, and conversed with his apostles, speaking to them of the things pertaining to the kingdom of God,[1] and giving them commission to preach the gospel to all nations;[2] forty days after his resurrection, he, in our nature, and as our head, triumphing over enemies, visibly went up into the highest heavens,[3] there to receive gifts for men,[4] to raise up our affections thither,[5] and to prepare a place for us,[6] where himself is, and shall continue till his second coming at the end of the world.[7]

1. Acts 1:2, 3. Until the day on which he was taken up, after that he through the Holy Ghost had given commandments unto the apostles whom he had chosen: to whom also he shewed himself alive after his passion by many infallible proofs, being seen of them forty days, and speaking of the things pertaining to the kingdom of God.
2. Matt. 28:19, 20. Go ye therefore, and teach all nations . . . teaching them to observe all things whatsoever I have commanded you.
Acts 1:8.
3. Heb. 6:20. Whither the forerunner is for us entered, *even* Jesus, made an high priest for ever.
Eph. 4:8. Wherefore he saith, When he ascended up on high, he led captivity captive, and gave gifts unto men.
Acts 1:9. While they beheld, he was taken up; and a cloud received him out of their sight.
4. Ps. 68:18. Thou hast ascended on high . . . thou hast received gifts for men; yea, *for* the rebellious also, that the LORD God might dwell *among them*.
5. Col. 3:1, 2. If ye then be risen with Christ, seek those things which are above, where Christ sitteth on the right hand of God. Set your affections on things above, not on things on the earth.
6. John 14:2. I go to prepare a place for you.
7. Acts 3:21. Whom the heaven must receive until the times of restitution of all things, which God hath spoken by the mouth of all his holy prophets since the world began.

Q. 54. *How is Christ exalted in his sitting at the right hand of God?*

A. Christ is exalted in his sitting at the right hand of God, in that as God-man he is advanced to the highest favor with God the Father,[1] with all fullness of joy,[2] glory,[3] and power over all things in heaven and earth;[4] and doth gather and defend his church, and subdue their enemies; furnisheth his ministers and people with gifts and graces,[5] and maketh intercession for them.[6]

1. Phil. 2:9. Wherefore God also hath highly exalted him, and given him a name which is above every name.

2. Acts 2:28. Thou shalt make me full of joy with thy countenance.
Compare Ps. 16:11.

3. John 17:5. And now, O Father, glorify thou me with thine own self with the glory which I had with thee before the world was.

4. Eph. 1:22. And hath put all *things* under his feet, and gave him *to be* the head over all *things* to the church.
I Peter 3:22.

5. Eph. 4:11, 12. And he gave some, apostles; and some, prophets; and some, evangelists; and some, pastors and teachers; for the perfecting of the saints, for the work of the ministry, for the edifying of the body of Christ.
See citations under Q. 45.

6. Rom. 8:34. Who *is* he that condemneth? *It is* Christ that died, yea rather, that is risen again, who is even at the right hand of God, who also maketh intercession for us.
See citations under Q. 44.

Q. 55. *How doth Christ make intercession?*

A. Christ maketh intercession, by his appearing in our nature continually before the Father in heaven,[1] in the merit of his obedience and sacrifice on earth;[2] declaring his will to have it applied to all believers;[3] answering all accusations against them;[4] and procuring for them quiet of conscience, notwithstanding daily failings,[5] access with boldness to the throne of grace,[6] and acceptance of their persons[7] and services.[8]

1. Heb. 9:24. For Christ is not entered into the holy places made with hands, *which are* the figures of the true; but into heaven itself, now to appear in the presence of God for us.

2. Heb. 1:3. When he had by himself purged our sins, sat down on the right hand of the Majesty on high.

3. John 17:9, 20, 24. I pray for them: I pray not for the world, but for them which thou hast given me; for they are thine. . . . Neither pray I for these alone, but for them also which shall believe on me through their word . . . Father, I will that they also, whom thou hast given me, be with me where I am; that they may behold my glory, which thou hast given me.

4. Rom. 8:33, 34. Who shall lay any thing to the charge of God's elect? *It is* God that justifieth. Who *is* he that condemneth? *It is* Christ that died, yea rather, that is risen again, who is even at the right hand of God, who also maketh intercession for us.

5. Rom. 5:1, 2. Therefore being justified by faith, we have peace with God through our Lord Jesus Christ: by whom also we have access by faith into this grace wherein we stand, and rejoice in hope of the glory of God.

6. Heb. 4:16. Let us therefore come boldly unto the throne of grace, that we may obtain mercy, and find grace to help in time of need.

7. Eph. 1:6. To the praise of the glory of his grace, wherein he hath made us accepted in the beloved.

8. I Peter 2:5. Ye also, as lively stones, are built up a spiritual house, an holy priesthood, to offer up spiritual sacrifices, acceptable to God by Jesus Christ.
Rev. 8:3, 4.

Q. 56. *How is Christ to be exalted in his coming again to judge the world?*

A. Christ is to be exalted in his coming again to judge the world, in that he, who was unjustly judged and condemned by wicked men, shall come again at the last day in great power, and in the full manifestation of his own glory, and of his Father's, with all his holy angels, with a shout, with the voice of the archangel, and with the trumpet of God, to judge the world in righteousness.[1]

> 1. Matt. 24:30. And then shall all the tribes of the earth mourn, and they shall see the Son of man coming in the clouds of heaven with power and great glory.
>
> Luke 9:26. For whosoever shall be ashamed of me and of my words, of him shall the Son of man be ashamed, when he shall come in his own glory, and *in his* Father's, and of the holy angels.
>
> I Thess. 4:16. For the Lord himself shall descend from heaven with a shout, with the voice of the archangel, and with the trump of God.
>
> Acts 17:31. Because he hath appointed a day, in the which he will judge the world in righteousness by *that* man whom he hath ordained; *whereof* he hath given assurance unto all *men*, in that he hath raised him from the dead.
>
> Matt. 25:31.

Q. 57. *What benefits hath Christ procured by his mediation?*

A. Christ by his mediation hath procured redemption, with all other benefits of the covenant of grace.[1]

> 1. Heb. 9:12. Neither by the blood of goats and calves, but by his own blood he entered in once into the holy place, having obtained eternal redemption *for us.*
>
> I Cor. 1:30. But of him are ye in Christ Jesus, who of God is made unto us wisdom, and righteousness, and sanctification, and redemption.
>
> Rom. 8:32. He that spared not his own Son, but delivered him up for us all, how shall he not with him also freely give us all things?
>
> II Cor. 1:20.

Q. 58. *How do we come to be made partakers of the benefits which Christ hath procured?*

A. We are made partakers of the benefits which Christ hath procured, by the application of them unto us, which is the work especially of God the Holy Ghost.[1]

> 1. John 1:12, 13. But as many as received him, to them gave he power to become the sons of God, *even* to them that believe on his name: which were born, not of blood, nor of the will of the flesh, nor of the will of man, but of God.
>
> John 3:5, 6. Jesus answered, Verily, verily, I say unto thee, Except a

man be born of water and *of* the Spirit, he cannot enter into the kingdom of God. That which is born of the flesh is flesh; and that which is born of the Spirit is spirit.

Titus 3:5, 6. But according to his mercy he saved us, by the washing of regeneration, and renewing of the Holy Ghost; which he shed on us abundantly through Jesus Christ our Saviour.

Q. 59. *Who are made partakers of redemption through Christ?*

A. Redemption is certainly applied, and effectually communicated, to all those for whom Christ hath purchased it;[1] who are in time by the Holy Ghost enabled to believe in Christ, according to the gospel.[2]

1. John 6:37, 39. All that the Father giveth me shall come to me; and him that cometh to me I will in no wise cast out. . . . And this is the Father's will which hath sent me, that of all which he hath given me I should lose nothing, but should raise it up again at the last day.

    John 10:15, 16. I lay down my life for the sheep. And other sheep I have, which are not of this fold: them also I must bring, and they shall hear my voice.

    Rom. 8:29, 30.

2. I Peter 1:2. Elect according to the foreknowledge of God the Father, through sanctification of the Spirit, unto obedience and sprinkling of the blood of Jesus Christ.

    II Thess. 2:13. But we are bound to give thanks alway to God for you, brethren beloved of the Lord, because God hath from the beginning chosen you to salvation through sanctification of the Spirit and belief of the truth.

Q. 60. *Can they who have never heard the gospel, and so know not Jesus Christ, nor believe in him, be saved by their living according to the light of nature?*

A. They who having never heard the gospel, know not Jesus Christ, and believe not in him, cannot be saved,[1] be they never so diligent to frame their lives according to the light of nature,[2] or the laws of that religion which they profess;[3] neither is there salvation in any other, but in Christ alone,[4] who is the Saviour only of his body the church.[5]

1. Rom. 10:14. How then shall they call on him in whom they have not believed? and how shall they believe in him of whom they have not heard? and how shall they hear without a preacher?

    II Thess. 1:8, 9. In flaming fire taking vengeance on them that know not God, and that obey not the gospel of our Lord Jesus Christ: who shall be punished with everlasting destruction from the presence of the Lord, and from the glory of his power.

    Acts 4:12. Neither is there salvation in any other: for there is none other name under heaven given among men, whereby we must be saved.

    Rom. 1:18-32.

2. I Cor. 1:21. For after that in the wisdom of God the world by wisdom knew not God, it pleased God by the foolishness of preaching to save them that believe.

Rom. 1:18-32; Rom. 3:9-19.

3. John 4:22. Ye worship ye know not what: we know what we worship: for salvation is of the Jews.

Phil. 3:4-10.

4. Acts 4:12. Neither is there salvation in any other: for there is none other name under heaven given among men, whereby we must be saved.

5. John 6:39, 44. And this is the Father's will which hath sent me, that of all which he hath given me I should lose nothing, but should raise it up again at the last day. . . . No man can come to me, except the Father which hath sent me draw him: and I will raise him up at the last day.

John 17:9. I pray for them: I pray not for the world, but for them which thou hast given me; for they are thine.

Q. 61. *Are all they saved who hear the gospel, and live in the church?*

A. All that hear the gospel, and live in the visible church, are not saved; but only they who are true members of the church invisible.[1]

1. Rom. 9:6. They *are* not all Israel, which are of Israel.

Matt. 7:21. Not every one that saith unto me, Lord, Lord, shall enter into the kingdom of heaven; but he that doeth the will of my Father which is in heaven.

Matt. 13:41, 42. The Son of man shall send forth his angels, and they shall gather out of his kingdom all things that offend, and them which do iniquity; and shall cast them into a furnace of fire: there shall be wailing and gnashing of teeth.

Q. 62. *What is the visible church?*

A. The visible church is a society made up of all such as in all ages and places of the world do profess the true religion,[1] and of their children.[2]

1. I Cor. 1:2. Unto the church of God which is at Corinth, to them that are sanctified in Christ Jesus, called *to be* saints, with all that in every place call upon the name of Jesus Christ our Lord, both their's and our's.

I Cor. 12:12, 13; Rom. 15:1-12.

2. Gen. 17:7. And I will establish my covenant between me and thee and thy seed after thee in their generations for an everlasting covenant, to be a God unto thee, and to thy seed after thee. (See the context.)

Compare Gal. 3:7, 9, 14; Rom. 4.

Acts 2:39. For the promise is unto you, and to your children.

I Cor. 7:14. For the unbelieving husband is sanctified by the wife, and the unbelieving wife is sanctified by the husband: else were your children unclean; but now are they holy.

Mark 10:13-16. And they brought young children to him, that he should touch them: and *his* disciples rebuked those that brought *them*. But when Jesus saw *it*, he was much displeased, and said unto them, Suffer the little children to come unto me, and forbid them not: for of such is the kingdom of God. Verily I say unto you, Whosoever shall not receive the kingdom of God as a little child, he shall not enter therein. And he took them up in his arms, put *his* hands upon them, and blessed them.

Q. 63. *What are the special privileges of the visible church?*

A. The visible church hath the privilege of being under God's special care and government;[1] of being protected and preserved in all ages, notwithstanding the opposition of all enemies;[2] and of enjoying the communion of saints, the ordinary means of salvation,[3] and offers of grace by Christ, to all members of it, in the ministry of the gospel, testifying that whosoever believes in him shall be saved,[4] and excluding none that will come unto him.[5]

1. I Cor. 12:28. And God hath set some in the church, first apostles, secondarily prophets, thirdly teachers, after that miracles, then gifts of healings, helps, governments, diversities of tongues.

   Eph. 4:11, 12; Acts 13:1, 2; Isa. 49:14-16.

2. Matt. 16:18. And upon this rock I will build my church; and the gates of hell shall not prevail against it.

   Isa. 31:4, 5; Ps. 115:9-18.

3. Acts 2:42. They continued stedfastly in the apostles' doctrine and fellowship, and in breaking of bread, and in prayers.

   Rom. 3:1, 2. What advantage then hath the Jew? or what profit *is there* of circumcision? Much every way: chiefly because that unto them were committed the oracles of God.

4. Ps. 147:19, 20. He sheweth his word unto Jacob, his statutes and his judgments unto Israel. He hath not dealt so with any nation: and *as for his* judgments, they have not known them.

   Rom. 9:4; Acts 16:31; Rev. 22:17.

5. John 6:37. And him that cometh to me I will in no wise cast out.

Q. 64. *What is the invisible church?*

A. The invisible church is the whole number of the elect, that have been, are, or shall be gathered into one under Christ the head.[1]

1. John 11:52. And not for that nation only, but that also he should gather together in one the children of God that were scattered abroad.

   John 10:16. And other sheep I have, which are not of this fold: them also I must bring, and they shall hear my voice; and there shall be one fold, *and* one shepherd.

   Eph. 1:10, 22, 23.

Q. 65. *What special benefits do the members of the invisible church enjoy by Christ?*

A. The members of the invisible church, by Christ, enjoy union and communion with him in grace and glory.[1]

1. John 17:21. That they all may be one; as thou, Father, *art* in me, and I in thee, that they also may be one in us.
   Eph. 2:5, 6.
   I John 1:3. And truly our fellowship *is* with the Father, and with his Son Jesus Christ.
   John 17:24. Father, I will that they also, whom thou hast given me, be with me where I am; that they may behold my glory.

Q. 66. *What is that union which the elect have with Christ?*

A. The union which the elect have with Christ is the work of God's grace,[1] whereby they are spiritually and mystically, yet really and inseparably, joined to Christ as their head and husband;[2] which is done in their effectual calling.[3]

1. Eph. 2:8. For by grace are ye saved through faith; and that not of your-selves: *it is* the gift of God. (See context.)
2. I Cor. 6:17. But he that is joined unto the Lord is one spirit.
   John 10:28. And I give unto them eternal life; and they shall never per-ish, neither shall any *man* pluck them out of my hand.
   Eph. 5:23, 30. Even as Christ is the head of the church . . . for we are members of his body, of his flesh, and of his bones.
   John 15:1-5.
3. I Cor. 1:9. God *is* faithful, by whom ye were called unto the fellowship of his Son Jesus Christ our Lord.
   I Peter 5:10.

Q. 67. *What is effectual calling?*

A. Effectual calling is the work of God's almighty power and grace,[1] whereby (out of his free and especial love to his elect, and from nothing in them moving him thereunto)[2] he doth in his accepted time invite and draw them to Jesus Christ, by his word and Spirit;[3] savingly enlightening their minds,[4] renewing and powerfully determining their wills,[5] so as they (although in themselves dead in sin) are hereby made willing and able, freely to answer his call, and to accept and embrace the grace offered and conveyed therein.[6]

1. Eph. 1:18-20. That ye may know what is the hope of his calling . . . and what *is* the exceeding greatness of his power to us-ward who believe, ac-cording to the working of his mighty power, which he wrought in Christ, when he raised him from the dead, and set *him* at his own right hand in the heavenly *places.*

II Tim. 1:9. Who hath saved us, and called *us* with an holy calling, not according to our works, but according to his own purpose and grace, which was given us in Christ Jesus before the world began.

2. Titus 3:4, 5. But after that the kindness and love of God our Saviour toward man appeared, not by works of righteousness which we have done, but according to his mercy he saved us, by the washing of regeneration, and renewing of the Holy Ghost.

Rom. 9:11. That the purpose of God according to election might stand, not of works, but of him that calleth.

Eph. 2:4-10.

3. II Cor. 5:20. Now then we are ambassadors for Christ, as though God did beseech *you* by us: we pray *you* in Christ's stead, be ye reconciled to God.

John 6:44. No man can come to me, except the Father which hath sent me draw him: and I will raise him up at the last day.

II Thess. 2:13, 14. But we are bound to give thanks alway to God for you, brethren beloved of the Lord, because God hath from the beginning chosen you to salvation through sanctification of the Spirit and belief of the truth: whereunto he called you by our gospel, to the obtaining of the glory of our Lord Jesus Christ.

4. Acts 26:18. To open their eyes, *and* to turn *them* from darkness to light, and *from* the power of Satan unto God, that they may receive forgiveness of sins, and inheritance among them which are sanctified by faith that is in me.

5. Ezek. 11:19. And I will put a new spirit within you; and I will take the stony heart out of their flesh, and will give them an heart of flesh.

Ezek. 36:26, 27.

6. John 6:45. And they shall be all taught of God. Every man therefore that hath heard, and hath learned of the Father, cometh unto me.

Phil. 2:13. For it is God which worketh in you both to will and to do of *his* good pleasure.

Deut. 30:6; Eph. 2:5.

Q. 68. *Are the elect only effectually called?*

A. All the elect, and they only, are effectually called;[1] although others may be, and often are, outwardly called by the ministry of the word,[2] and have some common operations of the Spirit,[3] who, for their willful neglect and contempt of the grace offered to them, being justly left in their unbelief, do never truly come to Jesus Christ.[4]

1. Acts 13:48. And as many as were ordained to eternal life believed.

John 6:39, 44. And this is the Father's will which hath sent me, that of all which he hath given me I should lose nothing, but should raise it up again at the last day. . . . No man can come to me, except the Father which hath sent me draw him: and I will raise him up at the last day.

John 17:9. I pray for them: I pray not for the world, but for them which thou hast given me; for they are thine.

2. Matt. 22:14. For many are called, but few *are* chosen.

3. Matt. 13:20, 21. But he that received the seed into stony places, the same is he that heareth the word . . . yet hath he not root in himself, but

dureth for awhile: for when tribulation or persecution ariseth because of the word, by and by he is offended.
Heb. 6:4-6.

4. Ps. 81:11, 12. But my people would not hearken to my voice; and Israel would none of me. So I gave them up unto their own hearts' lust: *and* they walked in their own counsels.

John 12:38-40. That the saying of Esaias the prophet might be fulfilled, which he spake, Lord, who hath believed our report? and to whom hath the arm of the Lord been revealed? Therefore they could not believe, because that Esaias said again, He hath blinded their eyes, and hardened their heart; that they should not see with *their* eyes, nor understand with *their* heart, and be converted, and I should heal them.

Acts 28:25-27; John 6:64, 65; Prov. 1:24-32; Ps. 95:9-11.

Q. 69. *What is the communion in grace, which the members of the invisible church have with Christ?*

A. The communion in grace, which the members of the invisible church have with Christ, is their partaking of the virtue of his mediation, in their justification,[1] adoption,[2] sanctification, and whatever else in this life manifests their union with him.[3]

1. Rom. 8:30. Moreover whom he did predestinate, them he also called: and whom he called, them he also justified: and whom he justified, them he also glorified.

2. Eph. 1:5. Having predestinated us unto the adoption of children by Jesus Christ to himself.

3. I Cor. 1:30. But of him are ye in Christ Jesus, who of God is made unto us wisdom, and righteousness, and sanctification, and redemption.

Q. 70. *What is justification?*

A. Justification is an act of God's free grace unto sinners, in which he pardoneth all their sin, accepteth and accounteth their persons righteous in his sight;[1] not for anything wrought in them, or done by them,[2] but only for the perfect obedience and full satisfaction of Christ, by God imputed to them,[3] and received by faith alone.[4]

1. II Cor. 5:19, 21. To wit, that God was in Christ, reconciling the world unto himself, not imputing their trespasses unto them . . . For he hath made him *to be* sin for us, who knew no sin; that we might be made the righteousness of God in him.

Rom. 3:22, 24, 25. Even the righteousness of God *which is* by faith of Jesus Christ unto all and upon all them that believe . . . being justified freely by his grace through the redemption that is in Christ Jesus: whom God hath set forth *to be* a propitiation through faith in his blood, to declare his righteousness for the remission of sins that are past, through the forbearance of God.

Rom. 4:5. But to him that worketh not, but believeth on him that justifieth the ungodly, his faith is counted for righteousness.

2. Eph. 1:6, 7. Wherein he hath made us accepted in the beloved. In whom we have redemption through his blood, the forgiveness of sins, according to the riches of his grace.

Rom. 3:28. Therefore we conclude that a man is justified by faith without the deeds of the law.

3. Rom. 3:24, 25. Being justified freely by his grace through the redemption that is in Christ Jesus: whom God hath set forth *to be* a propitiation through faith in his blood.

Rom. 5:17-19. Much more they which receive abundance of grace and of the gift of righteousness shall reign in life by one, Jesus Christ. Therefore as by the offence of one *judgment came* upon all men to condemnation; even so by the righteousness of one *the free gift came* upon all men unto justification of life. For as by one man's disobedience many were made sinners, so by the obedience of one shall many be made righteous.

Rom. 4:6-8. Even as David also describeth the blessedness of the man, unto whom God imputeth righteousness without works, *saying,* Blessed *are* they whose iniquities are forgiven, and whose sins are covered. Blessed *is* the man to whom the Lord will not impute sin.

4. Rom. 5:1. Therefore being justified by faith, we have peace with God.

Acts 10:43. To him give all the prophets witness, that through his name whosoever believeth in him shall receive remission of sins.

Gal. 2:16; Phil. 3:9; Rom. 3:25, 26.

Q. 71. *How is justification an act of God's free grace?*

A. Although Christ by his obedience and death, did make a proper, real, and full satisfaction to God's justice in the behalf of them that are justified: yet inasmuch as God accepteth the satisfaction from a surety, which he might have demanded of them; and did provide this surety, his only Son, imputing his righteousness to them, and requiring nothing of them for their justification, but faith, which also is his gift, their justification is to them of free grace.[1]

1. See citations under Question 70.

Q. 72. *What is justifying faith?*

A. Justifying faith is a saving grace,[1] wrought in the heart of a sinner, by the Spirit and word of God;[2] whereby he, being convinced of his sin and misery, and of the disability in himself and all other creatures to recover him out of his lost condition,[3] not only assenteth to the truth of the promise of the gospel,[4] but receiveth and resteth upon Christ and his righteousness therein held forth, for pardon of sin,[5] and for the accepting and accounting of his person righteous in the sight of God for salvation.[6]

1. Heb. 10:39. But we are not of them who draw back unto perdition; but of them that believe to the saving of the soul.

2. Rom. 10:14, 17. How shall they believe in him of whom they have not heard? . . . So then faith *cometh* by hearing, and hearing by the word of God.

II Thess. 2:13. But we are bound to give thanks alway to God for you, brethren beloved of the Lord, because God hath from the beginning chosen you to salvation through sanctification of the Spirit and belief of the truth.

3. John 16:8, 9. And when he is come, he will reprove the world of sin, and of righteousness, and of judgment: of sin, because they believe not on me.

Acts 16:30. Sirs, what must I do to be saved?

Acts 2:37; Eph. 2:1; Acts 4:12; Rom. 7:9.

4. Rom. 10:8-10. But what saith it? The word is nigh thee, *even* in thy mouth, and in thy heart: that is, the word of faith, which we preach; that if thou shalt confess with thy mouth the Lord Jesus, and shalt believe in thine heart that God hath raised him from the dead, thou shalt be saved. For with the heart man believeth unto righteousness; and with the mouth confession is made unto salvation.

5. Acts 10:43. To him give all the prophets witness, that through his name whosoever believeth in him shall receive remission of sins.

Gal. 2:15, 16. We *who are* Jews by nature, and not sinners of the Gentiles, knowing that a man is not justified by the works of the law, but by the faith of Jesus Christ, even we have believed in Jesus Christ, that we might be justified by the faith of Christ, and not by the works of the law: for by the works of the law shall no flesh be justified.

Acts 16:31.

6. Phil. 3:9. And be found in him, not having mine own righteousness, which is of the law, but that which is through the faith of Christ, the righteousness which is of God by faith.

Acts 15:11. But we believe that through the grace of the Lord Jesus Christ we shall be saved, even as they.

Q. 73. *How doth faith justify a sinner in the sight of God?*

A. Faith justifies a sinner in the sight of God, not because of those other graces which do always accompany it, or of good works that are the fruits of it;[1] nor as if the grace of faith, or any act thereof, were imputed to him for justification;[2] but only as it is an instrument, by which he receiveth and applieth Christ and his righteousness.[3]

1. Gal. 3:11. But that no man is justified by the law in the sight of God, *it is* evident: for, The just shall live by faith.

Rom. 3:28. Therefore we conclude that a man is justified by faith without the deeds of the law.

2. Titus 3:5-7. Not by works of righteousness which we have done, but according to his mercy he saved us, by the washing of regeneration, and renewing of the Holy Ghost; which he shed on us abundantly through Jesus Christ our Saviour; that being justified by his grace, we should be made heirs according to the hope of eternal life.

Rom. 4:5-8.

3. Phil. 3:9. And be found in him, not having mine own righteousness, which is of the law, but that which is through the faith of Christ, the righteousness which is of God by faith.

Q. 74. *What is adoption?*

A. Adoption is an act of the free grace of God,[1] in and for his only Son Jesus Christ,[2] whereby all those that are justified are received into the number of his children,[3] have his name put upon them,[4] the Spirit of his Son given to them,[5] are under his fatherly care and dispensations,[6] admitted to all the liberties and privileges of the sons of God, made heirs of all the promises, and fellow-heirs with Christ in glory.[7]

1. I John 3:1. Behold, what manner of love the Father hath bestowed upon us, that we should be called the sons of God.

2. Eph. 1:5. Having predestinated us unto the adoption of children by Jesus Christ to himself, according to the good pleasure of his will.

   Gal. 4:4, 5. But when the fulness of the time was come, God sent forth his Son, made of a woman, made under the law, to redeem them that were under the law, that we might receive the adoption of sons.

3. John 1:12. But as many as received him, to them gave he power to become the sons of God.

4. Rev. 3:12. And *I will write upon him* my new name.
   II Cor. 6:18.

5. Gal. 4:6. And because ye are sons, God hath sent forth the Spirit of his Son into your hearts, crying, Abba, Father.

6. Ps. 103:13. Like as a father pitieth *his* children, *so* the LORD pitieth them that fear him.

   Prov. 14:26. In the fear of the LORD *is* strong confidence: and his children shall have a place of refuge.

   Matt. 6:32. For your heavenly Father knoweth that ye have need of all these things.

7. Rom. 8:17. And if children, then heirs; heirs of God, and joint-heirs with Christ; if so be that we suffer with *him,* that we may be also glorified together.

   Heb. 6:12.

Q. 75. *What is sanctification?*

A. Sanctification is a work of God's grace, whereby they, whom God hath, before the foundation of the world, chosen to be holy, are, in time, through the powerful operation of his Spirit, applying the death and resurrection of Christ unto them, renewed in their whole man after the image of God;[1] having the seeds of repentance unto life, and all other saving graces, put into their hearts,[2] and those graces so stirred up, increased and strengthened,[3] as that they more and more die unto sin, and rise into newness of life.[4]

1. Eph. 1:4. According as he hath chosen us in him before the foundation of the world, that we should be holy and without blame before him in love.

I Cor. 6:11. And such were some of you: but ye are washed, but ye are sanctified, but ye are justified in the name of the Lord Jesus, and by the Spirit of our God.

II Thess. 2:13. But we are bound to give thanks alway to God for you, brethren beloved of the Lord, because God hath from the beginning chosen you to salvation through sanctification of the Spirit and belief of the truth.

Rom. 6:4-6. Therefore we are buried with him by baptism into death: that like as Christ was raised up from the dead by the glory of the Father, even so we also should walk in newness of life. For if we have been planted together in the likeness of his death, we shall be also *in the likeness* of *his* resurrection: knowing this, that our old man is crucified with *him,* that the body of sin might be destroyed, that hence forth we should not serve sin.

Eph. 4:23, 24. And be renewed in the spirit of your mind; and that ye put on the new man, which after God is created in righteousness and true holiness.

Phil. 3:10.

2. Acts 11:18. When they heard these things, they held their peace, and glorified God, saying, Then hath God also to the Gentiles granted repentance unto life.

I John 3:9. Whosoever is born of God doth not commit sin; for his seed remaineth in him: and he cannot sin, because he is born of God.

3. Jude 20. But ye, beloved, building up yourselves on your most holy faith, praying in the Holy Ghost.

Eph. 3:16-18. That he would grant you, according to the riches of his glory, to be strengthened with might by his Spirit in the inner man; that Christ may dwell in your hearts by faith; that ye, being rooted and grounded in love, may be able to comprehend with all saints.

Col. 1:10, 11. That ye might walk worthy of the Lord unto all pleasing, being fruitful in every good work, and increasing in the knowledge of God; strengthened with all might, according to his glorious power, unto all patience and longsuffering with joyfulness.

4. Rom. 6:4, 6, 14. Even so we also should walk in newness of life. . . . knowing this, that our old man is crucified with *him,* that the body of sin might be destroyed, that henceforth we should not serve sin. . . . For sin shall not have dominion over you: for ye are not under the law, but under grace.

Q. 76. *What is repentance unto life?*

A. Repentance unto life is a saving grace,[1] wrought in the heart of a sinner by the Spirit and word of God,[2] whereby out of the sight and sense, not only of the danger,[3] but also of the filthiness and odiousness of his sins,[4] and upon the apprehension of God's mercy in Christ to such as are penitent,[5] he so grieves for, and hates his sins,[6] as that he turns from them all to God,[7] purposing and endeavoring constantly to walk with him in all the ways of new obedience.[8]

1. II Tim. 2:25. If God peradventure will give them repentance to the acknowledging of the truth.
   Luke 24:47.

2. Acts 11:18, 20, 21. When they heard these things, they held their peace, and glorified God, saying, Then hath God also to the Gentiles granted repentance unto life. . . . And some of them were men of Cyprus and Cyrene, which, when they were come to Antioch, spake unto the Grecians, preaching the Lord Jesus. And the hand of the Lord was with them: and a great number believed, and turned unto the Lord.

Zech. 12:10. I will pour upon the house of David, and upon the inhabitants of Jerusalem, the spirit of grace and of supplications: and they shall look upon me whom they have pierced, and they shall mourn for him.

Acts 2:37.

3. Ezek. 18:30, 32. Repent, and turn *yourselves* from all your transgressions; so iniquity shall not be your ruin. . . . turn *yourselves,* and live ye.

Luke 15:17, 18. How many hired servants of my father's have bread enough and to spare, and I perish with hunger! I will arise and go to my father.

Hos. 2:6, 7.

4. Ezek. 36:31. Then shall ye remember your own evil ways, and your doings that *were* not good, and shall lothe yourselves in your own sight for your iniquities and for your abominations.

Ezek. 16:61, 63. Then thou shalt remember thy ways, and be ashamed . . . that thou mayest remember, and be confounded, and never open thy mouth any more because of thy shame.

Isa. 30:22.

5. Luke 22:61, 62. And the Lord turned, and looked upon Peter. And Peter remembered the word of the Lord, how he had said unto him, Before the cock crow, thou shalt deny me thrice. And Peter went out, and wept bitterly.

Zech. 12:10.

6. II Cor. 7:11. For behold this selfsame thing, that ye sorrowed after a godly sort, what carefulness it wrought in you, yea, *what* clearing of yourselves, yea, *what* indignation, yea, *what* fear, yea, *what* vehement desire, yea, *what* zeal, yea, *what* revenge!

Acts 2:37.

7. Acts 26:18. To open their eyes, *and* to turn *them* from darkness to light, and *from* the power of Satan unto God.

Ezek. 14:6. Repent, and turn *yourselves* from your idols; and turn away your faces from all your abominations.

I Kings 8:47, 48. If they shall bethink themselves . . . and *so* return unto thee with all their heart, and with all their soul.

I Sam. 7:3.

8. Ps. 119:59, 128. I thought on my ways, and turned my feet unto thy testimonies. . . . Therefore I esteem all *thy* precepts *concerning* all *things to be* right; *and* I hate every false way.

Q. 77. *Wherein do justification and sanctification differ?*

A. Although sanctification be inseparably joined with justification,[1] yet they differ in that God, in justification, imputeth the righteousness of Christ;[2] in sanctification, his Spirit infuseth grace, and enableth to the exercise thereof;[3] in the former, sin is pardoned;[4] in the other, it is subdued;[5] the one doth equally free all believers from the revenging wrath of God, and that perfectly in this life, that they never fall into condemnation;[6] the other is neither equal in all,[7] nor in this life perfect in any,[8] but growing up to perfection.[9]

1. I Cor. 6:11. And such were some of you: but ye are washed, but ye are sanctified, but ye are justified in the name of the Lord Jesus, and by the Spirit of our God.

   I Cor. 1:30. But of him are ye in Christ Jesus who of God is made unto us wisdom, and righteousness, and sanctification, and redemption. Rom. 8:30.

2. Rom. 4:6, 8. Even as David also describeth the blessedness of the man, unto whom God imputeth righteousness without works . . . Blessed *is* the man to whom the Lord will not impute sin.

   Phil. 3:8, 9. Yea doubtless, and I count all things *but* loss for the excellency of the knowledge of Christ Jesus my Lord: for whom I have suffered the loss of all things, and do count them *but* dung, that I may win Christ, and be found in him, not having mine own righteousness, which is of the law, but that which is through the faith of Christ, the righteousness which is of God by faith.

   II Cor. 5:21.

3. Ezek. 36:27. And I will put my Spirit within you, and cause you to walk in my statutes, and ye shall keep my judgments, and do *them*.

4. Rom. 3:24, 25. Being justified freely by his grace through the redemption that is in Christ Jesus: whom God hath set forth *to be* a propitiation through faith in his blood, to declare his righteousness for the remission of sins.

5. Rom. 6:6, 14. Knowing this, that our old man is crucified with *him*, that the body of sin might be destroyed, that henceforth we should not serve sin. . . . For sin shall not have dominion over you: for ye are not under the law, but under grace.

6. Rom. 8:1, 33, 34. *There is* therefore now no condemnation to them which are in Christ Jesus . . . Who shall lay any thing to the charge of God's elect? *It is* God that justifieth. Who *is* he that condemneth?

7. I Cor. 3:1, 2. And I, brethren, could not speak unto you as unto spiritual, but as unto carnal, *even* as unto babes in Christ. I have fed you with milk, and not with meat: for hitherto ye were not able *to bear it*, neither yet now are ye able.

   Mark 4:8, 28.

8. I John 1:8, 10. If we say that we have no sin, we deceive ourselves, and the truth is not in us. . . . If we say that we have not sinned, we make him a liar, and his word is not in us.

9. II Cor. 7:1. Having therefore these promises, dearly beloved, let us cleanse ourselves from all filthiness of the flesh and spirit, perfecting holiness in the fear of God.

   Phil. 3:12-14. Not as though I had already attained, either were already perfect: but I follow after, if that I may apprehend that for which also I am apprehended of Christ Jesus. Brethren, I count not myself to have apprehended: but *this* one thing I *do*, forgetting those things which are behind, and reaching forth unto those things which are before, I press toward the mark for the prize of the high calling of God in Christ Jesus. Eph. 4:11-15.

Q. 78. *Whence ariseth the imperfection of sanctification in believers?*

A. The imperfection of sanctification in believers ariseth from the remnants of sin abiding in every part of them, and the perpetual lusting of the flesh against the Spirit; whereby they are often foiled with temptations, and fall into many sins,[1] are hindered in all their spiritual services,[2] and their best works are imperfect and defiled in the sight of God.[3]

1. Rom. 7:18, 23. For I know that in me (that is, in my flesh,) dwelleth no good thing: for to will is present with me; but *how* to perform that which is good I find not . . . but I see another law in my members, warring against the law of my mind, and bringing me into captivity to the law of sin which is in my members.

2. Gal. 5:17. For the flesh lusteth against the Spirit . . . so that ye cannot do the things that ye would.
   Heb. 12:1. Let us lay aside every weight, and the sin which doth so easily beset *us*.

3. Exod. 28:38. And it shall be upon Aaron's forehead, that Aaron may bear the iniquity of the holy things, which the children of Israel shall hallow in all their holy gifts; and it shall be always upon his forehead, that they may be accepted before the Lord.
   Rom. 7:18, 23.

Q. 79. *May not true believers, by reason of their imperfections, and the many temptations and sins they are overtaken with, fall away from the state of grace?*

A. True believers, by reason of the unchangeable love of God,[1] and his decree and covenant to give them perseverence,[2] their inseparable union with Christ,[3] his continual intercession for them,[4] and the Spirit and seed of God abiding in them,[5] can neither totally nor finally fall away from the state of grace, but are kept by the power of God through faith unto salvation.[6]

1. Jer. 31:3. I have loved thee with an everlasting love.
   John 13:1.

2. I Cor. 1:8. Who shall also confirm you unto the end, *that ye may be* blameless in the day of our Lord Jesus Christ.
   Heb. 6:17. Wherein God, willing more abundantly to shew unto the heirs of promise the immutability of his counsel, confirmed *it* by an oath.
   Heb. 13:20, 21; Isa. 54:10.

3. I Cor. 12:27. Now ye are the body of Christ, and members in particular.
   Compare with Rom. 8:35-39.

4. Heb. 7:25. Wherefore he is able also to save them to the uttermost that come unto God by him, seeing he ever liveth to make intercession for them.
   Luke 22:32.

5. I John 3:9. Whosoever is born of God doth not commit sin; for his seed remaineth in him: and he cannot sin, because he is born of God.

I John 2:27. But the anointing which ye have received of him abideth in you, and ye need not that any man teach you: but as the same anointing teacheth you of all things, and is truth, and is no lie, and even as it hath taught you, ye shall abide in him.

6. Jer. 32:40. And I will make an everlasting covenant with them, that I will not turn away from them, to do them good; but I will put my fear in their hearts, that they shall not depart from me.

John 10:28. And I give unto them eternal life; and they shall never perish, neither shall any *man* pluck them out of my hand.

I Peter 1:5; Phil. 1:6.

Q. 80. *Can true believers be infallibly assured that they are in the estate of grace, and that they shall persevere therein unto salvation?*

A. Such as truly believe in Christ, and endeavor to walk in all good conscience before him, may, without extraordinary revelation, by faith grounded upon the truth of God's promises, and by the Spirit enabling them to discern in themselves those graces to which the promises of life are made, and bearing witness with their spirits that they are the children of God, be infallibly assured that they are in the estate of grace, and shall persevere therein unto salvation.[1]

1. I John 2:3. And hereby we do know that we know him, if we keep his commandments.

I Cor. 2:12. Now we have received, not the spirit of the world, but the Spirit which is of God; that we might know the things that are freely given to us of God.

I John 4:13, 16. Hereby know we that we dwell in him, and he in us, because he hath given us of his Spirit. . . . And we have known and believed the love that God hath to us. God is love; and he that dwelleth in love dwelleth in God, and God in him.

I John 3:14, 18, 19, 21, 24. We know that we have passed from death unto life, because we love the brethren. . . . let us not love in word, neither in tongue; but in deed and in truth. And hereby we know that we are of the truth, and shall assure our hearts before him. . . . Beloved, if our heart condemn us not, *then* have we confidence toward God. . . . And he that keepeth his commandments, dwelleth in him, and he in him. And hereby we know that he abideth in us, by the Spirit which he hath given us.

Rom. 8:16. The Spirit itself beareth witness with our spirit, that we are the children of God.

I John 5:13. These things have I written unto you that believe on the name of the Son of God; that ye may know that ye have eternal life.

Q. 81. *Are all true believers at all times assured of their present being in the estate of grace, and that they shall be saved?*

A. Assurance of grace and salvation not being of the essence of faith, true believers may wait long before they obtain it;[1] and, after the enjoyment thereof, may have it weakened and intermitted, through manifold distempers, sins, temptations, and desertions;[2] yet are they never left without such a presence and support of the Spirit of God, as keeps them from sinking into utter despair.[3]

1. Isa. 50:10. Who *is* among you that feareth the LORD, that obeyeth the voice of his servant, that walketh *in* darkness, and hath no light? let him trust in the name of the LORD, and stay upon his God.
   Ps. 88.
2. Ps. 31:22. For I said in my haste, I am cut off from before thine eyes.
   Ps. 77:1-12; Ps. 30:6, 7; Ps. 51:8, 12.
3. Job 13:15. Though he slay me, yet will I trust in him.
   Ps. 73:13-15, 23. Verily I have cleansed my heart *in* vain, and washed my hands in innocency. For all the day long have I been plagued, and chastened every morning. If I say, I will speak thus; behold, I should offend *against* the generation of thy children. . . . Nevertheless I *am* continually with thee: thou hast holden *me* by my right hand.
   I John 3:9; Isa. 54:7-11.

Q. 82. *What is the communion in glory which the members of the invisible church have with Christ?*

A. The communion in glory which the members of the invisible church have with Christ, is in this life,[1] immediately after death,[2] and at last perfected at the resurrection and day of judgment.[3]

1. II Cor. 3:18. But we all, with open face beholding as in a glass the glory of the Lord, are changed into the same image from glory to glory *even* as by the Spirit of the Lord.
2. Luke 23:43. And Jesus said unto him, Verily I say unto thee, To day shalt thou be with me in paradise.
3. I John 3:2. Beloved, now are we the sons of God, and it doth not yet appear what we shall be: but we know that, when he shall appear, we shall be like him; for we shall see him as he is.
   I Thess. 4:17; Rev. 22:3-5.

Q. 83. *What is the communion in glory with Christ, which the members of the invisible church enjoy in this life?*

A. The members of the invisible church have communicated to them, in this life, the first-fruits of glory with Christ, as they are members of him their head, and so in him are interested in that glory which he is fully possessed of;[1] and as an earnest thereof, enjoy the sense of God's love,[2] peace of conscience, joy in the Holy Ghost, and hope of glory.[3] As, on the contrary, the sense of God's revenging wrath, horror of conscience, and a fearful expectation of judgment, are to the wicked the beginning of the torment which they shall endure after death.[4]

1. Eph. 2:4-6. God . . . even when we were dead in sins, hath quickened us together with Christ . . . and hath raised *us* up together, and made *us* sit together in heavenly *places* in Christ Jesus.

2. Rom. 5:5. And hope maketh not ashamed; because the love of God is shed abroad in our hearts by the Holy Ghost which is given unto us.

II Cor. 1:22. Who hath also sealed us, and given the earnest of the Spirit in our hearts.

3. Rom. 5:1, 2. Therefore being justified by faith, we have peace with God through our Lord Jesus Christ: by whom also we have access by faith into this grace wherein we stand, and rejoice in hope of the glory of God.

Rom. 14:17. For the kingdom of God is not meat and drink; but righteousness, and peace, and joy in the Holy Ghost.

4. Gen. 4:13. And Cain said unto the Lord, My punishment *is* greater than I can bear.

Matt. 27:3-5. Then Judas, which had betrayed him, when he saw that he was condemned, repented himself, and brought again the thirty pieces of silver to the chief priests and elders, saying, I have sinned in that I have betrayed the innocent blood. And they said, What *is that* to us? see thou *to that*. And he cast down the pieces of silver in the temple, and departed, and went and hanged himself.

Heb. 10:27. But a certain fearful looking for of judgment and fiery indignation, which shall devour the adversaries.

Mark 9:44. Where their worm dieth not, and the fire is not quenched. Rom. 2:9.

Q. 84. *Shall all men die?*

A. Death being threatened as the wages of sin,[1] it is appointed unto all men once to die;[2] for that all have sinned.[3]

1. Rom. 6:23. For the wages of sin *is* death.

2. Heb. 9:27. And as it is appointed unto men once to die.

3. Rom. 5:12. So death passed upon all men, for that all have sinned.

Q. 85. *Death being the wages of sin, why are not the righteous delivered from death, seeing all their sins are forgiven in Christ?*

A. The righteous shall be delivered from death itself at the last day, and even in death are delivered from the sting and curse of it;[1] so that although they die, yet it is out of God's love,[2] to free them perfectly from sin and misery,[3] and to make them capable of further communion with Christ in glory, which they then enter upon.[4]

1. I Cor. 15:26, 55-57. The last enemy *that* shall be destroyed *is* death. . . . O death, where *is* thy sting? O grave, where *is* thy victory? The sting of death *is* sin; and the strength of sin *is* the law. But thanks *be* to God, which giveth us the victory through our Lord Jesus Christ.

Heb. 2:15.

2. Isa. 57:1, 2. The righteous is taken away from the evil *to come*. He shall enter into peace: they shall rest in their beds.

II Kings 22:20. Behold therefore, I will gather thee unto thy fathers, and thou shalt be gathered into thy grave in peace; and thine eyes shall not see all the evil which I will bring upon this place.

3. Luke 16:25. But Abraham said, Son, remember that thou in thy lifetime receivedst thy good things, and likewise Lazarus evil things: but now he is comforted, and thou art tormented.

II Cor. 5:1-8.

4. Luke 23:43. And Jesus said unto him, Verily I say unto thee, To day shalt thou be with me in paradise.

Phil. 1:23. For I am in a strait betwixt two, having a desire to depart, and to be with Christ; which is far better.

Q. 86. *What is the communion in glory with Christ, which the members of the invisible church enjoy immediately after death?*

A. The communion in glory with Christ, which the members of the invisible church enjoy immediately after death, is in that their souls are then made perfect in holiness, and received into the highest heavens, where they behold the face of God in light and glory;[1] waiting for the full redemption of their bodies,[2] which even in death continue united to Christ,[3] and rest in their graves as in their beds, till at the last day they be again united to their souls.[4] Whereas the souls of the wicked are at their death cast into hell, where they remain in torments and utter darkness; and their bodies kept in their graves, as in their prisons, until the resurrection and judgment of the great day.[5]

1. Luke 16:23. And in hell he lift up his eyes, being in torments, and seeth Abraham afar off, and Lazarus in his bosom.

Luke 23:43. And Jesus said unto him, Verily I say unto thee, To day shalt thou be with me in paradise.

Phil. 1:23; II Cor. 5:6-8.

2. Rom. 8:23. Waiting for the adoption, *to wit*, the redemption of our body. Ps. 16:9. My flesh also shall rest in hope.

3. I Thess. 4:14. For if we believe that Jesus died and rose again, even so them also which sleep in Jesus will God bring with him.

4. Rom. 8:23. And not only *they*, but ourselves also, which have the first fruits of the Spirit, even we ourselves groan within ourselves, waiting for the adoption, *to wit*, the redemption of our body.

5. Luke 16:23, 24. And in hell he lift up his eyes, being in torments, and seeth Abraham afar off, and Lazarus in his bosom. And he cried and said, Father Abraham . . . send Lazarus, that he may dip the tip of his finger in water, and cool my tongue; for I am tormented in this flame. Acts 1:25. From which Judas by transgression fell, that he might go to his own place.

Jude 6. He hath reserved in everlasting chains under darkness unto the judgment of the great day.

Q. 87. *What are we to believe concerning the resurrection?*

A. We are to believe that, at the last day, there shall be a general resurrection of the dead, both of the just and unjust;[1] when they that are then found alive shall in a moment be changed; and the self-same bodies of the dead which are laid in the grave, being then again united to their souls forever, shall be raised up by the power of Christ.[2] The bodies of the just, by the Spirit of Christ, and by virtue of his resurrection as their head, shall be raised in power, spiritual, and incorruptible, and made like to his glorious body:[3] and the bodies of the wicked shall be raised up in dishonor by him as an offended judge.[4]

1. Acts 24:15. There shall be a resurrection of the dead, both of the just and unjust.

2. I Cor. 15:51-53. Behold, I shew you a mystery; We shall not all sleep, but we shall all be changed, in a moment, in the twinkling of an eye, at the last trump: for the trumpet shall sound, and the dead shall be raised incorruptible, and we shall be changed. For this corruptible must put on incorruption, and this mortal *must* put on immortality.

I Thess. 4:15-17. For this we say unto you by the word of the Lord, that we which are alive *and* remain unto the coming of the Lord shall not prevent them which are asleep. For the Lord himself shall descend from heaven with a shout, with the voice of the archangel, and with the trump of God: and the dead in Christ shall rise first: then we which are alive *and* remain shall be caught up together with them in the clouds, to meet the Lord in the air: and so shall we ever be with the Lord.

John 5:28, 29.

3. I Cor. 15:21-23, 42-44. For since by man *came* death, by man *came* also the resurrection of the dead. For as in Adam all die, even so in Christ shall all be made alive. [It is evidently the scope of the apostle's argument in this passage, to prove, that as all the natural seed of Adam, their covenant-head, were subjected to death by his offence; so all the spiritual seed of Christ, their new covenant-head, shall be raised from death, to an immortal life of glory and blessedness, by virtue of his resurrection. It is therefore a perversion of the Scripture, to adduce this text as a proof of universal redemption.] But every man in his own order: Christ the firstfruits; afterward they that are Christ's at his coming. . . . So also *is* the resurrection of the dead. It is sown in corruption; it is raised in incorruption: it is sown in dishonour; it is raised in glory: it is sown in weakness; it is raised in power: it is sown a natural body; it is raised a spiritual body.

Phil. 3:21. Who shall change our vile body, that it may be fashioned like unto his glorious body.

4. John 5:28, 29. Marvel not at this: for the hour is coming, in the which all that are in the graves shall hear his voice, and shall come forth; they that have done good, unto the resurrection of life; and they that have done evil, unto the resurrection of damnation.

Dan. 12:2. And many of them that sleep in the dust of the earth shall awake, some to everlasting life, and some to shame *and* everlasting contempt.

Matt. 25:33.

Q. 88. *What shall immediately follow after the resurrection?*

A. Immediately after the resurrection shall follow the general and final judgment of angels and men,[1] the day and hour whereof no man knoweth, that all may watch and pray, and be ever ready for the coming of the Lord.[2]

1. II Peter 2:4. For if God spared not the angels that sinned, but cast *them* down to hell, and delivered *them* into chains of darkness, to be reserved unto judgment.

Rev. 20:11-13. And I saw a great white throne, and him that sat on it, from whose face the earth and the heaven fled away; and there was found no place for them. And I saw the dead, small and great, stand before God; and the books were opened: and another book was opened, which is *the book* of life: and the dead were judged out of those things which were written in the books, according to their works. And the sea gave up the dead which were in it; and death and hell delivered up the dead which were in them: and they were judged every man according to their works.

2. Matt. 24:36, 42, 44. But of that day and hour knoweth no *man,* no, not the angels of heaven, but my Father only. . . . Watch therefore: for ye know not what hour your Lord doth come. . . . Therefore be ye also ready: for in such an hour as ye think not the Son of man cometh.

Luke 21:35, 36.

Q. 89. *What shall be done to the wicked at the day of judgment?*

A. At the day of judgment, the wicked shall be set on Christ's left hand,[1] and upon clear evidence, and full conviction of their own consciences,[2] shall have the fearful but just sentence of condemnation pronounced against them;[3] and thereupon shall be cast out from the favorable presence of God, and the glorious fellowship with Christ, his saints, and all his holy angels, into hell, to be punished with unspeakable torments both of body and soul, with the devil and his angels forever.[4]

1. Matt. 25:33. And he shall set the sheep on his right hand, but the goats on the left.

2. Rom. 2:15, 16. Which shew the work of the law written in their hearts, their conscience also bearing witness, and *their* thoughts the mean while

accusing or else excusing one another; in the day when God shall judge the secrets of men by Jesus Christ according to my gospel.
(See the context.)

3. Matt. 25:41, 42. Then shall he say also unto them on the left hand, Depart from me, ye cursed, into everlasting fire, prepared for the devil and his angels: for I was an hungred, and ye gave me no meat.

4. Matt. 25:46. And these shall go away into everlasting punishment.
II Thess. 1:8, 9. In flaming fire taking vengeance on them that know not God, and that obey not the gospel of our Lord Jesus Christ: who shall be punished with everlasting destruction from the presence of the Lord, and from the glory of his power.
Luke 16:26; Mark 9:43, 44; Mark 14:21.

Q. 90. *What shall be done to the righteous at the day of judgment?*

A. At the day of judgment, the righteous, being caught up to Christ in the clouds,[1] shall be set on his right hand, and, there openly acknowledged and acquitted,[2] shall join with him in the judging of reprobate angels and men;[3] and shall be received into heaven,[4] where they shall be fully and forever freed from all sin and misery;[5] filled with inconceivable joy;[6] made perfectly holy and happy both in body and soul, in the company of innumerable saints and angels,[7] but especially in the immediate vision and fruition of God the Father, of our Lord Jesus Christ, and of the Holy Spirit, to all eternity.[8] And this is the perfect and full communion, which the members of the invisible church shall enjoy with Christ in glory, at the resurrection and day of judgment.

1. I Thess. 4:17. Then we which are alive *and* remain shall be caught up together with them in the clouds, to meet the Lord in the air.

2. Matt. 25:33. And he shall set the sheep on his right hand.
Matt. 10:32. Whosoever therefore shall confess me before men, him will I confess also before my Father which is in heaven.

3. I Cor. 6:2, 3. Do ye not know that the saints shall judge the world? . . . Know ye not that we shall judge angels?

4. Matt. 25:34, 46. Then shall the King say unto them on his right hand, Come, ye blessed of my Father, inherit the kingdom prepared for you from the foundation of the world . . . but the righteous into life eternal.

5. Eph. 5:27. That he might present it to himself a glorious church, not having spot, or wrinkle.
Rev. 7:17. And God shall wipe away all tears from their eyes.

6. Ps. 16:11. Thou wilt shew me the path of life: in thy presence *is* fulness of joy; at thy right hand *there are* pleasures for evermore.
I Cor. 2:9.

7. Heb. 12:22, 23. But ye are come unto mount Sion, and unto the city of the living God, the heavenly Jerusalem, and to an innumerable com-

pany of angels, to the general assembly and church of the firstborn, which are written in heaven, and to God the Judge of all, and to the spirits of just men made perfect.

8. I John 3:2. Beloved, now are we the sons of God, and it doth not yet appear what we shall be: but we know that, when he shall appear, we shall be like him; for we shall see him as he is.

I Cor. 13:12.

I Thess. 4:17, 18. So shall we ever be with the Lord. Wherefore comfort one another with these words.

Rev. 22:3-5.

Having Seen What the Scriptures Principally Teach Us to Believe Concerning God, It Follows to Consider What They Require as the Duty of Man

Q. 91. *What is the duty which God requireth of man?*

A. The duty which God requireth of man is obedience to his revealed will.[1]

1. Deut. 29:29. The secret *things belong* unto the LORD our God: but those *things which are* revealed *belong* unto us and to our children for ever, that *we* may do all the words of this law.

Micah 6:8; I Sam. 15:22.

Q. 92. *What did God at first reveal unto man as the rule of his obedience?*

A. The rule of obedience revealed to Adam in the estate of innocence, and to all mankind in him, besides a special command, not to eat of the fruit of the tree of the knowledge of good and evil, was the moral law.[1]

1. Rom. 10:5. For Moses describeth the righteousness which is of the law, That the man which doeth those things shall live by them.

Rom. 2:14, 15. When the Gentiles, which have not the law, do by nature the things contained in the law, these, having not the law, are a law unto themselves: which shew the work of the law written in their hearts.

Gen. 2:17.

Q. 93. *What is the moral law?*

A. The moral law is the declaration of the will of God to mankind, directing and binding everyone to personal, perfect, and perpetual conformity and obedience thereunto, in the frame and disposition of the whole man, soul and body, and in performance of all those duties of holiness and righteousness which he oweth to God and man:[1] promising life upon the fulfilling, and threatening death upon the breach of it.[2]

1. James 2:10. For whosoever shall keep the whole law, and yet offend in one *point*, he is guilty of all.

   Deut. 5:1, 31, 33; Luke 10:26, 27; I Thess. 5:23.
2. Rom. 10:5. The man which doeth those things shall live by them.

   Gal. 3:10. Cursed *is* every one that continueth not in all things which are written in the book of the law to do them.

Q. 94. *Is there any use of the moral law to man since the fall?*

A. Although no man since the fall can attain to righteousness and life by the moral law,[1] yet there is great use thereof, as well common to all men, as peculiar either to the unregenerate, or the regenerate.[2]

1. Rom. 8:3. For what the law could not do, in that it was weak through the flesh, God sending his own Son in the likeness of sinful flesh, and for sin, condemned sin in the flesh.

   Gal. 2:16. For by the works of the law shall no flesh be justified.
2. I Tim. 1:8. But we know that the law *is* good, if a man use it lawfully.

   Gal. 3:19, 24. Wherefore then *serveth* the law? It was added because of transgressions, till the seed should come to whom the promise was made; *and it was* ordained by angels in the hand of a mediator. . . . Wherefore the law was our schoolmaster *to bring us* unto Christ, that we might be justified by faith.

Q. 95. *Of what use is the moral law to all men?*

A. The moral law is of use to all men, to inform them of the holy nature and will of God,[1] and of their duty binding them to walk accordingly;[2] to convince them of their disability to keep it, and of the sinful pollution of their nature, hearts, and lives,[3] to humble them in the sense of their sin and misery,[4] and thereby help them to a clearer sight of the need they have of Christ,[5] and of the perfection of his obedience.

1. Rom. 7:12. Wherefore the law *is* holy, and the commandment holy, and just, and good.
2. Micah 6:8. What doth the Lord require of thee, but to do justly, and to love mercy, and to walk humbly with thy God?

   Luke 10:26, 28, 37. He said unto him, What is written in the law? how readest thou? . . . And he said unto him, Thou hast answered right: this do, and thou shalt live. . . . And he said, He that shewed mercy on him. Then said Jesus unto him, Go, and do thou likewise.
3. Ps. 19:11, 12. Moreover by them is thy servant warned . . . who can understand *his* errors?

   Rom. 3:20. For by the law *is* the knowledge of sin.

   Rom. 7:7. I had not known sin, but by the law: for I had not known lust, except the law had said, Thou shalt not covet.

4. Rom. 3:9, 23. What then? are we better *than they?* No, in no wise: for we have before proved both Jews and Gentiles, that they are all under sin . . . for all have sinned, and come short of the glory of God.

Rom. 7:9, 13. When the commandment came, sin revived, and I died. . . . that sin by the commandment might become exceeding sinful.

5. Gal. 3:21, 22. *Is* the law then against the promises of God? God forbid: for if there had been a law given which could have given life, verily righteousness should have been by the law. But the scripture hath concluded all under sin, that the promise by faith of Jesus Christ might be given to them that believe.

Q. 96. *What particular use is there of the moral law to unregenerate men?*

A. The moral law is of use to unregenerate men, to awaken their consciences to flee from the wrath to come,[1] and to drive them to Christ;[2] or, upon their continuance in the estate and way of sin, to leave them inexcusable,[3] and under the curse thereof.[4]

1. Rom. 7:9. For I was alive without the law once: but when the commandment came, sin revived, and I died.
I Tim. 1:9, 10.

2. Gal. 3:24. Wherefore the law was our schoolmaster *to bring us* unto Christ, that we might be justified by faith.

3. Rom. 1:20. So that they are without excuse. (Compare Rom. 2:15.)

4. Gal. 3:10. For as many as are of the works of the law are under the curse: for it is written, Cursed *is* every one that continueth not in all things which are written in the book of the law to do them.

Q. 97. *What special use is there of the moral law to the regenerate?*

A. Although they that are regenerate and believe in Christ be delivered from the moral law as a covenant of works, so as thereby they are neither justified nor condemned: yet, besides the general uses thereof common to them with all men, it is of special use to show them how much they are bound to Christ for his fulfilling it, and enduring the curse thereof, in their stead and for their good;[1] and thereby to provoke them to more thankfulness, and to express the same in their greater care to conform themselves thereunto as the rule of their obedience.[2]

1. Rom. 7:4, 6. Wherefore, my brethren, ye also are become dead to the law by the body of Christ; that ye should be married to another, *even* to him who is raised from the dead, that we should bring forth fruit unto God. . . . But now we are delivered from the law, that being dead wherein we were held; that we should serve in newness of spirit, and not *in* the oldness of the letter.
Rom. 6:14. For ye are not under the law, but under grace.

Rom. 3:20. Therefore by the deeds of the law there shall no flesh be justified in his sight.

Rom. 8:1, 34. *There is* therefore now no condemnation to them which are in Christ Jesus . . . Who *is* he that condemneth?

Gal. 3:13, 14. Christ hath redeemed us from the curse of the law, being made a curse for us . . . that we might receive the promise of the Spirit through faith.

Rom. 8:3, 4. For what the law could not do, in that it was weak through the flesh, God sending his own Son in the likeness of sinful flesh, and for sin, condemned sin in the flesh: that the righteousness of the law might be fulfilled in us.

II Cor. 5:21.

2. Col. 1:12-14. Giving thanks unto the Father, which hath made us meet to be partakers of the inheritance of the saints in light: who hath delivered us from the power of darkness, and hath translated *us* into the kingdom of his dear Son: in whom we have redemption through his blood, *even* the forgiveness of sins.

Rom. 7:22. For I delight in the law of God after the inward man.

Titus 2:11-14.

Q. 98. *Wherein is the moral law summarily comprehended?*

A. The moral law is summarily comprehended in the ten commandments,[1] which were delivered by the voice of God upon mount Sinai, and written by him on two tables of stone;[2] and are recorded in the twentieth chapter of Exodus; the first four commandments containing our duty to God, and the other six our duty to man.

1. Matt. 19:17-19. And he said unto him, Why callest thou me good? *there is* none good but one, *that is,* God: but if thou wilt enter into life, keep the commandments. He saith unto him, Which? Jesus said, Thou shalt do no murder, Thou shalt not commit adultery, Thou shalt not steal, Thou shalt not bear false witness. Honour thy father and *thy* mother: and, Thou shalt love thy neighbour as thyself.

2. Deut. 10:4. And he wrote on the tables, according to the first writing, the ten commandments.

Exod. 34:1-4.

Q. 99. *What rules are to be observed for the right understanding of the ten commandments?*

A. For the right understanding of the ten commandments, these rules are to be observed:

1. That the law is perfect, and bindeth everyone to full conformity in the whole man unto the righteousness thereof, and unto entire obedience forever; so as to require the utmost perfection of every duty, and to forbid the least degree of every sin.[1]

1. Ps. 19:7. The law of the LORD *is* perfect.

James 2:10. For whosoever shall keep the whole law, and yet offend in one *point*, he is guilty of all.

Matt. 5:22, 28, 37, 44. Whosoever shall say [to his brother], Thou fool, shall be in danger of hell fire. . . . whosoever looketh on a woman to lust after her hath committed adultery with her already in his heart. . . . But let your communication be, Yea, yea; Nay, nay: for whatsoever is more than these cometh of evil. . . . But I say unto you, Love your enemies, bless them that curse you, do good to them that hate you, and pray for them which despitefully use you, and persecute you.

2. That it is spiritual, and so reacheth the understanding, will, affections, and all other powers of the soul; as well as words, works, and gestures.[1]

1. Rom. 7:14. For we know that the law is spiritual.

Deut. 6:5. Thou shalt love the LORD thy God with all thine heart, and with all thy soul, and with all thy might.

Matt. 22:37-39; Matt. 12:36, 37.

See citations under Rule 1 above.

3. That one and the same thing, in divers respects, is required or forbidden in several commandments.[1]

1. Col. 3:5. Mortify therefore your members which are upon the earth; fornication, uncleanness, inordinate affection, evil concupiscence, and covetousness, which is idolatry.

I Tim. 6:10. For the love of money is the root of all evil: which while some coveted after, they have erred from the faith, and pierced themselves through with many sorrows.

Exod. 20:3-5; Amos 8:5.

4. That as, where a duty is commanded, the contrary sin is forbidden;[1] and where a sin is forbidden, the contrary duty is commanded:[2] so, where a promise is annexed, the contrary threatening is included;[3] and where a threatening is annexed, the contrary promise is included.[4]

1. Isa. 58:13. If thou turn away thy foot from the sabbath, *from* doing thy pleasure on my holy day; and call the sabbath a delight, the holy of the Lord, honourable; and shalt honour him, not doing thine own ways, nor finding thine own pleasure, nor speaking *thine own* words.

Matt. 15:4-6. For God commanded, saying, Honour thy father and mother: and, He that curseth father or mother, let him die the death. But ye say, Whosoever shall say to *his* father or *his* mother, *It is* a gift, by whatsoever thou mightest be profited by me; and honour not his father or his mother, *he shall be free.* Thus have ye made the commandment of God of none effect by your tradition.

Deut. 6:13. Compared with Matt. 4:9, 10.

2. Eph. 4:28. Let him that stole steal no more; but rather let him labour.

3. Exod. 20:12. Honour thy father and thy mother: that thy days may be long upon the land which the LORD thy God giveth thee. Compare with Prov. 30:17: The eye *that* mocketh at *his* father, and despiseth to obey

his mother, the ravens of the valley shall pick it out, and the young eagles shall eat it.

4. Jer. 18:7, 8. *At what* instant I shall speak concerning a nation, and concerning a kingdom, to pluck up, and to pull down, and to destroy *it;* if that nation, against whom I have pronounced, turn from their evil, I will repent of the evil that I thought to do unto them.

Exod. 20:7. Thou shalt not take the name of the Lord thy God in vain; for the Lord will not hold him guiltless that taketh his name in vain. Compare with Ps. 15:1, 4, 5; Ps. 24:4, 5.

5. That what God forbids, is at no time to be done;[1] what he commands is always our duty;[2] and yet every particular duty is not to be done at all times.[3]

1. Rom. 3:8. And not *rather,* (as we be slanderously reported, and as some affirm that we say,) Let us do evil, that good may come? whose damnation is just.
Heb. 11:25.

2. Deut. 4:9. Only take heed to thyself, and keep thy soul diligently, lest thou forget the things which thine eyes have seen, and lest they depart from thine heart all the days of thy life: but teach them thy sons, and thy sons' sons.

3. Matt. 12:7. But if ye had known what *this* meaneth, I will have mercy, and not sacrifice, ye would not have condemned the guiltless.
Mark 14:7.

6. That, under one sin or duty, all of the same kind are forbidden or commanded; together with all the causes, means, occasions, and appearances thereof, and provocations thereunto.[1]

1. I Thess. 5:22. Abstain from all appearance of evil.
Gal. 5:26. Let us not be desirous of vain glory, provoking one another, envying one another.
Heb. 10:24. Let us consider one another to provoke unto love and to good works.
Col. 3:21.

7. That what is forbidden or commanded to ourselves, we are bound, according to our places, to endeavor that it may be avoided or performed by others, according to the duty of their places.[1]

1. Exod. 20:10. But the seventh day *is* the sabbath of the Lord thy God: *in it* thou shalt not do any work, thou, nor thy son, nor thy daughter, thy manservant, nor thy maidservant, nor thy cattle, nor thy stranger that *is* within thy gates.
Deut. 6:6, 7. And these words, which I command thee this day, shall be in thine heart: and thou shalt teach them diligently unto thy children, and shalt talk of them when thou sittest in thine house, and when thou walkest by the way, and when thou liest down, and when thou risest up.
Josh. 24:15.

8. That in what is commanded to others, we are bound, according to our places and callings, to be helpful to them;[1] and

to take heed of partaking with others in what is forbidden them.[2]

1. Heb. 10:24. And let us consider one another to provoke unto love and to good works.
2. I Tim. 5:22. Lay hands suddenly on no man, neither be partaker of other men's sins: keep thyself pure.
   Eph. 5:11. And have no fellowship with the unfruitful works of darkness, but rather reprove *them*.

Q. 100. *What special things are we to consider in the ten commandments?*

A. We are to consider in the ten commandments: the preface, the substance of the commandments themselves, and the several reasons annexed to some of them the more to enforce them.

Q. 101. *What is the preface to the ten commandments?*

A. The preface to the ten commandments is contained in these words: *I am the Lord thy God, which have brought thee out of the land of Egypt, out of the house of bondage.*[1] Wherein God manifesteth his sovereignty, as being Jehovah, the eternal, immutable, and almighty God; having his being in and of himself, and giving being to all his words and works; and that he is a God in covenant, as with Israel of old, so with all his people; who as he brought them out of their bondage in Egypt, so he delivered us from our spiritual thralldom; and that therefore we are bound to take him for our God alone, and to keep all his commandments.

1. Exod. 20:2.

Q. 102. *What is the sum of the four commandments which contain our duty to God?*

A. The sum of the four commandments containing our duty to God is, to love the Lord our God with all our heart, and with all our soul, and with all our strength, and with all our mind.[1]

1. Luke 10:27. And he answering said, Thou shalt love the Lord thy God with all thy heart, and with all thy soul, and with all thy strength, and with all thy mind; and thy neighbour as thyself.

Q. 103. *Which is the first commandment?*

A. The first commandment is, *Thou shalt have no other gods before me.*[1]

1. Exod. 20:3.

Q. 104. *What are the duties required in the first commandment?*

A. The duties required in the first commandment[1] are: the knowing and acknowledging of God to be the only true God, and our God;[2] and to worship and glorify him accordingly;[3] by thinking,[4] meditating,[5] remembering,[6] highly esteeming,[7] honoring,[8] adoring,[9] choosing,[10] loving,[11] desiring,[12] fearing of him;[13] believing him;[14] trusting,[15] hoping,[16] delighting,[17] rejoicing in him;[18] being zealous for him;[19] calling upon him, giving all praise and thanks,[20] and yielding all obedience and submission to him with the whole man;[21] being careful in all things to please him,[22] and sorrowful when in anything he is offended;[23] and walking humbly with him.[24]

1. The exposition of the Ten Commandments contained in the answers to Questions 104 to 148 are deduced from the commandments themselves, and from the "Rules" set forth in Question 99. Texts under the specifications are given in order to show that the specifications are in accord with the general teaching of the Scriptures.

2. I Chron. 28:9. And thou, Solomon my son, know thou the God of thy father, and serve him with a perfect heart, and with a willing mind.

   Deut. 26:17. Thou hast avouched the LORD this day to be thy God.

   Isa. 43:10. Ye *are* my witnesses, saith the LORD, and my servant whom I have chosen: that ye may know and believe me, and understand that I *am* he: before me there was no God formed, neither shall there be after me.

   Jer. 14:22.

3. Ps. 95:6, 7. O come, let us worship and bow down: let us kneel before the LORD our maker. For he *is* our God; and we *are* the people of his pasture, and the sheep of his hand.

   Matt. 4:10. Thou shalt worship the Lord thy God, and him only shalt thou serve.

   Ps. 29:2. Give unto the LORD the glory due unto his name; worship the LORD in the beauty of holiness.

4. Mal. 3:16. Then they that feared the LORD spake often one to another: and the LORD hearkened, and heard *it;* and a book of remembrance was written before him for them that feared the LORD, and that thought upon his name.

5. Ps. 63:6. When I remember thee upon my bed, *and* meditate on thee in the *night* watches.

6. Eccl. 12:1. Remember now thy Creator in the days of thy youth.

7. Ps. 18:1, 2. I will love thee, O LORD, my strength. The LORD *is* my rock, and my fortress, and my deliverer; my God, my strength, in whom I will trust; my buckler, and the horn of my salvation, *and* my high tower.

8. Mal. 1:6. If then I *be* a father, where *is* mine honour?

9. Isa. 45:23. I have sworn by myself, the word is gone out of my mouth *in* righteousness, and shall not return, That unto me every knee shall bow, every tongue shall swear.

   Ps. 96.

10. Josh. 24:22. Ye *are* witnesses against yourselves that ye have chosen you the Lord, to serve him.

11. Deut. 6:5. And thou shalt love the LORD thy God.

12. Ps. 73:25. Whom have I in heaven *but thee?* and *there is* none upon earth *that* I desire beside thee.

13. Isa. 8:13. Sanctify the LORD of hosts himself; and *let* him *be* your fear, and *let* him *be* your dread.

14. Exod. 14:31. And the people feared the LORD, and believed the LORD.
Rom. 10:11; Acts 10:43.

15. Isa. 26:4. Trust ye in the LORD for ever.
Ps. 40:4.

16. Ps. 130:7. Let Israel hope in the LORD.

17. Ps. 37:4. Delight thyself also in the LORD.

18. Ps. 32:11. Be glad in the LORD, and rejoice, ye righteous: and shout for joy, all *ye that are* upright in heart.

19. Rom. 12:11. Fervent in spirit; serving the Lord.
Rev. 3:19. Be zealous therefore.
Num. 25:11.

20. Phil. 4:6. But in every thing by prayer and supplication with thanksgiving let your requests be made known unto God.

21. Jer. 7:23. But this thing commanded I them, saying, Obey my voice, and I will be your God, and ye shall be my people: and walk ye in all the ways that I have commanded you.
James 4:7. Submit yourselves therefore to God.
Rom. 12:1.

22. I John 3:22. And whatsoever we ask, we receive of him, because we keep his commandments, and do those things that are pleasing in his sight.

23. Neh. 13:8. And it grieved me sore.
Ps. 73:21. Thus my heart was grieved.
Ps. 119:136. Rivers of waters run down mine eyes, because they keep not thy law.
Jer. 31:18, 19.

24. Micah 6:8. And to walk humbly with thy God.

Q. 105. *What are the sins forbidden in the first commandment?*

A. The sins forbidden in the first commandment are: atheism, in denying or not having a God;[1] idolatry, in having or worshipping more gods than one, or any with, or instead of the true God;[2] the not having and vouching him for God, and our God;[3] the omission or neglect of anything due to him, required in this commandment;[4] ignorance,[5] forgetfulness,[6] misapprehensions, false opinions,[7] unworthy and wicked thoughts of him;[8] bold and curious searchings into his secrets;[9] all profaneness,[10] hatred of God,[11] self-love,[12] self-seeking,[13] and all other inordinate and immoderate setting of our mind, will, or affections upon other things, and taking them off from him in whole or in part;[14] vain credulity,[15] unbelief,[16] heresy,[17] misbelief,[18] distrust,[19] despair,[20] incorrigibleness, and insensibleness under judgments,[21] hardness of heart,[22] pride,[23] presumption,[24] carnal security,[25] tempting of God;[26] using unlawful means,[27] and trusting in lawful means;[28] carnal delights and joys,[29] corrupt, blind, and indiscreet zeal;[30] lukewarmness,[31] and deadness in the things of God;[32] estranging ourselves, and apostatizing from God;[33] praying or giving any religious worship to saints, angels, or any other creatures;[34] all compacts and consulting with the devil,[35] and hearkening to his suggestions;[36] making men the lords of our faith and conscience;[37] slighting and despising God, and his commands;[38] resisting and grieving of his Spirit,[39] discontent and impatience at his dispensations, charging him foolishly for the evils he inflicts on us;[40] and ascribing the praise of any good, we either are, have, or can do, to fortune, idols,[41] ourselves,[42] or any other creature.[43]

1. Ps. 14:1. The fool hath said in his heart, *There is* no God.

2. Jer. 2:27, 28. Saying to a stock, Thou *art* my father; and to a stone, Thou hast brought me forth . . . where *are* thy gods that thou hast made thee? . . . for *according to* the number of thy cities are thy gods, O Judah. Compare I Thess. 1:9.

3. Ps. 81:11. But my people would not hearken to my voice; and Israel would none of me.

4. Isa. 43:22, 23. But thou hast not called upon me, O Jacob; but thou hast been weary of me, O Israel. Thou hast not brought me the small cattle of thy burnt offerings; neither hast thou honoured me with thy sacrifices.

5. Jer. 4:22. For my people *is* foolish, they have not known me; they *are* sottish children, and they have none understanding: they *are* wise to do evil, but to do good they have no knowledge.
Hos. 4:1, 6. For the Lord hath a controversy with the inhabitants of the land, because *there is* no truth, nor mercy, nor knowledge of God in the land. . . . My people are destroyed for lack of knowledge.

6. Jer. 2:32. Can a maid forget her ornaments, *or* a bride her attire? yet my people have forgotten me days without number.
Ps. 50:22.

7. Acts 17:23, 29. For as I passed by, and beheld your devotions, I found an alter with this inscription, TO THE UNKNOWN GOD. Whom therefore ye ignorantly worship, him declare I unto you. . . . Forasmuch then as we are the offspring of God, we ought not to think that the Godhead is like unto gold, or silver, or stone, graven by art and man's device.

8. Ps. 50:21. These *things* hast thou done, and I kept silence; thou thoughtest that I was altogether *such an one* as thyself: *but* I will reprove thee, and set *them* in order before thine eyes.

9. Deut. 29:29. The secret *things belong* unto the LORD our God.

10. Titus 1:16. They profess that they know God; but in works they deny *him,* being abominable, and disobedient, and unto every good work reprobate.
Heb. 12:16.

11. Rom. 1:30. Backbiters, haters of God, despiteful, proud, boasters.

12. II Tim. 3:2. For men shall be lovers of their own selves, covetous.

13. Phil. 2:21. For all seek their own, not the things which are Jesus Christ's.

14. I John 2:15. Love not the world, neither the things *that are* in the world. If any man love the world, the love of the Father is not in him.

    I Sam. 2:29. And honourest thy sons above me.

    Col. 3:2, 5.

15. I John 4:1. Beloved, believe not every spirit, but try the spirits whether they are of God: because many false prophets are gone out into the world.

16. Heb. 3:12. Take heed, brethren, lest there be in any of you an evil heart of unbelief, in departing from the living God.

17. Gal. 5:20. Idolatry, witchcraft, hatred, variance, emulations, wrath, strife, seditions, heresies.

    Titus 3:10.

18. Acts 26:9. I verily thought with myself, that I ought to do many things contrary to the name of Jesus of Nazareth.

19. Ps. 78:22. Because they believed not in God, and trusted not in his salvation.

20. Ezek. 37:11. Then he said unto me, Son of man, these bones are the whole house of Israel: behold, they say, Our bones are dried, and our hope is lost: we are cut off for our parts.

21. Jer. 5:3. O Lord, *are* not thine eyes upon the truth? thou hast stricken them, but they have not grieved; thou hast consumed them, *but* they have refused to receive correction: they have made their faces harder than a rock; they have refused to return.

22. Rom. 2:5. But after thy hardness and impenitent heart treasurest up unto thyself wrath against the day of wrath and revelation of the righteous judgment of God.

23. Jer. 13:15. Hear ye, and give ear; be not proud: for the LORD hath spoken.

24. Ps. 19:13. Keep back thy servant also from presumptuous *sins* . . . then shall I be . . . innocent from the great transgression.

25. Zeph. 1:12. And punish the men that are settled on their lees: that say in their heart, The LORD will not do good, neither will he do evil.

26. Matt. 4:7. Thou shalt not tempt the Lord thy God.

27. Rom. 3:8. And not *rather,* (as we be slanderously reported, and as some affirm that we say,) Let us do evil, that good may come?

28. Jer. 17:5. Cursed *be* the man that trusteth in man, and maketh flesh his arm, and whose heart departeth from the LORD.

29. II Tim. 3:4. Traitors, heady, highminded, lovers of pleasures more than lovers of God.

30. Gal. 4:17. They zealously affect you, *but* not well.

    Rom. 10:2. For I bear them record that they have a zeal of God, but not according to knowledge.

    John 16:2; Luke 9:54, 55.

31. Rev. 3:16. So then because thou art lukewarm, and neither cold nor hot, I will spue thee out of my mouth.

32. Rev. 3:1. I know thy works, that thou hast a name that thou livest, and art dead.

33. Ezek. 14:5. Because they are all estranged from me through their idols.

    Isa. 1:4, 5. They have forsaken the LORD . . . they are gone away backward. Why should ye be stricken any more? ye will revolt more and more.

34. Hos. 4:12. My people ask counsel at their stocks, and their staff declareth unto them.

Rev. 19:10. And I fell at his feet to worship him. And he said unto me, See *thou do it* not: I am thy fellow servant, and of thy brethren that have the testimony of Jesus: worship God.

Col. 2:18. Let no man beguile you of your reward in a voluntary humility and worshipping of angels, intruding into those things which he hath not seen, vainly puffed up by his fleshly mind.

Rom. 1:25.

35. Lev. 20:6. And the soul that turneth after such as have familiar spirits, and after wizards, to go a whoring after them, I will even set my face against that soul, and will cut him off from among his people.

I Sam. 28:7-11. Compare I Chron. 10:13, 14.

36. Acts 5:3. But Peter said, Ananias, why hath Satan filled thine heart to lie to the Holy Ghost, and to keep back *part* of the price of the land?

37. Matt. 23:9. And call no *man* your father upon the earth: for one is your Father, which is in heaven.

38. Deut. 32:15. Then he forsook God *which* made him, and lightly esteemed the Rock of his salvation.

Prov. 13:13 Whoso despiseth the word shall be destroyed: but he that feareth the commandment shall be rewarded.

II Sam. 12:9.

39. Acts 7:51. Ye stiffnecked and uncircumcised in heart and ears, ye do always resist the Holy Ghost.

Eph. 4:30. And grieve not the Holy Spirit of God.

40. Ps. 73:2, 3. But as for me, my feet were almost gone; my steps had well nigh slipped. For I was envious at the foolish, *when* I saw the prosperity of the wicked.

See verses 13-15, 22.

41. Dan. 5:23. And thou hast praised the gods of silver, and gold, of brass, iron, wood, and stone, which see not, nor hear, nor know: and the God in whose hand thy breath *is* and whose *are* all thy ways, hast thou not glorified.

42. Deut. 8:17. And thou say in thine heart, My power and the might of *mine* hand hath gotten me this wealth.

Dan. 4:30.

43. Hab. 1:16. Therefore they sacrifice unto their net, and burn incense unto their drag.

Q. 106. *What are we especially taught by these words* (before me) *in the first commandment?*

A. These words (*before me,* or before my face) in the first commandment, teach us, that God, who seeth all things, taketh special notice of, and is much displeased with, the sin of having any other god: that so it may be an argument to dissuade from it, and to aggravate it as a most impudent provocation;[1] as also to persuade us to do as in his sight, whatever we do in his service.[2]

1. Ps. 44:20, 21. If we have forgotten the name of our God, or stretched out our hands to a strange god, shall not God search this out? for he knoweth the secrets of the heart.

Ezek. 8:5-18.

2. I Chron. 28:9. And thou, Solomon my son, know thou the God of thy father, and serve him with a perfect heart and with a willing mind: for the LORD searcheth all hearts, and understandeth all the imaginations of the thoughts.

Q. 107. *Which is the second commandment?*

A. The second commandment is, *Thou shalt not make unto thee any graven image, or any likeness of any thing that is in heaven above, or that is in the earth beneath, or that is in the water under the earth: thou shalt not bow down thyself to them, nor serve them: for I the Lord thy God am a jealous God, visiting the iniquity of the fathers upon the children unto the third and fourth generation of them that hate me; and shewing mercy unto thousands of them that love me, and keep my commandments.*[1]

1. Exod. 20:4-6.

Q. 108. *What are the duties required in the second commandment?*

A. The duties required in the second commandment are: the receiving, observing, and keeping pure and entire, all such religious worship and ordinances as God hath instituted in his word;[1] particularly prayer and thanksgiving in the name of Christ;[2] the reading, preaching, and hearing of the word;[3] the administration and receiving of the sacraments;[4] church government and discipline;[5] the ministry and maintenance thereof;[6] religious fasting;[7] swearing by the name of God;[8] and vowing unto him:[9] as also the disapproving, detesting, opposing all false worship;[10] and, according to each one's place and calling, removing it, and all monuments of idolatry.[11]

1. Deut. 32:46. Set your hearts unto all the words which I testify among you this day, which ye shall command your children to observe to do, all the words of this law.

Matt. 28:20. Teaching them to observe all things whatsoever I have commanded you.

I Tim. 6:13, 14. I give thee charge . . . that thou keep *this* commandment without spot, unrebukable, until the appearing of our Lord Jesus Christ.

Acts 2:42.

2. Phil. 4:6. Be careful for nothing; but in every thing by prayer and supplication with thanksgiving let your requests be made known unto God.
Eph. 5:20.

3. Deut. 17:18, 19. That he shall write him a copy of this law in a book . . .
and it shall be with him, and he shall read therein all the days of his life.
Acts 15:21. For Moses . . . hath in every city them that preach him, being read in the synagogues every sabbath day.
II Tim. 4:2. Preach the word; be instant in season, out of season; reprove, rebuke, exhort with all longsuffering and doctrine.
James 1:21. Receive with meekness the engrafted word, which is able to
save your souls.
Acts 10:33.

4. Matt. 28:19. Go ye therefore, and teach all nations, baptizing them in
the name of the Father, and of the Son, and of the Holy Ghost.
I Cor. 11:23-30.

5. Matt. 16:19. And I will give unto thee the keys of the kingdom of
heaven: and whatsoever thou shalt bind on earth shall be bound in
heaven: and whatsoever thou shalt loose on earth shall be loosed in
heaven.
Matt. 18:17. And if he shall neglect to hear them, tell *it* unto the church:
but if he neglect to hear the church, let him be unto thee as an heathen
man and a publican.
I Cor. 5; I Cor. 12:28; John 20:23.

6. Eph. 4:11, 12. And he gave some, apostles; and some, prophets; and
some, evangelists; and some, pastors and teachers; for the perfecting of
the saints, for the work of the ministry, for the edifying of the body of
Christ.
I Tim. 5:17, 18. Let the elders that rule well be counted worthy of double honour, especially they who labour in the word and doctrine. For
the scripture saith, Thou shalt not muzzle the ox that treadeth out the
corn. And, The labourer *is* worthy of his reward.
I Cor. 9:1-15.

7. Joel 2:12. Therefore also now, saith the LORD, Turn ye *even* to me
with all your heart, and with fasting, and with weeping, and with
mourning.
I Cor. 7:5.

8. Deut. 6:13. Thou shalt fear the LORD thy God, and serve him, and shalt
swear by his name.

9. Ps. 76:11. Vow, and pay unto the LORD your God.
Isa. 19:21; Ps. 116:14, 18.

10. Acts 17:16, 17. Now while Paul waited for them at Athens, his spirit was
stirred in him, when he saw the city wholly given to idolatry. Therefore
disputed he in the synagogue with the Jews, and with the devout persons, and in the market daily with them that met with him.
Ps. 16:4. Their sorrows shall be multiplied *that* hasten *after* another
god: their drink offerings of blood will I not offer, nor take up their
names into my lips.

11. Deut. 7:5. But thus shall ye deal with them; ye shall destroy their altars,
and break down their images, and cut down their groves, and burn their
graven images with fire.
Isa. 30:22. Ye shall defile also the covering of thy graven images of silver, and the ornament of thy molten images of gold: thou shalt cast
them away as a menstruous cloth; thou shalt say unto it, Get thee
hence.

Q. 109. *What are the sins forbidden in the second commandment?*

A. The sins forbidden in the second commandment are: all devising,[1] counselling,[2] commanding,[3] using,[4] and any wise approving any religious worship not instituted by God himself;[5] the making any representation of God, of all, or of any of the three Persons, either inwardly in our mind, or outwardly in any kind of image or likeness of any creature whatsoever;[6] all worshipping of it,[7] or God in it or by it;[8] the making of any representation of feigned deities,[9] and all worship of them, or service belonging to them;[10] all superstitious devices,[11] corrupting the worship of God,[12] adding to it, or taking from it,[13] whether invented and taken up of ourselves,[14] or received by tradition from others,[15] though under the title of antiquity,[16] custom,[17] devotion,[18] good intent, or any other pretense whatsoever;[19] simony,[20] sacrilege;[21] all neglect,[22] contempt,[23] hindering,[24] and opposing the worship and ordinances which God hath appointed.[25]

1. Num. 15:39. And it shall be unto you for a fringe, that ye may look upon it, and remember all the commandments of the LORD, and do them; and that ye seek not after your own heart and your own eyes, after which ye use to go a whoring.

2. Deut. 13:6, 8. If thy brother, the son of thy mother, or thy son, or thy daughter, or the wife of thy bosom, or thy friend, which *is* as thine own soul, entice thee secretly, saying, Let us go and serve other gods, which thou hast not known, thou, nor thy fathers . . . thou shalt not consent unto him, nor hearken unto him; neither shall thine eye pity him, neither shalt thou spare, neither shalt thou conceal him.

3. Hos. 5:11. Ephraim *is* oppressed *and* broken in judgment, because he willingly walked after the commandment.
   Micah 6:16. For the statutes of Omri are kept.

4. I Kings 11:33. Because that they have forsaken me, and have worshipped Ashtoreth.
   I Kings 12:33. So he offered upon the altar which he had made in Bethel the fifteenth day of the eighth month, *even* in the month which he had devised of his own heart; and ordained a feast unto the children of Israel: and he offered upon the altar, and burnt incense.

5. Deut. 12:30, 32. Take heed to thyself that thou be not snared by following them, after that they be destroyed from before thee; and that thou inquire not after their gods, saying, How did these nations serve their gods? even so will I do likewise. . . . What thing soever I command you, observe to do it: thou shalt not add thereto, nor diminish from it.

6. Deut. 4:15, 16. Take ye therefore good heed unto yourselves; for ye saw no manner of similitude on the day *that* the LORD spake unto you in Horeb out of the midst of the fire: lest ye corrupt *yourselves*, and make you a graven image, the similitude of any figure, the likeness of male or female.

Acts 17:29. Forasmuch then as we are the offspring of God, we ought not to think that the Godhead is like unto gold, or silver, or stone, graven by art and man's device.

Rom. 1:21-25.

7. Gal. 4:8. Howbeit then, when ye knew not God, ye did service unto them which by nature are no gods.

Dan. 3:18.

8. Exod. 32:5. And when Aaron saw *it*, he built an altar before it; and Aaron made proclamation, and said, To morrow *is* a feast to the LORD.

9. Exod. 32:8. They have made them a molten calf, and have worshipped it, and have sacrificed thereunto, and said, These *be* thy gods, O Israel, which have brought thee up out of the land of Egypt.

10. I Kings 18:26, 28. And they took the bullock which was given them, and they dressed *it*, and called on the name of Baal from morning even until noon, saying, O Baal, hear us. . . . And they cried aloud, and cut themselves after their manner with knives and lancets, till the blood gushed out upon them.

Isa. 65:11.

11. Acts 19:19. Many of them also which used curious arts brought their books together, and burned them before all *men:* and they counted the price of them, and found *it* fifty thousand *pieces* of silver.

12. Mal. 1:7, 8, 14. Ye offer polluted bread upon mine altar . . . And if ye offer the blind for sacrifice, *is it* not evil? and if ye offer the lame and sick, *is it* not evil? . . . But cursed *be* the deceiver, which hath in his flock a male, and voweth, and sacrificeth unto the Lord a corrupt thing: for I *am* a great King, saith the LORD of hosts, and my name *is* dreadful among the heathen.

13. Deut. 4:2. Ye shall not add unto the word which I command you, neither shall ye diminish *aught* from it, that ye may keep the commandments of the LORD your God which I command you.

14. Ps. 106:39. Thus were they defiled with their own works, and went a whoring with their own inventions.

15. Matt. 15:9. But in vain they do worship me, teaching *for* doctrines the commandments of men.

16. I Peter 1:18. Forasmuch as ye know that ye were not redeemed with corruptible things, *as* silver and gold, from your vain conversation *received* by tradition from your fathers.

17. Jer. 44:17. But we will certainly do whatsoever thing goeth forth out of our own mouth, to burn incense unto the queen of heaven, and to pour out drink offerings unto her, as we have done, we, and our fathers, our Kings, and our princes, in the cities of Judah, and in the streets of Jerusalem.

18. Isa. 65:3-5. A people that provoketh me to anger continually to my face; that sacrificeth in gardens, and burneth incense upon altars of brick . . . which eat swine's flesh, and broth of abominable *things is in* their vessels; which say, Stand by thyself, come not near to me; for I am holier than thou. These *are* a smoke in my nose, a fire that burneth all the day. Gal. 1:13, 14. How that beyond measure I persecuted the church of God, and wasted it: and profited in the Jews' religion above many my equals in mine own nation, being more exceedingly zealous of the traditions of my fathers.

19. I Sam. 13:12. I forced myself therefore, and offered a burnt offering. I Sam. 15:21. But the people [said Saul] took of the spoil, sheep and

oxen, the chief of the things which should have been utterly destroyed, to sacrifice unto the LORD thy God in Gilgal.

20. Acts 8:18. And when Simon saw that through laying on of the apostles' hands the Holy Ghost was given, he offered them money.

21. Rom. 2:22. Thou that abhorrest idols, dost thou commit sacrilege? Mal. 3:8. Will a man rob God? Yet ye have robbed me. But ye say, Wherein have we robbed thee? In tithes and offerings.

22. Exod. 4:24-26. And it came to pass by the way in the inn, that the LORD met him, and sought to kill him.

23. Matt. 22:5. But they made light of *it,* and went their ways, one to his farm, another to his merchandise.
Mal. 1:7, 12, 13. Ye offer polluted bread upon mine altar . . . ye say, The table of the LORD *is* polluted; and the fruit thereof, *even* his meat, *is* contemptible. Ye said also, Behold, what a weariness *is it!* and ye have snuffed at it, saith the LORD of hosts; and ye brought *that which was* torn, and the lame, and the sick.

24. Matt. 23:13. But woe unto you, scribes and Pharisees, hypocrites! for ye shut up the kingdom of heaven against men: for ye neither go in *yourselves,* neither suffer ye them that are entering to go in.

25. Acts 13:45. But when the Jews saw the multitudes, they were filled with envy, and spake against those things which were spoken by Paul, contradicting and blaspheming.
I Thess. 2:15, 16.

Q. 110. *What are the reasons annexed to the second commandment, the more to enforce it?*

A. The reasons annexed to the second commandment, the more to enforce it, contained in these words, *For I the Lord thy God am a jealous God, visiting the iniquity of the fathers upon the children unto the third and fourth generation of them that hate me; and shewing mercy unto thousands of them that love me, and keep my commandments;*[1] are, besides God's sovereignty over us, and propriety in us, his revengeful indignation against all false worship,[2] as being a spiritual whoredom;[3] accounting the breakers of this commandment such as hate him, and threatening to punish them unto divers generations,[4] and esteeming the observers of it such as love him and keep his commandments, and promising mercy to them unto many generations.[5]

1. Exod. 20:5, 6.
2. Exod. 34:13, 14. But ye shall destroy their altars, break their images, and cut down their groves: for thou shalt worship no other god: for the LORD, whose name *is* Jealous, *is* a jealous God.
3. I Cor. 10:20-22. But I *say,* that the things which the Gentiles sacrifice, they sacrifice to devils, and not to God: and I would not that ye should have fellowship with devils. Ye cannot drink the cup of the Lord, and the cup of devils: ye cannot be partakers of the Lord's table, and of the

table of devils. Do we provoke the Lord to jealousy? are we stronger than he?
Deut. 32:16-19; Jer. 7:18-20; Ezek. 16:26, 27.

4. Hos. 2:2-4. Plead with your mother, plead: for she *is* not my wife, neither *am* I her husband: let her therefore put away her whoredoms . . . and her adulteries from between her breasts; lest I strip her naked, and set her as in the day that she was born, and make her as a wilderness, and set her like a dry land, and slay her with thirst. And I will not have mercy upon her children; for they *be* the children of whoredoms.

5. Deut. 5:29. O that there were such an heart in them, that they would fear me, and keep all my commandments always, that it might be well with them, and with their children for ever!

Q. 111. *Which is the third commandment?*

A. The third commandment is, *Thou shalt not take the name of the Lord thy God in vain; for the Lord will not hold him guiltless that taketh his name in vain.*[1]

1. Exod. 20:7.

Q. 112. *What is required in the third commandment?*

A. The third commandment requires, that the name of God, his titles, attributes,[1] ordinances,[2] the word,[3] sacraments,[4] prayer,[5] oaths,[6] vows,[7] lots,[8] his works,[9] and whatsoever else there is whereby he makes himself known, be holily and reverently used in thought,[10] meditation,[11] word,[12] and writing;[13] by an holy profession,[14] and answerable conversation,[15] to the glory of God,[16] and the good of ourselves[17] and others.[18]

1. Matt. 6:9. After this manner therefore pray ye: Our Father which art in heaven, Hallowed be thy name.
Deut. 28:58. That thou mayest fear this glorious and fearful name, THE LORD THY GOD.
Ps. 68:4. Extol him that rideth upon the heavens by his name JAH.
Ps. 29:2; Rev. 15:3, 4.

2. Mal. 1:14. But cursed *be* the deceiver, which hath in his flock a male, and voweth, and sacrificeth unto the Lord a corrupt thing: for I *am* a great King, saith the LORD of hosts, and my name *is* dreadful among the heathen.

3. Ps. 138:2. I will worship toward thy holy temple, and praise thy name for thy lovingkindness and for thy truth: for thou hast magnified thy word above all thy name.

4. I Cor. 11:28, 29. But let a man examine himself, and so let him eat of *that* bread, and drink of *that* cup. For he that eateth and drinketh unworthily, eateth and drinketh damnation to himself, not discerning the Lord's body.
See context.

5. I Tim. 2:8. I will therefore that men pray every where, lifting up holy hands, without wrath and doubting.

6. Jer. 4:2. And thou shalt swear, The LORD liveth, in truth, in judgment, and in righteousness.

7. Ps. 76:11. Vow, and pay unto the LORD your God: let all that be round about him bring presents unto him that ought to be feared.

8. Acts 1:24, 26. And they prayed, and said, Thou, Lord, which knowest the hearts of all *men*, shew whether of these two thou hast chosen . . . And they gave forth their lots; and the lot fell upon Matthias.

9. Ps. 107:21, 22. Oh that *men* would praise the LORD *for* his goodness, and *for* his wonderful works to the children of men! And let them sacrifice the sacrifices of thanksgiving, and declare his works with rejoicing.

10. Mal. 3:16. And a book of remembrance was written before him for them that feared the LORD, and that thought upon his name.

11. Ps. 8.

12. Ps. 105:2, 5. Talk ye of all his wondrous works. . . . Remember his marvellous works that he hath done.
Col. 3:17.

13. Ps. 102:18. This shall be written for the generation to come: and the people which shall be created shall praise the LORD.

14. I Peter 3:15. *Be* ready always to *give* an answer to every man that asketh you a reason of the hope that is in you with meekness and fear.
Micah 4:5. We will walk in the name of the LORD our God for ever and ever.

15. Phil. 1:27. Only let your conversation be as it becometh the gospel of Christ.

16. I Cor. 10:31. Whether therefore ye eat, or drink, or whatsoever ye do, do all to the glory of God.

17. Jer. 32:39. And I will give them one heart, and one way, that they may fear me for ever, for the good of them.

18. I Peter 2:12. Having your conversation honest among the Gentiles: that, whereas they speak against you as evil doers, they may by *your* good works, which they shall behold, glorify God in the day of visitation.

Q. 113. *What are the sins forbidden in the third commandment?*

A. The sins forbidden in the third commandment are: the not using of God's name as is required;[1] and the abuse of it in an ignorant,[2] vain,[3] irreverent, profane,[4] superstitious,[5] or wicked mentioning or otherwise using the titles, attributes,[6] ordinances,[7] or works;[8] by blasphemy;[9] perjury;[10] all sinful cursing,[11] oaths,[12] vows,[13] and lots;[14] violating our oaths and vows, if lawful;[15] and fulfilling them, if of things unlawful;[16] murmuring and quarreling at,[17] curious prying into,[18] and misapplying of God's decrees[19] and providence;[20] misinterpreting,[21] misapplying,[22] or any way perverting the word, or any part of it,[23] to profane jests,[24] curious and unprofitable questions, vain janglings, or the maintaining of false doctrines;[25] abusing it, the creatures, or anything contained under the name of God, to charms,[26] or sinful lusts and practices;[27] the maligning,[28] scorning,[29] reviling,[30] or any way opposing of God's truth, grace, and ways;[31] making profession of religion in hypocrisy, or for sinister ends;[32] being ashamed of it,[33] or a shame to it, by uncomfortable,[34] unwise,[35] unfruitful,[36] and offensive walking[37] or backsliding from it.[38]

1. Mal. 2:2. If ye will not hear, and if ye will not lay *it* to heart, to give glory unto my name, saith the LORD of hosts, I will even send a curse upon you, and I will curse your blessings.

2. Acts 17:23. Whom therefore ye ignorantly worship.

3. Prov. 30:9. Lest I be full, and deny *thee*, and say, Who *is* the LORD? or lest I be poor, and steal, and take the name of my God *in vain*.

4. Mal. 1:6, 7, 12. If then I *be* a father, where *is* mine honour? and if I *be* a master, where *is* my fear? saith the LORD of hosts unto you, O priests, that despise my name. . . . Ye offer polluted bread upon mine altar; and ye say, Wherein have we polluted thee? In that ye say, The table of the Lord *is* contemptible. . . . But ye have profaned it, in that ye say, The table of the LORD *is* polluted; and the fruit thereof, *even* his meat, *is* contemptible.
Mal. 3:14.

5. Jer. 7:4. Trust ye not in lying words, saying, The temple of the LORD, The temple of the LORD, The temple of the LORD, *are* these.
See context.
Col. 2:20-22.

6. Exod. 5:2. Pharoah said, Who *is* the LORD, that I should obey his voice to let Israel go?
Ps. 139:20. For they speak against thee wickedly, *and* thine enemies take *thy name* in vain.

7. Ps. 50:16, 17. But unto the wicked God saith, What hast thou to do to declare my statutes, or *that* thou shouldest take my covenant in thy mouth? seeing thou hatest instruction, and castest my words behind thee.

8. Isa. 5:12. And the harp, and the viol, the tabret, and pipe, and wine, are in their feasts: but they regard not the work of the LORD, neither consider the operation of his hands.

9. II Kings 19:22. Whom hast thou reproached and blasphemed? and against whom hast thou exalted *thy* voice, and lifted up thine eyes on high? *even* against the Holy *One* of Israel.
Lev. 24:11.

10. Zech. 5:4. And it shall enter into the house of the thief, and into the house of him that sweareth falsely by my name: and it shall remain in the midst of his house, and shall consume it.

11. Rom. 12:14. Bless, and curse not.
I Sam. 17:43; II Sam. 16:5.

12. Jer. 5:7. Thy children have forsaken me, and sworn by *them that are* no gods.
Jer. 23:10. For because of swearing the land mourneth.

13. Deut. 23:18. Thou shalt not bring the hire of a whore, or the price of a dog, into the house of the LORD thy God for any vow.
Acts 23:12. And when it was day, certain of the Jews banded together, and bound themselves under a curse, saying that they would neither eat nor drink till they had killed Paul.

14. Esth. 3:7. They cast Pur, that *is,* the lot, before Haman, from day to day. Esth. 9:24. Because Haman . . . had devised against the Jews to destroy them, and had cast Pur, that *is,* the lot.

15. Ps. 24:4. Who hath not lifted up his soul into vanity, nor sworn deceitfully.
Ezek. 17:19. Surely mine oath that he hath despised, and my covenant that he hath broken, even it will I recompense upon his own head.
See context.

16. Mark 6:26. And the king was exceeding sorry; *yet* for his oath's sake, and for their sakes which sat with him, he would not reject her.
I Sam. 25:22, 32-34.

17. Rom. 9:14, 19, 20. *Is there* unrighteousness with God? God forbid. . . . Why doth he yet find fault? For who hath resisted his will? Nay but, O man, who art thou that repliest against God? Shall the thing formed say to him that formed *it,* Why hast thou made me thus?

18. Deut. 29:29. The secret *things belong* unto the LORD.

19. Rom. 3:5, 7. But if our unrighteousness commend the righteousness of God, what shall we say? *Is* God unrighteous who taketh vengeance? . . . For if the truth of God hath more abounded through my lie unto his glory; why yet am I also judged as a sinner?
See context.

20. Ps. 73:12, 13. Behold, these *are* the ungodly, who prosper in the world; they increase *in* riches. Verily I have cleansed my heart *in* vain, and washed my hands in innocency.

21. Matt. 5:21-48.

22. Ezek. 13:22. Because with lies ye have made the heart of the righteous sad, whom I have not made sad; and strengthened the hands of the wicked, that he should not return from his wicked way, by promising him life.

23. II Peter 3:16. In which are some things hard to be understood, which they that are unlearned and unstable wrest, as *they do* also the other scriptures, unto their own destruction.
Matt. 22:29. Ye do err, not knowing the scriptures, nor the power of God.
See context, verses 23-32.

24. Eph. 5:4. Neither filthiness, nor foolish talking, nor jesting, which are not covenient: but rather giving of thanks.

25. I Tim. 6:4, 5, 20. He is proud, knowing nothing, but doting about questions and strifes of words, whereof cometh envy, strife, railings, evil surmisings, perverse disputings of men of corrupt minds, and destitute of the truth . . . avoiding profane *and* vain babblings, and oppositions of science falsely so called.
II Tim. 2:14. Charging *them* before the Lord that they strive not about words to no profit, *but* to the subverting of the hearers.
Titus 3:9.

26. Deut. 18:10, 11. There shall not be found among you *any one* that maketh his son or his daughter to pass through the fire, *or* that useth divination, *or* an observer of times, or an enchanter, or a witch, or a charmer, or a consulter with familiar spirits, or a wizard, or a necromancer.
See context.
Acts 19:13.

27. II Tim. 4:3, 4. For the time will come when they will not endure sound doctrine; but after their own lusts shall they heap to themselves

teachers, having itching ears; and they shall turn away *their* ears from the truth, and shall be turned unto fables.
Jude 4; Rom. 13:13, 14; I Kings 21:9, 10.

28. Acts 13:45. But when the Jews saw the multitudes, they were filled with envy, and spake against those things which were spoken by Paul, contradicting and blaspheming.

29. II Peter 3:3. Knowing this first, that there shall come in the last day scoffers, walking after their own lusts.
Ps. 1:1. Nor sitteth in the seat of the scornful.

30. I Peter 4:4. Wherein they think it strange that ye run not with *them* to the same excess of riot, speaking evil of *you*.

31. Acts 13:50. But the Jews stirred up the devout and honourable women, and the chief men of the city, and raised persecution against Paul and Barnabas, and expelled them out of their coasts.
See verses 45, 46.
Acts 4:18. And commanded them not to speak at all nor teach in the name of Jesus.
Acts 19:9; I Thess. 2:16; Heb. 10:29.

32. II Tim. 3:5. Having a form of godliness, but denying the power thereof.
Matt. 23:14. Woe unto you, scribes and Pharisees, hypocrites! for ye devour widows' houses, and for a pretence make long prayer.
Matt. 6:1-3, 5, 16.

33. Mark 8:38. Whosoever therefore shall be ashamed of me and of my words in this adulterous and sinful generation; of him also shall the Son of man be ashamed, when he cometh in the glory of his Father with the holy angels.

34. Ps. 73:14, 15. For all the day long have I been plagued, and chastened every morning. If I say, I will speak thus; behold, I should offend *against* the generation of thy children.

35. Eph. 5:15, 17. See then that ye walk circumspectly, not as fools, but as wise . . . Wherefore be ye not unwise, but understanding what the will of the Lord *is*.
I Cor. 6:5, 6.

36. Isa. 5:4. What could have been done more to my vineyard, that I have not done in it? wherefore, when I looked that it should bring forth grapes, brought it forth wild grapes?
II Peter 1:8, 9.

37. Rom. 2:23, 24. Thou that makest thy boast of the law, through breaking the law dishonourest thou God? For the name of God is blasphemed among the Gentiles through you.

38. Gal. 3:1, 3. O foolish Galatians, who hath bewitched you, that ye should not obey the truth, before whose eyes Jesus Christ hath been evidently set forth, crucified among you? . . . Are ye so foolish? having begun in the Spirit, are ye now made perfect by the flesh?
Heb. 6:6.

Q. 114. *What reasons are annexed to the third commandment?*

A. The reasons annexed to the third commandment, in these words: *"the Lord thy God,"* and, *"for the Lord will not hold him guiltless that taketh his name in vain,"*[1] are because he is the

Lord and our God, therefore his name is not to be profaned, or any way abused by us;[2] especially because he will be so far from acquitting and sparing the transgressors of this commandment, as that he will not suffer them to escape his righteous judgment,[3] albeit many such escape the censures and punishments of men.[4]

1. Exod. 20:7.
2. Lev. 19:12. And ye shall not swear by my name falsely, neither shalt thou profane the name of thy God: I *am* the LORD.
3. Deut. 28:58, 59. If thou wilt not observe to do all the words of this law that are written in this book, that thou mayest fear this glorious and fearful name, THE LORD THY GOD; then the LORD will make thy plagues wonderful, and the plagues of thy seed, *even* great plagues, and of long continuance.
   Zech. 5:2-4; Ezek. 36:21-23.
4. I Sam. 2:12, 17, 22.

Q. 115. *Which is the fourth commandment?*

A. The fourth commandment is, *Remember the sabbath day, to keep it holy. Six days shalt thou labour, and do all thy work: but the seventh day is the sabbath of the Lord thy God: in it thou shalt not do any work, thou, nor thy son, nor thy daughter, thy manservant, nor thy maidservant, nor thy cattle, nor thy stranger that is within thy gates; for in six days the Lord made heaven and earth, the sea, and all that in them is, and rested the seventh day: wherefore the Lord blessed the sabbath day, and hallowed it.*[1]

1. Exod. 20:8-11.

Q. 116. *What is required in the fourth commandment?*

A. The fourth commandment requireth of all men the sanctifying or keeping holy to God such set times as he hath appointed in his word, expressly one whole day in seven;[1] which was the seventh from the beginning of the world to the resurrection of Christ,[2] and the first day of the week ever since, and so to continue to the end of the world; which is the Christian Sabbath,[3] and in the New Testament called *The Lord's day.*

1. Isa. 56:2, 4, 6, 7. Blessed *is* the man *that* doeth this, and the son of man *that* layeth hold on it; that keepeth the sabbath from polluting it, and keepeth his hand from doing any evil. . . . For thus saith the LORD unto the eunuchs that keep my sabbaths, and choose *the things* that please me, and take hold of my covenant . . . Also the sons of the stranger, that join themselves to the Lord, to serve him, and to love the name of the LORD, to be his servants, every one that keepeth the sabbath from pol-

luting it, and taketh hold of my covenant; even them will I bring to my holy mountain, and make them joyful in my house of prayer: their burnt offerings and their sacrifices *shall be* accepted upon mine altar; for mine house shall be called an house of prayer for all people.

2. Gen. 2:3. And God blessed the seventh day, and sanctified it: because that in it he had rested from all his work which God created and made.
   Luke 23:56. And rested the sabbath day according to the commandment.

3. I Cor. 16:2. Upon the first *day* of the week let every one of you lay by him in store, as *God* hath prospered him.
   Acts 20:7. And upon the first *day* of the week, when the disciples came together to break bread, Paul preached unto them, ready to depart on the morrow.
   John 20:19-27.

Q. 117. *How is the Sabbath or Lord's day to be sanctified?*

A. The Sabbath, or Lord's day, is to be sanctified by an holy resting all that day,[1] not only from such works as are at all times sinful, but even from such worldly employments and recreations as are on other days lawful;[2] and making it our delight to spend the whole time (except so much of it as is to be taken up in works of necessity and mercy)[3] in the public and private exercise of God's worship.[4] And, to that end, we are to prepare our hearts, and with such foresight, diligence, and moderation, to dispose, and seasonably to dispatch our worldly business, that we may be the more free and fit for the duties of the day.[5]

1. Exod. 20:8, 10. Remember the sabbath day, to keep it holy. . . . *in it* thou shalt not do any work, thou, nor thy son.

2. Jer. 17:21, 22. Thus saith the LORD; Take heed to yourselves, and bear no burden on the sabbath day, nor bring *it* in by the gates of Jerusalem; neither carry forth a burden out of your houses on the sabbath day, neither do ye any work, but hallow ye the sabbath day, as I commanded your fathers.
   Exod. 16:25-29; Neh. 13:15-22.

3. Matt. 12:1-14.

4. Lev. 23:3. Six days shall work be done: but the seventh day *is* the sabbath of rest, an holy convocation.
   Isa. 58:13. And call the sabbath a delight, the holy of the LORD, honourable; and shalt honour him, not doing thine own ways, nor finding thine own pleasure, nor speaking *thine own* words.
   Luke 4:16. And, as his custom was, he went into the synagogue on the sabbath day, and stood up for to read.
   Acts 20:7.

5. Exod. 20:8. Remember the sabbath day, to keep it holy.
   Luke 23:54, 56. And that day was the preparation, and the sabbath drew on. . . . And they returned, and prepared spices and ointments; and resteth the sabbath day according to the commandment.
   Neh. 13:19. And it came to pass, that when the gates of Jerusalem began to be dark before the sabbath, I commanded that the gates should be shut, and charged that they should not be opened till after the sabbath.

Q. 118. *Why is the charge of keeping the Sabbath more specially directed to governors of families and other superiors?*

A. The charge of keeping the Sabbath is more specially directed to governors of families and other superiors, because they are bound not only to keep it themselves, but to see that it be observed by all those that are under their charge; and because they are prone ofttimes to hinder them by employments of their own.[1]

1. These statements are necessary inferences from the relations which exist between governors and the governed.

Q. 119. *What are the sins forbidden in the fourth commandment?*

A. The sins forbidden in the fourth commandment are: all omissions of the duties required,[1] all careless, negligent, and unprofitable performing of them, and being weary of them;[2] all profaning the day by idleness, and doing that which is in itself sinful;[3] and by all needless works, words, and thoughts about our worldly employments and recreations.[4]

1. Ezek. 22:26. Her priests have violated my law, and have profaned mine holy things . . . and have hid their eyes from my sabbaths, and I am profaned among them.
2. Ezek. 33:31, 32. And they come unto thee as the people cometh, and they sit before thee *as* my people, and they hear thy words, but they will not do them: for with their mouth they shew much love, *but* their heart goeth after their covetousness. And, lo, thou *art* unto them as a very lovely song of one that hath a pleasant voice, and can play well on an instrument: for they hear thy words, but they do them not.
   Mal. 1:13. Ye said also, Behold, what a weariness *is it!* and ye have snuffed at it, saith the LORD of hosts; and ye brought *that which was* torn, and the lame, and the sick.
   Amos 8:5.
3. Ezek. 23:38. Moreover this they have done unto me: they have defiled my sanctuary in the same day, and have profaned my sabbaths.
4. Jer. 17:27. But if ye will not hearken unto me to hallow the sabbath day, and not to bear a burden . . . then will I kindle a fire in the gates thereof, and it shall devour the palaces of Jerusalem, and it shall not be quenched.
   See context.
   Isa. 58:13, 14.

Q. 120. *What are the reasons annexed to the fourth commandment, the more to enforce it?*

A. The reasons annexed to the fourth commandment, the more to enforce it, are taken from the equity of it, God allowing us six days of seven for our own affairs, and reserving but one for himself, in these words, *Six days shalt thou labour, and do all thy work:*[1] from God's challenging a special propriety in that day, *the seventh day is the sabbath of the Lord thy God:*[2] from the example of God who *in six days . . . made heaven and earth, the sea, and all that in them is, and rested the seventh day:* and from that blessing which God put upon that day, not only in sanctifying it to be a holy day for his service, but in ordaining it to be a means of blessing to us in our sanctifying it, *wherefore the Lord blessed the sabbath day, and hallowed it.*[3]

1. Exod. 20:9.
2. Exod. 20:10.
3. Exod. 20:11.

Q. 121. *Why is the word* remember *set in the beginning of the fourth commandment?*

A. The word *remember* is set in the beginning of the fourth commandment,[1] partly because of the great benefit of remembering it, we being thereby helped in our preparation to keep it;[2] and, in keeping it, better to keep all the rest of the commandments,[3] and to continue a thankful remembrance of the two great benefits of creation and redemption, which contain a short abridgement of religion:[4] and partly because we are ready to forget it,[5] for that there is less light of nature for it, and yet it restraineth our natural liberty in things at other times lawful;[6] that it cometh but once in seven days, and many worldly businesses come between, and too often take off our minds from thinking of it, either to prepare for it, or to sanctify it;[7] and that Satan with his instruments much labor to blot out the glory, and even the memory of it, and to bring in all irreligion and impiety.[8]

1. Exod. 20:8.
2. Exod. 16:23. To morrow *is* the rest of the holy sabbath unto the Lord: bake *that* which ye will bake *to day,* and seethe that ye will seethe.
   Luke 23:54. And that day was the preparation, and the sabbath drew on. Compare Mark 15:42. And now when the even was come, because it was the preparation, that is, the day before the sabbath.
   Neh. 13:19.
3. Ezek. 20:12, 20. Moreover also I gave them my sabbaths, to be a sign between me and them, that they might know that I *am* the LORD that sanctify them. . . . and hallow my sabbaths; and they shall be a sign between me and you, that ye may know that I *am* the LORD your God.

4. Gen. 2:2, 3. And on the seventh day God ended his work which he had made; and he rested on the seventh day from all his work which he had made. And God blessed the seventh day, and sanctified it: because that in it he had rested from all his work which God created and made.

Ps. 118:22, 24. The stone *which* the builders refused is become the head stone of the corner. . . . This *is* the day *which* the LORD hath made; we will rejoice and be glad in it.

Heb. 4:9.

5. Num. 15:37, 38, 40. And the LORD spake unto Moses, saying, Speak unto the children of Israel . . . that ye may remember, and do all my commandments, and be holy unto your God.

See context.

6. Exod. 34:21. Six days thou shalt work, but on the seventh day thou shalt rest: in earing time and in harvest thou shalt rest.

7. See citation under figure 5 above.

8. Lam. 1:7. Jerusalem remembered in the days of her affliction and of her miseries all her pleasant things that she had in the days of old, when her people fell into the hand of the enemy, and none did help her: the adversaries saw her, *and* did mock at her sabbaths.

Neh. 13:15-23; Jer. 17:21-23.

Q. 122. *What is the sum of the six commandments which contain our duty to man?*

A. The sum of the six commandments which contain our duty to man is, to love our neighbor as ourselves,[1] and to do to others what we would have them to do to us.[2]

1. Matt. 22:39. And the second *is* like unto it, Thou shalt love thy neighbour as thyself.

2. Matt. 7:12. Therefore all things whatsoever ye would that men should do to you, do ye even so to them: for this is the law and the prophets.

Q. 123. *Which is the fifth commandment?*

A. The fifth commandment is, *Honour thy father and thy mother: that thy days may be long upon the land which the Lord thy God giveth thee.*[1]

1. Exod. 20:12.

Q. 124. *Who are meant by* father *and* mother, *in the fifth commandment?*

A. By *father* and *mother,* in the fifth commandment, are meant not only natural parents, but all superiors in age[1] and gifts;[2] and especially such as by God's ordinance are over us in place of authority, whether in family,[3] church,[4] or commonwealth.[5]

1. I Tim. 5:1, 2. Rebuke not an elder, but entreat *him* as a father; *and* the

younger men as brethren; the elder women as mothers; the younger as sisters.

2. Gen. 4:20, 21. And Adah bare Jabal: he was the father of such as dwell in tents, and *of such as have* cattle. And his brother's name *was* Jubal: he was the father of all such as handle the harp and organ.

Gen. 45:8. And he hath made me a father to Pharoah.

3. II Kings 5:13. And his servants came near, and spake unto him, and said, My father, *if* the prophet had bid thee *do some* great thing, wouldst thou not have done it?

4. Gal. 4:19. My little children, of whom I travail in birth again until Christ be formed in you.

II Kings 2:12. And Elisha saw *it,* and he cried, My father, my father, the chariot of Israel, and the horsemen thereof.

II Kings 13:14.

5. Isa. 49:23. And kings shall be thy nursing fathers, and their queens thy nursing mothers.

Q. 125. *Why are superiors styled* father *and* mother?

A. Superiors are styled *father* and *mother,* both to teach them in all duties towards their inferiors, like natural parents, to express love and tenderness to them, according to their several relations,[1] and to work inferiors to a greater willingness and cheerfulness in performing their duties to their superiors, as to their parents.[2]

1. Eph. 6:4. And, ye fathers, provoke not your children to wrath: but bring them up in the nurture and admonition of the Lord.

I Thess. 2:7, 8, 11. But we were gentle among you, even as a nurse cherisheth her children: so being affectionately desirous of you, we were willing to have imparted unto you, not the gospel of God only, but also our own souls, because ye were dear unto us. . . . As ye know how we exhorted and comforted and charged every one of you, as a father *doth* his children.

Num. 11:11, 12, 16.

2. I Cor. 4:14-16. I write not these things to shame you, but as my beloved sons I warn *you.* For though ye have ten thousand instructors in Christ, yet *have ye* not many fathers: for in Christ Jesus I have begotten you through the gospel. Wherefore I beseech you, be ye followers of me.

Q. 126. *What is the general scope of the fifth commandment?*

A. The general scope of the fifth commandment is, the performance of those duties which we mutually owe in our several relations, as inferiors, superiors, or equals.[1]

1. Eph. 5:21. Submitting yourselves one to another in the fear of God.

I Peter 2:17. Honour all *men.* Love the brotherhood. Fear God. Honour the king.

Rom. 12:10. *Be* kindly affectioned one to another with brotherly love; in honour preferring one another.

Q. 127. *What is the honor which inferiors owe to superiors?*

A. The honor which inferiors owe to their superiors is: all due reverence in heart,[1] word,[2] and behavior;[3] prayer and thanksgiving for them;[4] imitation of their virtues and graces;[5] willing obedience to their lawful commands and counsels,[6] due submission to their corrections;[7] fidelity to,[8] defense and maintenance of their persons and authority, according to their several ranks, and the nature of their places;[9] bearing with their infirmities, and covering them in love,[10] that so they may be an honor to them and to their government.[11]

1. Mal. 1:6. A son honoureth *his* father, and a servant his master: if then I *be* a father, where *is* mine honour? and if I *be* a master, where *is* my fear?

   Lev. 19:3. Ye shall fear every man his mother, and his father.

2. Prov. 31:28. Her children arise up, and call her blessed; her husband *also*, and he praiseth her.

   I Peter 3:6. Even as Sarah obeyed Abraham, calling him lord.

3. Lev. 19:32. Thou shalt rise up before the hoary head, and honour the face of the old man.

   I Kings 2:19. And she sat on his right hand.

4. I Tim 2:1, 2. I exhort therefore, that, first of all, supplications, prayers, intercessions, *and* giving of thanks, be made for all men; for kings, and *for* all that are in authority.

5. Heb. 13:7. Remember them which have the rule over you, who have spoken unto you the word of God: whose faith follow, considering the end of *their* conversation.

   Phil. 3:17. Brethren, be followers together of me, and mark them which walk so as ye have us for an ensample.

6. Eph. 6:1, 5-7. Children, obey your parents in the Lord . . . Servants, be obedient to them that are *your* masters according to the flesh.

   I Peter 2:13, 14. Submit yourselves to every ordinance of man for the Lord's sake: whether it be to the king, as supreme; or unto governors . . .
   Rom. 13:1-6; Heb. 13:17; Prov. 4:3, 4; Prov. 23:22.

7. Heb. 12:9. Furthermore we have had fathers of our flesh which corrected *us*, and we gave *them* reverence.

   I Peter 2:18-20. Servants, *be* subject to *your* masters with all fear . . . but if, when ye do well, and suffer *for it*, ye take it patiently, this *is* acceptable with God.

8. Titus 2:9, 10. *Exhort* servants to be obedient unto their own masters, *and* to please *them* well in all *things*; not answering again; not purloining, but shewing all good fidelity; that they may adorn the doctrine of God our Saviour in all things.

9. Matt. 22:21. Render therefore unto Cæsar the things which are Cæsar's.

   Rom. 13:6, 7. For this cause pay ye tribute also: for they are God's ministers, attending continually upon this very thing. Render therefore to all their dues: tribute to whom tribute *is due*; custom to whom custom; fear to whom fear; honour to whom honour.

I Tim. 5:17, 18. Let the elders that rule well be counted worthy of double honour, especially they who labour in the word and doctrine. . . . Thou shalt not muzzle the ox that treadeth out the corn. And, The labourer *is* worthy of his reward.

Gal. 6:6; Gen. 45:11; Gen 47:12.

10. Gen. 9:23. And Shem and Japheth took a garment, and laid *it* upon both their shoulders, and went backward, and covered the nakedness of their father; and their faces *were* backward, and they saw not their father's nakedness.

I Peter 2:18; Prov. 23:22.

11. Ps. 127:3, 5. Lo, children *are* an heritage of the LORD . . . Happy *is* the man that hath his quiver full of them: they shall not be ashamed, but they shall speak with the enemies in the gate.

Prov. 31:23. Her husband is known in the gates, when he sitteth among the elders of the land.

Q. 128. *What are the sins of inferiors against their superiors?*

A. The sins of inferiors against their superiors are: all neglect of the duties required toward them;[1] envying at,[2] contempt of,[3] and rebellion[4] against their persons[5] and places,[6] in their lawful counsels,[7] commands, and corrections;[8] cursing, mocking,[9] and all such refractory and scandalous carriage, as proves a shame and dishonor to them and their government.[10]

1. Matt. 15:5, 6. But ye say, Whosoever shall say to *his* father or *his* mother, *It is* a gift, by whatsoever thou mightest be profited by me; and honour not his father or his mother, *he shall be free.* Thus have ye made the commandment of God of none effect by your tradition.

2. Ps. 106:16. They envied Moses also in the camp, *and* Aaron the saint of the LORD.

3. I Sam. 8:7. For they have not rejected thee, but they have rejected me, that I should not reign over them.
Isa. 3:5. The child shall behave himself proudly against the ancient, and the base against the honourable.

4. II Sam. 15:1-12.

5. Exod. 21:15. And he that smiteth his father, or his mother, shall be surely put to death.

6. I Sam. 10:27. But the children of Belial said, How shall this man save us? And they despised him, and brought him no presents.

7. I Sam. 2:25. Notwithstanding they hearkened not unto the voice of their father, because the LORD would slay them.

8. Deut. 21:18, 20, 21. If a man have a stubborn and rebellious son, which will not obey the voice of his father, or the voice of his mother, and *that,* when they have chastened him, will not hearken unto them . . . and they shall say unto the elders of his city, This our son *is* stubborn and rebellious, he will not obey our voice; *he is* a glutton, and a drunkard. And all the men of his city shall stone him with stones, that he die.

9. Prov. 30:11, 17. *There is* a generation *that* curseth their father, and doth not bless their mother. . . . The eye *that* mocketh at *his* father, and

despiseth to obey *his* mother, the ravens of the valley shall pick it out, and the young eagles shall eat it.

10. Prov. 19:26. He that wasteth *his* father, *and* chaseth away *his* mother, *is* a son that causeth shame, and bringeth reproach.

Q. 129. *What is required of superiors towards their inferiors?*

A. It is required of superiors, according to that power they receive from God, and that relation wherein they stand, to love,[1] pray for,[2] and bless their inferiors;[3] to instruct,[4] counsel, and admonish them;[5] countenancing,[6] commending, and rewarding such as do well;[7] and discountenancing,[8] reproving, and chastising such as do ill;[9] protecting, and providing for them all things necessary for soul and body;[10] and, by grave, wise, holy, and exemplary carriage, to procure glory to God,[11] honor to themselves,[12] and so to preserve that authority which God hath put upon them.[13]

1. Col. 3:19. Husbands, love *your* wives, and be not bitter against them.
   Titus 2:4.
2. I Sam. 12:23. Moreover as for me, God forbid that I should sin against the LORD in ceasing to pray for you.
   Job 1:5.
3. I Kings 8:55, 56. And he stood, and blessed all the congregation of Israel with a loud voice.
   Gen. 49:28.
4. Deut. 6:6, 7. And these words, which I command thee this day, shall be in thine heart: and thou shalt teach them diligently unto thy children, and shalt talk of them when thou sittest in thine house, and when thou walkest by the way, and when thou liest down, and when thou risest up.
5. Eph. 6:4. And, ye fathers, provoke not your children to wrath: but bring them up in the nurture and admonition of the Lord.
6. I Peter 3:7. Likewise, ye husbands, dwell with *them* according to knowledge, giving honour unto the wife, as unto the weaker vessel, and as being heirs together of the grace of life; that your prayers be not hindered.
7. Rom. 13:3. For rulers are not a terror to good works, but to the evil. . . . do that which is good, and thou shalt have praise of the same.
   I Peter 2:14.
8. Rom. 13:4. He is the minister of God . . . a revenger to *execute* wrath upon him that doeth evil.
9. Prov. 29:15. The rod and reproof give wisdom: but a child left *to himself* bringeth his mother to shame.
   Rom. 13:4.
10. I Tim. 5:8. But if any provide not for his own, and specially for those of his own house, he hath denied the faith, and is worse than an infidel.
    Isa. 1:10, 17. Hear the word of the LORD, ye rulers of Sodom; give ear unto the law of our God, ye people of Gomorrah. . . . Learn to do well; seek judgment, relieve the oppressed, judge the fatherless, plead for the widow.

Eph. 6:4. And, ye fathers, provoke not your children to wrath: but bring them up in the nurture and admonition of the Lord.

11. I Tim. 4:12. Let no man despise thy youth; but be thou an example of the believers, in word, in conversation, in charity, in spirit, in faith, in purity.
Titus 2:2-14.

12. I Kings 3:28. And all Israel heard of the judgment which the king had judged; and they feared the king: for they saw that the wisdom of God *was* in him, to do judgment.

13. Titus 2:15. These things speak, and exhort, and rebuke with all authority. Let no man despise thee.

Q. 130. *What are the sins of superiors?*

A. The sins of superiors are, besides the neglect of the duties required of them,[1] an inordinate seeking of themselves,[2] their own glory,[3] ease, profit, or pleasure;[4] commanding things unlawful,[5] or not in the power of inferiors to perform;[6] counselling,[7] encouraging,[8] or favoring them in that which is evil;[9] dissuading, discouraging, or discountenancing them in that which is good;[10] correcting them unduly;[11] careless exposing or leaving them to wrong, temptation, and danger;[12] provoking them to wrath;[13] or any way dishonoring themselves, or lessening their authority, by an unjust, indiscreet, rigorous, or remiss behavior.[14]

1. Ezek. 34:2, 4. Should not the shepherds feed the flocks? . . . The diseased have ye not strengthened, neither have ye healed that which was sick, neither have ye bound up *that which was* broken, neither have ye brought again that which was driven away, neither have ye sought that which was lost.

2. Phil. 2:21. For all seek their own, not the things which are Jesus Christ's.

3. John 5:44. How can ye believe, which receive honour one of another, and seek not the honour that *cometh* from God only?
John 7:18.

4. Isa. 56:10, 11. His watchmen *are* blind: they are all ignorant, they *are* all dumb dogs, they cannot bark; sleeping, lying down, loving to slumber. Yea, *they are* greedy dogs *which* can never have enough.
Deut. 17:17. Neither shall he greatly multiply to himself silver and gold.

5. Acts 4:18. And they called them, and commanded them not to speak at all nor teach in the name of Jesus.
Dan. 3:4-6.

6. Exod. 5:10-19; Matt. 23:2, 4.

7. Matt. 14:8 compared with Mark 6:24. And she went forth, and said unto her mother, What shall I ask? And she said, The head of John the Baptist.

8. Jer. 5:30, 31. A wonderful and horrible thing is committed in the land; the prophets prophesy falsely, and the priests bear rule by their means; and my people love *to have it* so: and what will ye do in the end thereof?
II Sam. 13:28.

9. Jer. 6:13, 14. From the prophet even unto the priest every one dealeth falsely. They have healed also the hurt *of the daughter* of my people slightly, saying, Peace, peace; when *there is* no peace.
Ezek. 13:9, 10.

10. John 7:46-49. The officers answered, Never man spake like this man. Then answered them the Pharisees, Are ye also decieved? Have any of the rulers or of the Pharisees believed on him? But this people who knoweth not the law are cursed.

John 9:28. Then they reviled him, and said, Thou art his disciple; but we are Moses' disciples.

11. I Peter 2:19, 20. For this *is* thankworthy, if a man for conscience toward God endure grief, suffering wrongfully. For what glory *is it,* if, when ye be buffeted for your faults, ye shall take it patiently? but if, when ye do well, and suffer *for it,* ye take it patiently, this *is* acceptable with God.
Heb. 12:10. They verily for a few days chastened *us* after their own pleasure; but he for *our* profit, that *we* might be partakers of his holiness.
Deut. 25:3.

12. Lev. 19:29. Do not prostitute thy daughter.

Isa. 58:7. *Is it* not to deal thy bread to the hungry, and that thou bring the poor that are cast out to thy house? when thou seest the naked, that thou cover him; and that thou hide not thyself from thine own flesh?
Gen. 38:11, 26.

13. Eph. 6:4. And, ye fathers, provoke not your children to wrath.

14. Gen. 9:21. And he drank of the wine, and was drunken; and he was uncovered within his tent.

I Kings 12:13, 14. And the king [Rehoboam] answered the people roughly, and forsook the old men's counsel that they gave him; and spake to them after the counsel of the young men, saying, My father made your yoke heavy, and I will add to your yoke: my father *also* chastised you with whips, but I will chastise you with scorpions.

I Kings 1:6. And his father had not displeased him at any time in saying, Why hast thou done so?

I Sam. 3:13. For I have told him [Eli] that I will judge his house for ever for the iniquity which he knoweth; because his sons made themselves vile, and he restrained them not.

Q. 131. *What are the duties of equals?*

A. The duties of equals are: to regard the dignity and worth of each other,[1] in giving honor to go one before another;[2] and to rejoice in each other's gifts and advancement as their own.[3]

1. I Peter 2:17. Honour all *men.* Love the brotherhood.

2. Rom. 12:10. In honour preferring one another.
Phil. 2:3. In lowliness of mind let each esteem other better than themselves.

3. Rom. 12:15, 16. Rejoice with them that do rejoice, and weep with them that weep. *Be* of the same mind one toward another.
Phil. 2:4. Look not every man on his own things, but every man also on the things of others.

Q. 132. *What are the sins of equals?*

A. The sins of equals are, besides the neglect of the duties required,[1] the undervaluing of the worth,[2] envying the gifts,[3] grieving at the advancement or prosperity one of another;[4] and usurping pre-eminence one over another.[5]

1. Rom. 13:8. Owe no man any thing, but to love one another: for he that loveth another hath fulfilled the law.

2. Prov. 14:21. He that despiseth his neighbour sinneth: but he that hath mercy on the poor, happy *is* he.
   Isa. 65:5. Which say, Stand by thyself, come not near to me; for I am holier than thou.
   II Tim. 3:3.

3. Acts 7:9. And the patriarchs, moved with envy, sold Joseph into Egypt: but God was with him.
   Gal. 5:26. Let us not be desirous of vain glory, provoking one another, envying one another.

4. I John 3:12. Not as Cain, *who* was of that wicked one, and slew his brother. And wherefore slew he him? Because his own works were evil, and his brother's righteous.
   Matt. 20:15. Is thine eye evil, because I am good?
   Num. 12:2; Luke 15:28, 29.

5. Matt. 20:25-27. But Jesus called them *unto him,* and said, Ye know that the princes of the Gentiles exercise dominion over them, and they that are great exercise authority upon them. But it shall not be so among you.
   III John 9; Luke 22:24-26.

Q. 133. *What is the reason annexed to the fifth commandment, the more to enforce it?*

A. The reason annexed to the fifth commandment in these words: *"that thy days may be long upon the land which the Lord thy God giveth thee,"*[1] is an express promise of long life and prosperity, as far as it shall serve for God's glory and their own good, to all such as keep this commandment.[2]

1. Exod. 20:12.

2. Eph. 6:2, 3. Honour thy father and mother; which is the first commandment with promise; that it may be well with thee, and thou mayest live long on the earth.
   Deut. 5:16; I Kings 8:25.

Q. 134. *Which is the sixth commandment?*

A. The sixth commandment is, *Thou shalt not kill.*[1]

1. Exod. 20:13.

Q. 135. *What are the duties required in the sixth commandment?*

A. The duties required in the sixth commandment are: all
careful studies, and lawful endeavors, to preserve the life of ourselves[1] and others,[2] by resisting all thoughts and purposes,[3] subduing all passions,[4] and avoiding all occasions,[5] temptations,[6] and
practices, which tend to the unjust taking away the life of any;[7]
by just defense thereof against violence;[8] patient bearing of the
hand of God;[9] quietness of mind,[10] cheerfulness of spirit,[11] a
sober use of meat,[12] drink,[13] physic,[14] sleep,[15] labor,[16] and recreation;[17] by charitable thoughts,[18] love,[19] compassion,[20] meekness,
gentleness, kindness;[21] peaceable,[22] mild, and courteous speeches
and behavior;[23] forbearance, readiness to be reconciled, patient
bearing and forgiving of injuries, and requiting good for evil;[24]
comforting and succoring the distressed, and protecting and defending the innocent.[25]

1. Eph. 5:29. No man ever yet hated his own flesh; but nourisheth and
cherisheth it.
Matt. 10:23.

2. Ps. 82:4. Deliver the poor and needy: rid *them* out of the hand of the
wicked.
Deut. 22:8. When thou buildest a new house, then thou shalt make a
battlement for thy roof, that thou bring not blood upon thine house,
if any man fall from thence.

3. Matt. 5:22. But I say unto you, That whosoever is angry with his brother
without a cause shall be in danger of the judgment: and whosoever shall
say to his brother, Raca, shall be in danger of the council: but whosoever
shall say, Thou fool, shall be in danger of hell fire.
Jer. 26:15, 16.

4. Eph. 4:26. Be ye angry, and sin not: let not the sun go down upon your
wrath.

5. Prov. 22:24, 25. Make no friendship with an angry man; and with a
furious man thou shalt not go: lest thou learn his ways, and get a snare to
thy soul.
I Sam. 25:32, 33; Deut. 22:8.

6. Prov. 1:10, 11, 15. My son, if sinners entice thee, consent thou not. If
they say, Come with us, let us lay wait for blood, let us lurk privily for
the innocent without cause . . . My son, walk not thou in the way with
them; refrain thy foot from their path.
Matt. 4:6, 7.

7. I Kings 21:9, 10, 19. And she [Jezebel] wrote in the letters, saying, Proclaim a fast, and set Naboth on high among the people: and set two men,
sons of Belial, before him, to bear witness against him, saying, Thou
didst blaspheme God and the king. And *then* carry him out, and stone
him, that he may die. . . . Hast thou [Ahab] killed, and also taken pos-

session? . . . Thus saith the LORD, In the place where dogs licked the blood of Naboth shall dogs lick thy blood, even thine.

Gen. 37:21, 22; I Sam. 24:12, and 26:9-11.

8. Prov. 24:11, 12. If thou forbear to deliver *them that are* drawn unto death, and *those that are* ready to be slain; if thou sayest, Behold, we knew it not; doth not he that pondereth the heart consider *it?* and he that keepeth thy soul, doth *not* he know *it?* and shall *not* he render to *every* man according to his works?

I Sam. 14:45.

9. Luke 21:19. In your patience posses ye your souls.

James 5:8. Be ye also patient; stablish your hearts: for the coming of the Lord draweth nigh.

Heb. 12:5. My son, despise not thou the chastening of the Lord, nor faint when thou art rebuked of him.

10. Ps. 37:8, 11. Cease from anger, and forsake wrath: fret not thyself in any wise to do evil. . . . the meek shall inherit the earth; and shall delight themselves in the abundance of peace.

I Peter 3:3, 4. Whose adorning . . . *let it be* the hidden man of the heart, in that which is not corruptible, *even the ornament* of a meek and quiet spirit, which is in the sight of God of great price.

11. Prov. 17:22. A merry heart doeth good *like* a medicine: but a broken spirit drieth the bones.

I Thess. 5:16. Rejoice evermore.

12. Prov 23:20. Be not . . . among riotous eaters of flesh.

Prov. 25:16.

13. Prov. 23:29, 30. Who hath woe? who hath sorrow? who hath contentions? who hath babbling? who hath wounds without cause? who hath redness of eyes? They that tarry long at the wine; they that go to seek mixed wine.

I Tim. 5:23.

14. Matt. 9:12. But when Jesus heard *that,* he said unto them, They that be whole need not a physician, but they that are sick.

Isa. 38:21.

15. Ps. 127:2. *It is* vain for you to rise up early, to sit up late, to eat the bread of sorrows: *for* so he giveth his beloved sleep.

16. II Thess. 3:10, 12. For even when we were with you, this we commanded you, that if any would not work, neither should he eat. . . . Now them that are such we command and exhort by our Lord Jesus Christ, that with quietness they work, and eat their own bread.

17. Mark 6:31. And he said unto them, Come ye yourselves apart into a desert place, and rest a while: for there were many coming and going, and they had no leisure so much as to eat.

I Tim. 4:8.

18. I Cor. 13:4, 5. Charity . . . thinketh no evil.

I Sam. 19:4, 5.

19. Rom. 13:10. Love worketh no ill to his neighbour.

Prov. 10:12. Hatred stirreth up strifes: but love covereth all sins.

20. Zech. 7:9. Thus speaketh the LORD of hosts, saying . . . shew mercy and compassion every man to his brother.

Luke 10:33, 34.

21. Col. 3:12. Put on therefore, as the elect of God, holy and beloved, bowels of mercies, kindness, humbleness of mind, meekness, longsuffering.

22. Rom. 12:18. If it be possible, as much as lieth in you, live peaceably with all men.

23. I Peter 3:8, 9. *Be* pitiful, *be* courteous: not rendering evil for evil, or railing for railing: but contrariwise blessing.

I Cor. 4:12, 13. Being reviled, we bless; being persecuted, we suffer it: being defamed, we entreat.

24. Col. 3:13. Forbearing one another, and forgiving one another, if any man have a quarrel against any: even as Christ forgave you, so also *do* ye.

James 3:17. The wisdom that is from above is . . . gentle, *and* easy to be entreated.

I Peter 2:20. If, when ye do well, and suffer *for it*, ye take it patiently, this *is* acceptable with God.

Rom. 12:20, 21. If thine enemy hunger, feed him; if he thirst, give him drink: for in so doing thou shalt heap coals of fire on his head. Be not overcome of evil, but overcome evil with good.

Matt. 5:24.

25. I Thess. 5:14. Comfort the feebleminded, support the weak.

Matt. 25:35, 36. I was an hungred, and ye gave me meat: I was thirsty, and ye gave me drink: I was a stranger, and ye took me in: naked, and ye clothed me: I was sick, and ye visited me: I was in prison, and ye came unto me.

Prov. 31:8, 9. Open thy mouth for the dumb in the cause of all such as are appointed to destruction. . . . plead the cause of the poor and needy.

Isa. 58:7.

Q. 136. *What are the sins forbidden in the sixth commandment?*

A. The sins forbidden in the sixth commandment are: all taking away the life of ourselves,[1] or of others,[2] except in case of public justice,[3] lawful war,[4] or necessary defense;[5] the neglecting or withdrawing the lawful or necessary means of preservation of life;[6] sinful anger,[7] hatred,[8] envy,[9] desire of revenge;[10] all excessive passions;[11] distracting cares;[12] immoderate use of meat, drink,[13] labor,[14] and recreation;[15] provoking words;[16] oppression,[17] quarreling,[18] striking, wounding,[19] and whatsoever else tends to the destruction of the life of any.[20]

1. Acts 16:28. But Paul cried with a loud voice, saying, Do thyself no harm: for we are all here.

   Prov. 1:18.

2. Gen. 9:6. Whoso sheddeth man's blood, by man shall his blood be shed: for in the image of God made he man.

3. Exod. 21:14. If a man come presumptuously upon his neighbour, to slay him with guile; thou shalt take him from mine altar, that he may die.

   Num. 35:31, 33.

4. Deut. 20:1. When thou goest out to battle against thine enemies, and seest horses, and chariots, *and* a people more than thou, be not afraid of

them: for the LORD thy God *is* with thee, which brought thee up out of the land of Egypt.

Heb. 11:32-34. The time would fail me to tell of Gedeon, and *of* Barak, and *of* Samson, and *of* Jephthae; *of* David also, and Samuel, and *of* the prophets: who through faith subdued kingdoms . . . out of weakness were made strong, waxed valiant in fight, turned to flight the armies of the aliens.

Jer. 48:10.

5. Exod. 22:2. If a thief be found breaking up, and be smitten that he die, *there shall* no blood *be shed* for him.

6. Matt. 25:42, 43. I was an hungred, and ye gave me no meat: I was thirsty, and ye gave me no drink: I was a stranger, and ye took me not in: naked, and ye clothed me not: sick, and in prison, and ye visited me not.

James 2:15, 16.

7. Matt. 5:22. I say unto you, That whosoever is angry with his brother without a cause shall be in danger of the judgment.

8. I John 3:15. Whosoever hateth his brother is a murderer.

Prov. 10:12. Hatred stirreth up strifes.

Lev. 19:17.

9. Prov. 14:30. A sound heart *is* the life of the flesh: but envy the rottenness of the bones.

10. Rom. 12:19. Dearly beloved, avenge not yourselves, but *rather* give place unto wrath.

11. James 4:1. From whence *come* wars and fighting among you? *come they* not hence, *even* of your lusts that war in your members?

Eph. 4:31.

12. Matt. 6:34. Take therefore no thought for the morrow . . . Sufficient unto the day *is* the evil thereof.

13. Luke 21:34. And take heed to yourselves, lest at any time your hearts be overcharged with surfeiting, and drunkenness.

14. Exod. 20:9, 10. Six days shalt thou labour, and do all thy work: but the seventh day *is* the sabbath of the LORD thy God: *in it* thou shalt not do any work, thou, nor thy son, nor thy daughter, thy manservant, nor thy maidservant, nor thy cattle, nor thy stranger that *is* within thy gates.

15. I Peter 4:3, 4. For the time past of *our* life may suffice us to have wrought the will of the Gentiles, when we walked in lasciviousness, lusts, excess of wine, revellings, banquetings, and abominable idolatries: wherein they think it strange that ye run not with *them* to the same excess of riot, speaking evil of *you.*

16. Prov. 15:1. Grievous words stir up anger.

Prov. 12:18.

17. Isa. 3:15. What mean ye *that* ye beat my people to pieces, and grind the faces of the poor? saith the Lord GOD of hosts.

Exod. 1:14.

18. Gal. 5:15. But if ye bite and devour one another, take heed that ye be not comsumed one of another.

19. Num. 35:16. And if he smite him with an instrument of iron, so that he die, he *is* a murderer: the murderer shall surely be put to death.

20. Prov. 28:17. A man that doeth violence to the blood of *any* person shall flee to the pit; let no man stay him.

Exod. 21:18-36.

Q. 137. *Which is the seventh commandment?*

A. The seventh commandment is, *Thou shalt not commit adultery.*[1]

1. Exod. 20:14.

Q. 138. *What are the duties required in the seventh commandment?*

A. The duties required in the seventh commandment are: chastity in body, mind, affections,[1] words,[2] and behavior;[3] and the preservation of it in ourselves and others;[4] watchfulness over the eyes and all the senses;[5] temperance,[6] keeping of chaste company,[7] modesty in apparel,[8] marriage by those that have not the gift of continency,[9] conjugal love,[10] and cohabitation;[11] diligent labor in our callings;[12] shunning of all occasions of uncleanness, and resisting temptations thereunto.[13]

1. Thess. 4:4, 5. Every one of you should know how to possess his vessel in sanctification and honour; not in the lust of concupiscence.
2. Eph. 4:29. Let no corrupt communication proceed out of your mouth, but that which is good to the use of edifying.
   Col. 4:6.
3. I Peter 3:2. While they behold your chaste conversation *coupled* with fear.
4. I Cor. 7:2. Nevertheless, *to avoid* fornication, let every man have his own wife, and let every woman have her own husband.
   Titus 2:4, 5. That they may teach the young women . . . *to be* discreet, chaste, keepers at home.
5. Matt. 5:28. Whosoever looketh on a woman to lust after her hath committed adultery with her already in his heart.
6. Prov. 23:31, 33. Look not thou upon the wine when it is red . . . Thine eyes shall behold strange women.
   Jer. 5:7. When I had fed them to the full, they then committed adultery, and assembled themselves by troops in the harlots' houses.
7. Prov. 2:16, 20. To deliver thee from the strange woman, *even* from the stranger *which* flattereth with her words . . . That thou mayest walk in the way of good *men*, and keep the paths of the righteous.
   I Cor. 5:9. I wrote unto you in an epistle not to company with fornicators.
8. I Tim. 2:9. In like manner also, that women adorn themselves in modest apparel, with shamefacedness and sobriety.
9. I Cor. 7:9. But if they cannot contain, let them marry.
10. Prov. 5:18, 19. Rejoice with the wife of thy youth. *Let her be as* the loving hind and pleasant roe; let her breasts satisfy thee at all times; and be thou ravished always with her love.
11. I Peter 3:7. Likewise, ye husbands, dwell with *them* according to knowledge.

I Cor. 7:5. Defraud ye not one the other, except *it be* with consent for a time . . . and come together again, that Satan tempt you not for your incontinency.

12. I Tim. 5:13, 14. And withal they learn *to be* idle . . . I will therefore that the younger women marry, bear children, guide the house.
Prov. 31:27.

13. Prov. 5:8. Remove thy way far from her, and come not nigh the door of her house.

Q. 139. *What are the sins forbidden in the seventh commandment?*

A. The sins forbidden in the seventh commandment, besides the neglect of the duties required,[1] are: adultery, fornication,[2] rape, incest,[3] sodomy, and all unnatural lusts;[4] all unclean imaginations, thoughts, purposes, and affections;[5] all corrupt or filthy communications, or listening thereunto;[6] wanton looks,[7] impudent or light behavior, immodest apparel,[8] prohibiting of lawful,[9] and dispensing with unlawful marriages;[10] allowing, tolerating, keeping of stews, and resorting to them;[11] entangling vows of single life,[12] undue delay of marriage;[13] having more wives or husbands than one at the same time;[14] unjust divorce[15] or desertion;[16] idleness, gluttony, drunkenness,[17] unchaste company;[18] lascivious songs, books, pictures, dancings, stageplays,[19] and all other provocations to, or acts of, uncleanness either in ourselves or others.[20]

1. Prov. 5:7. Hear me now therefore, O ye children, and depart not from the words of my mouth.
Prov. 4:23, 27.

2. Heb. 13:4. Whoremongers and adulterers God will judge.
Eph. 5:5. For this ye know, that no whoremonger, nor unclean person . . . hath any inheritance in the kingdom of Christ and of God.
Gal. 5:19.

3. II Sam. 13:14. Howbeit he would not hearken unto her voice: but, being stronger than she, forced her, and lay with her.
Mark 6:18. John had said unto Herod, It is not lawful for thee to have thy brother's wife.
I Cor. 5:1, 13.

4. Rom. 1:26, 27. For this cause God gave them up unto vile affections: for even their women did change the natural use into that which is against nature: and likewise also the men, leaving the natural use of the woman, burned in their lust one toward another.
Lev. 20:15, 16. If a man lie with a beast, he shall surely be put to death: and ye shall slay the beast. And if a woman approach unto any beast, and lie down thereto, thou shalt kill the woman, and the beast: they shall surely be put to death; their blood *shall be* upon them.

5. Matt. 15:19. Out of the heart proceed evil thoughts, murders, adulteries, fornications.

Col. 3:5. Mortify therefore your members which are upon the earth; fornication, uncleanness, inordinate affection, evil concupiscence, and covetousness, which is idolatry.

Matt. 5:28.

6. Eph. 5:3, 4. But fornication, and all uncleanness, or covetousness, let it not be once named among you, as becometh saints; neither filthiness, nor foolish talking, nor jesting, which are not convenient.

Prov. 7:5, 21. That they may keep thee from the strange woman, from the stranger *which* flattereth with her words. . . . With her much fair speech she caused him to yield.

Prov. 19:27.

7. Isa. 3:16. The daughters of Zion are haughty, and walk with stretched forth necks and wanton eyes.

II Peter 2:14. Having eyes full of adultery, and that cannot cease from sin.

8. Prov. 7:10, 13. And behold, there met him a woman *with* the attire of an harlot, and subtil of heart. . . . So she caught him, and kissed him, *and* with an impudent face said unto him, . . .

9. I Tim. 4:3. Forbidding to marry . . .

10. Lev. 18:1-21.

11. II Kings 23:7. He [Josiah] brake down the houses of the sodomites, that *were* by the house of the LORD.

Lev. 19:29. Do not prostitute thy daughter, to cause her to be a whore; lest the land fall to whoredom, and the land become full of wickedness.

Jer. 5:7. How shall I pardon thee for this? thy children have forsaken me . . . when I had fed them to the full, they then committed adultery, and assembled themselves by troops in the harlots' houses.

12. Matt. 19:10-12. His disciples say unto him, If the case of the man be so with *his* wife, it is not good to marry. But he said unto them, All *men* cannot receive this saying, save *they* to whom it is given. For there are some eunuchs, which were so born from *their* mother's womb: and there are some eunuchs, which were made eunuchs of men: and there be eunuchs, which have made themselves eunuchs for the kingdom of heaven's sake. He that is able to receive *it*, let him receive *it*.

13. I Tim. 5:14, 15. I will therefore that the younger women marry . . . for some are already turned aside after Satan.

Gen. 38:26.

14. Matt. 19:5. For this cause shall a man leave father and mother, and shall cleave to his wife: and they twain shall be one flesh.

I Cor. 7:2.

15. Matt. 5:32. But I say unto you, That whosoever shall put away his wife, saving for the cause of fornication, causeth her to commit adultery: and whosoever shall marry her that is divorced committeth adultery.

Mal. 2:16.

16. See citations under Question 138.

I Cor. 7:12, 13.

17. Ezek. 16:49. Behold, this was the iniquity of thy sister Sodom, pride, fulness of bread, and abundance of idleness was in her.

Jer. 5:7.

18. **Eph. 5:11.** And have no fellowship with the unfruitful works of darkness.

    Prov. 5:8.

19. **Rom. 13:13.** Let us walk honestly, as in the day; not in rioting and drunkenness, not in chambering and wantonness.

    I Peter 4:3. For the time past of *our* life may suffice us to have wrought the will of the Gentiles, when we walked in lasciviousness, lusts, excess of wine, revellings, banquetings.

    Mark 6:22.

20. **Rom. 13:14.** Make not provision for the flesh, to *fulfil* the lusts *thereof.*
    II Peter 2:17, 18. To whom the mist of darkness is reserved for ever. For when they speak great swelling *words* of vanity, they allure through the lusts of the flesh, *through much* wantonness, those that were clean escaped from them who live in error.

Q. 140. *Which is the eighth commandment?*

A. The eighth commandment is, *Thou shalt not steal.*[1]

1. Exod. 20:15.

Q. 141. *What are the duties required in the eighth commandment?*

A. The duties required in the eighth commandment are: truth, faithfulness, and justice in contracts and commerce between man and man;[1] rendering to everyone his due;[2] restitution of goods unlawfully detained from the right owners thereof;[3] giving and lending freely, according to our abilities, and the necessities of others;[4] moderation of our judgments, wills, and affections, concerning worldly goods;[5] a provident care and study to get,[6] keep, use, and dispose of those things which are necessary and convenient for the sustentation of our nature, and suitable to our condition;[7] a lawful calling,[8] and diligence in it;[9] frugality;[10] avoiding unnecessary lawsuits,[11] and suretyship, or other like engagements;[12] and an endeavor by all just and lawful means to procure, preserve, and further the wealth and outward estate of others, as well as our own.[13]

1. **Ps. 15:2, 4.** He that walketh uprightly, and worketh righteousness . . . *He that* sweareth to *his own* hurt, and changeth not.

   Micah 6:8. What doth the Lord require of thee, but to do justly?

   Zech. 8:16.

2. **Rom. 13:7.** Render . . . to all their dues: tribute to whom tribute.

3. **Lev. 6:4, 5.** He shall restore that which he took violently away, or the thing which he hath deceitfully gotten, or that which was delivered him

to keep, or the lost thing which he found, or all that about which he hath sworn falsely.

Luke 19:8.

4. Deut. 15:7, 8, 10. Thou shalt not harden thine heart, nor shut thine hand from thy poor brother: but thou shalt open thine hand wide unto him, and shalt surely lend him sufficient for his need, *in that* which he wanteth. . . . Thou shalt surely give him, and thine heart shall not be grieved when thou givest unto him.

Gal. 6:10; Luke 6:30, 38.

5. I Tim. 6:8, 9. Having food and raiment let us be therewith content. But they that will be rich fall into temptation and a snare, and *into* many foolish and hurtful lusts, which drown men in destruction and perdition.

6. I Tim. 5:8. But if any provide not for his own, and specially for those of his own house, he hath denied the faith, and is worse than an infidel.

7. Prov. 27:23, 24. Be thou diligent to know the state of thy flocks, *and* look well to thy herds. For riches *are* not for ever.

I Tim. 6:17, 18. Charge them that are rich in this world . . . that they do good, that they be rich in good works, ready to distribute, willing to communicate.

8. Eph. 4:28. Let him labour, working with *his* hands the thing which is good.

Rom. 12:5-8.

9. Prov. 10:4. The hand of the diligent maketh rich.

Rom. 12:11. Not slothful in business; fervent in spirit; serving the Lord.

10. Prov. 12:27. The substance of a diligent man *is* precious.

Prov. 21:20. *There is* treasure to be desired and oil in the dwelling of the wise; but a foolish man spendeth it up.

John 6:12.

11. I Cor. 6:7. Now therefore there is utterly a fault among you, because ye go to law one with another.

12. Prov. 11:15. He that is surety for a stranger shall smart *for it:* and he that hateth suretiship is sure.

Prov. 6:1-5.

13. Lev. 25:35. And if thy brother be waxen poor, and fallen in decay with thee; then thou shalt relieve him: *yea, though he be* a stranger, or a sojourner.

Phil. 2:4. Look not every man on his own things, but every man also on the things of others.

Deut. 22:1-4; Exod. 23:4, 5.

Q. 142. *What are the sins forbidden in the eighth commandment?*

A. The sins forbidden in the eighth commandment, besides the neglect of the duties required,[1] are: theft,[2] robbery,[3] man-stealing,[4] and receiving anything that is stolen;[5] fraudulent dealing,[6] false weights and measures,[7] removing landmarks,[8] injustice and unfaithfulness in contracts between man and man,[9] or in matters of trust;[10] oppression,[11] extortion, usury,[12] bribery,[13] vexatious lawsuits,[14] unjust enclosures and depopulations;[15] engrossing commodities to enhance the price,[16] unlawful callings,[17] and all other unjust or sinful ways of taking or withholding from our neighbor what belongs to him, or of enriching ourselves;[18] covetousness,[19] inordinate prizing and affecting worldly goods;[20] distrustful and distracting cares and studies in getting, keeping, and using them;[21] envying at the prosperity of others;[22] as likewise idleness,[23] prodigality, wasteful gaming, and all other ways whereby we do unduly prejudice our own outward estate;[24] and defrauding ourselves of the due use and comfort of that estate which God hath given us.[25]

1. Prov. 23:21. Drowsiness shall clothe *a man* with rags.

   I John 3:17. But whoso hath this world's good, and seeth his brother have need, and shutteth up his bowels *of compassion* from him, how dwelleth the love of God in him?

   James 2:15, 16.

2. Eph. 4:28. Let him that stole steal no more.

3. Ps. 62:10. Become not vain in robbery.

4. I Tim. 1:10. [The law is made] for whoremongers, for them that defile themselves with mankind, for menstealers.

   Exod. 21:16.

5. Prov. 29:24. Whoso is partner with a thief hateth his own soul.

   Ps. 50:18. When thou sawest a thief, then thou consentedst with him.

6. I Thess. 4:6. That no *man* go beyond and defraud his brother in *any* matter: because that the Lord *is* the avenger of all such.

7. Prov. 11:1. A false balance *is* abomination to the LORD.

   Prov. 20:10. Divers weights, *and* divers measures, both of them *are* alike abomination to the LORD.

8. Deut. 19:14. Thou shalt not remove thy neighbour's landmark, which they of old time have set in thine inheritance.

   Prov. 23:10.

9. Amos 8:5. Making the ephah small, and the shekel great, and falsifying the balances by deceit.

   Ps. 37:21. The wicked borroweth, and payeth not again.

10. Luke 16:11. If therefore ye have not been faithful in the unrighteous mammon, who will commit to your trust the true *riches?*

11. Ezek. 22:29. The people of the land have used oppression.

    Lev. 25:17. Ye shall not therefore oppress one another; but thou shalt fear thy God.

12. Matt. 23:25. Woe unto you, scribes and Pharisees, hypocrites! for ye make clean the outside of the cup and of the platter, but within they are full of extortion and excess.

Ezek. 22:12. Thou hast greedily gained of thy neighbours by extortion, and hast forgotten me, saith the LORD God.

13. Isa. 33:15. He that walketh righteously, and speaketh uprightly; he that despiseth the gain of oppressions, that shaketh his hands from holding of bribes, that stoppeth his ears from hearing of blood, and shutteth his eyes from seeing evil.

14. Prov. 3:30. Strive not with a man without cause, if he have done thee no harm.

I Cor. 6:7.

15. Isa. 5:8. Woe unto them that join house to house, *that* lay field to field, till *there be* no place, that they may be placed alone in the midst of the earth!

Micah 2:2. They covet fields, and take *them* by violence; and houses, and take *them* away.

16. Prov. 11:26. He that withholdeth corn, the people shall curse him: but blessing *shall be* upon the head of him that selleth *it.*

17. Acts 19:19. Many of them also which used curious arts brought their books together, and burned them before all *men.*

See context.

18. James 5:4. Behold, the hire of the labourers who have reaped down your fields, which is of you kept back by fraud, crieth: and the cries of them which have reaped are entered into the ears of the Lord of sabaoth.

Prov. 21:6. The getting of treasures by a lying tongue *is* a vanity tossed to and fro of them that seek death.

19. Luke 12:15. Take heed, and beware of covetousness.

Prov. 1:19.

20. I John 2:15, 16. Love not the world, neither the things *that are* in the world. If any man love the world, the love of the Father is not in him. For all that *is* in the world, the lust of the flesh, and the lust of the eyes, and the pride of life, is not of the Father, but is of the world.

Prov. 23:5; Ps. 62:10.

21. Matt. 6:25, 34. Take no thought for your life, what ye shall eat, or what ye shall drink; nor yet for your body, what ye shall put on. . . . Take therefore no thought for the morrow: for the morrow shall take thought for the things of itself. Sufficient unto the day *is* the evil thereof.

22. Ps. 73:3. I was envious at the foolish, *when* I saw the prosperity of the wicked.

James 5:9. Grudge not one against another, brethren, lest ye be condemned.

23. II Thess. 3:11. We hear that there are some which walk among you disorderly, working not at all, but are busybodies.

Prov. 18:9.

24. Prov. 21:17. He that loveth pleasure *shall be* a poor man: he that loveth wine and oil shall not be rich.

Prov. 23:20, 21. Be not among winebibbers; among riotous eaters of flesh: for the drunkard and the glutton shall come to poverty.

Prov. 28:19.

25. Deut. 12:7. And there ye shall eat before the LORD your God, and ye shall rejoice in all that ye put your hand unto, ye and your households, wherein the LORD thy God hath blessed thee.

Deut. 16:14. And thou shalt rejoice in thy feast, thou, and thy son, and thy daughter, and thy manservant, and thy maidservant, and the Levite, the stranger, and the fatherless, and the widow, that *are* within thy gates

Q. 143. *Which is the ninth commandment?*

A. The ninth commandment is, *Thou shalt not bear false witness against thy neighbour.*[1]

1. Exod. 20:16.

Q. 144. *What are the duties required in the ninth commandment?*

A. The duties required in the ninth commandment are: the preserving and promoting of truth between man and man,[1] and the good name of our neighbor, as well as our own;[2] appearing and standing for the truth;[3] and from the heart, sincerely,[4] freely,[5] clearly,[6] and fully,[7] speaking the truth, and only the truth, in matters of judgment and justice,[8] and in all other things whatsoever;[9] a charitable esteem of our neighbors;[10] loving, desiring, and rejoicing in their good name;[11] sorrowing for,[12] and covering of their infirmities;[13] freely acknowledging of their gifts and graces,[14] defending their innocency;[15] a ready receiving of a good report,[16] and unwillingness to admit of an evil report concerning them;[17] discouraging talebearers,[18] flatterers,[19] and slanderers;[20] love and care of our own good name, and defending it when need requireth;[21] keeping of lawful promises;[22] studying and practicing of whatsoever things are true, honest, lovely, and of good report.[23]

1. Eph. 4:25. Putting away lying, speak every man truth with his neighbour: for we are members one of another.

2. III John 12. Demetrius hath good report of all *men,* and of the truth itself: yea, and we *also* bear record; and ye know that our record is true.

3. Prov. 31:9. Open thy mouth, judge righteously, and plead the cause of the poor and needy.

4. Ps. 15:2. He that walketh uprightly, and worketh righteousness, and speaketh the truth in his heart.

5. Jer. 9:3. They are not valiant for the truth upon the earth.

6. Jer. 42:4. Whatsoever thing the LORD shall answer you, I will declare *it* unto you; I will keep nothing back from you.
   Acts 20:20.

7. Acts 20:27. I have not shunned to declare unto you all the counsel of God.

8. Lev. 19:15. Thou shalt not respect the person of the poor, nor honour the person of the mighty: *but* in righteousness shalt thou judge thy neighbour.
   Prov. 14:5. A faithful witness will not lie: but a false witness will utter lies.

9. Isa. 63:8. Surely they *are* my people, children *that* will not lie.

Col. 3:9. Lie not one to another, seeing that ye have put off the old man with his deeds.

II Cor. 1:17.

10. Heb. 6:9. But, beloved, we are persuaded better things of you, and things that accompany salvation, though we thus speak.

I Cor. 13:4, 5. Charity . . . thinketh no evil.

11. III John 4. I have no greater joy than to hear that my children walk in truth.

Rom. 1:8.

12. II Cor. 12:21. *And* lest, when I come again, my God will humble me among you, and *that* I shall bewail many which have sinned already, and have not repented of the uncleanness and fornication and lasciviousness which they have committed.

Ps. 119:158.

13. Prov. 17:9. He that covereth a transgression seeketh love.

I Peter 4:8.

14. I Cor. 1:4, 5. I thank my God always on your behalf, for the grace of God which is given you by Jesus Christ; that in every thing ye are enriched by him, in all utterance, and *in* all knowledge.

II Tim. 1:4, 5.

15. Psa. 82:3. Defend the poor and fatherless: do justice to the afflicted and needy.

16. I Cor. 13:4, 6, 7. Charity . . . rejoiceth not in iniquity, but rejoiceth in the truth . . . believeth all things, hopeth all things.

17. Psa. 15:3. Nor taketh up a reproach against his neighbour.

18. Prov. 25:23. The north wind driveth away rain: so *doth* an angry countenance a backbiting tongue.

19. Prov. 26:24, 25. He that hateth dissembleth with his lips, and layeth up deceit within him; when he speaketh fair, believe him not: for *there are* seven abominations in his heart.

20. Ps. 101:5. Whoso privily slandereth his neighbour, him will I cut off.

21. II Cor. 11:18, 23. Seeing that many glory after the flesh, I will glory also. . . . Are they ministers of Christ? . . . I *am* more; in labours more abundant, in stripes above measure, in prisons more frequent.

Prov. 22:1; John 8:49.

22. Ps. 15:4. *He that* sweareth to *his own* hurt, and changeth not.

23. Phil. 4:8. Finally, brethren, whatsoever things are true, whatsoever things *are* honest, whatsoever things *are* just, whatsoever things *are* pure, whatsoever things *are* lovely, whatsoever things *are* of good report; if *there be* any virtue, and if *there be* any praise, think on these things.

Q. 145. *What are the sins forbidden in the ninth commandment?*

A. The sins forbidden in the ninth commandment are: all prejudicing of the truth, and the good name of our neighbors as well as our own,[1] especially in public judicature;[2] giving false evidence,[3] suborning false witnesses,[4] wittingly appearing and pleading for an evil cause, outfacing and overbearing the truth;[5] passing unjust sentence,[6] calling evil good, and good evil; rewarding the wicked according to the work of the righteous, and the righteous according to the work of the wicked;[7] forgery,[8] concealing the truth, undue silence in a just cause,[9] and holding our peace when iniquity calleth for either a reproof from ourselves,[10] or complaint to others;[11] speaking the truth unseasonably,[12] or maliciously to a wrong end,[13] or perverting it to a wrong meaning,[14] or in doubtful and equivocal expression, to the prejudice of truth or justice;[15] speaking untruth,[16] lying,[17] slandering,[18] backbiting,[19] detracting,[20] talebearing,[21] whispering,[22] scoffing,[23] reviling;[24] rash,[25] harsh,[26] and partial censuring;[27] misconstruing intentions, words, and actions;[28] flattering,[29] vainglorious boasting,[30] thinking or speaking too highly or too meanly of ourselves or others; denying the gifts and graces of God;[31] aggravating smaller faults;[32] hiding, excusing, or extenuating of sins, when called to a free confession;[33] unnecessarily discovering of infirmities;[34] raising false rumors;[35] receiving and countenancing evil reports,[36] and stopping our ears against just defense;[37] evil suspicion;[38] envying or grieving at the deserved credit of any;[39] endeavoring or desiring to impair it,[40] rejoicing in their disgrace and infamy;[41] scornful contempt,[42] fond admiration;[43] breach of lawful promises;[44] neglecting such things as are of good report;[45] and practicing or not avoiding ourselves, or not hindering what we can in others, such things as procure an ill name.[46]

1. Luke 3:14. And he said unto them, Do violence to no man, neither accuse *any* falsely.

2. Lev. 19:15. Ye shall do no unrighteousness in judgment.
   Hab. 1:4.

3. Prov. 19:5. A false witness shall not be unpunished, and *he that* speaketh lies shall not escape.
   Prov. 6:16, 19.

4. Acts 6:13. And set up false witnesses, which said, This man ceaseth not to speak blasphemous words against this holy place, and the law.

5. Jer. 9:3. And they bend their tongues *like* their bow *for* lies: but they are not valiant for the truth upon the earth.
   Ps. 12:3, 4. The LORD shall cut off . . . the tongue that speaketh proud things: who have said, With our tongue will we prevail; our lips *are* our own: who *is* lord over us?
   Ps. 52:1-4.

6. Prov. 17:15. He that justifieth the wicked, and he that condemneth the just, even they both *are* abomination to the LORD.

7. Isa. 5:23. [Woe unto them] which justify the wicked for reward, and take away the righteousness of the righteous from him!

8. I Kings 21:8.

9. Lev. 5:1. And if a soul sin, and hear the voice of swearing, and *is* a witness, whether he hath seen or known *of it;* if he do not utter *it,* then he shall bear his iniquity.

   Acts 5:3. Peter said, Ananias, why hath Satan filled thine heart to lie to the Holy Ghost, and to keep back *part* of the price of the land?

10. Lev. 19:17. Thou shalt in any wise rebuke thy neighbour, and not suffer sin upon him.

    Isa. 58:1. Cry aloud, spare not, lift up thy voice like a trumpet, and shew my people their transgression, and the house of Jacob their sins.

11. Isa. 59:4. None calleth for justice, nor *any* pleadeth for truth: they trust in vanity.

12. Prov. 29:11. A fool uttereth all his mind: but a wise *man* keepeth it in till afterwards.

13. I Sam. 22:9, 10. Then answered Doeg the Edomite, which was set over the servants of Saul, and said, I saw the son of Jesse coming to Nob, to Ahimelech the son of Ahitub. And he inquired of the LORD for him, and gave him . . . the sword of Goliath the Philistine.

    Ps. 52:1. Why boasteth thou thyself in mischief, O mighty man?

14. Ps. 56:5. Every day they wrest my words.

    Matt. 26:60, 61. At the last came two false witnesses, and said, This *fellow* said, I am able to destroy the temple of God, and to build it in three days. Compare John 2:19.

15. Gen. 3:5. God doth know that in the day ye eat thereof, then your eyes shall be opened, and ye shall be as gods, knowing good and evil.

    Gen. 26:7, 9.

16. Isa. 59:13. Conceiving and uttering from the heart words of falsehood.

17. Col. 3:9. Lie not one to another, seeing that ye have put off the old man with his deeds.

    Lev. 19:11.

18. Ps. 50:20. Thou sittest *and* speakest against thy brother; thou slanderest thine own mother's son.

19. Ps. 15:3. *He that* backbiteth not with his tongue.

    Rom. 1:30. Backbiters, haters of God.

20. James 4:11. Speak not evil one of another, brethren.

    Titus 3:2. To speak evil of no man.

21. Lev. 19:16. Thou shalt not go up and down *as* a talebearer among thy people.

22. Rom. 1:29. Full of . . . deceit, malignity; whisperers.

    Prov. 16:28.

23. Isa. 28:22. Now therefore be ye not mockers, lest your bands be made strong.

    Gen. 21:9; Gal. 4:29.

24. I Cor. 6:10. Nor drunkards, nor revilers . . . shall inherit the kingdom of God.

25. Matt. 7:1. Judge not, that ye be not judged.

26. James 2:13. He shall have judgment without mercy, that hath shewed no mercy.

27. John 7:24. Judge not according to the appearance, but judge righteous judgment.
Rom. 2:1.

28. Rom. 3:8. And not *rather,* (as we be slanderously reported, and as some affirm that we say,) Let us do evil, that good may come? whose damnation is just.
Ps. 69:10. When I wept, *and chastened* my soul with fasting, that was to my reproach.

29. Ps. 12:2, 3. *With* flattering lips *and* with a double heart do they speak. The LORD shall cut off all flattering lips.

30. II Tim. 3:2. For men shall be lovers of their own selves . . . boasters.

31. Luke 18:11. The Pharisee stood and prayed thus with himself, God, I thank thee, that I am not as other men *are,* extortioners, unjust, adulterers, or even as this publican.
Gal. 5:26. Let us not be desirous of vainglory, provoking one another, envying one another.
Exod. 4:10, 14. And Moses said unto the LORD, O my LORD, I *am* not eloquent, neither heretofore, nor since thou hast spoken unto thy servant: but I *am* slow of speech, and of a slow tongue. . . . And the anger of the LORD was kindled against Moses.
Acts 12:22.

32. Isa. 29:20, 21. All that watch for iniquity are cut off: that make a man an offender for a word.
Matt. 7:3.

33. Gen. 3:12, 13. And the man said, The woman whom thou gavest *to be* with me, she gave me of the tree, and I did eat. . . . And the woman said, The serpent beguiled me, and I did eat.
Prov. 28:13. He that covereth his sins shall not prosper.
Gen. 4:9.

34. Prov. 25:9. Debate thy cause with thy neighbour *himself;* and discover not a secret to another.
Gen. 9:22.

35. Exod. 23:1. Thou shalt not raise a false report.

36. Jer. 20:10. I heard the defaming of many . . . Report, *say they,* and we will report it. All my familiars watched for my halting, *saying,* Peradventure he will be enticed, and we shall prevail against him, and we shall take our revenge on him.
Prov. 29:12.

37. Acts 7:57. Then they cried out with a loud voice, and stopped their ears.

38. I Cor. 13:4, 5. Charity . . . thinketh no evil.
I Tim. 6:4.

39. Matt. 21:15. And when the chief priests and scribes saw the wonderful things that he did, and the children crying in the temple, and saying, Hosanna to the son of David; they were sore displeased.
Num. 11:29.

40. Dan. 6:3, 4. Then this Daniel was preferred above the presidents and

princes . . . Then the presidents and princes sought to find occasion against Daniel concerning the kingdom.
Ezra 4:12, 13.

41. Jer. 48:27. For was not Israel a derision unto thee? was he found among thieves? for since thou spakest of him, thou skippedst for joy.

42. Matt. 27:28, 29. And they stripped him, and put on him a scarlet robe. And when they had platted a crown of thorns, they put *it* upon his head, and a reed in his right hand: and they bowed the knee before him, and mocked him, saying, Hail, King of the Jews!
Ps. 35:15, 16.

43. I Cor. 3:21. Let no man glory in men.
Jude 16. Having men's persons in admiration because of advantage.
Acts 12:22.

44. Rom. 1:31. Without understanding, covenantbreakers.
II Tim. 3:3.

45. II Sam. 12:14. Thou hast given great occasion to the enemies of the LORD to blaspheme.
I Sam. 2:24.

46. Phil. 3:18, 19. For many walk, of whom I have told you often, and now tell you even weeping, *that they are* the enemies of the cross of Christ: whose end *is* destruction, whose god *is their* belly, and *whose* glory *is* in their shame, who mind earthly things.
II Peter 2:2. And many shall follow their pernicious ways; by reason of whom the way of truth shall be evil spoken of.
II Sam. 12:13, 14.

Q. 146. *Which is the tenth commandment?*

A. The tenth commandment is, *Thou shalt not covet thy neighbour's house, thou shalt not covet thy neighbour's wife, nor his manservant, nor his maidservant, nor his ox, nor his ass, nor any thing that is thy neighbour's.*[1]

1. Exod. 20:17.

Q. 147. *What are the duties required in the tenth commandment?*

A. The duties required in the tenth commandment are: such a full contentment with our own condition,[1] and such a charitable frame of the whole soul towards our neighbor, as that all our inward motions and affections touching him, tend unto and further all that good which is his.[2]

1. Heb. 13:5. *Let your* conversation *be* without covetousness; *and be* content with such things as ye have: for he hath said, I will never leave thee.
I Tim. 6:6.
2. Rom. 12:15. Rejoice with them that do rejoice, and weep with them that weep.
Phil. 2:4. Look not every man on his own things, but every man also on the things of others.
I Tim. 1:5.

Q. 148. *What are the sins forbidden in the tenth commandment?*

A. The sins forbidden in the tenth commandment are: discontentment with our own estate;[1] envying,[2] and grieving at the good of our neighbor,[3] together with all inordinate motions and affections to anything that is his.[4]

1. I Cor. 10:10. Neither murmur ye, as some of them also murmured, and were destroyed of the destroyer.

2. Gal. 5:26. Let us not be desirous of vain glory, provoking one another, envying one another.

   James 3:14, 16. But if ye have bitter envying and strife in your hearts, glory not, and lie not against the truth. . . . For where envying and strife *is*, there *is* confusion and every evil work.

3. Ps. 112:9, 10. His horn shall be exalted with honour. The wicked shall see *it*, and be grieved.

   Neh 2:10.

4. Rom. 7:7. I had not known sin, but by the law: for I had not known lust, except the law had said, Thou shalt not covet.

   Deut. 5:21. Neither shalt thou desire thy neighbour's wife, neither shalt thou covet thy neighbour's house, his field, or his manservant, or his maidservant, his ox, or his ass, or any *thing* that *is* thy neighbour's.

   Col. 3:5. Mortify . . . inordinate affection, evil concupiscence, and covetousness, which is idolatry.

   Rom. 13:9.

Q. 149. *Is any man able perfectly to keep the commandments of God?*

A. No man is able, either of himself,[1] or by any grace received in this life, perfectly to keep the commandments of God;[2] but doth daily break them in thought,[3] word, and deed.[4]

1. James 3:2. In many things we offend all.

   John 15:5. Without me ye can do nothing.

2. I Kings 8:46. For *there is* no man that sinneth not.

   Ps. 17:15. As for me, I will behold thy face in righteousness: I shall be satisfied, when I awake, with thy likeness.

   I John 1:8—2:6.

3. Gen. 8:21. The imagination of man's heart *is* evil from his youth.

   James 1:14. Every man is tempted, when he is drawn away of his own lust, and enticed.

   Gen. 6:5.

   See citations under figure 2 above.

4. Ps. 19:12. Who can understand *his* errors? cleanse thou me from secret *faults*.

   James 3:2, 8. In many things we offend all. . . . the tongue can no man tame; *it is* an unruly evil, full of deadly poison.

Q. 150. *Are all transgressions of the law of God equally heinous in themselves, and in the sight of God?*

A. All transgressions of the law of God are not equally heinous; but some sins in themselves, and by reason of several aggravations, are more heinous in the sight of God than others.[1]

> 1. Heb. 2:2, 3. If the word spoken by angels was stedfast, and every transgression and disobedience received a just recompense of reward; how shall we escape, if we neglect so great salvation; which at the first began to be spoken by the Lord?
> Ezra 9:14; Ps. 78:17, 32, 56.

Q. 151. *What are those aggravations that make some sins more heinous than others?*

A. Sins receive their aggravations,

1. From the persons offending:[1] if they be of riper age, greater experience, or grace;[2] eminent for profession,[3] gifts,[4] place, office,[5] guides to others,[6] and whose example is likely to be followed by others.[7]

2. From the parties offended:[8] if immediately against God,[9] his attributes,[10] and worship;[11] against Christ, and his grace;[12] the Holy Spirit, his witness, and workings;[13] against superiors, men of eminency,[14] and such as we stand especially related and engaged unto;[15] against any of the saints,[16] particularly weak brethren, the souls of them or any other;[17] and the common good of all or many.[18]

3. From the nature and quality of the offense:[19] if it be against the express letter of the law,[20] break many commandments, contain in it many sins:[21] if not only conceived in the heart, but break forth in words and actions,[22] scandalize others,[23] and admit of no reparation:[24] if against means,[25] mercies,[26] judgments,[27] light of nature,[28] conviction of conscience,[29] public or private admonition,[30] censures of the church,[31] civil punishments;[32] and our prayers, purposes, promises, vows, covenants, and engagements to God or men:[33] if done deliberately, willfully,[34] presumptuously, impudently, boastingly,[35] maliciously,[36] frequently,[37] obstinately,[38] with light,[39] continuance,[40] or relapsing after repentance.[41]

4. From circumstances of time,[42] and place:[43] if on the Lord's day,[44] or other times of divine worship;[45] or immediately be-

fore,[46] or after these,[47] or other helps to prevent or remedy such miscarriages:[48] if in public, or in the presence of others, who are thereby likely to be provoked or defiled.[49]

1. Jer. 2:8. The priests said not, Where *is* the LORD? and they that handle the law knew me not: the pastors also transgressed against me, and the prophets prophesied by Baal.

2. I Kings 11:9. And the LORD was angry with Solomon, because his heart was turned from the LORD God of Israel, which had appeared unto him twice.

3. II Sam. 12:14. By this deed thou hast given great occasion to the enemies of the LORD to blaspheme.

   I Cor. 5:1.

4. James 4:17. To him that knoweth to do good, and doeth *it* not, to him it is sin.

   Luke 12:47. That servant, which knew his Lord's will, and prepared not *himself*, neither did according to his will, shall be beaten with many *stripes*.

5. John 3:10. Jesus answered and said unto him, Art thou a master of Israel, and knowest not these things?

   Jer. 5:4, 5.

   II Sam. 12:7-9; Ezek. 8:11, 12.

6. Rom. 2:21, 22, 24. Thou therefore which teachest another, teachest thou not thyself? thou that preachest a man should not steal, dost thou steal? thou that sayest a man should not commit adultery, dost thou commit adultery? . . . For the name of God is blasphemed among the Gentiles through you.

7. Gal. 2:14. But when I saw that they walked not uprightly according to the truth of the gospel, I said unto Peter before *them* all, If thou, being a Jew, livest after the manner of Gentiles, and not as do the Jews, why compellest thou the Gentiles to live as do the Jews?

   II Peter 2:2.

8. I John 5:10. He that believeth on the Son of God hath the witness in himself: he that believeth not God hath made him a liar; because he believeth not the record that God gave of his Son.

   Matt. 21:38, 39.

9. I Sam. 2:25. If one man sin against another, the judge shall judge him: but if a man sin against the LORD, who shall entreat for him?

   Acts 5:4. Thou hast not lied unto men, but unto God.

10. Rom. 2:4. Or despisest thou the riches of his goodness and forbearance and longsuffering; not knowing that the goodness of God leadeth thee to repentance?

11. Mal. 1:14. Cursed *be* the deceiver, which hath in his flock a male, and voweth, and sacrificeth unto the Lord a corrupt thing.

    I Cor. 10:21, 22. Ye cannot be partakers of the Lord's table, and of the table of devils. Do we provoke the LORD to jealousy? are we stronger than he?

12. John 3:18, 36. He that believeth not is condemned already, because he hath not believed in the name of the only begotten Son of God. . . . he that believeth not the Son shall not see life; but the wrath of God abideth on him.

    Heb. 12:25.

13. Heb. 6:4-6. For *it is* impossible for those who were once enlightened . . . and were made partakers of the Holy Ghost . . . if they shall fall away, to renew them again unto repentance.

Heb. 10:29. Of how much sorer punishment, suppose ye, shall he be thought worthy, who hath trodden under foot the Son of God . . . and hath done despite unto the Spirit of grace?

Matt. 12:31, 32; Eph. 4:30.

14. Num. 12:8. Wherefore then were ye not afraid to speak against my servant Moses?

Jude 8.

15. Prov. 30:17. The eye *that* mocketh at *his* father, and despiseth to obey *his* mother, the ravens of the valley shall pick it out, and the young eagles shall eat it.

Ps. 41:9. Yea, mine own familiar friend, in whom I trusted, which did eat of my bread, hath lifted up *his* heel against me.

Ps. 55:12-14.

16. Zech. 2:8. He that toucheth you toucheth the apple of his eye.

17. I Cor. 8:11, 12. And through thy knowledge shall the weak brother perish, for whom Christ died? But when ye sin so against the brethren, and wound their weak conscience, ye sin against Christ.

Rom. 14:13, 15, 21.

18. I Thess. 2:15, 16. Who both killed the Lord Jesus, and their own prophets, and have persecuted us . . . to fill up their sins alway: for the wrath is come upon them to the uttermost.

Matt. 23:34-38.

19. Isa. 3:9. They declare their sin as Sodom, they hide *it* not.

20. Ezek. 20:12, 13. I gave them my sabbaths to be a sign between me and them . . . and my sabbaths they greatly polluted.

21. Col. 3:5. Mortify therefore your members which are upon the earth; fornication, uncleanness, inordinate affection, evil concupiscence, and covetousness, which is idolatry.

I Tim. 6:10.

22. Micah 2:1, 2. Woe to them that devise iniquity, and work evil upon their beds! when the morning is light, they practice it, because it is in the power of their hand. And they covet fields, and take *them* by violence.

23. Rom. 2:23, 24. Thou that makest thy boast of the law, through breaking the law dishonourest thou God? For the name of God is blasphemed among the Gentiles through you, as it is written.

Matt. 18:7.

24. Prov. 6:32-35. *But* whoso committeth adultery with a woman . . . a wound and dishonour shall he get; and his reproach shall not be wiped away. For jealousy *is* the rage of a man: therefore he will not spare in the day of vengeance. He will not regard any ransom.

Matt. 16:26. What is a man profited, if he shall gain the whole world, and lose his own soul? or what shall a man give in exchange for his soul?

25. Matt. 11:21-24. Woe unto thee, Chorazin! woe unto thee, Bethsaida! for if the mighty works, which were done in you, had been done in Tyre and Sidon, they would have repented long ago in sackcloth and ashes But I say unto you, It shall be more tolerable for Tyre and Sidon at the day of judgment, than for you. . . .

John 15:22.

26. Deut. 32:6. Do ye thus requite the LORD, O foolish people and unwise?

is not he thy father *that* hath bought thee? hath he not made thee, and established thee?

Isa. 1:2, 3; Ezra 9:13, 14.

27. Jer. 5:3. O LORD, *are* not thine eyes upon the truth? thou hast stricken them, but they have not grieved; thou hast consumed them, *but* they have refused to receive correction: they have made their faces harder than a rock; they have refused to return.

Amos 4:8-11.

28. Rom. 1:20, 21. For the invisible things of him from the creation of the world are clearly seen, being understood by the things that are made, *even* his eternal power and Godhead; so that they are without excuse.

29. Rom. 1:32. Who knowing the judgment of God, that they which commit such things are worthy of death, not only do the same, but have pleasure in them that do them.

Dan. 5:22.

30. Prov. 29:1. He, that being often reproved hardeneth *his* neck, shall suddenly be destroyed, and that without remedy.

31. Matt. 18:17. If he neglect to hear the church, let him be unto thee as an heathen man and a publican.

Titus 3:10.

32. Rom. 13:1-5.

33. Ps. 78:34, 36, 37; Jer. 42:5, 6, 20-22; Prov. 20:25; Lev. 26:25; Jer. 31:32; Prov. 2:17; Ezek. 17:18.

34. Ps. 36:4. He deviseth mischief upon his bed; he setteth himself in a way *that is* not good; he abhorreth not evil.

Jer. 6:16. Thus saith the LORD, Stand ye in the ways, and see, and ask for the old paths, where *is* the good way, and walk therein, and ye shall find rest for your souls. But they said, We will not walk *therein*.

35. Num. 15:30. But the soul that doeth *ought* presumptuously, *whether he be* born in the land, or a stranger, the same reproacheth the LORD; and that soul shall be cut off from among his people.

Jer. 6:15. Were they ashamed when they had committed abomination? nay, they were not at all ashamed, neither could they blush: therefore they shall fall among them that fall.

Ps. 52:1. Why boastest thou thyself in mischief, O mighty man?

36. Ezek. 35:5, 6. Because thou hast had a perpetual hatred, and hast shed *the blood of* the children of Israel by the force of the sword in the time of their calamity, in the time *that their* iniquity *had* an end: therefore, *as* I live, saith the LORD God, I will prepare thee unto blood.

III John 10.

37. Num. 14:22. Have tempted me now these ten times, and have not hearkened to my voice.

38. Zech. 7:11, 12. But they refused to hearken, and pulled away the shoulder, and stopped their ears, that they should not hear. Yea, they made their hearts *as* an adamant stone.

39. Prov. 2:14. Who rejoice to do evil, *and* delight in the frowardness of the wicked.

40. Jer. 9:3, 5. They proceed from evil to evil, and they know not me, saith the LORD. . . . *and* weary themselves to commit iniquity.

Isa. 57:17.

41. II Peter 2:20, 21. For if after they have escaped the pollutions of the world through the knowledge of the Lord and Saviour Jesus Christ, they

are again entangled therein, and overcome, the latter end is worse with them than the beginning. For it had been better for them not to have known the way of righteousness, than, after they have known *it,* to turn from the holy commandment delivered unto them.

Heb. 6:4, 6.

42. Isa. 22:12-14. And in that day did the Lord God of hosts call to weeping, and to mourning, and to baldness, and to girding with sackcloth: and behold joy and gladness, slaying oxen, and killing sheep, eating flesh, and drinking wine . . . Surely this iniquity shall not be purged from you till ye die, saith the Lord God of hosts.

II Kings 5:26.

43. Jer. 7:10, 11. And come and stand before me in this house, which is called by my name, and say, We are delivered to do all these abominations? Is this house, which is called by my name, become a den of robbers in your eyes?

44. Ezek. 23:38. They have defiled my sanctuary in the same day, and have profaned my sabbaths.

45. Isa. 58:3, 4. Behold, in the day of your fast ye find pleasure, and exact all your labours. Behold, ye fast for strife and debate, and to smite with the fist of wickedness.

46. I Cor. 11:20, 21. When ye come together therefore into one place, *this* is not to eat the Lord's supper. For in eating every one taketh before *other* his own supper: and one is hungry, and another is drunken.

Jer. 7:9, 10. Will ye steal, murder . . . and come and stand before me in this house?

47. Prov. 7:14, 15. *I have* peace offerings with me; this day have I paid my vows. Therefore came I forth to meet thee, diligently to seek thy face, and I have found thee.

48. Neh. 9:13-16. Thou camest down also upon mount Sinai . . . and madest known unto them thy holy sabbath . . . and gavest them bread from heaven for their hunger, and broughtest forth water for them out of the rock for their thirst . . . But they and our fathers dealt proudly, and hardened their necks, and hearkened not to thy commandments.

II Chron. 36:15, 16.

49. Isa. 3:9. They declare their sin as Sodom, they hide *it* not. Woe unto their soul! for they have rewarded evil unto themselves.

I Sam. 2:22-24.

Q. 152. *What doth every sin deserve at the hands of God?*

A. Every sin, even the least,[1] being against the sovereignty,[2] goodness,[3] and holiness of God,[4] and against his righteous law,[5] deserveth his wrath and curse,[6] both in this life,[7] and that which is to come;[8] and cannot be expiated but by the blood of Christ.[9]

1. James 2:10, 11. Whosoever shall keep the whole law, and yet offend in one *point,* he is guilty of all. For he that said, Do not commit adultery, said also, Do not kill.

2. Mal. 1:14. But cursed *be* the deceiver, which hath in his flock a male, and voweth, and sacrificeth unto the Lord a corrupt thing: for I *am* a great King, saith the Lord of hosts, and my name *is* dreadful among the heathen.

3. Deut. 32:6. Do ye thus requite the Lord, O foolish people and unwise? *is* not he thy father *that* hath bought thee? hath he not made thee, and established thee?

4. Hab. 1:13. *Thou art* of purer eyes than to behold evil, and canst not look on iniquity: wherefore lookest thou upon them that deal treacherously?
I Peter 1:15, 16. As he which hath called you is holy, so be ye holy in all manner of conversation; because it is written, Be ye holy; for I am holy. Lev. 11:45.

5. I John 3:4. Whosoever committeth sin transgresseth also the law: for sin is the transgression of the law.
Rom. 7:12. The law *is* holy, and the commandment holy, and just, and good.

6. Gal. 3:10. For as many as are of the works of the law are under the curse: for it is written, Cursed *is* every one that continueth not in all things which are written in the book of the law to do them.
Eph. 5:6.

7. Deut. 28:15. But it shall come to pass, if thou wilt not hearken unto the voice of the Lord thy God, to observe to do all his commandments and his statutes which I command thee this day; that all these curses shall come upon thee, and overtake thee.
Prov. 13:21.

8. Matt. 25:41. Depart from me, ye cursed, into everlasting fire, prepared for the devil and his angels.
Rom. 6:21, 23. The end of those things *is* death. . . . the wages of sin *is* death.

9. Heb. 9:22. And almost all things are by the law purged with blood; and without shedding of blood is no remission.
I John 1:7. And the blood of Jesus Christ his Son cleanseth us from all sin.
I Peter 1:18, 19.

Q. 153. *What doth God require of us, that we may escape his wrath and curse due to us by reason of the transgression of the law?*

A. That we may escape the wrath and curse of God due to us by reason of the transgression of the law, he requireth of us repentance towards God, and faith towards our Lord Jesus Christ,[1] and the diligent use of the outward means whereby Christ communicates to us the benefits of his mediation.[2]

1. Acts 20:21. Testifying both to the Jews, and also to the Greeks, repentance toward God, and faith toward our Lord Jesus Christ.
Mark 1:15. Repent ye, and believe the gospel.
John 3:18. He that believeth on him is not condemned: but he that believeth not is condemned already, because he hath not believed in the name of the only begotten Son of God.

2. See texts cited under Q. 154.

Q. 154. *What are the outward means whereby Christ communicates to us the benefits of his mediation?*

A. The outward and ordinary means, whereby Christ communicates to his church the benefits of his mediation, are all his ordinances; especially the word, sacraments, and prayer; all which are made effectual to the elect for their salvation.[1]

> 1. Matt. 28:19, 20. Go ye therefore, and teach all nations, baptizing them in the name of the Father, and of the Son, and of the Holy Ghost: teaching them to observe all things whatsoever I have commanded you: and, lo, I am with you alway, *even* unto the end of the world.
>
> Acts 2:42, 46. And they continued stedfastly in the apostles' doctrine and fellowship, and in breaking of bread, and in prayers. . . . And they, continuing daily with one accord in the temple, and breaking bread from house to house, did eat their meat with gladness and singleness of heart. I Tim. 4:16; I Cor. 1:21; Eph. 5:19, 20; Eph. 6:17, 18.

Q. 155. *How is the word made effectual to salvation?*

A. The Spirit of God maketh the reading, but especially the preaching of the word, an effectual means of enlightening, convincing, and humbling sinners,[1] of driving them out of themselves, and drawing them unto Christ:[2] of conforming them to his image,[3] and subduing them to his will;[4] of strengthening them against temptations and corruptions;[5] of building them up in grace,[6] and establishing their hearts in holiness and comfort through faith unto salvation.[7]

> 1. Jer. 23:28, 29. And he that hath my word, let him speak my word faithfully. . . . *Is* not my word like as a fire? saith the Lord; and like a hammer *that* breaketh the rock in pieces?
>
> Heb. 4:12. The word of God *is* quick, and powerful, and sharper than any twoedged sword, piercing even to the dividing asunder of soul and spirit, and of the joints and marrow, and *is* a discerner of the thoughts and intents of the heart.
>
> Acts 17:11, 12. These were more noble than those in Thessalonica, in that they received the word with all readiness of mind, and searched the scriptures daily, whether those things were so. Therefore many of them believed; also of honourable women which were Greeks, and of men, not a few.
>
> Acts 26:18. To open their eyes, *and* to turn *them* from darkness to light, and *from* the power of Satan unto God.
>
> 2. Acts 2:37, 41. Now when they heard *this,* they were pricked in their heart, and said unto Peter and to the rest of the apostles, Men *and* brethren, what shall we do? . . . Then they that gladly received his word were baptized: and the same day there were added *unto them* about three thousand souls.
>
> Acts 8:27-38.
>
> 3. II Cor. 3:18. But we all, with open face beholding as in a glass the glory

of the Lord, are changed into the same image from glory to glory, *even* as by the Spirit of the Lord.

Col. 1:27.

4. II Cor. 10:4, 5. (For the weapons of our warfare *are* not carnal, but mighty through God to the pulling down of strongholds;) casting down imaginations, and every high thing that exalteth itself against the knowledge of God, and bringing into captivity every thought to the obedience of Christ.

Rom. 6:17.

5. Ps. 19:11. Moreover by them is thy servant warned.

Col. 1:28. Whom we preach, warning every man.

Eph. 6:16, 17. Above all, taking the shield of faith, wherewith ye shall be able to quench all the fiery darts of the wicked. And take the helmet of salvation, and the sword of the Spirit, which is the word of God.

Matt. 4:7, 10.

6. Eph. 4:11, 12. And he gave some, apostles . . . and some, pastors and teachers; for the perfecting of the saints, for the work of the ministry, for the edifying of the body of Christ.

Acts 20:32. And now, brethren, I commend you to God, and to the word of his grace, which is able to build you up.

II Tim. 3:15, 16; I Cor. 3:9-11.

7. Rom. 16:25. Now to him that is of power to stablish you according to my gospel, and the preaching of Jesus Christ, according to the revelation of the mystery, which was kept secret since the world began.

I Thess. 3:2, 13. And sent Timotheus, our brother, and minister of God, and our fellow-labourer in the gospel of Christ, to establish you, and to comfort you concerning your faith . . . to the end he may stablish your hearts unblameable in holiness before God, even our Father, at the coming of our Lord Jesus Christ with all his saints.

Rom. 10:14-17.

Q. 156. *Is the word of God to be read by all?*

A. Although all are not permitted to read the word publicly to the congregation, yet all sorts of people are bound to read it apart by themselves,[1] and with their families;[2] to which end, the holy Scriptures are to be translated out of the original into the language of every people unto whom they come.[3]

1. Deut. 17:18, 19. And it shall be, when he sitteth upon the throne of his kingdom, that he shall write him a copy of this law in a book out of *that which is* before the priests the Levites: and it shall be with him, and he shall read therein all the days of his life.

Isa. 34:16. Seek ye out of the book of the LORD, and read.

John 5:39. Search the scriptures.

Rev. 1:3. Blessed *is* he that readeth, and they that hear the words of this prophecy, and keep those things which are written therein.

2. Deut. 6:6, 7. And these words, which I command thee this day, shall be in thine heart: and thou shalt teach them diligently unto thy children, and shalt talk of them when thou sittest in thine house, and when thou

walkest by the way, and when thou liest down, and when thou risest up.

Ps. 78:5, 6. For he established a testimony in Jacob, and appointed a law in Israel, which he commanded our fathers, that they should make them known to their children: that the generation to come might know *them, even* the children *which* should be born; *who* should arise and declare *them* to their children.

3. I Cor. 14:18, 19. I thank my God, I speak with tongues more than ye all: yet in the church I had rather speak five words with my understanding, that *by my voice* I might teach others also, than ten thousand words in an *unknown* tongue. (See context.)

Q. 157. *How is the word of God to be read?*

A. The holy Scriptures are to be read with an high and reverent esteem of them;[1] with a firm persuasion that they are the very word of God,[2] and that he only can enable us to understand them;[3] with desire to know, believe, and obey, the will of God revealed in them;[4] with diligence,[5] and attention to the matter and scope of them;[6] with meditation,[7] application,[8] self-denial,[9] and prayer.[10]

1. Ps. 119:97. O how love I thy law!

   Neh. 8:5. And Ezra opened the book in the sight of all the people . . . and when he opened it, all the people stood up.

   Isa. 66:2. But to this *man* will I look, *even* to *him that is* poor and of a contrite spirit, and trembleth at my word.

2. I Thess. 2:13. For this cause also thank we God without ceasing, because, when ye received the word of God which ye heard of us, ye received *it* not *as* the word of men, but as it is in truth, the word of God, which effectually worketh also in you that believe.

   II Peter 1:16-21.

3. Ps. 119:18. Open thou mine eyes, that I may behold wondrous things out of thy law.

   Luke 24:44-48.

4. James 1:21, 22. Receive with meekness the engrafted word, which is able to save your souls. But be ye doers of the word, and not hearers only, deceiving your own selves.

   I Peter 2:2. As newborn babies, desire the sincere milk of the word, that ye may grow thereby.

   Mark 4:20.

5. Acts 17:11. These [Bereans] were more noble than those in Thessalonica, in that they received the word with all readiness of mind, and searched the scriptures daily, whether those things were so.

   Deut. 11:13.

6. Acts 8:30, 34. And Philip . . . said, Understandest thou what thou readest? . . . And the eunuch answered Philip . . . of whom speaketh the prophet this? of himself, or of some other man?

   Matt. 13:23.

7. Ps. 1:2. But his delight *is* in the law of the Lord; and in his law doth he meditate day and night.

Ps. 119:97. O how love I thy law! it *is* my meditation all the day.

8. Acts 2:38, 39. Repent and be baptized every one of you . . . for the promise is unto you, and to your children.

II Sam. 12:7; II Chron. 34:21.

9. Gal. 1:15, 16. But when it pleased God . . . to reveal his Son in me, that I might preach him among the heathen; immediately I conferred not with flesh and blood.

Prov. 3:5.

10. Ps. 119:18. Open thou mine eyes, that I may behold wondrous things out of thy law.

Luke 24:45.

Q. 158. *By whom is the word of God to be preached?*

A. The word of God is to be preached only by such as are sufficiently gifted,[1] and also duly approved and called to that office.[2]

1. I Tim. 3:2, 6. A bishop . . . must be blameless . . . apt to teach . . . not a novice.

II Tim 2:2. And the things that thou hast heard of me among many witnesses, the same commit thou to faithful men, who shall be able to teach others also.

Mal. 2:7.

2. Rom. 10:15. And how shall they preach, except they be sent?

I Tim. 4:14. Neglect not the gift that is in thee, which was given thee by prophecy, with the laying on of the hands of the presbytery.

Q. 159. *How is the word of God to be preached by those that are called thereunto?*

A. They that are called to labor in the ministry of the word are to preach sound doctrine,[1] diligently, in season, and out of season;[2] plainly,[3] not in the enticing word of man's wisdom, but in demonstration of the Spirit, and of power;[4] faithfully,[5] making known the whole counsel of God;[6] wisely,[7] applying themselves to the necessities and capacities of the hearers;[8] zealously,[9] with fervent love to God,[10] and the souls of his people;[11] sincerely,[12] aiming at his glory,[13] and their conversion,[14] edification,[15] and salvation.[16]

1. Titus 2:1, 8. But speak thou the things which become sound doctrine . . . sound speech, that cannot be condemned.

2. Acts 18:25. Being fervent in the spirit, he spake and taught diligently the things of the Lord.

II Tim. 4:2. Preach the word; be instant in season, out of season.

3. I Cor. 14:9. Except ye utter by the tongue words easy to be understood, how shall it be known what is spoken? for ye shall speak into the air.

4. I Cor. 2:4. And my speech and my preaching *was* not with enticing words of man's wisdom, but in demonstration of the Spirit and of power.

5. Jer. 23:28. He that hath my word, let him speak my word faithfully.

I Cor. 4:1, 2. Let a man so account of us, as of the ministers of Christ, and stewards of the mysteries of God. Moreover it is required in stewards, that a man be found faithful.

Matt. 24:45-47.

6. Acts 20:27. For I have not shunned to declare unto you all the counsel of God.

7. Col. 1:28. Whom we preach, warning every man, and teaching every man in all wisdom.

II Tim. 2:15. Study to shew thyself approved unto God, a workman that needeth not to be ashamed, rightly dividing the word of truth.

8. I Cor. 3:2. I have fed you with milk, and not with meat: for hitherto ye were not able *to bear it,* neither yet now are ye able.

Heb. 5:12-14; I Thess. 2:7; Luke 12:42.

9. Acts 18:25. This man was instructed in the way of the Lord; and being fervent in the spirit, he spake and taught diligently the things of the Lord, knowing only the baptism of John.

II Tim. 4:5.

10. II Cor. 5:13, 14. For whether we be beside ourselves, *it is* to God: or whether we be sober, *it is* for your cause. For the love of Christ constraineth us; because we thus judge, that if one died for all, then were all dead.

Phil. 1:15-17.

11. II Cor. 12:15. And I will very gladly spend and be spent for you; though the more abundantly I love you, the less I be loved.

I Thess. 3:12.

12. II Cor. 4:2. But have renounced the hidden things of dishonesty, not walking in craftiness, nor handling the word of God deceitfully; but by manifestation of the truth commending ourselves to every man's conscience in the sight of God.

II Cor. 2:17.

13. John 7:18. He that speaketh of himself seeketh his own glory: but he that seeketh his glory that sent him, the same is true, and no unrighteousness is in him.

I Thess. 2:4-6.

14. I Cor. 9:19-22. For though I be free from all *men,* yet have I made myself servant unto all, that I might gain the more. And unto the Jews I become as a Jew, that I might gain the Jews; to them that are under the law, as under the law, that I might gain them that are under the law . . . I am made all things to all *men,* that I might by all means save some.

15. II Cor. 12:19. But *we do* all things, dearly beloved, for your edifying.

Eph. 4:12.

16. I Tim. 4:16. Take heed unto thyself, and unto the doctrine; continue in them: for in doing this thou shalt both save thyself, and them that hear thee.

II Tim. 2:10. Therefore I endure all things for the elect's sakes, that they may also obtain the salvation which is in Christ Jesus with eternal glory.

Acts 26:16-18.

Q. 160. *What is required of those that hear the word preached?*

A. It is required of those that hear the word preached, that they attend upon it with diligence,[1] preparation,[2] and prayer;[3] examine what they hear by the Scriptures;[4] receive the truth with faith,[5] love,[6] meekness,[7] and readiness of mind,[8] as the word of God;[9] meditate,[10] and confer of it;[11] hide it in their hearts,[12] and bring forth the fruit of it in their lives.[13]

1. Ps. 84:1, 2, 4. How amiable *are* thy tabernacles, O LORD of hosts! My soul longeth, yea, even fainteth for the courts of the LORD . . . Blessed *are* they that dwell in thy house: they will be still praising thee.
   Ps. 27:4; Prov. 8:34.

2. Luke 8:18. Take heed therefore how ye hear.
   I Peter 2:1, 2. Wherefore laying aside all malice, and all guile, and hypocrisies, and envies, and all evil speakings, as newborn babes, desire the sincere milk of the word, that ye may grow thereby.
   James 1:21.

3. Ps. 119:18. Open thou mine eyes, that I may behold wondrous things out of thy law.
   Eph. 6:18, 19.

4. Acts 17:11. And searched the scriptures daily, whether those things were so.

5. Heb. 4:2. For unto us was the gospel preached, as well as unto them: but the word preached did not profit them, not being mixed with faith in them that heard *it*.

6. II Thess. 2:10. They received not the love of the truth, that they might be saved.

7. James 1:21. Receive with meekness the engrafted word.
   Ps. 25:9.

8. Acts 17:11. These were more noble than those in Thessalonica, in that they received the word with all readiness of mind.
   Acts 2:41.

9. I Thess. 2:13. For this cause also thank we God without ceasing, because, when ye received the word of God which ye heard of us, ye received *it* not *as* the word of men, but as it is in truth, the word of God.

10. Heb. 2:1. Therefore we ought to give the more earnest heed to the things which we have heard, lest at any time we should let *them* slip.

11. Deut. 6:6, 7. And these words, which I command thee this day, shall be in thine heart: and thou shalt teach them diligently unto thy children, and shalt talk of them when thou sittest in thine house, and when thou walkest by the way, and when thou liest down, and when thou risest up.

12. Ps. 119:11. Thy word have I hid in mine heart, that I might not sin against thee.
    Prov. 2:1-5.

13. Luke 8:15. But that on the good ground are they, which in an honest and good heart, having heard the word, keep *it*, and bring forth fruit with patience.
    James 1:25.

Q. 161. *How do the sacraments become effectual means of salvation?*

A. The sacraments become effectual means of salvation, not by any power in themselves or any virtue derived from the piety or intention of him by whom they are administered; but only by the working of the Holy Ghost, and the blessing of Christ by whom they are instituted.[1]

1. I Peter 3:21. The like figure whereunto *even* baptism doth also now save us (not the putting away of the filth of the flesh, but the answer of a good conscience toward God,) by the resurrection of Jesus Christ.

Acts 8:13. Then Simon himself believed also: and when he was baptized, he continued with Philip, and wondered, beholding the miracles and signs which were done. [His baptism, notwithstanding, was ineffectual to any saving purpose, for Peter said to him] vs. 23. I perceive that thou art in the gall of bitterness, and *in* the bond of iniquity.

I Cor. 3:7. So then neither is he that planteth any thing, neither he that watereth; but God that giveth the increase.

I Cor. 6:11. But ye are washed, but ye are sanctified, but ye are justified in the name of the Lord Jesus, and by the Spirit of our God.

Q. 162. *What is a sacrament?*

A. A sacrament is an holy ordinance instituted by Christ in his church,[1] to signify, seal, and exhibit[2] unto those that are within the covenant of grace,[3] the benefits of his mediation;[4] to strengthen and increase their faith and all other graces;[5] to oblige them to obedience;[6] to testify and cherish their love and communion one with another,[7] and to distinguish them from those that are without.[8]

1. Matt. 28:19. Go ye therefore, and teach all nations, baptizing them in the name of the Father, and of the Son, and of the Holy Ghost.

Matt. 26:26, 27. And as they were eating, Jesus took bread, and blessed *it*, and brake *it*, and gave *it* to the disciples, and said, Take, eat; this is my body. And he took the cup, and gave thanks, and gave *it* to them, saying, Drink ye all of it.

2. Rom. 4:11. And he [Abraham] received the sign of circumcision, a seal of the righteousness of the faith which *he had yet* being uncircumcised: that he might be the father of all them that believe, though they be not circumcised; that righteousness might be imputed unto them also.

I Cor. 11:24, 25.

3. Rom. 9:8. The children of the promise are counted for the seed.

Gal. 3:27, 29. For as many of you as have been baptized into Christ have put on Christ. . . . And if *ye be* Christ's, then are ye Abraham's seed, and heirs according to the promise.

Gal. 5:6. For in Christ Jesus neither circumcision availeth any thing, nor uncircumcision; but faith which worketh by love.

Gal. 6:15. For in Christ Jesus neither circumcision availeth any thing, nor uncircumcision, but a new creature.

4. Acts 2:38. Then Peter said unto them, Repent, and be baptized every one of you in the name of Jesus Christ for the remission of sins, and ye shall receive the gift of the Holy Ghost.

I Cor. 10:16. The cup of blessing which we bless, is it not the communion of the blood of Christ? The bread which we break, is it not the communion of the body of Christ?

Acts 22:16.

5. I Cor. 11:24-26.

6. Rom. 6:4. Therefore we are buried with him by baptism into death: that like as Christ was raised up from the dead by the glory of the Father, even so we also should walk in newness of life.

I Cor. 10:21. Ye cannot drink the cup of the Lord, and the cup of devils: ye cannot be partakers of the Lord's table, and of the table of devils.

7. I Cor. 12:13. For by one Spirit are we all baptized into one body, whether *we be* Jews or Gentiles, whether *we be* bond or free; and have been all made to drink into one Spirit.

I Cor. 10:17. We *being* many are one bread, *and* one body: for we are all partakers of that one bread.

Eph. 4:3-5.

8. I Cor. 10:21. Ye cannot drink the cup of the Lord, and the cup of devils: ye cannot be partakers of the Lord's table, and of the table of devils.

Q. 163. *What are the parts of a sacrament?*

A. The parts of a sacrament are two: the one, an outward and sensible sign used according to Christ's own appointment; the other, an inward and spiritual grace thereby signified.[1]

1. See Confession of Faith, Chapter XXIX, Section 2, and passages there cited.

Q. 164. *How many sacraments hath Christ instituted under the New Testament?*

A. Under the New Testament Christ hath instituted in his church only two sacraments, baptism, and the Lord's supper.[1]

1. Matt. 28:19; Matt. 26:26, 27; I Cor. 11:23-26.

Q. 165. *What is baptism?*

A. Baptism is a sacrament of the New Testament, wherein Christ hath ordained the washing with water in the name of the Father, and of the Son, and of the Holy Ghost,[1] to be a sign and seal of ingrafting into himself,[2] of remission of sins by his blood,[3] and regeneration by his Spirit;[4] of adoption,[5] and resurrection unto everlasting life:[6] and whereby the parties baptized are solemnly admitted into the visible church,[7] and enter into an open and professed engagement to be wholly and only the Lord's.[8]

1. Matt. 28:19. Go ye therefore, and teach all nations, baptizing them in the name of the Father, and of the Son, and of the Holy Ghost.
2. Gal. 3:27. For as many of you as have been baptized into Christ have put on Christ.
   Rom. 6:3.
3. Acts 22:16. Arise, and be baptized, and wash away thy sins.
   Mark 1:4. John did baptize in the wilderness, and preach the baptism of repentance for the remission of sins.
   Rev. 1:5.
4. John 3:5. Except a man be born of water and of the Spirit, he cannot enter into the kingdom of God.
   Titus 3:5. According to his mercy he saved us, by the washing of regeneration, and renewing of the Holy Ghost.
5. Gal. 3:26, 27. For ye are all the children of God by faith in Christ Jesus. For as many of you as have been baptized into Christ have put on Christ.
6. I Cor. 15:29. Else what shall they do which are baptized for the dead, if the dead rise not at all? why are they then baptized for the dead?
7. Acts 2:41. Then they that gladly received his word were baptized: and the same day there were added *unto them* about three thousand souls.
8. Rom. 6:4. Therefore we are buried with him by baptism into death: that like as Christ was raised up from the dead by the glory of the Father, even so we also should walk in newness of life.

Q. 166. *Unto whom is baptism to be administered?*

A. Baptism is not to be administered to any that are out of the visible church, and so strangers from the covenant of promise, till they profess their faith in Christ, and obedience to him;[1] but infants descending from parents, either both or but one of them, professing faith in Christ, and obedience to him, are, in that respect, within the covenant, and are to be baptized.[2]

1. Acts 2:41. Then they that gladly received his word were baptized.
2. Acts 2:38, 39. Then Peter said unto them, Repent, and be baptized every one of you in the name of Jesus Christ for the remission of sins, and ye shall receive the . . . Holy Ghost. For the promise is unto you, and to your children, and to all that are afar off, *even* as many as the Lord our God shall call.
   I Cor. 7:14. The unbelieving husband is sanctified by the wife, and the unbelieving wife is sanctified by the husband: else were your children unclean; but now are they holy.
   Luke 18:16; Rom. 11:16; Gen. 17:7-9, compared with Col. 2:11, 12; Gal. 3:17, 18, 29.

Q. 167. *How is our baptism to be improved by us?*

A. The needful but much neglected duty of improving our baptism, is to be performed by us all our life long, especially in the time of temptation,[1] and when we are present at the administration of it to others, by serious and thankful consideration of the nature of it, and of the ends for which Christ instituted it, the privileges and benefits conferred and sealed thereby, and our solemn vow made therein;[2] by being humbled for our sinful defilement, our falling short of, and walking contrary to, the grace of baptism and our engagements;[3] by growing up to assurance of pardon of sin, and of all other blessings sealed to us in that sacrament;[4] by drawing strength from the death and resurrection of Christ, into whom we are baptized, for the mortifying of sin, and quickening of grace;[5] and by endeavoring to live by faith,[6] to have our conversation in holiness and righteousness,[7] as those that have therein given up their names to Christ, and to walk in brotherly love, as being baptized by the same Spirit into one body.[8]

1. Ps. 22:10, 11. I was cast upon thee from the womb: thou *art* my God from my mother's belly. Be not far from me; for trouble *is* near.

2. Rom. 6:3-5.

3. Rom. 6:2, 3. God forbid. How shall we, that are dead to sin, live any longer therein? Know ye not, that so many of us as were baptized into Jesus Christ were baptized into his death?
   I Cor. 1:11-13.

4. I Peter 3:21. The like figure whereunto *even* baptism doth also now save us (not the putting away of the filth of the flesh, but the answer of a good conscience toward God,) by the resurrection of Jesus Christ.
   Rom. 4:11, 12.

5. Rom. 6:2-4. How shall we, that are dead to sin, live any longer therein? know ye not, that so many of us as were baptized into Jesus Christ were baptized into his death? Therefore we are buried with him by baptism into death: that like as Christ was raised up from the dead by the glory of the Father, even so we also should walk in newness of life.

6. Gal. 3:26, 27. For ye are all the children of God by faith in Christ Jesus. For as many of you as have been baptized into Christ have put on Christ.

7. Rom. 6:22. But now being made free from sin, and become servants to God, ye have your fruit unto holiness, and the end everlasting life.

8. I Cor. 12:13, 25, 26. For by one Spirit are we all baptized into one body, whether *we be* Jews or Gentiles, whether *we be* bond or free . . . that there should be no schism in the body; but *that* the members should have the same care one for another. And whether one member suffer, all the members suffer with it; or one member be honoured, all the members rejoice with it.
   See context.

Q. 168. *What is the Lord's supper?*

A. The Lord's supper is a sacrament of the New Testament, wherein by giving and receiving bread and wine according to the appointment of Jesus Christ, his death is showed forth;[1] and

they that worthily communicate, feed upon his body and blood
to their spiritual nourishment and growth in grace;[2] have their
union and communion with him confirmed; testify and renew
their thankfulness and engagement to God,[3] and their mutual love and fellowship each with other, as members of the
same mystical body.[4]

1. I Cor. 11:26. For as often as ye eat this bread, and drink this cup, ye do
shew the Lord's death till he come.

2. Matt. 26:26, 27. And said, Take, eat; this is my body. And he took the
cup, and gave thanks, and gave *it* to them, saying, Drink ye all of it.
I Cor. 11:23-27.

3. I Cor. 10:16, 21. The cup of blessing which we bless, is it not the communion of the blood of Christ? The bread which we break, is it not the
communion of the body of Christ? . . . Ye cannot drink the cup of the
Lord, and the cup of devils: ye cannot be partakers of the Lord's table,
and of the table of devils.

4. I Cor. 10:17. For we *being* many are one bread, *and* one body: for we are
all partakers of that one bread.

Q. 169. *How hath Christ appointed bread and wine to be given and received in the sacrament of the Lord's supper?*

A. Christ hath appointed the ministers of his word, in the administration of this sacrament of the Lord's supper, to set apart
the bread and wine from common use by the word of institution,
thanksgiving, and prayer; to take and break the bread, and to
give both the bread and the wine to the communicants; who are
by the same appointment to take and eat the bread, and to drink
the wine; in thankful remembrance that the body of Christ was
broken and given, and his blood shed for them.[1]

1. See General Note, p. 145.

Q. 170. *How do they that worthily communicate in the Lord's supper feed upon the body and blood of Christ therein?*

A. As the body and blood of Christ are not corporally or carnally present in, with, or under the bread and wine in the Lord's
supper;[1] and yet are spiritually present to the faith of the re-
ceiver, no less truly and really than the elements themselves are
to their outward senses;[2] so they that worthily communicate in
the sacrament of the Lord's supper, do therein feed upon the
body and blood of Christ, not after a corporal or carnal, but in
a spiritual manner; yet truly and really,[3] while by faith they re-

ceive and apply unto themselves Christ crucified, and all the benefits of his death.[4]

1. The specifications enumerated in answers to Questions 170 to 175 are deduced from the nature of the Lord's supper as set forth in the New Testament. The texts are given to show that these specifications are in accord with the general tenor of the Scriptures.
Acts 3:21. Whom the heaven must receive until the times of restitution of all things.

2. Gal. 3:1. O foolish Galatians . . . before whose eyes Jesus Christ hath been evidently set forth, crucified among you.
Heb. 11:1.

3. John 6:51, 53. I am the living bread which came down from heaven: if any man eat of this bread, he shall live for ever: and the bread that I will give is my flesh, which I will give for the life of the world. . . . Except ye eat the flesh of the Son of man, and drink his blood, ye have no life in you.
See context.

4. I Cor. 10:16. The cup of blessing which we bless, is it not the communion of the blood of Christ? The bread which we break, is it not the communion of the body of Christ?

Q. 171. *How are they that receive the sacrament of the Lord's supper to prepare themselves before they come unto it?*

A. They that receive the sacrament of the Lord's supper are, before they come, to prepare themselves thereunto: by examining themselves,[1] of their being in Christ,[2] of their sins and wants;[3] of the truth and measure of their knowledge,[4] faith,[5] repentance,[6] love to God and the brethren,[7] charity to all men,[8] forgiving those that have done them wrong;[9] of their desires after Christ,[10] and of their new obedience;[11] and by renewing the exercise of these graces,[12] by serious meditation,[13] and fervent prayer.[14]

1. I Cor. 11:28. But let a man examine himself, and so let him eat of *that* bread, and drink of *that* cup.

2. II Cor. 13:5. Examine yourselves, whether ye be in the faith; prove your own selves. Know ye not your own selves, how that Jesus Christ is in you, except ye be reprobates?

3. I Cor. 5:7. Purge out therefore the old leaven, that ye may be a new lump, as ye are unleaven. For even Christ our passover is sacrificed for us. Compare Exod. 12:15.

4. I Cor. 11:29. For he that eateth and drinketh unworthily, eateth and drinketh damnation to himself, not discerning the Lord's body.

5. II Cor. 13:5. See citation under figure 2 above.

6. I Cor. 11:31. For if we would judge ourselves, we should not be judged.

7. I Cor. 10:17. For we *being* many are one bread, *and* one body: for we are all partakers of that one bread.

8. I Cor. 5:8. Therefore let us keep the feast, not with old leaven, neither with the leaven of malice and wickedness; but with the unleavened *bread* of sincerity and truth.

I Cor. 11:18, 20.

9. Matt. 5:23, 24. Therefore if thou bring thy gift to the altar, and there rememberest that thy brother hath ought against thee; leave there thy gift before the altar, and go thy way; first be reconciled to thy brother, and then come and offer thy gift.

10. John 7:37. Jesus stood and cried, saying, If any man thirst, let him come unto me, and drink.

Luke 1:53. He hath filled the hungry with good things.
Isa. 55:1.

11. I Cor. 5:8. Therefore let us keep the feast, not with old leaven . . . but with the unleavened *bread* of sincerity and truth.

12. Heb. 10:21, 22, 24. And *having* an high priest over the house of God; let us draw near with a true heart in the full assurance of faith, having our hearts sprinkled from an evil conscience, and our bodies washed with pure water. . . . And let us consider one another to provoke unto love and good works.

Ps. 26:6.

13. I Cor. 11:24. This do in remembrance of me.

14. Matt. 26:26. Jesus took bread, and blessed *it*.

II Chron. 30:18, 19.

Q. 172. *May one who doubteth of his being in Christ, or of his due preparation, come to the Lord's supper?*

A. One who doubteth of his being in Christ, or of his due preparation to the sacrament of the Lord's supper, may have true interest in Christ, though he be not yet assured thereof;[1] and in God's account hath it, if he be duly affected with the apprehension of the want of it,[2] and unfeignedly desirous to be found in Christ,[3] and to depart from iniquity;[4] in which case (because promises are made, and this sacrament is appointed, for the relief even of weak and doubting Christians)[5] he is to bewail his unbelief,[6] and labor to have his doubts resolved;[7] and so doing, he may and ought to come to the Lord's supper, that he may be further strengthened.[8]

1. Isa. 50:10. Who *is* among you that feareth the LORD, that obeyeth the voice of his servant, that walketh *in* darkness, and hath no light? let him trust in the name of the LORD, and stay upon his God.

2. Isa. 54:7, 8, 10. For a small moment have I forsaken thee; but with great mercies will I gather thee. In a little wrath I hid my face from thee for a moment; but with everlasting kindness will I have mercy on thee, saith the LORD thy Redeemer. . . . For the mountains shall depart, and the hills be removed; but my kindness shall not depart from thee, neither shall the covenant of my peace be removed, saith the LORD that hath mercy on thee.

Matt. 5:3, 4; Ps. 31:22.

3. Ps. 42:11. Why art thou cast down, O my soul? and why art thou dis-
quieted within me? hope thou in God: for I shall yet praise him, *who is*
the health of my countenance, and my God.

4. II Tim. 2:19. Nevertheless the foundation of God standeth sure, having
this seal, The Lord knoweth them that are his. And, Let every one that
nameth the name of Christ depart from iniquity.

Rom. 7:24, 25. O wretched man that I am! who shall deliver me from the
body of this death? I thank God through Jesus Christ our Lord.

5. Matt. 26:28. For this is my blood of the new testament, which is shed for
many for the remission of sins.

Matt. 11:28. Come unto me, all *ye* that labour and are heavy laden,
and I will give you rest.

Isa. 40:11, 29, 31.

6. Mark 9:24. And said with tears, Lord, I believe; help thou mine unbelief.

7. Acts 16:30. And brought them out, and said, Sirs, what must I do to be
saved?

Acts 9:6.

8. I Cor. 11:28. But let a man examine himself, and so let him eat of *that*
bread, and drink of *that* cup.

Matt. 11:28.

Q. 173. *May any who profess the faith, and desire to come to the Lord's supper, be kept from it?*

A. Such as are found to be ignorant or scandalous, notwithstanding their profession of the faith, and desire to come to the
Lord's supper, may and ought to be kept from that sacrament by
the power which Christ hath left in his church,[1] until they receive instruction, and manifest their reformation.[2]

1. I Cor. 11:29. For he that eateth and drinketh unworthily, eateth and
drinketh damnation [judgment] to himself, not discerning the Lord's
body.

I Cor. 5:11. But now I have written unto you not to keep company, if
any man that is called a brother be a fornicator, or covetous, or an idola-
tor, or a railer, or a drunkard, or an extortioner; with such an one no not
to eat.

Matt. 7:6.

2. I Cor. 5:4, 5; II Cor. 2:5-8.

Q. 174. *What is required of them that receive the sacrament of the Lord's supper, in the time of the administration of it?*

A. It is required of them that receive the sacrament of the
Lord's supper that, during the time of the administration of it,
with all holy reverence and attention, they wait upon God in
that ordinance; diligently observe the sacramental elements and
actions;[1] heedfully discern the Lord's body,[2] and affectionately

meditate on his death and sufferings,[3] and thereby stir up themselves to a vigorous exercise of their graces; in judging themselves,[4] and sorrowing for sin;[5] in earnest hungering and thirsting
after Christ,[6] feeding on him by faith,[7] receiving of his fullness,[8]
trusting in his merits,[9] rejoicing in his love,[10] giving thanks for
his grace;[11] in renewing of their covenant with God,[12] and love
to all the saints.[13]

1. Gal. 3:1. Before whose eyes Jesus Christ hath been evidently set forth,
   crucified among you.
2. I Cor. 11:29. For he that eateth and drinketh unworthily, eateth and
   drinketh damnation to himself, not discerning the Lord's body.
3. Luke 22:19. And he took bread, and gave thanks, and brake *it*, and gave
   unto them, saying, This is my body which is given for you: this do in remembrance of me.
4. I Cor. 11:31. For if we would judge ourselves, we should not be judged.
5. Zech. 12:10. And they shall look upon me whom they have pierced, and
   they shall mourn.
6. Ps. 63:1, 2. O God, thou *art* my God; early will I seek thee: my soul
   thirsteth for thee, my flesh longeth for thee in a dry and thirsty land,
   where no water is; to see thy power and thy glory, so *as* I have seen thee
   in the sanctuary.
7. Gal. 2:20. And the life which I now live in the flesh I live by the faith of
   the Son of God, who loved me, and gave himself for me.
   John 6:35.
8. John 1:16. And of his fulness have all we received, and grace for grace.
   Col. 1:19.
9. Phil. 3:9. And be found in him, not having mine own righteousness,
   which is of the law, but that which is through the faith of Christ, the
   righteousness which is of God by faith.
10. I Peter 1:8. Whom having not seen, ye love; in whom, though now ye see
    him not, yet believing, ye rejoice with joy unspeakable and full of glory.
    I Chron. 30:21.
11. Ps. 22:26. The meek shall eat and be satisfied: they shall praise the
    LORD that seek him: your heart shall live for ever.
12. Jer. 50:5. Come, and let us join ourselves to the LORD in a perpetual
    covenant *that* shall not be forgotten.
    Ps. 50:5.
13. I Cor. 10:17. For we *being* many are one bread, *and* one body: for we are
    all partakers of that one bread.
    Acts 2:42.

Q. 175. *What is the duty of Christians after they have received the sacrament of the Lord's supper?*

A. The duty of Christians after they have received the sacrament of the Lord's supper, is seriously to consider how they have
behaved themselves therein, and with what success;[1] if they find

quickening and comfort, to bless God for it,[2] beg the continuance of it, watch against relapse,[3] fulfill their vows,[4] and encourage themselves to a frequent attendance on that ordinance:[5] but if they find no present benefit, more exactly to review their preparation to, and carriage at, the sacrament;[6] in both which if they can approve themselves to God and their own consciences, they are to wait for the fruit of it in due time;[7] but if they see that they have failed in either, they are to be humbled,[8] and to attend upon it afterward with more care and diligence.[9]

1. I Cor. 11:17, 30, 31. Now in this that I declare *unto you* I praise *you* not, that ye come together not for the better, but for the worse. . . . For this cause many *are* weak and sickly among you, and many sleep. For if we would judge ourselves, we should not be judged.

2. II Cor. 2:14. Now thanks *be* unto God, which always causeth us to triumph in Christ.

   Acts 2:42, 46, 47.

3. I Cor. 10:12. Wherefore let him that thinketh he standeth take heed lest he fall.

   Rom. 11:20.

4. Ps. 50:14. Offer unto God thanksgiving; and pay thy vows unto the most High.

5. I Cor. 11:25, 26; Ps. 27:4; Acts 2:42.

6. Ps. 77:6. I commune with mine own heart: and my spirit made diligent search.

   Ps. 139:23, 24. Search me, O God, and know my heart: try me, and know my thoughts: and see if *there be any* wicked way in me, and lead me in the way everlasting.

7. Ps. 123:1, 2. Unto thee lift I up mine eyes, O thou that dwellest in the heavens. Behold, as the eyes of servants *look* unto the hand of their masters, *and* as the eyes of a maiden unto the hand of her mistress; so our eyes *wait* upon the Lord our God, until that he have mercy upon us. Isa. 8:17.

8. Hos. 14:2. Take with you words, and turn to the Lord: say unto him, take away all iniquity, and receive *us* graciously: so will we render the calves of our lips.

   Hos. 6:1, 2.

9. II Cor. 7:11. For behold this selfsame thing, that ye sorrowed after a godly sort, what carefulness it wrought in you, yea, *what* clearing of yourselves, yea, *what* indignation, yea, *what* fear, yea, *what* vehement desire, yea, *what* zeal, yea *what* revenge! In all *things* ye have approved yourselves to be clear in this matter.

   I Chron. 15:12-14.

Q. 176. *Wherein do the sacraments of baptism and the Lord's supper agree?*

A. The sacraments of baptism and the Lord's supper agree, in that the author of both is God;[1] the spiritual part of both is

Christ and his benefits;[2] both are seals of the same covenant,[3] are to be dispensed by ministers of the gospel and by none other,[4] and to be continued in the church of Christ until his second coming.[5]

1. Matt. 28:19. Go ye therefore, and teach all nations, baptizing them in the name of the Father, and of the Son, and of the Holy Ghost.

   I Cor. 11:23. For I have received of the Lord that which also I delivered unto you, That the Lord Jesus the *same* night in which he was betrayed took bread.

2. Rom. 6:3, 4. Know ye not, that so many of us as were baptized into Jesus Christ were baptized into his death? Therefore we are buried with him by baptism into death: that like as Christ was raised up from the dead by the glory of the Father, even so we also should walk in newness of life.

   I Cor. 10:16. The cup of blessing which we bless, is it not the communion of the blood of Christ? The bread which we break, is it not the communion of the body of Christ?

3. Col. 2:11, 12. In whom also ye are circumcised with the circumcision made without hands, in putting off the body of the sins of the flesh by the circumcision of Christ: buried with him in baptism, wherein also ye are risen with *him* through the faith of the operation of God, who hath raised him from the dead. Compared with Rom. 4:11.

   Matt. 26:27, 28. And he took the cup, and gave thanks, and gave *it* to them, saying, Drink ye all of it; for this is my blood of the new testament, which is shed for many for the remission of sins.

4. See General Note, page 145.

5. Matt. 28:20. Teaching them [all nations] to observe all things whatsoever I have commanded you: and, lo, I am with you alway, *even* unto the end of the world.

   I Cor. 11:26. For as often as ye eat this bread, and drink this cup, ye do shew the Lord's death till he come.

Q. 177. *Wherein do the sacraments of baptism and the Lord's supper differ?*

A. The sacraments of baptism and the Lord's supper differ, in that baptism is to be administered but once, with water, to be a sign and seal of our regeneration and ingrafting into Christ,[1] and that even to infants;[2] whereas the Lord's supper is to be administered often, in the elements of bread and wine, to represent and exhibit Christ as spiritual nourishment to the soul,[3] and to confirm our continuance and growth in him,[4] and that only to such as are of years and ability to examine themselves.[5]

1. Matt. 3:11. I indeed baptize you with water unto repentance: but he that cometh after me is mightier than I, whose shoes I am not worthy to bear: he shall baptize you with the Holy Ghost, and *with* fire.

   Gal. 3:27. For as many of you as have been baptized into Christ have put on Christ.

   Titus 3:5.

2. Acts 2:38, 39. Repent, and be baptized every one of you . . . For the promise is unto you, and to your children.

I Cor. 7:14. The unbelieving wife is sanctified by the husband: else were your children unclean; but now are they holy.

See citations under Question 166, figure 2.

3. I Cor. 11:26. For as often as ye eat this bread, and drink this cup, ye do shew the Lord's death till he come.

Col. 2:19. Not holding the Head, from which all the body by joints and bands having nourishment ministered, and knit together, increaseth with the increase of God.

4. I Cor. 10:16. The cup of blessing which we bless, is it not the communion of the blood of Christ? The bread which we break, is it not the communion of the body of Christ?

John 6:51-53.

5. I Cor. 11:28. But let a man examine himself, and so let him eat of *that* bread, and drink of *that* cup.

Q. 178. *What is prayer?*

A. Prayer is an offering up of our desires unto God,[1] in the name of Christ,[2] by the help of his Spirit,[3] with confession of our sins,[4] and thankful acknowledgment of his mercies.[5]

1. Ps. 62:8. Trust in him at all times; ye people, pour out your heart before him: God *is* a refuge for us.

2. John 16:23, 24. Whatsoever ye shall ask the Father in my name, he will give *it* you. Hitherto have ye asked nothing in my name: ask, and ye shall receive, that your joy may be full.

3. Rom. 8:26. Likewise the Spirit also helpeth our infirmities: for we know not what we should pray for as we ought: but the Spirit itself maketh intercession for us with groanings which cannot be uttered.

4. Dan. 9:4. And I prayed unto the LORD my God, and made my confession. Ps. 32:5, 6. I said, I will confess my transgressions unto the Lord; and thou forgavest the iniquity of my sin. Selah. For this shall every one that is godly pray unto thee in a time when thou mayest be found.

5. Phil. 4:6. In every thing by prayer and supplication with thanksgiving let your requests be made known unto God.

Q. 179. *Are we to pray unto God only?*

A. God only being able to search the heart,[1] hear the requests,[2] pardon the sins,[3] and fulfill the desires of all,[4] and only to be believed in,[5] and worshipped with religious worship;[6] prayer, which is a special part thereof,[7] is to be made by all to him alone, and to none other.[8]

1. I Kings 8:39. Thou, *even* thou only, knowest the hearts of all the children of men.

Acts 1:24. And they prayed, and said, Thou, Lord, which knowest the hearts of all *men*, shew whether of these two thou hast chosen.

Rom. 8:27.

2. Ps. 65:2. O thou that hearest prayer, unto thee shall all flesh come.

3. Micah 7:18. Who *is* a God like unto thee, that pardoneth iniquity, and passeth by the transgression of the remnant of his heritage?

4. Ps. 145:16, 19. Thou openest thine hand, and satisfiest the desire of every living thing. . . . He will fulfil the desire of them that fear him.

5. II Sam. 22:32. For who *is* God, save the Lord? and who *is* a rock, save our God?

   John 14:1. Let not your heart be troubled: ye believe in God.

6. Matt. 4:10. Then saith Jesus unto him, Get thee hence, Satan: for it is written, Thou shalt worship the Lord thy God, and him only shalt thou serve.

7. I Cor. 1:2. Unto the church of God which is at Corinth, to them that are sanctified in Christ Jesus, called *to be* saints, with all that in every place call upon the name of Jesus Christ our Lord, both theirs and ours.

8. Luke 4:8. And Jesus answered and said unto him, Get thee behind me, Satan: for it is written, Thou shalt worship the Lord thy God, and him only shalt thou serve.

   Isa. 42:8. I *am* the Lord: that *is* my name: and my glory will I not give to another, neither my praise to graven images.

   Jer. 3:23.

Q. 180. *What is it to pray in the name of Christ?*

A. To pray in the name of Christ is, in obedience to his command, and in confidence on his promises, to ask mercy for his sake:[1] not by bare mentioning of his name;[2] but by drawing our encouragement to pray, and our boldness, strength, and hope of acceptance in prayer, from Christ and his mediation.[3]

1. John 14:13, 14. And whatsoever ye shall ask in my name, that will I do, that the Father may be glorified in the Son. If ye shall ask any thing in my name, I will do *it*.
   Dan. 9:17.

2. Luke 6:46. And why call ye me, Lord, Lord, and do not the things which I say?
   Matt. 7:21.

3. Heb. 4:14-16. Seeing then that we have a great high priest, that is passed into the heavens, Jesus the Son of God, let us hold fast *our* profession. For we have not an high priest which cannot be touched with the feeling of our infirmities; but was in all points tempted like as *we are, yet* without sin. Let us therefore come boldly unto the throne of grace, that we may obtain mercy, and find grace to help in time of need.
   I John 5:13-15.

Q. 181. *Why are we to pray in the name of Christ?*

A. The sinfulness of man, and his distance from God by reason thereof, being so great, as that we can have no access into his presence without a mediator, and there being none in heaven or earth appointed to, or fit for, that glorious work but Christ alone, we are to pray in no other name but his only.[1]

1. John 14:6. Jesus saith unto him, I am the way, the truth, and the life: no man cometh unto the Father, but by me.

Eph. 3:12. In whom we have boldness and access with confidence by the faith of him.

I Tim. 2:5. For *there is* one God, and one mediator between God and men, the man Christ Jesus.

John 6:27.

Col. 3:17. And whatsoever ye do in word or deed, *do* all in the name of the Lord Jesus, giving thanks to God and the Father by him.

Heb. 7:25-27; 13:15.

Q. 182. *How doth the Spirit help us to pray?*

A. We not knowing what to pray for as we ought, the Spirit helpeth our infirmities, by enabling us to understand both for whom, and what, and how prayer is to be made; and by working and quickening in our hearts (although not in all persons, nor at all times in the same measure) those apprehensions, affections, and graces, which are requisite for the right performance of that duty.[1]

1. Rom. 8:26. Likewise the Spirit also helpeth our infirmities: for we know not what we should pray for as we ought: but the Spirit itself maketh intercession for us with groanings which cannot be uttered.

Psa. 80:18. Quicken us, and we will call upon thy name.

Psa. 10:17; Zech. 12:10.

Q. 183. *For whom are we to pray?*

A. We are to pray for the whole church of Christ upon earth,[1] for magistrates,[2] and ministers,[3] for ourselves,[4] our brethren,[5] yea, our enemies,[6] and for all sorts of men living,[7] or that shall live hereafter;[8] but not for the dead.[9]

1. Eph. 6:18. Praying always with all prayer and supplication in the Spirit, and watching thereunto with all perseverance and supplication for all saints.

Ps. 28:9. Save thy people, and bless thine inheritance: feed them also, and lift them up for ever.

2. I Tim. 2:1, 2. I exhort therefore, that, first of all, supplications, prayers, intercessions, *and* giving of thanks, be made for all men; for kings, and *for* all that are in authority.

3. II Thess. 3:1. Finally, brethren, pray for us, that the word of the Lord may have *free* course, and be glorified, even as *it is* with you.

Col. 4:3.

4. Gen. 32:11. Deliver me, I pray thee, from the hand of my brother, from the hand of Esau: for I fear him, lest he will come and smite me, *and* the mother with the children.

5. James 5:16. Pray one for another, that ye may be healed.
II Thess. 1:11.
6. Matt. 5:44. Pray for them which despitefully use you, and persecute you.
7. I Tim. 2:1, 2. See under figure 2 above.
8. John 17:20. Neither pray I for these alone, but for them also which shall believe on me through their word.
II Sam. 7:29.
9. This statement is based on the absence of any command to pray for the dead, and of any example in the Scriptures of such prayer.

Q. 184. *For what things are we to pray?*

A. We are to pray for all things tending to the glory of God,[1] the welfare of the church,[2] our own[3] or others' good;[4] but not for anything that is unlawful.[5]

1. Matt. 6:9. Our Father which art in heaven, Hallowed be thy name.
2. Ps. 51:18. Do good in thy good pleasure unto Zion: build thou the walls of Jerusalem.
Ps. 122:6. Pray for the peace of Jerusalem: they shall prosper that love thee.
3. Matt. 7:11. If ye then, being evil, know how to give good gifts unto your children, how much more shall your Father which is in heaven give good things to them that ask him?
4. Ps. 125:4. Do good, O Lord, unto *those that be* good, and to *them that are* upright in their hearts.
I Thess. 5:23; II Thess. 3:16.
5. I John 5:14. And this is the confidence that we have in him, that, if we ask any thing according to his will, he heareth us.
James 4:3. Ye ask, and receive not, because ye ask amiss.

Q. 185. *How are we to pray?*

A. We are to pray with an awful apprehension of the majesty of God,[1] and deep sense of our own unworthiness,[2] necessities,[3] and sins;[4] with penitent,[5] thankful,[6] and enlarged hearts;[7] with understanding,[8] faith,[9] sincerity,[10] fervency,[11] love,[12] and perseverance,[13] waiting upon him[14] with humble submission to his will.[15]

1. Ps. 33:8. Let all the earth fear the Lord: let all the inhabitants of the world stand in awe of him.
Ps. 95:6. O come, let us worship and bow down: let us kneel before the Lord our maker.
2. Gen. 18:27. And Abraham answered and said, Behold now, I have taken upon me to speak unto the Lord, which *am but* dust and ashes.
Ps. 144:3.

3. Ps. 86:1. Bow down thine ear, O LORD, hear me: for I *am* poor and needy. Luke 15:17-19.

4. Ps. 130:3. If thou, LORD, shouldest mark iniquities, O Lord, who shall stand?

   Luke 18:13. And the publican, standing afar off, would not lift up so much as *his* eyes unto heaven, but smote upon his breast, saying, God be merciful to me a sinner.

5. Ps. 51:17. The sacrifices of God *are* a broken spirit: a broken and a contrite heart, O God, thou wilt not despise.

   Zech. 12:10-14.

6. Phil. 4:6. In every thing by prayer and supplication with thanksgiving let your requests be made known unto God.

   I Thess. 5:18.

7. Ps. 81:10. Open thy mouth wide, and I will fill it.

   Eph. 3:20, 21. Now unto him that is able to do exceeding abundantly above all that we ask or think, according to the power that worketh in us, unto him *be* glory in the church by Christ Jesus throughout all ages. . .

8. I Cor. 14:15. What is it then? I will pray with the spirit, and I will pray with the understanding also.

9. Heb. 10:22. Let us draw near . . . in full assurance of faith.

   James 1:6. But let him ask in faith, nothing wavering.

10. Heb. 10:22. Let us draw near with a true heart.

    Ps. 145:18. The LORD *is* nigh unto all them that call upon him . . . in truth.

    Ps. 17:1; John 4:24.

11. James 5:16. The effectual fervent prayer of a righteous man availeth much.

12. I Tim. 2:8. I will therefore that men pray every where, lifting up holy hands, without wrath and doubting.

    Matt. 5:23, 24.

13. Eph. 6:18. Praying always with all prayer and supplication in the Spirit, and watching thereunto with all perseverence.

14. Micah 7:7. Therefore I will look unto the LORD; I will wait for the God of my salvation: my God will hear me.

15. Matt. 26:39. And he went a little farther, and fell on his face, and prayed, saying, O my Father, if it be possible, let this cup pass from me: nevertheless not as I will, but as thou *wilt*.

Q. 186. *What rule hath God given for our direction in the duty of prayer?*

A. The whole word of God is of use to direct us in the duty of praying;[1] but the special rule of direction is that form of prayer which our Saviour Christ taught his disciples, commonly called, *the Lord's prayer.*[2]

1. II Tim 3:16, 17. All scripture *is* given by inspiration of God, and *is* profitable for doctrine . . . that the man of God may be perfect, throughly furnished unto all good works.

   I John 5:14.

2. Matt. 6:9-13; Luke 11:2-4.

Q. 187. *How is the Lord's prayer to be used?*

A. The Lord's prayer is not only for direction, as a pattern according to which we are to make other prayers; but may be also used as a prayer so that it be done with understanding, faith, reverence, and other graces necessary to the right performance of the duty of prayer.[1]

1. Matt. 6:9. After this manner therefore pray ye.
   Luke 11:2. When ye pray, say, Our Father.

Q. 188. *Of how many parts doth the Lord's prayer consist?*

A. The Lord's prayer consists of three parts: a preface, petitions, and a conclusion.

Q. 189. *What doth the preface of the Lord's prayer teach us?*

A. The preface of the Lord's prayer (contained in these words, *Our Father which art in heaven*)[1] teacheth us, when we pray, to draw near to God with confidence of his fatherly goodness, and our interest therein;[2] with reverence, and all other childlike dispositions,[3] heavenly affections,[4] and due apprehensions of his sovereign power, majesty, and gracious condescension:[5] as also to pray with and for others.[6]

1. Matt. 6:9.
2. Luke 11:13. If ye then, being evil, know how to give good gifts unto your children: how much more shall *your* heavenly Father give the Holy Spirit to them that ask him?
   Rom. 8:15.
3. Ps. 95:6, 7. Let us kneel before the LORD our maker. For he *is* our God; and we *are* the people of his pasture, and the sheep of his hand.
   Isa. 64:9.
4. Ps. 123:1. Unto thee lift I up mine eyes, O thou that dwellest in the heavens.
   Lam. 3:41. Let us lift up our hearts with *our* hands unto God in the heavens.
5. Ps. 104:1. Bless the LORD, O my soul. O LORD my God, thou art very great; thou art clothed with honour and majesty.
   Isa. 63:15. Look down from heaven, and behold from the habitation of thy holiness and of thy glory: where *is* thy zeal and thy strength, the sounding of thy bowels and of thy mercies toward me? are they restrained?
   Ps. 113:4-6.
6. Acts 12:5. Peter therefore was kept in prison: but prayer was made without ceasing of the church unto God for him.
   Zech. 8:21.

Q. 190. *What do we pray for in the first petition?*

A. In the first petition (which is, *Hallowed be thy name*),[1] acknowledging the utter inability and indisposition that is in ourselves and all men to honor God aright,[2] we pray: that God would by his grace enable and incline us and others to know, to acknowledge, and highly esteem him,[3] his titles,[4] attributes,[5] ordinances, word,[6] works, and whatsoever he is pleased to make himself known by;[7] and to glorify him in thought, word,[8] and deed;[9] that he would prevent and remove atheism,[10] ignorance,[11] idolatry,[12] profaneness,[13] and whatsoever is dishonorable to him;[14] and by his overruling providence, direct and dispose of all things to his own glory.[15]

1. Matt. 6:9.
2. II Cor. 3:5. Not that we are sufficient of ourselves to think any thing as of ourselves; but our sufficiency *is* of God.

    Ps. 51:15. O Lord, open thou my lips; and my mouth shall shew forth thy praise.
3. Ps. 67:2, 3. That thy way may be known upon earth, thy saving health among all nations. Let the people praise thee, O God; let all the people praise thee.

    Ps. 72:19. Let the whole earth be filled *with* his glory.

    Eph. 3:20, 21.
4. Ps. 83:18. That *men* may know that thou, whose name alone *is* JEHO-VAH, *art* the most high over all the earth.
5. Ps. 145:6-8. And *men* shall speak of the might of thy terrible acts: and I will declare thy greatness. They shall abundantly utter the memory of thy great goodness, and shall sing of thy righteousness. The LORD *is* gracious, and full of compassion; slow to anger, and of great mercy.

    Ps. 86:10, 15.
6. II Thess. 3:1. Finally, brethren, pray for us, that the word of the Lord may have *free* course, and be glorified, even as *it is* with you.

    Ps. 107:32. Let them exalt him also in the congregation of the people, and praise him in the assembly of the elders.

    II Cor. 2:14.
7. Ps. 8 and 145, throughout.
8. Ps. 19:14. Let the words of my mouth, and the meditations of my heart, be acceptable in thy sight, O LORD, my strength, and my redeemer.
9. Phil. 1:11. Being filled with the fruits of righteousness, which are by Jesus Christ, unto the glory and praise of God.
10. Ps. 79:10. Wherefore should the heathen say, Where *is* their God? let him be known among the heathen in our sight.

    Ps. 67:1-4.
11. Eph. 1:17, 18. That the God of our Lord Jesus Christ, the Father of glory, may give unto you the spirit of wisdom and revelation in the knowledge of him: the eyes of your understanding being enlightened.
12. Ps. 97:7. Confounded be all they that serve graven images, that boast themselves of idols: worship him, all *ye* gods.

13. Ps. 74:18, 22. Remember this, *that* the enemy hath reproached, O LORD, and *that* the foolish people have blasphemed thy name. . . . Arise, O God, plead thine own cause: remember how the foolish man reproacheth thee daily.

14. Jer. 14:21. For thy name's sake, do not disgrace the throne of thy glory. II Kings 19:16.

15. Isa. 64:1, 2. Oh that thou wouldest rend the heavens, that thou wouldest come down, that the mountains might flow down at thy presence . . . to make thy name known to thine adversaries, *that* the nations may tremble at thy presence! II Chron. 20:6, 10-12.

Q. 191. *What do we pray for in the second petition?*

A. In the second petition (which is, *Thy kingdom come*),[1] acknowledging ourselves and all mankind to be by nature under the dominion of sin and Satan,[2] we pray: that the kingdom of sin and Satan may be destroyed,[3] the gospel propagated throughout the world,[4] the Jews called,[5] the fullness of the Gentiles brought in;[6] that the church may be furnished with all gospel-officers and ordinances,[7] purged from corruption,[8] countenanced and maintained by the civil magistrate; that the ordinances of Christ may be purely dispensed, and made effectual to the converting of those that are yet in their sins, and the confirming, comforting, and building up of those that are already converted;[9] that Christ would rule in our hearts here,[10] and hasten the time of his second coming, and our reigning with him forever;[11] and that he would be pleased so to exercise the kingdom of his power in all the world, as may best conduce to these ends.[12]

1. Matt. 6:10.

2. Eph. 2:2, 3. Wherein in time past ye walked according to the course of this world, according to the prince of the power of the air, the spirit that now worketh in the children of disobedience: among whom also we all had our conversation in times past in the lusts of our flesh, fulfilling the desires of the flesh and of the mind; and were by nature the children of wrath, even as others.

3. Ps. 68:1. Let God arise, let his enemies be scattered: let them also that hate him flee before him.
Rev. 12:9.

4. II Thess. 3:1. Finally, brethren, pray for us, that the word of the Lord may have *free* course, and be glorified, even as *it is* with you.

5. Rom. 10:1. Brethren, my heart's desire and prayer to God for Israel is, that they might be saved.
Ps. 67:2.

6. Rom. 11:25. For I would not, brethren, that ye should be ignorant of this mystery . . . that blindness in part is happened to Israel, until the fulness of the Gentiles be come in.

Ps. 67:1-7.

7. Matt. 9:38. Pray ye therefore the Lord of the harvest, that he will send forth labourers into his harvest.

8. Eph. 5:26, 27. That he might sanctify and cleanse it with the washing of water by the word, that he might present it to himself a glorious church, not having spot, or wrinkle, or any such thing; but that it should be holy and without blemish.

Mal. 1:11.

9. II Cor. 4:2. Nor handling the word of God deceitfully; but by manifestation of the truth commending ourselves to every man's conscience in the sight of God.

Acts 26:18. To open their eyes, *and* to turn *them* from darkness to light, and *from* the power of Satan unto God, that they may receive forgiveness of sins, and inheritance among them which are sanctified.

II Thess. 2:16, 17. Now our Lord Jesus Christ himself, and God, even our Father . . . comfort your hearts, and stablish you in every good word and work.

10. Eph. 3:14, 17. For this cause I bow my knees unto the Father of our Lord Jesus Christ . . . that Christ may dwell in your hearts by faith.

11. Rev. 22:20. He which testifieth these things saith, Surely I come quickly. Amen. Even so, come, Lord Jesus.

12. Isa. 64:1, 2. Oh that thou wouldest rend the heavens, that thou wouldest come down, that the mountains might flow down at thy presence, as *when* the melting fire burneth, the fire causeth the waters to boil, to make thy name known to thine adversaries, *that* the nations may tremble at thy presence!

II Chron. 20:6, 10-12.

Q. 192. *What do we pray for in the third petition?*

A. In the third petition (which is, *Thy will be done on earth as it is in heaven*),[1] acknowledging that by nature we and all men are not only utterly unable and unwilling to know and do the will of God,[2] but prone to rebel against his word,[3] to repine and murmur against his providence,[4] and wholly inclined to do the will of the flesh, and of the devil:[5] we pray that God would by his Spirit take away from ourselves and others all blindness,[6] weakness,[7] indisposedness,[8] and perverseness of heart,[9] and by his grace make us able and willing to know, do, and submit to his will in all things,[10] with the like humility,[11] cheerfulness,[12] faithfulness,[13] diligence,[14] zeal,[15] sincerity,[16] and constancy,[17] as the angels do in heaven.[18]

1. Matt. 6:10.

2. I Cor. 2:14. The natural man receiveth not the things of the Spirit of

God: for they are foolishness unto him: neither can he know *them*, because they are spiritually discerned.

Rom. 8:5, 8.

3. Rom. 8:7. Because the carnal mind *is* enmity against God: for it is not subject to the law of God, neither indeed can be.

4. Matt. 20:11, 12. And when they had received *it*, they murmured against the goodman of the house, saying, These last have wrought *but* one hour, and thou hast made them equal unto us, which have borne the burden and heat of the day.

Ps. 73:3. I was envious at the foolish, *when* I saw the prosperity of the wicked.

5. Titus 3:3. For we ourselves also were sometimes foolish, disobedient, deceived, serving divers lusts and pleasures, living in malice and envy.

Eph. 2:2, 3.

See Question 191 under figure 2.

6. Eph. 1:17, 18. That the God of our Lord Jesus Christ, the Father of glory, may give unto you the spirit of wisdom and revelation in the knowledge of him: the eyes of your understanding being enlightened.

7. Eph. 3:16. That he would grant you, according to the riches of his glory, to be strengthened with might by his Spirit in the inner man.

8. Matt. 26:40, 41. And he cometh unto the disciples, and findeth them asleep, and saith unto Peter, What, could ye not watch with me one hour? Watch and pray, that ye enter not into temptation: the spirit indeed *is* willing, but the flesh *is* weak.

Rom. 7:24, 25.

9. Ezek. 11:19. And I will take the stony heart out of their flesh, and will give them an heart of flesh.

Jer. 31:18. Thou hast chastised me, and I was chastised, as a bullock unaccustomed *to the yoke:* turn thou me, and I shall be turned; for thou *art* the Lord my God.

10. Ps. 119:35. Make me to go in the path of thy commandments: for therein do I delight.

Acts 21:14. And when he would not be persuaded, we ceased, saying, The will of the Lord be done.

I Sam. 3:18.

11. Ps. 123:2. Behold, as the eyes of servants *look* unto the hand of their masters, *and* as the eyes of a maiden unto the hand of her mistress; so our eyes *wait* upon the Lord our God.

Ps. 131:2; Micah 6:8.

12. Ps. 100:2. Serve the Lord with gladness: come before his presence with singing.

13. Isa. 38:3. Remember now, O Lord, I beseech thee, how I have walked before thee in truth and with a perfect heart, and have done *that which is* good in thy sight.

Eph. 6:6. Doing the will of God from the heart.

14. Ps. 119:4. Thou has commanded *us* to keep thy precepts diligently.

15. Rom. 12:11. Not slothful in business; fervent in spirit; serving the Lord.

16. II Cor. 1:12. Our rejoicing is this, the testimony of our conscience, that

in simplicity and godly sincerity, not with fleshly wisdom, but by the grace of God, we have had our conversation in the world.

17. Ps. 119:112. I have inclined mine heart to perform thy statutes alway, *even unto* the end.

Rom. 2:7. To them who by patient continuance in well doing seek for glory and honour and immortality, eternal life.

18. Ps. 103:20-22. Bless the LORD, ye his angels, that excel in strength, that do his commandments, hearkening unto the voice of his word. Bless ye the LORD, all *ye* his hosts; *ye* ministers of his, that do his pleasure. . . . bless the LORD, O my soul.

Dan. 7:10.

Q. 193. *What do we pray for in the fourth petition?*

A. In the fourth petition (which is, *Give us this day our daily bread*),[1] acknowledging that in Adam, and by our own sin, we have forfeited our right to all the outward blessings of this life, and deserve to be wholly deprived of them by God, and to have them cursed to us in the use of them;[2] and that neither they of themselves are able to sustain us,[3] nor we to merit,[4] or by our own industry to procure them,[5] but prone to desire,[6] get,[7] and use them unlawfully:[8] we pray for ourselves and others, that both they and we, waiting upon the providence of God from day to day in the use of lawful means may, of his free gift, and as to his fatherly wisdom shall seem best, enjoy a competent portion of them,[9] and have the same continued and blessed unto us in our holy and comfortable use of them,[10] and contentment in them;[11] and be kept from all things that are contrary to our temporal support and comfort.[12]

1. Matt. 6:11.

2. Gen. 3:17. And unto Adam he said . . . cursed *is* the ground for thy sake; in sorrow shalt thou eat *of* it all the days of thy life.

   Lam. 3:22. *It is of* the LORD's mercies that we are not consumed, because his compassions fail not.

   Deut. 28:15-68.

3. Deut. 8:3. And he humbled thee, and suffered thee to hunger, and fed thee with manna . . . that he might make thee know that man doth not live by bread only, but by every *word* that proceedeth out of the mouth of the LORD doth man live.

4. Gen. 32:10. I am not worthy of the least of all the mercies, and of all the truth, which thou hast shewed unto thy servant.

5. Deut. 8:18. But thou shalt remember the LORD thy God: for *it is* he that giveth thee power to get wealth.

   Prov. 10:22.

6. Luke 12:15. Take heed, and beware of covetousness.

   Jer. 6:13.

7. Hos. 12:7. *He is* a merchant, the balances of deceit *are* in his hand: he loveth to oppress.

8. James 4:3. Ye ask, and receive not, because ye ask amiss, that ye may consume *it* upon your lusts.

9. Gen. 28:20, 21. And Jacob vowed a vow, saying, If God will be with me, and will keep me in this way that I go, and will give me bread to eat, and raiment to put on . . . then shall the Lord be my God.

James 4:13, 15. Go to now, ye that say, To day or to morrow we will go into such a city . . . and continue there a year, and buy and sell, and get gain . . . for that ye *ought* to say, If the Lord will, we shall live, and do this, or that.

Ps. 90:17. And let the beauty of the Lord our God be upon us: and establish thou the work of our hands upon us; yea, the work of our hands establish thou it.

Ps. 144:12-15.

10. I Tim. 4:4, 5. Every creature of God *is* good, and nothing to be refused, if it be received with thanksgiving: for it is sanctified by the word of God and prayer.

Prov. 10:22.

11. I Tim. 6:6, 8. Godliness with contentment is great gain. . . . And having food and raiment let us be therewith content.

12. Prov. 30:8, 9. Remove far from me vanity and lies . . . feed me with food convenient for me: lest I be full, and deny *thee,* and say, Who *is* the Lord? or lest I be poor, and steal, and take the name of my God *in vain.*

Q. 194. *What do we pray for in the fifth petition?*

A. In the fifth petition (which is, *Forgive us our debts, as we forgive our debtors*),[1] acknowledging that we and all others are guilty both of original and actual sin, and thereby become debtors to the justice of God, and that neither we nor any other creature can make the least satisfaction for that debt:[2] we pray for ourselves and others, that God of his free grace would, through the obedience and satisfaction of Christ apprehended and applied by faith, acquit us both from the guilt and punishment of sin,[3] accept us in his Beloved,[4] continue his favor and grace to us,[5] pardon our daily failings,[6] and fill us with peace and joy, in giving us daily more and more assurance of forgiveness;[7] which we are the rather emboldened to ask, and encouraged to expect, when we have this testimony in ourselves, that we from the heart forgive others their offenses.[8]

1. Matt. 6:12.

2. Matt. 18:24. And when he had begun to reckon, one was brought unto him, which owed him ten thousand talents.

Rom. 5:19. By one man's disobedience many were made sinners.

Rom. 3:9, 19. We have before proved both Jews and Gentiles, that they are all under sin . . . that every mouth may be stopped, and all the world may become guilty before God.

See context.

Ps. 130:3. If thou, Lord, shouldest mark iniquities, O Lord, who shall stand?

Micah 6:6, 7.

3. Rom. 5:19. By the obedience of one shall many be made righteous.

Rom. 3:24, 25. Being justified freely by his grace through the redemption that is in Christ Jesus: whom God hath set forth *to be* a propitiation through faith in his blood, to declare his righteousness for the remission of sins that are past, through the forbearance of God.

Acts 13:39.

4. Eph. 1:6. To the praise of the glory of his grace, wherein he hath made us accepted in the beloved.

5. II Peter 1:2. Grace and peace be multiplied unto you through the knowledge of God, and of Jesus our Lord.

6. Hos. 14:2. Take with you words, and turn to the Lord: say unto him, take away all iniquity, and receive *us* graciously.

Ps. 143:2. Enter not into judgment with thy servant: for in thy sight shall no man living be justified.

Ps. 130:3.

7. Rom. 15:13. Now the God of hope fill you with all joy and peace in believing, that ye may abound in hope, through the power of the Holy Ghost.

Rom. 5:1, 2; Ps. 51:7-12.

8. Luke 11:4. And forgive us our sins; for we also forgive every one that is indebted to us.

Matt. 18:35. So likewise shall my heavenly Father do also unto you, if ye from your hearts forgive not every one his brother their trespasses.

Matt. 6:14, 15.

Q. 195. *What do we pray for in the sixth petition?*

A. In the sixth petition (which is, *And lead us not into temptation, but deliver us from evil*),[1] acknowledging that the most wise, righteous, and gracious God, for divers holy and just ends, may so order things that we may be assaulted, foiled, and for a time led captive by temptations;[2] that Satan,[3] the world,[4] and the flesh, are ready powerfully to draw us aside and ensnare us;[5] and that we, even after the pardon of our sins, by reason of our corruption,[6] weakness, and want of watchfulness,[7] are not only subject to be tempted, and forward to expose ourselves unto temptations,[8] but also of ourselves unable and unwilling to resist them, to recover out of them, and to improve them;[9] and worthy to be left under the power of them;[10] we pray: that God would so overrule the world and all in it,[11] subdue the flesh,[12] and restrain Satan,[13] order all things,[14] bestow and bless all means of grace,[15] and quicken us to watchfulness in the use of them, that we and all his people may by his providence be kept from being tempted to sin;[16] or, if tempted, that by his Spirit we may be powerfully supported and enabled to stand in the hour of temptation;[17] or, when fallen, raised again and recovered out of it,[18] and have a sanctified use and improvement thereof;[19] that our sanctification and salvation may be perfected,[20] Satan trodden under our feet,[21] and we fully freed from sin, temptation, and all evil forever.[22]

1. Matt. 6:13.

2. II Chron. 32:31. God left him, to try him, that he might know all *that was* in his heart.
   Job 2:6. And the LORD said unto Satan, Behold, he *is* in thine hand; but save his life.

3. I Peter 5:8. Be sober, be vigilant; because your adversary the devil, as a roaring lion, walketh about, seeking whom he may devour.
   Job 2:2.

4. Luke 21:34. And take heed to yourselves, lest at any time your hearts be overcharged with surfeiting, and drunkenness, and cares of this life, and *so* that day come upon you unawares.
   Mark 4:19.

5. James 1:14. Every man is tempted, when he is drawn away of his own lust, and enticed.

6. Gal. 5:17. For the flesh lusteth against the Spirit, and the Spirit against the flesh: and these are contrary the one to the other: so that ye cannot do the things that ye would.
   Rom. 7:18.

7. Matt. 26:41. Watch and pray, that ye enter not into temptation: the spirit indeed *is* willing, but the flesh *is* weak.

8. I Tim. 6:9. They that will be rich fall into temptation and a snare, and *into* many foolish and hurtful lusts.
   Prov. 7:22.

9. Rom. 7:18, 19. For I know that in me (that is, in my flesh,) dwelleth no good thing: for to will is present with me; but *how* to perform that which is good I find not. For the good that I would I do not: but the evil which I would not, that I do.

10. Ps. 81:11, 12. But my people would not hearken to my voice; and Israel would none of me. So I gave them up unto their own hearts' lust: *and* they walked in their own counsels.

11. John 17:15. I pray not that thou shouldest take them out of the world, but that thou shouldest keep them from the evil.
    Rom. 8:28.

12. Ps. 51:10. Create in me a clean heart, O God; and renew a right spirit within me.
    Ps. 119:133. Let not any iniquity have dominion over me.

13. Heb. 2:18. For in that he himself hath suffered being tempted, he is able to succour them that are tempted.

   I Cor. 10:13. God *is* faithful, who will not suffer you to be tempted above that ye are able.

   II Cor. 12:8.

14. Rom. 8:28. And we know that all things work together for good to them that love God, to them who are the called according to *his* purpose.

15. Heb. 13:20, 21. Now the God of peace . . . make you perfect in every good work to do his will, working in you that which is wellpleasing in his sight, through Jesus Christ.

   Eph. 4:11, 12.

16. Matt. 26:41. Watch and pray, that ye enter not into temptation.

   Ps. 19:13. Keep back thy servant also from presumptuous *sins;* let them not have dominion over me.

17. I Cor. 10:13. God *is* faithful, who will not suffer you to be tempted above that ye are able; but will with the temptation also make a way to escape, that ye may be able to bear *it.*

   Eph. 3:14-16.

18. Ps. 51:12. Restore unto me the joy of thy salvation; and uphold me *with thy* free spirit.

19: I Peter 5:10. But the God of all grace, who hath called us unto his eternal glory by Christ Jesus, after that ye have suffered a while, make you perfect, stablish, strengthen, settle *you.*

   I Peter 1:6, 7. Wherein ye greatly rejoice, though now for a season, if need be, ye are in heaviness through manifold temptations: that the trial of your faith, being much more precious than of gold that perisheth, though it be tried with fire, might be found unto praise and honour and glory at the appearing of Jesus Christ.

20. I Thess. 3:13. To the end he may stablish your hearts unblamable in holiness before God, even our Father, at the coming of our Lord Jesus Christ with all his saints.

21. Rom. 16:20. And the God of peace shall bruise Satan under your feet shortly.

22. I Thess. 5:23. And the very God of peace sanctify you wholly; and I *pray God* your whole spirit and soul and body be preserved blameless unto the coming of our Lord Jesus Christ.

Q. 196. *What doth the conclusion of the Lord's prayer teach us?*

A. The conclusion of the Lord's prayer (which is, *For thine is the kingdom, and the power, and the glory, for ever. Amen.*),[1] teacheth us to enforce our petitions with arguments,[2] which are to be taken, not from any worthiness in ourselves, or in any other creature, but from God;[3] and with our prayers to join praises,[4] ascribing to God alone eternal sovereignty, omnipotency, and glorious excellency;[5] in regard whereof, as he is able and willing to help us,[6] so we by faith are emboldened to plead with him that he would,[7] and quietly to rely upon him that he will, fulfill our requests.[8] And to testify our desires and assurance, we say, *Amen.*[9]

1. Matt. 6:13.

2. Job 23:3, 4. Oh that I knew where I might find him! *that* I might come *even* to his seat! I would order *my* cause before him, and fill my mouth with arguments.

   Jer. 14:20, 21. We acknowledge, O LORD, our wickedness, *and* the iniquity of our fathers: for we have sinned against thee. Do not abhor *us,* for thy name's sake, do not disgrace the throne of thy glory: remember, break not thy covenant with us.

3. Dan. 9:4, 7-9, 16, 19. And I prayed unto the LORD my God, and made my confession, and said, O Lord, the great and dreadful God, keeping the covenant and mercy to them that love him, and to them that keep his commandments . . . O Lord, righteousness *belongeth* unto thee, but unto us confusion of faces, as at this day . . . O Lord, to us *belongeth* confusion of face, to our kings, to our princes, and to our fathers, because we have sinned against thee. To the Lord our God *belong* mercies and forgivenesses, though we have rebelled against him . . . O Lord, hear; O Lord, forgive; O Lord, hearken and do; defer not, for thine own sake, O my God.

4. Phil. 4:6. In every thing by prayer and supplication with thanksgiving let your requests be made known unto God.

5. I Chron. 29:10-13. And David said, Blessed *be* thou, LORD God of Israel our father, for ever and ever. Thine, O LORD, *is* the greatness, and the power, and the glory and the victory, and the majesty: for all *that is* in the heaven and in the earth *is thine;* thine *is* the kingdom, O LORD, and thou art exalted as head above all. Both riches and honour *come* of thee, and thou reignest over all; and in thine hand *is* power and might; and in thine hand *it is* to make great, and to give strength unto all. Now therefore, our God, we thank thee, and praise thy glorious name.

6. Eph. 3:20, 21. Now unto him that is able to do exceeding abundantly above all that we ask or think, according to the power that worketh in us, unto him *be* glory in the church by Christ Jesus throughout all ages, world without end. Amen.

   Luke 11:13. If ye then, being evil, know how to give good gifts unto your children: how much more shall *your* heavenly Father give the Holy Spirit to them that ask him?

   Ps. 84:11.

7. Eph. 3:12. In whom we have boldness and access with confidence by the faith of him.

   Heb. 10:19-22. Having therefore, brethren, boldness to enter into the holiest by the blood of Jesus, by a new and living way, which he hath consecrated for us, through the veil, that is to say, his flesh; and *having* an high priest over the house of God; let us draw near with a true heart in full assurance of faith, having our hearts sprinkled from an evil conscience, and our bodies washed with pure water.

8. I John 5:14. And this is the confidence that we have in him, that, if we ask any thing according to his will, he heareth us.

Rom. 8:32. He that spared not his own Son, but delivered him up for us all, how shall he not with him also freely give us all things?

9. I Cor. 14:16. Else when thou shalt bless with the spirit, how shall he that occupieth the room of the unlearned say Amen at thy giving of thanks, seeing he understandeth not what thou sayest?

Rev. 22:20, 21. He which testifieth these things saith, Surely I come quickly. Amen. Even so, come, Lord Jesus. The grace of our Lord Jesus Christ be with you all. Amen.

THE
SHORTER CATECHISM

With Scripture Proofs approved by the General Assembly of 1910

THE
SHORTER CATECHISM

✠

Q. 1. *What is the chief end of man?*

A. Man's chief end is to glorify God,[1] and to enjoy him forever.[2]

1. I Cor., 10:31. Whether therefore ye eat, or drink, or whatsoever ye do, do all to the glory of God.

   Rom. 11:36. For of him, and through him, and to him, *are* all things: to whom *be* glory for ever. Amen.

2. Ps. 73:24-26. Thou shalt guide me with thy counsel, and afterward receive me *to* glory. Whom have I in heaven *but thee?* and *there is* none upon earth *that* I desire beside thee. My flesh and my heart faileth: *but* God *is* the strength of my heart, and my portion for ever.

   John 17:22, 24. And the glory which thou gavest me I have given them; that they may be one, even as we are one . . . Father, I will that they also, whom thou hast given me, be with me where I am; that they may behold my glory, which thou hast given me: for thou lovedst me before the foundation of the world.

Q. 2. *What rule hath God given to direct us how we may glorify and enjoy him?*

A. The word of God, which is contained in the Scriptures of the Old and New Testaments, is the only rule to direct us how we may glorify and enjoy him.[1]

1. Gal. 1:8, 9. But though we, or an angel from heaven, preach any other gospel unto you than that which we have preached unto you, let him be accursed. As we said before, so say I now again, If any *man* preach any other gospel unto you than that ye have received, let him be accursed.

   Isa. 8:20. To the law and to the testimony: if they speak not according to this word, *it is* because *there is* no light in them.

   Luke 16:29, 31; II Tim. 3:15-17.

Q. 3. *What do the Scriptures principally teach?*

A. The Scriptures principally teach, what man is to believe concerning God, and what duty God requires of man.[1]

1. Micah 6:8. He hath shewed thee, O man, what *is* good; and what doth the LORD require of thee, but to do justly, and to love mercy, and to walk humbly with thy God?

   John 20:31. But these are written, that ye might believe that Jesus is the Christ, the Son of God; and that believing ye might have life through his name.

John 3:16. For God so loved the world, that he gave his only begotten Son, that whosoever believeth in him should not perish, but have everlasting life.

Q. 4. *What is God?*

A. God is a Spirit,[1] infinite, eternal, and unchangeable, in his being,[2] wisdom,[3] power,[4] holiness,[5] justice,[6] goodness,[7] and truth.[8]

1. John 4:24. God *is* a Spirit: and they that worship him must worship *him* in spirit and in truth.

2. Ps. 90:2. From everlasting to everlasting, thou *art* God.

   Mal. 3:6. For I *am* the LORD, I change not; therefore ye sons of Jacob are not consumed.

   James 1:17. The Father of lights, with whom is no variableness, neither shadow of turning.

   I Kings 8:27. But will God indeed dwell on the earth? behold, the heaven and heaven of heavens cannot contain thee; how much less this house that I have builded?

   Jer. 23:24. Can any hide himself in secret places that I shall not see him? saith the LORD. Do not I fill heaven and earth? saith the LORD.

   Isa. 40:22.

3. Ps. 147:5. Great *is* our Lord, and of great power: his understanding *is* infinite.

   Rom. 16:27. To God only wise, *be* glory through Jesus Christ for ever. Amen.

4. Gen. 17:1. The LORD appeared to Abram, and said unto him, I *am* the Almighty God; walk before me, and be thou perfect.

   Rev. 19:6. The Lord God omnipotent reigneth.

5. Isa. 57:15. For thus saith the high and lofty One that inhabiteth eternity, whose name *is* Holy; I dwell in the high and holy *place*, with him also *that is* of a contrite and humble spirit, to revive the spirit of the humble, and to revive the heart of the contrite ones.

   John 17:11. Holy Father, keep through thine own name those whom thou hast given me, that they may be one, as we *are*.

   Rev. 4:8. Holy, holy, holy, Lord God Almighty, which was, and is, and is to come.

6. Deut. 32:4. *He is* the Rock, his work *is* perfect: for all his ways *are* judgment: a God of truth and without iniquity, just and right *is* he.

7. Ps. 100:5. For the LORD *is* good; his mercy *is* everlasting; and his truth *endureth* to all generations.

   Rom. 2:4. Or despisest thou the riches of his goodness and forbearance and longsuffering; not knowing that the goodness of God leadeth thee to repentance?

8. Exod. 34:6. The LORD, The LORD God, merciful and gracious, longsuffering, and abundant in goodness and truth.

   Ps. 117:2. For his merciful kindness is great toward us: and the truth of the LORD *endureth* for ever. Praise ye the LORD.

Q. 5. *Are there more gods than one?*

A. There is but one only, the living and true God.[1]

1. Deut. 6:4. Hear, O Israel: The LORD our God *is* one LORD.
   Jer. 10:10. But the LORD *is* the true God, he *is* the living God, and an everlasting king.

Q. 6. *How many persons are there in the Godhead?*

A. There are three persons in the Godhead: the Father, the Son, and the Holy Ghost; and these three are one God, the same in substance, equal in power and glory.[1]

1. II Cor. 13:14. The grace of the Lord Jesus Christ, and the love of God, and the communion of the Holy Ghost, *be* with you all. Amen.
   Matt. 28:19. Go ye therefore, and teach all nations, baptizing them in the name of the Father, and of the Son, and of the Holy Ghost.
   Matt. 3:16, 17. And Jesus, when he was baptized, went up straightway out of the water: and, lo, the heavens were opened unto him, and he saw the Spirit of God descending like a dove, and lighting upon him: and lo a voice from heaven, saying, This is my beloved Son, in whom I am well pleased.

Q. 7. *What are the decrees of God?*

A. The decrees of God are, his eternal purpose, according to the counsel of his will, whereby, for his own glory, he hath fore-ordained whatsoever comes to pass.[1]

1. Eph. 1:11. In whom also we have obtained an inheritance, being predestinated according to the purpose of him who worketh all things after the counsel of his own will.
   Acts 4:27, 28. For of a truth against thy holy child Jesus, whom thou hast anointed, both Herod, and Pontius Pilate, with the Gentiles, and the people of Israel, were gathered together, for to do whatsoever thy hand and thy counsel determined before to be done.
   Ps. 33:11. The counsel of the LORD standeth for ever, the thoughts of his heart to all generations.
   Eph. 2:10; Rom. 9:22, 23; 11:33.

Q. 8. *How doth God execute his decrees?*

A. God executeth his decrees in the works of creation and providence.[1]

1. Rev. 4:11. Thou hast created all things, and for thy pleasure they are and were created.
   Eph. 1:11. In whom also we have obtained an inheritance, being predestinated according to the purpose of him who worketh all things after the counsel of his own will.

Q. 9. *What is the work of creation?*

A. The work of creation is, God's making all things of nothing, by the word of his power, in the space of six days, and all very good.[1]

> 1. Heb. 11:3. Through faith we understand that the worlds were framed by the word of God, so that things which are seen were not made of things which do appear.
>   Rev. 4:11; Gen. 1:1-31.

Q. 10. *How did God create man?*

A. God created man, male and female, after his own image,[1] in knowledge, righteousness, and holiness,[2] with dominion over the creatures.[3]

> 1. Gen. 1:27. So God created man in his *own* image, in the image of God created he him; male and female created he them.
> 2. Col. 3:10. And have put on the new *man*, which is renewed in knowledge after the image of him that created him.
>   Eph. 4:24. And that ye put on the new man, which after God is created in righteousness and true holiness.
> 3. Gen. 1:28. And God blessed them, and God said unto them, Be fruitful, and multiply, and replenish the earth, and subdue it: and have dominion over the fish of the sea, and over the fowl of the air, and over every living thing that moveth upon the earth.

Q. 11. *What are God's works of providence?*

A. God's works of providence are, his most holy,[1] wise,[2] and powerful preserving[3] and governing all his creatures, and all their actions.[4]

> 1. Ps. 145:17. The LORD *is* righteous in all his ways, and holy in all his works.
> 2. Ps. 104:24. O LORD, how manifold are thy works! in wisdom hast thou made them all: the earth is full of thy riches.
> 3. Heb. 1:3. Upholding all things by the word of his power.
> 4. Ps. 103:19. His kingdom ruleth over all.
>   Matt. 10:29, 30. Are not two sparrows sold for a farthing? and one of them shall not fall on the ground without your Father. But the very hairs of your head are all numbered.
>   Job, chapters 38-41.

Q. 12. *What special act of providence did God exercise towards man, in the estate wherein he was created?*

A. When God had created man, he entered into a covenant of life with him, upon condition of perfect obedience;[1] forbidding him to eat of the tree of the knowledge of good and evil, upon pain of death.[2]

1. Compare Gen. 2:16, 17 with Rom. 5:12-14; Rom. 10:5; Luke 10:25-28, and with the covenants made with Noah and Abraham.

2. Gen. 2:17. But of the tree of the knowledge of good and evil, thou shalt not eat of it: for in the day that thou eatest thereof thou shalt surely die.

Q. 13. *Did our first parents continue in the estate wherein they were created?*

A. Our first parents, being left to the freedom of their own will, fell from the estate wherein they were created, by sinning against God.[1]

1. Gen. 3:6-8, 13. And when the woman saw that the tree *was* good for food, and that it *was* pleasant to the eyes, and a tree to be desired to make *one* wise, she took of the fruit thereof, and did eat, and gave also unto her husband with her; and he did eat. And the eyes of them both were opened, and they knew that they *were* naked; and they sewed fig leaves together, and made themselves aprons. And they heard the voice of the LORD God walking in the garden in the cool of the day: and Adam and his wife hid themselves from the presence of the LORD God amongst the trees of the garden. . . . And the LORD God said unto the woman, What *is* this *that* thou hast done? And the woman said, The serpent beguiled me, and I did eat.
II Cor. 11:3.

Q. 14. *What is sin?*

A. Sin is any want of conformity unto, or transgression of, the law of God.[1]

1. I John 3:4. Whosoever committeth sin trangresseth also the law: for sin is the transgression of the law.
James 4:17. Therefore to him that knoweth to do good, and doeth *it* not, to him it is sin.
Rom. 3:23. For all have sinned, and come short of the glory of God.

Q. 15. *What was the sin whereby our first parents fell from the estate wherein they were created?*

A. The sin whereby our first parents fell from the estate wherein they were created, was their eating the forbidden fruit.[1]

1. See proof to Answer 13. Gen. 3:6.

Q. 16. *Did all mankind fall in Adam's first transgression?*

A. The covenant being made with Adam, not only for himself, but for his posterity,[1] all mankind, descending from him by ordinary generation, sinned in him, and fell with him in his first transgression.[2]

1. Acts 17:26. And hath made of one blood all nations of men for to dwell on all the face of the earth, and hath determined the times before appointed, and the bounds of their habitation.
   See under Question 12.

2. Gen. 2:17. But of the tree of the knowledge of good and evil, thou shalt not eat of it: for in the day that thou eatest thereof thou shalt surely die.
   Compare Rom. 5:12-20; I Cor. 15:21, 22.

Q. 17. *Into what estate did the fall bring mankind?*

A. The fall brought mankind into an estate of sin and misery.[1]

1. Rom. 5:12. Wherefore, as by one man sin entered into the world, and death by sin; and so death passed upon all men, for that all have sinned.
   Gal. 3:10. For as many as are of the works of the law are under the curse: for it is written, Cursed *is* every one that continueth not in all things which are written in the book of the law to do them.

Q. 18. *Wherein consists the sinfulness of that estate whereinto man fell?*

A. The sinfulness of that estate whereinto man fell, consists in the guilt of Adam's first sin,[1] the want of original righteousness, and the corruption of his whole nature, which is commonly called original sin;[2] together with all actual transgressions which proceed from it.[3]

1. Rom. 5:12, 19. Wherefore, as by one man sin entered into the world, and death by sin; and so death passed upon all men, for that all have sinned . . . by one man's disobedience many were made sinners.
   I Cor. 15:22.

2. Rom. 5:6. For when we were yet without strength, in due time Christ died for the ungodly.
   Eph. 2:1-3. And you *hath he quickened,* who were dead in trespasses and sins; wherein in time past ye walked according to the course of this world, according to the prince of the power of the air, the spirit that now worketh in the children of disobedience: among whom also we all had our conversation in times past in the lusts of our flesh, fulfilling the desires of the flesh and of the mind; and were by nature the children of wrath, even as others.
   Rom. 8:7, 8. Because the carnal mind *is* enmity against God: for it is not subject to the law of God, neither indeed can be. So then they that are in the flesh cannot please God.
   Gen. 6:5. And GOD saw that the wickedness of man *was* great in the earth, and *that* every imagination of the thoughts of his heart *was* only evil continually.
   Rom. 3:10-20; Ps. 51:5; 58:3.

3. James 1:14, 15. But every man is tempted, when he is drawn away of his own lust, and enticed. Then when lust hath conceived, it bringeth forth sin: and sin, when it is finished, bringeth forth death.

Matt. 15:19. For out of the heart proceed evil thoughts, murders, adulteries, fornications, thefts, false witness, blasphemies.

Q. 19. *What is the misery of that estate whereinto man fell?*

A. All mankind, by their fall, lost communion with God,[1] are under his wrath and curse,[2] and so made liable to all miseries in this life, to death itself, and to the pains of hell forever.[3]

1. Gen. 3:8, 24. Adam and his wife hid themselves from the presence of the LORD God amongst the trees of the garden. . . . So he drove out the man.

2. Eph. 2:3. And were by nature the children of wrath, even as others.

3. Rom. 5:14. Nevertheless death reigned from Adam to Moses, even over them that had not sinned after the similitude of Adam's transgression, who is the figure of him that was to come.

Rom. 6:23. The wages of sin *is* death.

Q. 20. *Did God leave all mankind to perish in the estate of sin and misery?*

A. God having, out of his mere good pleasure, from all eternity, elected some to everlasting life,[1] did enter into a covenant of grace, to deliver them out of the estate of sin and misery, and to bring them into an estate of salvation, by a Redeemer.[2]

1. Eph. 1:4-7. According as he hath chosen us in him before the foundation of the world, that we should be holy and without blame before him in love: having predestinated us unto the adoption of children by Jesus Christ to himself, according to the good pleasure of his will, to the praise of the glory of his grace, wherein he hath made us accepted in the beloved. In whom we have redemption through his blood, the forgiveness of sins, according to the riches of his grace.

2. Titus 3:4-7. But after that the kindness and love of God our Saviour toward man appeared, not by works of righteousness which we have done, but according to his mercy he saved us, by the washing of regeneration, and renewing of the Holy Ghost; which he shed on us abundantly through Jesus Christ our Saviour; that being justified by his grace, we should be made heirs according to the hope of eternal life.

Titus 1:2. In hope of eternal life, which God, that cannot lie, promised before the world began.

Gal. 3:21; Rom. 3:20-22.

Q. 21. *Who is the Redeemer of God's elect?*

A. The only Redeemer of God's elect is the Lord Jesus Christ,[1] who, being the eternal Son of God, became man,[2] and so was, and continueth to be, God and man, in two distinct natures, and one person, forever.[3]

1. I Tim. 2:5. For *there is* one God, and one mediator between God and men, the man Christ Jesus.

2. John 1:1, 14. In the beginning was the Word, and the Word was with God, and the Word was God. . . . And the Word was made flesh, and dwelt among us.

   John 10:30. I and *my* Father are one.

   Phil. 2:6. Who, being in the form of God, thought it not robbery to be equal with God.

   Gal. 4:4. But when the fulness of the time was come, God sent forth his Son, made of a woman, made under the law.

3. See texts just cited; also Phil. 2:5-11.

Q. 22. *How did Christ, being the Son of God, become man?*

A. Christ, the Son of God, became man, by taking to himself a true body and a reasonable soul,[1] being conceived by the power of the Holy Ghost, in the womb of the Virgin Mary, and born of her,[2] yet without sin.[3]

1. John 1:14. And the Word was made flesh, and dwelt among us, (and we beheld his glory, the glory as of the only begotten of the Father,) full of grace and truth.

   Heb. 2:14. Forasmuch then as the children are partakers of flesh and blood, he also himself likewise took part of the same.

   Matt. 26:38. Then saith he unto them, My soul is exceeding sorrowful, even unto death.

2. Luke 1:31, 35, 41, 42. Behold, thou shalt conceive in thy womb, and bring forth a son, and shalt call his name JESUS. . . . The Holy Ghost shall come upon thee, and the power of the Highest shall overshadow thee: therefore also that holy thing which shall be born of thee shall be called the Son of God. . . . And Elisabeth was filled with the Holy Ghost: and she spake out with a loud voice, and said, Blessed *art* thou among women, and blessed *is* the fruit of thy womb.

   Gal. 4:4. But when the fulness of the time was come, God sent forth his Son, made of a woman, made under the law.

3. Heb. 4:15. For we have not an high priest which cannot be touched with the feeling of our infirmities; but was in all points tempted like as *we are,* yet without sin.

   Heb. 7:26. Such an high priest became us, *who is* holy, harmless, undefiled, separate from sinners.

Q. 23. *What offices doth Christ execute as our Redeemer?*

A. Christ, as our Redeemer, executeth the offices of a prophet,[1] of a priest,[2] and of a king, both in his estate of humiliation and exaltation.[3]

1. Acts 3:22. Moses truly said unto the fathers, A prophet shall the Lord

your God raise up unto you of your brethren, like unto me; him shall ye hear in all things whatsoever he shall say unto you.
Luke 4:18, 21.

2. Heb. 5:5, 6. So also Christ glorified not himself to be made an high priest; but he that said unto him, Thou art my Son, to day have I begotten thee. As he saith also in another *place,* Thou *art* a priest for ever after the order of Melchisedec.
Heb. 4:14, 15.

3. Rev. 19:16. And he hath on *his* vesture and on his thigh a name written, KING OF KINGS, AND LORD OF LORDS.
Isa. 9:6, 7; Ps. 2:6.

Q. 24. *How doth Christ execute the office of a prophet?*

A. Christ executeth the office of a prophet, in revealing to us,[1] by his word and Spirit, the will of God for our salvation.[2]

1. John 1:1, 4. In the beginning was the Word, and the Word was with God, and the Word was God. . . . In him was life; and the life was the light of men.

2. John 15:15. Henceforth I call you not servants; for the servant knoweth not what his lord doeth: but I have called you friends; for all things that I have heard of my Father I have made known unto you.
John 20:31. But these are written, that ye might believe that Jesus is the Christ, the Son of God; and that believing ye might have life through his name.
II Peter 1:21. For the prophecy came not in old time by the will of man: but holy men of God spake *as they were* moved by the Holy Ghost.
John 14:26.

Q. 25. *How doth Christ execute the office of a priest?*

A. Christ executeth the office of a priest, in his once offering up of himself a sacrifice to satisfy divine justice,[1] and reconcile us to God,[2] and in making continual intercession for us.[3]

1. Heb. 9:14, 28. How much more shall the blood of Christ, who through the eternal Spirit offered himself without spot to God, purge your conscience from dead works to serve the living God? . . . Christ was once offered to bear the sins of many.
Rom. 3:26. To declare, *I say,* at this time his righteousness: that he might be just, and the justifier of him which believeth in Jesus.
Rom. 10:4. For Christ *is* the end of the law for righteousness to every one that believeth.

2. Heb. 2:17. In all things it behoved him to be made like unto *his* brethren, that he might be a merciful and faithful high priest in things *pertaining* to God, to make reconciliation for the sins of the people.

3. Heb. 7:25. He is able also to save them to the uttermost that come unto God by him, seeing he ever liveth to make intercession for them.

Q. 26. *How doth Christ execute the office of a king?*

A. Christ executeth the office of a king, in subduing us to himself,[1] in ruling and defending us,[2] and in restraining and conquering all his and our enemies.[3]

1. Ps. 110:3. Thy people *shall be* willing in the day of thy power.
2. Isa. 33:22. The LORD *is* our judge, the LORD *is* our lawgiver, the LORD *is* our king; he will save us.
3. I Cor. 15:25. For he must reign, till he hath put all enemies under his feet.
   Acts 12:17; 18:9, 10.

Q. 27. *Wherein did Christ's humiliation consist?*

A. Christ's humiliation consisted in his being born, and that in a low condition,[1] made under the law,[2] undergoing the miseries of this life,[3] the wrath of God,[4] and the cursed death of the cross,[5] in being buried and continuing under the power of death for a time.[6]

1. Luke 2:7. And she brought forth her firstborn son, and wrapped him in swaddling clothes, and laid him in a manger.
   Phil. 2:6-8; II Cor. 8:9.
2. Gal. 4:4. God sent forth his Son, made of a woman, made under the law.
3. Isa. 53:3. He is despised and rejected of men; a man of sorrows, and acquainted with grief.
4. Matt. 27:46. And about the ninth hour Jesus cried with a loud voice, saying . . . My God, my God, why hast thou forsaken me?
   Luke 22:41-44.
5. Gal. 3:13. Christ hath redeemed us from the curse of the law, being made a curse for us: for it is written, Cursed *is* every one that hangeth on a tree.
   Phil. 2:8. He humbled himself, and became obedient unto death, even the death of the cross.
6. I Cor. 15:3, 4. For I delivered unto you first of all that which I also received, how that Christ died for our sins according to the scriptures; and that he was buried, and that he rose again the third day according to the scriptures.

Q. 28. *Wherein consisteth Christ's exaltation?*

A. Christ's exaltation consisteth in his rising again from the dead on the third day,[1] in ascending up into heaven, in sitting at the right hand of God the Father,[2] and in coming to judge the world at the last day.[3]

1. See last quoted text.
2. Acts 1:9. And when he had spoken these things, while they beheld, he was taken up; and a cloud received him out of their sight.

Eph. 1:19, 20. His mighty power, which he wrought in Christ, when he raised him from the dead, and set *him* at his own right hand in the heavenly *places.*

3. Acts 1:11. Which also said, Ye men of Galilee, why stand ye gazing up into heaven? this same Jesus, which is taken up from you into heaven, shall so come in like manner as ye have seen him go into heaven.

Acts 17:31. He hath appointed a day, in the which he will judge the world in righteousness by *that* man whom he hath ordained; *whereof* he hath given assurance unto all *men,* in that he hath raised him from the dead.

Q. 29. *How are we made partakers of the redemption purchased by Christ?*

A. We are made partakers of the redemption purchased by Christ, by the effectual application of it to us by his Holy Spirit.[1]

1. John 1:12, 13. As many as received him, to them gave he power to become the sons of God, *even* to them that believe on his name: which were born, not of blood, nor of the will of the flesh, nor of the will of man, but of God.

John 3:5, 6. Except a man be born of water and *of* the Spirit, he cannot enter into the kingdom of God. That which is born of the flesh is flesh; and that which is born of the Spirit is spirit.

Titus 3:5, 6. Not by works of righteousness which we have done, but according to his mercy he saved us, by the washing of regeneration, and renewing of the Holy Ghost; which he shed on us abundantly through Jesus Christ our Saviour.

Q. 30. *How doth the Spirit apply to us the redemption purchased by Christ?*

A. The Spirit applieth to us the redemption purchased by Christ, by working faith in us,[1] and thereby uniting us to Christ in our effectual calling.[2]

1. Eph. 2:8. By grace are ye saved through faith; and that not of yourselves: *it is* the gift of God.

2. John 15:5. I am the vine, ye *are* the branches: He that abideth in me, and I in him, the same bringeth forth much fruit: for without me ye can do nothing.

I Cor. 6:17. But he that is joined unto the Lord is one spirit.

I Cor. 1:9. God *is* faithful, by whom ye were called unto the fellowship of his Son Jesus Christ.

I Peter 5:10. But the God of all grace, who hath called us unto his eternal glory by Christ Jesus, after that ye have suffered a while, make you perfect, stablish, strengthen, settle *you.*

Q. 31. *What is effectual calling?*

A. Effectual calling is the work of God's Spirit,[1] whereby, convincing us of our sin and misery,[2] enlightening our minds in the knowledge of Christ,[3] and renewing our wills,[4] he doth persuade and enable us to embrace Jesus Christ freely offered to us in the gospel.[5]

1. II Tim. 1:8, 9. Be thou partaker of the afflictions of the gospel according to the power of God; who hath saved us, and called *us* with an holy calling.

Eph. 1:18-20. The eyes of your understanding being enlightened; that ye may know what is the hope of his calling, and what the riches of the glory of his inheritance in the saints, and what *is* the exceeding greatness of his power to us-ward who believe, according to the working of his mighty power, which he wrought in Christ, when he raised him from the dead, and set *him* at his own right hand in the heavenly *places*.

2. Acts 2:37. Now when they heard *this,* they were pricked in their heart, and said unto Peter and to the rest of the apostles, Men *and* brethren, what shall we do?

3. Acts 26:18. To open their eyes, *and* to turn *them* from darkness to light, and *from* the power of Satan unto God.

4. Ezek. 11:19. And I will give them one heart, and I will put a new spirit within you; and I will take the stony heart out of their flesh, and will give them an heart of flesh.
Ezek. 36:26, 27.

5. John 6:44, 45. No man can come to me, except the Father which hath sent me draw him . . . Every man therefore that hath heard, and hath learned of the Father, cometh unto me.
Phil. 2:13; Deut. 30:6; Eph. 2:5.

Q. 32. *What benefits do they that are effectually called partake of in this life?*

A. They that are effectually called do in this life partake of justification,[1] adoption,[2] sanctification, and the several benefits which, in this life, do either accompany or flow from them.[3]

1. Rom. 8:30. Moreover whom he did predestinate, them he also called: and whom he called, them he also justified: and whom he justified, them he also glorified.

2. Eph. 1:5. Having predestinated us unto the adoption of children by Jesus Christ to himself.

3. I Cor. 1:30. But of him are ye in Christ Jesus, who of God is made unto us wisdom, and righteousness, and sanctification, and redemption.

Q. 33. *What is justification?*

A. Justification is an act of God's free grace, wherein he pardoneth all our sins,[1] and accepteth us as righteous in his sight,[2] only for the righteousness of Christ, imputed to us,[3] and received by faith alone.[4]

1. Eph. 1:7. In whom we have redemption through his blood, the forgiveness of sins, according to the riches of his grace.

2. II Cor. 5:19, 21. God was in Christ, reconciling the world unto himself, not imputing their trespasses unto them; and hath committed unto us the word of reconciliation. . . . For he hath made him *to be* sin for us, who knew no sin; that we might be made the righteousness of God in him.

Rom. 4:5. But to him that worketh not, but believeth on him that justifieth the ungodly, his faith is counted for righteousness.

Rom. 3:22, 24, 25.

3. Rom. 5:17-19. For if by one man's offence death reigned by one; much more they which receive abundance of grace and of the gift of righteousness shall reign in life by one, Jesus Christ. Therefore as by the offence of one *judgment came* upon all men to condemnation; even so by the righteousness of one *the free gift came* upon all men unto justification of life. For as by one man's disobedience many were made sinners, so by the obedience of one shall many be made righteous.

Rom. 4:6-8.

4. Rom. 5:1. Therefore being justified by faith, we have peace with God through our Lord Jesus Christ.

Acts 10:43. To him give all the prophets witness, that through his name whosoever believeth in him shall receive remission of sins.

Gal. 2:16; Phil. 3:9.

Q. 34. *What is adoption?*

A. Adoption is an act of God's free grace,[1] whereby we are received into the number, and have a right to all the privileges, of the sons of God.[2]

1. I John 3:1. Behold, what manner of love the Father hath bestowed upon us, that we should be called the sons of God.

2. John 1:12. As many as received him, to them gave he power to become the sons of God, *even* to them that believe on his name.

Rom. 8:17. And if children, then heirs; heirs of God, and joint-heirs with Christ.

Q. 35. *What is sanctification?*

A. Sanctification is the work of God's free grace,[1] whereby we are renewed in the whole man after the image of God,[2] and are enabled more and more to die unto sin, and live unto righteousness.[3]

1. II Thess. 2:13. God hath from the beginning chosen you to salvation through sanctification of the Spirit and belief of the truth.

2. Eph. 4:23, 24. And be renewed in the spirit of your mind; and that ye put on the new man, which after God is created in righteousness and true holiness.

3. Rom. 6:4, 6, 14. Therefore we are buried with him by baptism into death: that like as Christ was raised up from the dead by the glory of the Father, even so we also should walk in newness of life. . . . knowing this, that our old man is crucified with *him*, that the body of sin might

be destroyed, that henceforth we should not serve sin. . . . For sin shall not have dominion over you: for ye are not under the law, but under grace.

Rom. 8:4. That the righteousness of the law might be fulfilled in us, who walk not after the flesh, but after the Spirit.

Q. 36. *What are the benefits which in this life do accompany or flow from justification, adoption, and sanctification?*

A. The benefits which in this life do accompany or flow from justification, adoption, and sanctification, are: assurance of God's love, peace of conscience, joy in the Holy Ghost,[1] increase of grace,[2] and perseverance therein to the end.[3]

1. Rom. 5:1, 2, 5. Being justified by faith, we have peace with God through our Lord Jesus Christ: by whom also we have access by faith into this grace wherein we stand, and rejoice in hope of the glory of God. . . . and hope maketh not ashamed; because the love of God is shed abroad in our hearts by the Holy Ghost which is given unto us.

    Rom. 14:17. For the kingdom of God is not meat and drink; but righteousness, and peace, and joy in the Holy Ghost.

2. Col. 1:10, 11. That ye might walk worthy of the Lord unto all pleasing, being fruitful in every good work, and increasing in the knowledge of God; strengthened with all might, according to his glorious power, unto all patience and longsuffering with joyfulness.

    Prov. 4:18. The path of the just *is* as the shining light, that shineth more and more unto the perfect day.

    Eph. 3:16-18; II Peter 3:18.

3. Jer. 32:40. And I will make an everlasting covenant with them, that I will not turn away from them, to do them good; but I will put my fear in their hearts, that they shall not depart from me.

    I John 2:19, 27. They went out from us, but they were not of us; for if they had been of us, they would *no doubt* have continued with us: but *they went out,* that they might be made manifest that they were not all of us. . . . But the anointing which ye have received of him abideth in you, and ye need not that any man teach you: but as the same anointing teacheth you of all things, and is truth, and is no lie, and even as it hath taught you, ye shall abide in him.

    Rev. 14:12. Here is the patience of the saints: here *are* they that keep the commandments of God, and the faith of Jesus.

    I Peter 1:5. Who are kept by the power of God through faith unto salvation ready to be revealed in the last time.

    I John 5:13.

Q. 37. *What benefits do believers receive from Christ at death?*

A. The souls of believers are at their death made perfect in holiness, and do immediately pass into glory;[1] and their bodies, being still united to Christ,[2] do rest in their graves till the resurrection.[3]

1. Luke 23:43. And Jesus said unto him, Verily I say unto thee, To day shalt thou be with me in paradise.

Luke 16:23. And in hell he lift up his eyes, being in torments, and seeth Abraham afar off, and Lazarus in his bosom.
Phil. 1:23. Having a desire to depart, and to be with Christ.
II Cor. 5:6-8.

2. I Thess. 4:14. Them also which sleep in Jesus will God bring with him.

3. Rom. 8:23. And not only *they*, but ourselves also, which have the first-fruits of the Spirit, even we ourselves groan within ourselves, waiting for the adoption, *to wit*, the redemption of our body.
I Thess. 4:14. For if we believe that Jesus died and rose again, even so them also which sleep in Jesus will God bring with him.

Q. 38. *What benefits do believers receive from Christ at the resurrection?*

A. At the resurrection, believers, being raised up in glory,[1] shall be openly acknowledged, and acquitted in the day of judgment,[2] and made perfectly blessed in the full enjoying of God[3] to all eternity.[4]

1. I Cor. 15:42, 43. So also *is* the resurrection of the dead. It is sown in corruption; it is raised in incorruption: it is sown in dishonour; it is raised in glory: it is sown in weakness; it is raised in power.

2. Matt. 25:33, 34. And he shall set the sheep on his right hand, but the goats on the left. Then shall the King say unto them on his right hand, Come, ye blessed of my Father, inherit the kingdom prepared for you from the foundation of the world.
Matt. 10:32. Whosoever . . . shall confess me before men, him will I confess also before my Father which is in heaven.

3. Ps. 16:11. Thou wilt shew me the path of life: in thy presence *is* fulness of joy; at thy right hand *there are* pleasures for evermore.
I Cor. 2:9.

4. I Thess. 4:17. And so shall we ever be with the Lord. See preceding context.

Q. 39. *What is the duty which God requireth of man?*

A. The duty which God requireth of man, is, obedience to his revealed will.[1]

1. Deut. 29:29. The secret *things belong* unto the LORD our God: but those *things which are* revealed *belong* unto us and to our children for ever, that *we* may do all the words of this law.
Micah 6:8. He hath shewed thee, O man, what *is* good; and what doth the LORD require of thee, but to do justly, and to love mercy, and to walk humbly with thy God?
I Sam. 15:22.

Q. 40. *What did God at first reveal to man for the rule of his obedience?*

A. The rule which God at first revealed to man for his obedience, was the moral law.[1]

1. Rom. 2:14, 15. For when the Gentiles, which have not the law, do by na-

ture the things contained in the law, these, having not the law, are a law
unto themselves: which shew the work of the law written in their hearts.
Rom. 10:5. For Moses describeth the righteousness which is of the law,
That the man which doeth those things shall live by them.

Q. 41. *Wherein is the moral law summarily comprehended?*

A. The moral law is summarily comprehended in the ten commandments.[1]

> 1. Matt. 19:17-19. If thou wilt enter into life, keep the commandments. He
> saith unto him, Which? Jesus said, Thou shalt do no murder, Thou shalt
> not commit adultery, Thou shalt not steal, Thou shalt not bear false wit-
> ness, Honour thy father and *thy* mother: and, Thou shalt love thy neigh-
> bour as thyself.

Q. 42. *What is the sum of the ten commandments?*

A. The sum of the ten commandments is, to love the Lord our
God, with all our heart, with all our soul, with all our strength,
and with all our mind; and our neighbor as ourselves.[1]

> 1. Matt. 22:37-40. Thou shalt love the Lord thy God with all thy heart,
> and with all thy soul, and with all thy mind. This is the first and great
> commandment. And the second *is* like unto it, Thou shalt love thy neigh-
> bour as thyself. On these two commandments hang all the law and the
> prophets.

Q. 43. *What is the preface to the ten commandments?*

A. The preface to the ten commandments is in these words,
*I am the Lord thy God, which have brought thee out of the
land of Egypt, out of the house of bondage.*[1]

> 1. Exod. 20:2.

Q. 44. *What doth the preface to the ten commandments teach us?*

A. The preface to the ten commandments teacheth us, that
because God is the Lord, and our God, and Redeemer, therefore we are bound to keep all his commandments.

Q. 45. *Which is the first commandment?*

A. The first commandment is, *Thou shalt have no other gods
before me.*[1]

> 1. Exod. 20:3.

Q. 46. *What is required in the first commandment?*

A. The first commandment requireth us[1] to know and acknowledge God to be the only true God, and our God,[2] and to worship and glorify him accordingly.[3]

1. The exposition of the Ten Commandments found in answers to Questions 46-81 are deductions from the commandments themselves and the rules set forth in the Larger Catechism, Q. 99. The texts under the specifications are given to show that they are in accord with the general teaching of the Scriptures.

2. I Chron. 28:9. And thou, Solomon my son, know thou the God of thy father.

   Deut. 26:17. Thou hast avouched the LORD this day to be thy God, and to walk in his ways, and to keep his statutes, and his commandments, and his judgments, and to hearken unto his voice.

3. Matt. 4:10. Thou shalt worship the Lord thy God, and him only shalt thou serve.

   Ps. 95:6, 7. O come, let us worship and bow down: let us kneel before the LORD our maker. For he *is* our God; and we *are* the people of his pasture, and the sheep of his hand.

   Ps. 29:2. Give unto the LORD the glory due unto his name; worship the LORD in the beauty of holiness.

Q. 47. *What is forbidden in the first commandment?*

A. The first commandment forbiddeth the denying,[1] or not worshipping and glorifying, the true God, as God,[2] and our God;[3] and the giving the worship and glory to any other, which is due to him alone.[4]

1. Ps. 14:1. The fool hath said in his heart, *There is* no God.

2. Rom. 1:20, 21. So that they are without excuse: because that, when they knew God, they glorified *him* not as God.

3. Ps. 81:11. But my people would not hearken to my voice; and Israel would none of me.

4. Rom. 1:25. Who changed the truth of God into a lie, and worshipped and served the creature more than the Creator.

Q. 48. *What are we especially taught by these words, "before me," in the first commandment?*

A. These words, *"before me,"* in the first commandment, teach us that God, who seeth all things, taketh notice of, and is much displeased with, the sin of having any other god.[1]

1. I Chron. 28:9. And, thou, Solomon my son, know thou the God of thy father, and serve him with a perfect heart and with a willing mind: for the LORD searcheth all hearts, and understandeth all the imaginations of the thoughts: if thou seek him, he will be found of thee; but if thou forsake him, he will cast thee off for ever.

   Ps. 44:20, 21. If we have forgotten the name of our God, or stretched out our hands to a strange god; shall not God search this out?

Q. 49. *Which is the second commandment?*

A. The second commandment is, *Thou shalt not make unto thee any graven image, or any likeness of any thing that is in heaven above, or that is in the earth beneath, or that is in the water under the earth: thou shalt not bow down thyself to them, nor serve them: for I the Lord thy God am a jealous God, visiting the iniquity of the fathers upon the children unto the third and fourth generation of them that hate me; and shewing mercy unto thousands of them that love me, and keep my commandments.*[1]

1. Exod. 20:4-6.

Q. 50. *What is required in the second commandment?*

A. The second commandment requireth the receiving, observing, and keeping pure and entire, all such religious worship and ordinances as God hath appointed in his word.[1]

    1. Deut. 12:32. What thing soever I command you, observe to do it: thou shalt not add thereto, nor diminish from it.

    Deut. 32:46. Set your hearts unto all the words which I testify among you this day, which ye shall command your children to observe to do, all the words of this law.

    Matt. 28:20. Teaching them to observe all things whatsoever I have commanded you.

Q. 51. *What is forbidden in the second commandment?*

A. The second commandment forbiddeth the worshipping of God by images,[1] or any other way not appointed in his word.[2]

    1. Deut. 4:15, 16. Take ye therefore good heed unto yourselves; for ye saw no manner of similitude on the day *that* the LORD spake unto you in Horeb . . . lest ye corrupt *yourselves,* and make you a graven image.

    See verses 17-19; Acts 17:29.

    2. Deut. 12:30-32. Take heed to thyself that thou be not snared by following them, after that they be destroyed from before thee; and that thou enquire not after their gods, saying, How did these nations serve their gods? even so will I do likewise. Thou shalt not do so unto the LORD thy God: for every abomination to the LORD, which he hateth, have they done unto their gods; for even their sons and their daughters they have burnt in the fire to their gods. What thing soever I command you, observe to do it: thou shalt not add thereto, nor diminish from it.

Q. 52. *What are the reasons annexed to the second commandment?*

A. The reasons annexed to the second commandment are:

God's sovereignty over us,[1] his propriety in us,[2] and the zeal he hath to his own worship.[3]

1. Ps. 95:2, 3. Let us come before his presence with thanksgiving, and make a joyful noise unto him with psalms. For the LORD *is* a great God, and a great King above all gods.

2. Ps. 45:11. He *is* thy Lord; and worship thou him.

3. Exod. 34:14. Thou shalt worship no other god: for the LORD, whose name *is* Jealous, *is* a jealous God.

Q. 53. Which is the third commandment?

A. The third commandment is, *Thou shalt not take the name of the Lord thy God in vain; for the Lord will not hold him guiltless that taketh his name in vain.*[1]

1. Exod. 20:7.

Q. 54. What is required in the third commandment?

A. The third commandment requireth the holy and reverent use of God's names,[1] titles, attributes,[2] ordinances,[3] word,[4] and works.[5]

1. Ps. 29:2. Give unto the LORD the glory due unto his name.
   Matt. 6:9. After this manner therefore pray ye: Our Father which art in heaven, Hallowed be thy name.

2. Rev. 15:3, 4. Great and marvellous *are* thy works, Lord God Almighty; just and true *are* thy ways, thou King of saints. Who shall not fear thee, O Lord, and glorify thy name?

3. Mal. 1:14. But cursed *be* the deceiver, which hath in his flock a male, and voweth, and sacrificeth unto the Lord a corrupt thing: for I *am* a great King, saith the LORD of hosts, and my name *is* dreadful among the heathen.

4. Ps. 138:2. I will worship toward thy holy temple, and praise thy name for thy lovingkindness and for thy truth: for thou hast magnified thy word above all thy name.

5. Ps. 107:21, 22. Oh that *men* would praise the LORD *for* his goodness, and *for* his wonderful works to the children of men! And let them sacrifice the sacrifices of thanksgiving, and declare his works with rejoicing.

Q. 55. What is forbidden in the third commandment?

A. The third commandment forbiddeth all profaning or abusing of anything whereby God maketh himself known.[1]

1. Mal. 2:2. If ye will not hear, and if ye will not lay *it* to heart, to give glory unto my name, saith the LORD of hosts, I will even send a curse upon you.
   Isa. 5:12. And the harp, and the viol, the tabret, and pipe, and wine, are in their feasts: but they regard not the work of the LORD, neither consider the operation of his hands.

Q. 56. *What is the reason annexed to the third commandment?*

A. The reason annexed to the third commandment is, that however the breakers of this commandment may escape punishment from men, yet the Lord our God will not suffer them to escape his righteous judgment.[1]

1. Deut. 28:58, 59. If thou wilt not observe to do all the words of this law that are written in this book, that thou mayest fear this glorious and fearful name, THE LORD THY GOD; then the LORD will make thy plagues wonderful.

Q. 57. *Which is the fourth commandment?*

A. The fourth commandment is, *Remember the sabbath day, to keep it holy. Six days shalt thou labour, and do all thy work: but the seventh day is the sabbath of the Lord thy God: in it thou shalt not do any work, thou, nor thy son, nor thy daughter, thy manservant, nor thy maidservant, nor thy cattle, nor thy stranger that is within thy gates: for in six days the Lord made heaven and earth, the sea, and all that in them is, and rested the seventh day: wherefore the Lord blessed the sabbath day, and hallowed it.*[1]

1. Exod. 20:8-11.

Q. 58. *What is required in the fourth commandment?*

A. The fourth commandment requireth the keeping holy to God such set times as he hath appointed in his word; expressly one whole day in seven, to be a holy Sabbath to himself.[1]

1. Lev. 19:30. Ye shall keep my sabbaths, and reverence my sanctuary: I *am* the LORD.
   Deut. 5:12. Keep the sabbath day to sanctify it, as the LORD thy God hath commanded thee.
   Isa. 56:2-7.

Q. 59. *Which day of the seven hath God appointed to be the weekly Sabbath?*

A. From the beginning of the world to the resurrection of Christ, God appointed the seventh day of the week to be the weekly Sabbath;[1] and the first day of the week, ever since, to continue to the end of the world, which is the Christian Sabbath.[2]

1. Gen. 2:3. And God blessed the seventh day, and sanctified it: because that in it he had rested from all his work which God created and made.

Luke 23:56. And they returned, and prepared spices and ointments; and rested the sabbath day according to the commandment.

2. Acts 20:7. And upon the first *day* of the week, when the disciples came together to break bread, Paul preached unto them.

I Cor. 16:1, 2. Now concerning the collection for the saints, as I have given order to the churches of Galatia, even so do ye. Upon the first *day* of the week let every one of you lay by him in store, as *God* hath prospered him, that there be no gatherings when I come.

John 20:19-26.

Q. 60. *How is the Sabbath to be sanctified?*

A. The Sabbath is to be sanctified by a holy resting all that day, even from such worldly employments and recreations as are lawful on other days;[1] and spending the whole time in the public and private exercises of God's worship,[2] except so much as is to be taken up in the works of necessity and mercy.[3]

1. Lev. 23:3. Six days shall work be done: but the seventh day *is* the sabbath of rest, an holy convocation; ye shall do no work *therein*.
   Exod. 16:25-29; Jer. 17:21, 22.

2. Ps. 92:1, 2. (A Psalm *or* Song for the sabbath day.) *It is* a good *thing* to give thanks unto the LORD, and to sing praises unto thy name, O most High: to shew forth thy lovingkindness in the morning, and thy faithfulness every night.
   Luke 4:16. And he came to Nazareth, where he had been brought up: and, as his custom was, he went into the synagogue on the sabbath day, and stood up for to read.
   Isa. 58:13; Acts 20:7.

3. Matt. 12:11, 12. What man shall there be among you, that shall have one sheep, and if it fall into a pit on the sabbath day, will he not lay hold on it, and lift *it* out? How much then is a man better than a sheep? Wherefore it is lawful to do well on the sabbath days.
   See context.

Q. 61. *What is forbidden in the fourth commandment?*

A. The fourth commandment forbiddeth the omission, or careless performance, of the duties required,[1] and the profaning the day by idleness, or doing that which is in itself sinful,[2] or by unnecessary thoughts, words, or works, about our worldly employments or recreations.[3]

1. Ezek. 22:26. Her priests have violated my law, and have profaned mine holy things: they have put no difference between the holy and profane, neither have they shewed *difference* between the unclean and the clean, and have hid their eyes from my sabbaths, and I am profaned among them.
   Mal. 1:13. Ye said also, Behold, what a weariness *is it!* and ye have snuffed at it, saith the LORD of hosts; and ye brought *that which was* torn,

and the lame, and the sick; thus ye brought an offering: should I accept this of your hand? saith the LORD.
Amos 8:5.

2. Ezek. 23:38. They have defiled my sanctuary in the same day, and have profaned my sabbaths.

3. Isa. 58:13. If thou turn away thy foot from the sabbath, *from* doing thy pleasure on my holy day; and call the sabbath a delight, the holy of the LORD, honourable; and shalt honour him, not doing thine own ways, nor finding thine own pleasure, nor speaking *thine own* words.
Jer. 17:24, 27.

Q. 62. *What are the reasons annexed to the fourth commandment?*

A. The reasons annexed to the fourth commandment are, God's allowing us six days of the week for our own employments,[1] his challenging a special propriety in the seventh,[2] his own example,[3] and his blessing the Sabbath day.[4]

1. Exod. 31:15, 16. Six days may work be done; but in the seventh *is* the sabbath of rest . . . Wherefore the children of Israel shall keep the sabbath.

2. Lev. 23:3. Ye shall do no work *therein*: it *is* the sabbath of the LORD in all your dwellings.

3. Exod. 31:17. It *is* a sign between me and the children of Israel for ever: for *in* six days the LORD made heaven and earth, and on the seventh day he rested, and was refreshed.

4. Gen. 2:3. And God blessed the seventh day, and sanctified it.

Q. 63. *Which is the fifth commandment?*

A. The fifth commandment is, *Honour thy father and thy mother: that thy days may be long upon the land which the Lord thy God giveth thee.*[1]

1. Exod. 20:12.

Q. 64. *What is required in the fifth commandment?*

A. The fifth commandment requireth the preserving the honor, and performing the duties, belonging to everyone in their several places and relations, as superiors, inferiors, or equals.[1]

1. Eph. 5:21, 22. Submitting yourselves one to another in the fear of God. Wives, submit yourselves unto your own husbands, as unto the Lord.

Eph. 6:1, 5, 9. Children, obey your parents in the Lord . . . Servants, be obedient to them that are *your* masters according to the flesh . . . And, ye masters, do the same things unto them, forbearing threatening: knowing that your Master also is in heaven.

Rom. 13:1. Let every soul be subject unto the higher powers.

Rom. 12:10. *Be* kindly affectioned one to another with brotherly love; in honour preferring one another.

Q. 65. *What is forbidden in the fifth commandment?*

A. The fifth commandment forbiddeth the neglecting of, or doing anything against, the honor and duty which belongeth to everyone in their several places and relations.[1]

1. Rom. 13:7, 8. Render therefore to all their dues: tribute to whom tribute *is due;* custom to whom custom; fear to whom fear; honour to whom honour. Owe no man any thing, but to love one another.

Q. 66. *What is the reason annexed to the fifth commandment?*

A. The reason annexed to the fifth commandment is, a promise of long life and prosperity (as far as it shall serve for God's glory, and their own good) to all such as keep this commandment.[1]

1. Eph. 6:2, 3. Honour thy father and mother; which is the first commandment with promise; that it may be well with thee, and thou mayest live long on the earth.

Q. 67. *Which is the sixth commandment?*

A. The sixth commandment is, *Thou shalt not kill.*[1]

1. Exod. 20:13.

Q. 68. *What is required in the sixth commandment?*

A. The sixth commandment requireth all lawful endeavors to preserve our own life,[1] and the life of others.[2]

1. Eph. 5:29. For no man ever yet hateth his own flesh; but nourisheth and cherisheth it.
Matt. 10:23.
2. Ps. 82:3, 4. Defend the poor and fatherless . . . Deliver the poor and needy.
Job 29:13. The blessing of him that was ready to perish came upon me.
I Kings 18:4.

Q. 69. *What is forbidden in the sixth commandment?*

A. The sixth commandment forbiddeth the taking away of our own life,[1] or the life of our neighbor unjustly,[2] or whatsoever tendeth thereunto.[3]

1. Acts 16:28. Paul cried with a loud voice, saying, Do thyself no harm.
2. Gen. 9:6. Whoso sheddeth man's blood, by man shall his blood be shed.
3. Matt. 5:22. But I say unto you, That whosoever is angry with his brother without a cause shall be in danger of the judgment: and whosoever shall say to his brother, Raca, shall be in danger of the council: but whosoever shall say, Thou fool, shall be in danger of hell fire.

I John 3:15. Whosoever hateth his brother is a murderer: and ye know that no murderer hath eternal life abiding in him.

Gal. 5:15. But if ye bite and devour one another, take heed that ye be not consumed one of another.

Prov. 24:11, 12.

Exod. 21:18-32.

Q. 70. *Which is the seventh commandment?*

A. The seventh commandment is, *Thou shalt not commit adultery.*[1]

1. Exod. 20:14.

Q. 71. *What is required in the seventh commandment?*

A. The seventh commandment requireth the preservation of our own[1] and our neighbor's chastity,[2] in heart,[3] speech,[4] and behavior.[5]

1. I Thess. 4:4, 5. That every one of you should know how to possess his vessel in sanctification and honour; not in the lust of concupiscence, even as the Gentiles which know not God.
2. I Cor. 7:2. Nevertheless, *to avoid* fornication, let every man have his own wife, and let every woman have her own husband.
   Eph. 5:11, 12.
3. Matt. 5:28. But I say unto you, That whosoever looketh on a woman to lust after her hath committed adultery with her already in his heart.
4. Eph. 4:29. Let no corrupt communication proceed out of your mouth, but that which is good to the use of edifying, that it may minister grace unto the hearers.
   Col. 4:6.
5. I Peter 3:2. While they behold your chaste conversation *coupled* with fear.

Q. 72. *What is forbidden in the seventh commandment?*

A. The seventh commandment forbiddeth all unchaste thoughts,[1] words,[2] and actions.[3]

1. Matt. 5:28. Whosoever looketh on a woman to lust after her hath committed adultery with her already in his heart.
2. Eph. 5:4. Neither filthiness, nor foolish talking, nor jesting, which are not convenient.
3. Eph. 5:3. Fornication, and all uncleanness . . . let it not be once named among you.

Q. 73. *Which is the eighth commandment?*

A. The eighth commandment is, *Thou shalt not steal.*[1]

1. Exod. 20:15.

Q. 74. *What is required in the eighth commandment?*

A. The eighth commandment requireth the lawful procuring and furthering the wealth and outward estate of ourselves[1] and others.[2]

1. II Thess. 3:10-12. For even when we were with you, this we commanded you, that if any would not work, neither should he eat. For we hear that there are some which walk among you disorderly, working not at all, but are busybodies. Now them that are such we command and exhort by our Lord Jesus Christ, that with quietness they work, and eat their own bread.
   Rom. 12:17; Prov. 27:23.
2. Lev. 25:35. If thy brother be waxen poor, and fallen in decay with thee; then thou shalt relieve him.
   Phil. 2:4. Look not every man on his own things, but every man also on the things of others.
   Prov. 13:4. The soul of the sluggard desireth, and *hath* nothing: but the soul of the diligent shall be made fat.
   Prov. 20:4. The sluggard will not plow by reason of the cold; *therefore* shall he beg in harvest, and *have* nothing.
   Prov. 24:30-34.

Q. 75. *What is forbidden in the eighth commandment?*

A. The eighth commandment forbiddeth whatsoever doth, or may, unjustly hinder our own[1] or our neighbor's wealth or outward estate.[2]

1. I Tim. 5:8. If any provide not for his own, and specially for those of his own house, he hath denied the faith, and is worse than an infidel.
2. Eph. 4:28. Let him that stole steal no more: but rather let him labour, working with *his* hands the thing which is good, that he may have to give to him that needeth.
   Prov. 21:6; II Thess. 3:7-10.

Q. 76. *Which is the ninth commandment?*

A. The ninth commandment is, *Thou shalt not bear false witness against thy neighbour.*[1]

1. Exod. 20:16.

Q. 77. *What is required in the ninth commandment?*

A. The ninth commandment requireth the maintaining and promoting of truth between man and man,[1] and of our own[2] and our neighbor's good name,[3] especially in witness-bearing.[4]

1. Zech. 8:16. Speak ye every man the truth to his neighbour.
2. I Peter 3:16. Having a good conscience; that, whereas they speak evil of you, as of evildoers, they may be ashamed that falsely accuse your good conversation in Christ.

Acts 25:10. Then said Paul, I stand at Cæsar's judgment seat . . . to the Jews have I done no wrong.

3. III John 12. Demetrius hath good report of all *men*, and of the truth itself: yea, and we *also* bare record.

4. Prov. 14:5, 25. A faithful witness will not lie . . . A true witness delivereth souls.

Q. 78. *What is forbidden in the ninth commandment?*

A. The ninth commandment forbiddeth whatsoever is prejudicial to truth,[1] or injurious to our own or our neighbor's good name.[2]

1. Prov. 19:5. A false witness shall not be unpunished, and *he that* speaketh lies shall not escape.
   Prov. 6:16-19.

2. Luke 3:14. And the soldiers likewise demanded of him, saying, And what shall we do? And he said unto them, Do violence to no man, neither accuse *any* falsely; and be content with your wages.
   Ps. 15:3. *He that* backbiteth not with his tongue, nor doeth evil to his neighbour, nor taketh up a reproach against his neighbour.

Q. 79. *Which is the tenth commandment?*

A. The tenth commandment is, *Thou shalt not covet thy neighbour's house, thou shalt not covet thy neighbour's wife, nor his manservant, nor his maidservant, nor his ox, nor his ass, nor any thing that is thy neighbour's.*[1]

1. Exod. 20:17.

Q. 80. *What is required in the tenth commandment?*

A. The tenth commandment requireth full contentment with our own condition,[1] with a right and charitable frame of spirit toward our neighbor, and all that is his.[2]

1. Heb. 13:5. *Let your* conversation *be* without covetousness; *and be* content with such things as ye have.

2. Rom. 12:15. Rejoice with them that do rejoice, and weep with them that weep.
   Phil. 2:4. Look not every man on his own things, but every man also on the things of others.
   I Cor. 13:4-6.

Q. 81. *What is forbidden in the tenth commandment?*

A. The tenth commandment forbiddeth all discontentment with our own estate,[1] envying or grieving at the good of our neighbor,[2] and all inordinate motions and affections to anything that is his.[3]

1. I Cor. 10:10. Neither murmur ye, as some of them also murmured, and were destroyed of the destroyer.
2. Gal. 5:26. Let us not be desirous of vain glory, provoking one another, envying one another
3. Col. 3:5. Mortify therefore your members which are upon the earth; fornication, uncleanness, inordinate affection, evil concupiscence, and covetousness, which is idolatry.

Q. 82. *Is any man able perfectly to keep the commandments of God?*

A. No mere man, since the fall, is able, in this life, perfectly to keep the commandments of God;[1] but doth daily break them, in thought,[2] word,[3] and deed.[4]

1. I Kings 8:46. If they sin against thee, (for *there is* no man that sinneth not,) and thou be angry with them, and deliver them to the enemy, so that they carry them away captives unto the land of the enemy, far or near.
   I John 1:8—2:6.
2. Gen. 8:21. The imagination of man's heart *is* evil from his youth.
3. James 3:8. The tongue can no man tame; *it is* an unruly evil, full of deadly poison.
4. James 3:2. In many things we offend all.

Q. 83. *Are all transgressions of the law equally heinous?*

A. Some sins in themselves, and by reason of several aggravations, are more heinous in the sight of God than others.[1]

1. Ps. 19:13. Keep back thy servant also from presumptuous *sins;* let them not have dominion over me: then shall I be upright, and I shall be innocent from the great transgression.
   John 19:11. He that delivered me unto thee hath the greater sin.

Q. 84. *What doth every sin deserve?*

A. Every sin deserveth God's wrath and curse, both in this life, and that which is to come.[1]

1. Gal. 3:10. Cursed *is* every one that continueth not in all things which are written in the book of the law to do them.
   Matt. 25:41. Then shall he say also unto them on the left hand, Depart from me, ye cursed, into everlasting fire, prepared for the devil and his angels.

Q. 85. *What doth God require of us, that we may escape his wrath and curse, due to us for sin?*

A. To escape the wrath and curse of God, due to us for sin,

God requireth of us faith in Jesus Christ, repentance unto life,[1] with the diligent use of all the outward means whereby Christ communicateth to us the benefits of redemption.[2]

1. Acts 20:21. Testifying both to the Jews, and also to the Greeks, repentance toward God, and faith toward our Lord Jesus Christ.
   Mark 1:15; John 3:18.
2. See under Question 88 below.

Q. 86. *What is faith in Jesus Christ?*

A. Faith in Jesus Christ is a saving grace,[1] whereby we receive[2] and rest upon him alone for salvation,[3] as he is offered to us in the gospel.[4]

1. Heb. 10:39. We are not of them who draw back unto perdition; but of them that believe to the saving of the soul.
2. John 1:12. As many as received him, to them gave he power to become the sons of God, *even* to them that believe on his name.
3. Phil. 3:9. And be found in him, not having mine own righteousness, which is of the law, but that which is through the faith of Christ, the righteousness which is of God by faith.
4. John 6:40. And this is the will of him that sent me, that every one which seeth the Son, and believeth on him, may have everlasting life: and I will raise him up at the last day.

Q. 87. *What is repentance unto life?*

A. Repentance unto life is a saving grace,[1] whereby a sinner, out of a true sense of his sin,[2] and apprehension of the mercy of God in Christ,[3] doth, with grief and hatred of his sin, turn from it unto God,[4] with full purpose of, and endeavor after, new obedience.[5]

1. Acts 11:18. Then hath God also to the Gentiles granted repentance unto life.
2. Acts 2:37. When they heard *this,* they were pricked in their heart, and said unto Peter and to the rest of the apostles, Men *and* brethren, what shall we do?
3. Joel 2:13. Rend your heart, and not your garments, and turn unto the LORD your God: for he *is* gracious and merciful, slow to anger, and of great kindness, and repenteth him of the evil.
4. II Cor. 7:11. For behold this selfsame thing, that ye sorrowed after a godly sort, what carefulness it wrought in you, yea, *what* clearing of yourselves, yea, *what* indignation, yea, *what* fear, yea, *what* vehement desire, yea, *what* zeal, yea, *what* revenge! In all *things* ye have approved yourselves to be clear in this matter.
   Jer. 31:18, 19. Turn thou me, and I shall be turned; for thou *art* the LORD my God. Surely after that I was turned, I repented; and after that I was instructed, I smote upon *my* thigh: I was ashamed, yea, even confounded, because I did bear the reproach of my youth.

Acts. 26:18. To open their eyes, *and* to turn *them* from darkness to light, and *from* the power of Satan unto God, that they may receive forgiveness of sins, and inheritance among them which are sanctified by faith that is in me.

5. Ps. 119:59. I thought on my ways, and turned my feet unto thy testimonies.

Q. 88. *What are the outward and ordinary means whereby Christ communicateth to us the benefits of redemption?*

A. The outward and ordinary means whereby Christ communicateth to us the benefits of redemption are, his ordinances, especially the word, sacraments, and prayer;[1] all of which are made effectual to the elect for salvation.

1. Matt. 28:19, 20. Go ye therefore, and teach all nations, baptizing them in the name of the Father, and of the Son, and of the Holy Ghost: teaching them to observe all things whatsoever I have commanded you: and, lo, I am with you alway, *even* unto the end of the world. Amen.

Acts 2:41, 42. Then they that gladly received his word were baptized . . . And they continued stedfastly in the apostles' doctrine and fellowship, and in breaking of bread, and in prayers.

Q. 89. *How is the word made effectual to salvation?*

A. The Spirit of God maketh the reading, but especially the preaching, of the word, an effectual means of convincing and converting sinners,[1] and of building them up in holiness and comfort through faith unto salvation.[2]

1. Ps. 19:7. The law of the LORD *is* perfect, converting the soul: the testimony of the LORD *is* sure, making wise the simple.

Ps. 119:130. The entrance of thy words giveth light; it giveth understanding unto the simple.

Heb 4:12.

2. I Thess. 1:6. And ye became followers of us, and of the Lord, having received the word in much affliction, with joy of the Holy Ghost.

Rom. 1:16. I am not ashamed of the gospel of Christ: for it is the power of God unto salvation to every one that believeth.

Rom. 16:25. Now to him that is of power to stablish you according to my gospel, and the preaching of Jesus Christ, according to the revelation of the mystery, which was kept secret since the world began.

Acts 20:32. And now, brethren, I commend you to God, and to the word of his grace, which is able to build you up, and to give you an inheritance among all them which are sanctified.

Q. 90. *How is the word to be read and heard, that it may become effectual to salvation?*

A. That the word may become effectual to salvation, we must attend thereunto with diligence,[1] preparation,[2] and prayer;[3] receive it with faith[4] and love,[5] lay it up in our hearts,[6] and practice it in our lives.[7]

1. Prov. 8:34. Blessed *is* the man that heareth me, watching daily at my gates, waiting at the posts of my doors.

2. Luke 8:18. Take heed therefore how ye hear: for whosoever hath, to him shall be given; and whosoever hath not, from him shall be taken even that which he seemeth to have.

   I Peter 2:1, 2. Wherefore laying aside all malice, and all guile, and hypocrisies, and envies, and all evil speakings, as newborn babes, desire the sincere milk of the word, that ye may grow thereby.

3. Ps. 119:18. Open thou mine eyes, that I may behold wondrous things out of thy law.

4. Heb. 4:2. The word preached did not profit them, not being mixed with faith in them that heard *it*.

5. II Thess. 2:10. They received not the love of the truth, that they might be saved.

6. Ps. 119:11. Thy word have I hid in mine heart, that I might not sin against thee.

7. Luke 8:15. But that on the good ground are they, which in an honest and good heart, having heard the word, keep *it*, and bring forth fruit with patience.

   James 1:25. But whoso looketh into the perfect law of liberty, and continueth *therein,* he being not a forgetful hearer, but a doer of the work, this man shall be blessed in his deed.

Q. 91. *How do the sacraments become effectual means of salvation?*

A. The sacraments become effectual means of salvation, not from any virtue in them, or in him that doth administer them; but only by the blessing of Christ, and the working of his Spirit in them that by faith receive them.[1]

1. I Peter 3:21. The like figure whereunto *even* baptism doth also now save us (not the putting away of the filth of the flesh, but the answer of a good conscience toward God,) by the resurrection of Jesus Christ.

   Acts 8:13, 23. Then Simon himself believed also: and when he was baptized, he continued with Philip, and wondered, beholding the miracles and signs which were done. . . . For I perceive that thou art in the gall of bitterness, and *in* the bond of iniquity.
   See intervening context.

   I Cor. 3:7. So then neither is he that planteth any thing, neither he that watereth; but God that giveth the increase.

   I Cor. 6:11. And such were some of you: but ye are washed, but ye are sanctified, but ye are justified in the name of the Lord Jesus, and by the Spirit of our God.

   I Cor. 12:13. For by one Spirit are we all baptized into one body . . . and have been all made to drink into one Spirit.

Q. 92. *What is a sacrament?*

A. A sacrament is a holy ordinance instituted by Christ, wherein, by sensible signs, Christ and the benefits of the new covenant are represented,[1] sealed, and applied to believers.[2]

1. Matt. 28:19. Go ye therefore, and teach all nations, baptizing them in the name of the Father, and of the Son, and of the Holy Ghost.

   Matt. 26:26-28. And as they were eating, Jesus took bread, and blessed *it*, and brake *it*, and gave *it* to the disciples, and said, Take, eat; this is my body. And he took the cup, and gave thanks, and gave *it* to them, saying, Drink ye all of it; for this is my blood of the new testament, which is shed for many for the remission of sins.

2. Rom. 4:11. And he received the sign of circumcision, a seal of the righteousness of the faith which *he had yet* being uncircumcised.

Q. 93. *Which are the sacraments of the New Testament?*

A. The sacraments of the New Testament are, baptism,[1] and the Lord's supper.[2]

1. Matt. 28:19. Go ye therefore, and teach all nations, baptizing them in the name of the Father, and of the Son, and of the Holy Ghost.

2. I Cor. 11:23. For I have received of the Lord that which also I delivered unto you, That the Lord Jesus the *same* night in which he was betrayed took bread.

   See the context.

Q. 94. *What is baptism?*

A. Baptism is a sacrament, wherein the washing with water, in the name of the Father, and of the Son, and of the Holy Ghost,[1] doth signify and seal our ingrafting into Christ, and partaking of the benefits of the covenant of grace,[2] and our engagement to be the Lord's.[3]

1. See Matt. 28:19 cited under Question 93 above.

2. Gal. 3:27. For as many of you as have been baptized into Christ have put on Christ.

   Rom. 6:3. Know ye not, that so many of us as were baptized into Jesus Christ were baptized into his death?

3. Rom. 6:4. Therefore we are buried with him by baptism into death: that like as Christ was raised up from the dead by the glory of the Father, even so we also should walk in newness of life.

Q. 95. *To whom is baptism to be administered?*

A. Baptism is not to be administered to any that are out of the visible church, till they profess their faith in Christ, and obedience to him;[1] but the infants of such as are members of the visible church, are to be baptized.[2]

1. Acts 2:41. Then they that gladly received his word were baptized.

2. Gen. 17:7, 10. And I will establish my covenant between me and thee and thy seed after thee in their generations for an everlasting covenant, to be a God unto thee, and to thy seed after thee. . . . This *is* my covenant, which ye shall keep, between me and you and thy seed after thee; Every man child among you shall be circumcised.

Gal. 3:17, 18, 29. And this I say, *that* the covenant, that was confirmed before of God in Christ, the law, which was four hundred and thirty years after, cannot disannul, that it should make the promise of none effect. For if the inheritance *be* of the law, *it is* no more of promise: but God gave *it* to Abraham by promise. . . . And if ye *be* Christ's, then are ye Abraham's seed, and heirs according to the promise.

Acts 2:38, 39. Then Peter said unto them, Repent, and be baptized every one of you in the name of Jesus Christ for the remission of sins, and ye shall receive the gift of the Holy Ghost. For the promise is unto you, and to your children, and to all that are afar off, *even* as many as the Lord our God shall call.

Q. 96. *What is the Lord's supper?*

A. The Lord's supper is a sacrament, wherein, by giving and receiving bread and wine, according to Christ's appointment, his death is showed forth;[1] and the worthy receivers are, not after a corporal and carnal manner, but by faith, made partakers of his body and blood, with all his benefits, to their spiritual nourishment and growth in grace.[2]

1. Matt. 26:26, 27. And as they were eating, Jesus took bread, and blessed *it*, and brake *it*, and gave *it* to the disciples, and said, Take, eat; this is my body. And he took the cup, and gave thanks, and gave *it* to them, saying, Drink ye all of it.

I Cor. 11:26. For as often as ye eat this bread, and drink this cup, ye do shew the Lord's death till he come.

2. I Cor. 10:16. The cup of blessing which we bless, is it not the communion of the blood of Christ? The bread which we break, is it not the communion of the body of Christ?

Eph. 3:17. That Christ may dwell in your hearts by faith.

Q. 97. *What is required to the worthy receiving of the Lord's supper?*

A. It is required of them that would worthily partake of the Lord's supper, that they examine themselves, of their knowledge to discern the Lord's body,[1] of their faith to feed upon him,[2]

of their repentance,[3] love[4] and new obedience;[5] lest coming unworthily, they eat and drink judgment to themselves.[6]

1. I Cor. 11:28, 29. But let a man examine himself, and so let him eat of
   that bread, and drink of *that* cup. For he that eateth and drinketh unworthily, eateth and drinketh damnation to himself, not discerning the
   Lord's body.

2. John 6:53-56. Then Jesus said unto them, Verily, verily, I say unto you,
   Except ye eat the flesh of the Son of man, and drink his blood, ye have
   no life in you. Whoso eateth my flesh, and drinketh my blood, hath eternal life; and I will raise him up at the last day. For my flesh is meat indeed, and my blood is drink indeed. He that eateth my flesh, and drinketh my blood, dwelleth in me, and I in him.

3. Zech. 12:10. And I will pour upon the house of David, and upon the inhabitants of Jerusalem, the spirit of grace and of supplications: and
   they shall look upon me whom they have pierced, and they shall mourn
   for him, as one mourneth for *his* only *son*, and shall be in bitterness for
   him, as one that is in bitterness for *his* firstborn.

4. I John 4:19. We love him, because he first loved us.
   Gal. 5:6. For in Jesus Christ neither circumcision availeth any thing, nor
   uncircumcision; but faith which worketh by love.

5. Rom. 6:4. Therefore we are buried with him by baptism into death:
   that like as Christ was raised up from the dead by the glory of the Father,
   even so we also should walk in newness of life.
   Rom. 6:17-22.

6. I Cor. 11:27. Wherefore whosoever shall eat this bread, and drink *this*
   cup of the Lord, unworthily, shall be guilty of the body and blood of the
   Lord.

Q. 98. *What is prayer?*

A. Prayer is an offering up of our desires unto God,[1] for
things agreeable to his will,[2] in the name of Christ,[3] with confession of our sins,[4] and thankful acknowledgment of his mercies.[5]

1. Ps. 62:8. Trust in him at all times; ye people, pour out your heart before him: God *is* a refuge for us.
   Ps. 10:17. Lord, thou hast heard the desire of the humble.

2. I John 5:14. And this is the confidence that we have in him, that, if we
   ask any thing according to his will, he heareth us.
   Matt. 26:39; John 6:38.

3. John 16:23. Whatsoever ye shall ask the Father in my name, he will give
   it you.

4. Dan. 9:4. And I prayed unto the Lord my God, and made my confession.

5. Phil. 4:6. Be careful for nothing; but in every thing by prayer and supplication with thanksgiving let your requests be made known unto God.

Q. 99. *What rule hath God given for our direction in prayer?*

A. The whole word of God is of use to direct us in prayer;[1] but the special rule of direction is that form of prayer, which Christ taught his disciples, commonly called, *the Lord's prayer.*[2]

1. II Tim. 3:16, 17. All scripture *is* given by inspiration of God, and *is* profitable for doctrine, for reproof, for correction, for instruction in righteousness: that the man of God may be perfect, throughly furnished unto all good works.

   I John 5:14.

2. Matt. 6:9. After this manner therefore pray ye: Our Father which art in heaven, Hallowed by thy name.

Q. 100. *What doth the preface of the Lord's prayer teach us?*

A. The preface of the Lord's prayer, which is, *"Our Father which art in heaven,"* teacheth us to draw near to God, with all holy reverence and confidence, as children to a father, able and ready to help us;[1] and that we should pray with and for others.[2]

1. Isa. 64:9. Be not wroth very sore, O LORD, neither remember iniquity for ever: behold, see, we beseech thee, we *are* all thy people.

   Luke 11:13. If ye then, being evil, know how to give good gifts unto your children: how much more shall *your* heavenly Father give the Holy Spirit to them that ask him?

   Rom. 8:15. For ye have not received the spirit of bondage again to fear; but ye have received the Spirit of adoption, whereby we cry, Abba, Father.

2. Eph. 6:18. Praying always with all prayer and supplication in the Spirit, and watching thereunto with all perseverance and supplication for all saints.

   Acts 12:5; Zech. 8:21.

Q. 101. *What do we pray for in the first petition?*

A. In the first petition, which is, *"Hallowed be thy name,"* we pray, that God would enable us, and others, to glorify him in all that whereby he maketh himself known,[1] and that he would dispose all things to his own glory.[2]

1. Ps. 67:1-3. God be merciful unto us, and bless us; *and* cause his face to shine upon us; that thy way may be known upon earth, thy saving health among all nations. Let the people praise thee, O God; let all the people praise thee.

   II Thess. 3:1. Finally, brethren, pray for us, that the word of the Lord may have *free* course, and be glorified, even as *it is* with you.

   Ps. 145.

2. Isa. 64:1, 2. Oh that thou wouldest rend the heavens, that thou wouldest come down, that the mountains might flow down at thy presence, as . . . *when* the melting fire burneth, the fire causeth the waters to boil, to

make thy name known to thine adversaries, *that* the nations may tremble at thy presence!

Rom. 11:36. For of him, and through him, and to him, *are* all things: to
whom *be* glory for ever. Amen.

Q. 102. *What do we pray for in the second petition?*

A. In the second petition, which is, *"Thy kingdom come,"* we
pray, that Satan's kingdom may be destroyed,[1] and that the
kingdom of grace may be advanced, ourselves and others brought
into it, and kept in it,[2] and that the kingdom of glory may be
hastened.[3]

1. Ps. 68:1. Let God arise, let his enemies be scattered: let them also that
hate him flee before him.

2. II Thess. 3:1. Finally, brethren, pray for us, that the word of the Lord
may have *free* course, and be glorified, even as *it is* with you.
Ps. 51:18; 67:1-3; Rom. 10:1.

3. Rev. 22:20. He which testifieth these things saith, Surely I come quickly.
Amen. Even so, come, Lord Jesus.
II Peter 3:11-13.

Q. 103. *What do we pray for in the third petition?*

A. In the third petition, which is, *"Thy will be done in earth,
as it is in heaven,"* we pray, that God, by his grace, would make
us able and willing to know, obey, and submit to his will in all
things[1] as the angels do in heaven.[2]

1. Ps. 119:34-36. Give me understanding, and I shall keep thy law; yea, I
shall observe it with *my* whole heart. Make me to go in the path of thy
commandments; for therein do I delight. Incline my heart unto thy
testimonies.
Acts 21:14. And when he would not be persuaded, we ceased, saying,
The will of the Lord be done.

2. Ps. 103:20-22. Bless the LORD, ye his angels, that excel in strength, that
do his commandments, hearkening unto the voice of his word. Bless ye
the LORD, all *ye* his hosts; *ye* ministers of his, that do his pleasure. Bless
the LORD, all his works in all places of his dominion: bless the LORD, O
my soul.

Q. 104. *What do we pray for in the fourth petition?*

A. In the fourth petition, which is, *"Give us this day our
daily bread,"* we pray, that, of God's free gift, we may receive
a competent portion of the good things of this life,[1] and enjoy his
blessing with them.[2]

1. Prov. 30:8. Remove far from me vanity and lies: give me neither poverty
nor riches; feed me with food convenient for me.

2. I Tim. 4:4, 5. For every creature of God *is* good, and nothing to be refused, if it be received with thanksgiving: for it is sanctified by the word of God and prayer.

Prov. 10:22.

Q. 105. *What do we pray for in the fifth petition?*

A. In the fifth petition, which is, *"And forgive us our debts, as we forgive our debtors,"* we pray, that God, for Christ's sake, would freely pardon all our sins;[1] which we are the rather encouraged to ask, because by his grace we are enabled from the heart to forgive others.[2]

1. Ps. 51:1. Have mercy upon me, O God, according to thy lovingkindness: according unto the multitude of thy tender mercies blot out my transgressions.

   Rom. 3:24, 25.

2. Luke 11:4. And forgive us our sins; for we also forgive every one that is indebted to us.

   Matt. 18:35; Matt. 6:14, 15.

Q. 106. *What do we pray for in the sixth petition?*

A. In the sixth petition, which is, *"And lead us not into temptation, but deliver us from evil,"* we pray, that God would either keep us from being tempted to sin,[1] or support and deliver us when we are tempted.[2]

1. Matt. 26:41. Watch and pray, that ye enter not into temptation.

   Ps. 19:13. Keep back thy servant also from presumptuous *sins;* let them not have dominion over me.

2. I Cor. 10:13. There hath no temptation taken you but such as is common to man: but God *is* faithful, who will not suffer you to be tempted above that ye are able; but will with the temptation also make a way to escape, that ye may be able to bear *it.*

   Ps. 51:10, 12. Create in me a clean heart, O God; and renew a right spirit within me. . . . Restore unto me the joy of thy salvation; and uphold me *with thy* free spirit.

Q. 107. *What doth the conclusion of the Lord's prayer teach us?*

A. The conclusion of the Lord's prayer, which is, *"For thine is the kingdom, and the power, and the glory, for ever, Amen,"* teacheth us to take our encouragement in prayer from God only,[1] and in our prayers to praise him, ascribing kingdom, power, and glory to him,[2] and in testimony of our desire and assurance to be heard, we say, *Amen.*[3]

1. Dan. 9:18, 19. We do not present our supplications before thee for our righteousness, but for thy great mercies. O Lord, hear; O Lord, forgive; O Lord, hearken and do; defer not, for thine own sake, O my God.

2. I Chron. 29:11-13. Thine, O LORD, *is* the greatness, and the power, and the glory, and the victory, and the majesty: for all *that is* in the heaven and in the earth *is thine;* thine *is* the kingdom, O LORD, and thou art exalted as head above all. Both riches and honour *come* of thee, and thou reignest over all; and in thine hand *is* power and might; and in thine hand *it is* to make great, and to give strength unto all. Now therefore, our God, we thank thee, and praise thy glorious name.

3. Rev. 22:20, 21. He which testifieth these things saith, Surely I come quickly. Amen. Even so, come, Lord Jesus. The grace of our Lord Jesus Christ *be* with you all. Amen.

I Cor. 14:16.

☦

THE TEN COMMANDMENTS

God spake all these words, saying, I am the Lord thy God, which have brought thee out of the land of Egypt, out of the house of bondage.

I. Thou shalt have no other gods before me.

II. Thou shalt not make unto thee any graven image, or any likeness of any thing that is in heaven above, or that is in the earth beneath, or that is in the water under the earth: thou shalt not bow down thyself to them, nor serve them: for I the Lord thy God am a jealous God, visiting the iniquity of the fathers upon the children unto the third and fourth generation of them that hate me; and shewing mercy unto thousands of them that love me, and keep my commandments.

III. Thou shalt not take the name of the Lord thy God in vain; for the Lord will not hold him guiltless that taketh his name in vain.

IV. Remember the sabbath day, to keep it holy. Six days shalt thou labour, and do all thy work: but the seventh day is the sabbath of the Lord thy God: in it thou shalt not do any work, thou, nor thy son, nor thy daughter, thy manservant, nor thy maidservant, nor thy cattle, nor thy stranger that is within thy gates: for in six days the Lord made heaven and earth, the sea, and all that in them is, and rested the seventh day: wherefore the Lord blessed the sabbath day, and hallowed it.

V. Honour thy father and thy mother: that thy days may be long upon the land which the Lord thy God giveth thee.

VI. Thou shalt not kill.

VII. Thou shalt not commit adultery.

VIII. Thou shalt not steal.

IX. Thou shalt not bear false witness against thy neighbour.

X. Thou shalt not covet thy neighbour's house, thou shalt not covet thy neighbour's wife, nor his manservant, nor his maidservant, nor his ox, nor his ass, nor any thing that is thy neighbour's.

✠

THE LORD'S PRAYER

MATTHEW VI

Our Father which art in heaven, Hallowed be thy name. Thy kingdom come. Thy will be done in earth, as it is in heaven. Give us this day our daily bread. And forgive us our debts, as we forgive our debtors. And lead us not into temptation, but deliver us from evil: For thine is the kingdom, and the power, and the glory, for ever. Amen.

✠

THE CREED

I believe in God the Father almighty, maker of heaven and earth; and in Jesus Christ his only Son, our Lord; which was conceived by the Holy Ghost, born of the Virgin Mary, suffered under Pontius Pilate, was crucified, dead, and buried; he descended into hell;* the third day he rose again from the dead; he ascended into heaven, and sitteth on the right hand of God the Father almighty; from thence he shall come to judge the quick and the dead. I believe in the Holy Ghost; the holy catholic church; the communion of saints; the forgiveness of sins; the resurrection of the body; and the life everlasting. Amen.

---

* *I.e.* Continued in the state of the dead, and under the power of death, until the third day. See the answer to Question 50 in the Larger Catechism, p. 168.

A BRIEF STATEMENT OF BELIEF

Adopted by the General Assembly of May, 1962

REPORT OF AD INTERIM COMMITTEE TO PREPARE A BRIEF STATEMENT OF BELIEF

Foreword

The Committee desires to express its understanding of the task assigned it by the 1958 Assembly. It has labored under the impression that it was asked to prepare in the language of our day a Brief Statement of Faith, which if adopted, would replace the Brief Statement of 1913, and be used in like manner.

That there may be clear understanding as to the place and function of the offered Brief Statement, the Committee suggests the following resolution:

Resolved:

1. That the General Assembly of 1962 adopt the Brief Statement of Faith offered by the Ad Interim Committee with the understanding that it shall not be considered a substitute for or an amendment to our Standards.

2. That the Board of Christian Education be instructed to print sufficient quantities to meet demands, to list the Brief Statement along with other educational materials, to place it in the back of future printings of *The Confession of Faith*.

3. That the Committee's foreword and this resolution be included in all printings of the Brief Statement as expressing the understanding of the 1962 Assembly in adopting the Brief Statement of Faith.

The Brief Statement

This statement of belief has been prepared to present in the language of our time the historic Christian doctrine set forth in Scripture and affirmed by the Presbyterian Church. In a brief statement it has not been possible to treat all doctrines, or to cover fully the doctrines which have been treated. The conditions of history and the limitations of human mind and language are such that no statement of Christian doctrine can be either final or complete. Nevertheless, this affirmation is submitted in the hope that it will be used for the glory of God and the edification of the church.

CHARLES L. KING, *Chairman*
FELIX B. GEAR, *Vice Chairman*
JOHN H. LEITH, *Secretary*
WADE H. BOGGS, JR.
MARY L. BONEY
KENNETH J. FOREMAN
ROLAND M. FRYE
WARNER L. HALL

T. B. JACKSON
ASHBY JOHNSON
LAURENCE F. KINNEY
JAMES G. LEYBURN
J. R. McCAIN
HARRY M. MOFFETT, JR.
DAVID L. STITT

A Brief Statement of Belief

GOD AND REVELATION

The Word of God

The living and only true God has made himself known to all mankind through nature, mind, conscience, and history. He has especially revealed himself and his purpose for man in the variety of ways recorded in the Old and New Testaments. The Bible, as the written Word of God, sets forth what God has done and said in revealing his righteous judgment and love, culminating in Christ. The Spirit of God who inspired the writers of Scripture also illumines readers of Scripture as they seek his saving truth. The Bible calls men to an obedient response to the Gospel and is the supreme authority and indispensable guide for Christian faith and life.

God

God has revealed himself as the Creator, Sustainer, and Ruler of all that exists. In the exercise of his sovereign power in creation, history, and redemption, God is holy and perfect, abundant in goodness, and the source of all truth and freedom. He is just in his dealings with all the world; he requires that men live and act in justice; and he visits his wrath on all sin. He is gracious and merciful and does not desire that any should perish. Both his judgments and his mercies are expressions of his character as he pursues his redemptive purposes for man.

Trinity

God is personal, and he reveals himself as the Trinity of Father, Son, and Holy Spirit. It is the witness of the Scriptures, confirmed in Christian experience, that the God who creates and sustains us is the God who redeems us in Christ, and the God who works in our hearts as the Holy Spirit; and we believe that this threefold revelation manifests the true nature of God.

MAN AND SIN

God created man in his own image. As a created being, man is finite and dependent upon his Creator.

331

The
Image
of God

Man can distinguish between right and wrong, and is morally responsible for his own actions. He reflects the image of God insofar as he lives in obedience to the will of God. A unique creature standing both within nature and above it, he is placed by God in authority over the world. It is, therefore, his responsibility to use all things for the glory of God. Although made in the image of God, man has fallen; and we, like all mankind before us, sin in our refusal to accept God as sovereign. We rebel against the will of God

Original
Sin

by arrogance and by despair. We thrust God from the center of life, rejecting divine control both of human life and the universe. From this perversity arises every specific sin, whether of negligence, perfunctory performance, or outright violation of the will of God.

Sin permeates and corrupts our entire being and burdens us more and more with fear, hostility, guilt,

Total
Depravity

and misery. Sin operates not only within individuals but also within society as a deceptive and oppressive power, so that even men of good will are unconsciously and unwillingly involved in the sins of society. Man cannot destroy the tyranny of sin in himself or in his world; his only hope is to be delivered from it by God.

CHRIST AND SALVATION

God, loving men and hating the sin which enslaves them, has acted for their salvation in history and es-

The Gospel:
Incarnation

pecially through his covenant people. In the fullness of time, he sent his only, eternally begotten Son, born of the Virgin Mary. As truly God and truly man, Jesus Christ enables us to see God as he is and man as he

and
Atonement

ought to be. Through Christ's life, death, resurrection, and ascension, God won for man the decisive victory over sin and death and established his Kingdom among men. Through Christ, bearing on the cross the consequences of our sin, God exposed the true nature of sin as our repudiation of God. Through Christ, bearing on the cross the guilt of our sin, God forgives us and reconciles us to himself. By raising his Son from the dead, God conquers sin and death for us.

God has an eternal, inclusive purpose for his world,

The Sovereign Purpose of God and Election

which embraces the free and responsible choices of man and everything which occurs in all creation. This purpose of God will surely be accomplished. In executing his purpose, God chooses men in Christ and calls forth the faith which unites them with Christ, releasing them from bondage to sin and death into freedom, obedience, and life. Likewise God in his sovereign purpose executes judgment upon sinful man.

Justification by Faith

Man cannot earn or deserve God's salvation but receives it through faith by the enabling power of the Holy Spirit. In faith, man believes and receives God's promise of grace and mercy in Christ, is assured of his acceptance for Christ's sake in spite of his sinfulness, and responds to God in grateful love and loyalty.

Repentance and Sanctification

In repentance, man, through the work of the Holy Spirit, recognizes himself as he is, turns from his sin, and redirects his life increasingly in accordance with God's will. The Christian life is a continuing process of growth which reaches its final fulfillment only in the life to come.

THE CHURCH AND THE MEANS OF GRACE

The true Church is the whole community, on earth and in heaven, of those called by God into fellowship with him and with one another to know and do his will. As the body of Christ, the Church on earth is the instrument through which God continues to proclaim and apply the benefits of his redemptive work and to establish his Kingdom.

The Form of the Church

The Church in the world has many branches, all of which are subject to sin and to error. Depending on how closely they conform to the will of Christ as head of the Church, denominations and congregations are more or less pure in worship, doctrine, and practice. The Presbyterian Church follows scriptural precedent in its representative government by elders (presbyters). These elders govern only in courts of regular gradation. The form of government of a church, however, is not essential to its validity. The visible church is composed of those who profess their faith in Jesus Christ, together with their children.

The Means of Grace

Through the Church, God provides certain means for developing the Christian mind and conscience and for maturing faith, hope, and love. Primary among these means are the preaching, teaching, and study of the Word; public and private prayer; and the sacraments.

The Bible

The Bible becomes a means of grace through preaching, teaching, and private study, as the Holy Spirit speaks to human needs and reveals the living Word of God who is Jesus Christ. It illuminates man's thought and experience as it provides an occasion for the Holy Spirit's work of redemption and as it testifies to the working of God, but it is not intended to be a substitute for science and inquiry. In preaching and teaching, the Church proclaims and interprets the mighty acts of God in history and seeks to relate them to every phase of human life. The prayerful and diligent study of the Scripture guides the Christian in his relationships with God and his fellow man, and in his personal life.

Prayer

Christian prayer is communion with God in the name of Jesus Christ through the inspiration and guidance of the Holy Spirit. In prayers, alone or with others, we acknowledge God's greatness and goodness, confess our sins, express our love to him, rejoice in his blessings, present our needs and those of others, receive from him guidance and strength, and joyfully dedicate ourselves to his will. To pray in the name of Christ, our Mediator, is not to repeat a formula, but to trust his redemptive work, to ask for his intercession, to depend upon his presence with us, and to desire what he has taught us to value and believe.

The Sacraments

Christ gave to the Church through his apostles the sacraments of Baptism and the Lord's Supper as visible signs and assurances of the Gospel. Baptism sets forth, by the symbolic use of water, the cleansing and regenerating love of God through the work of the Holy Spirit; in this sacrament we and our children are assured that we are members of the covenant family of God, and are publicly accepted into fellowship with Christ and his Church. The Lord's Supper sets forth, by the symbolic use of bread and wine, the death of Christ for our salvation; in this sacrament we have communion with the risen Christ, who gives himself to us as we receive in faith the bread and wine for the nourishment of our Christian life. Being assured of his forgiving and sustaining love, we renew our dedication and enjoy fellowship with the whole people of God. The Lord's table is open to members of all churches who have publicly professed Jesus Christ as Saviour and Lord and who come in penitence and faith.

CHRISTIAN LIFE AND WORK

Vocation

Each Christian is called to be a servant of God in all of life, so that we must seek God's will for the work we do and for the manner in which we do it. Christian vocation may be found in any work where our own abilities and interests best meet the legitimate needs of God's world. The Church is charged under God with the obligation to seek out the most responsible and effective Christian leadership. It is the special role of the ordained ministry, including elders and deacons, to perform particular services in the life of the Church and to strengthen every Christian in the discharge of the responsibilities of the priesthood of all believers in the Church and the world. For the Christian, all life becomes significant as he does his daily work with dedication and diligence out of love for God and for his neighbor.

Social Responsibility

The range of Christian responsibility is as wide as human life. The Christian must recognize, but not accept as inevitable, the world as it is, distorted and torn by sin. Christians as individuals and as groups have the right and the duty to examine in the light of the Word of God the effects on human personality of social institutions and practices. As servants of the sovereign will of God, Christians are under obligation to their fellow men and to unborn generations to shape and influence these institutions and practices so that the world may be brought more nearly into conformity with the purpose of God for his creation. The Church's concern for the reign of God in the world is essential to its basic responsibility both for evangelism and for Christian nurture.

Providence and Suffering

We believe that our destiny and that of the world are not subject to chance or fate, but to the just and loving sovereignty of God. In this assurance we face the problems of suffering and evil. Faith in the purpose and providence of God assures us of his presence in suffering and of his power to give it meaning. We are confident that no form of evil can separate us from the love of God, that God works in all things for good, and that evil will ultimately be overcome. Therefore, while we cannot fully understand the pain and evil of the present world, we can offer ourselves as active instruments of God's will in their conquest.

JUDGMENT AND THE LIFE TO COME

Resurrection

Eternal life is the gift of God. We are assured by the promises of the Gospel, by our relation to Christ, and by his resurrection that death does not put an end to personal existence, but that we too shall be raised from the dead. Those who have accepted the forgiving love of God in Christ enter into eternal life in fellowship with God and his people. This new life begins in the present world and is fulfilled in the resurrection of the body and the world to come. Those who have rejected the love of God bring upon themselves his judgment and shut themselves outside the fellowship of God and his people.

Return of Christ and God's Triumph

As Christ came once in humility, he will return in glory for the final judgment and for the consummation of his universal Kingdom. The work and promises of Jesus Christ give assurance that the age-long struggle between sin and grace will in God's good time have an end; all the power of evil will be destroyed, and God's holy, wise, and loving purposes will be accomplished.